Deviance, Conformity, and Social Control in Canada

Third Edition

Tami M. Bereska

Grant MacEwan University

Pearson Canada
Toronto

Library and Archives Canada Cataloguing in Publication

Bereska, Tami M. (Tami Marie), 1968–

   Deviance, conformity, and social control in Canada / Tami M. Bereska. — 3rd ed.

Includes bibliographical references and index.

ISBN 978-0-13-245931-0

   1. Deviant behaviour—Textbooks. 2. Conformity—Textbooks. 3. Social control—Textbooks.
4. Canada—Social conditions—Textbooks. I. Title.

HM811.B47 2011   302.5'420971   C2009-905992-4

ISBN 978-0-13-245931-0

Vice President, Editorial Director: Gary Bennett
Editor-in-Chief: Ky Pruesse
Editor, Humanities and Social Sciences: Joel Gladstone
Marketing Manager: Arthur Gee
Associate Editor: Ben Zaporozan
Managing Editor: Söğüt Y. Güleç
Project Management: Raj Singh / MPS Limited, A Macmillan Company
Copy Editor: Judy Sturrup
Proofreader: Tara Tovell
Production Coordinator: Avinash Chandra
Composition: MPS Limited, A Macmillan Company
Photo Research: Sandy Cooke
Assistant Art Director: Miguel Acevedo
Cover Design: Kerrin Hands
Cover Image: iStock

For permission to reproduce other copyrighted material, the publisher gratefully acknowledges the copyright
holders listed on page 346, which is considered an extension of this copyright page.

Statistics Canada information is used with the permission of the Minister of Industry, as Minister responsible for
Statistics Canada. Information on the availability of the wide range of data from Statistics Canada can be
obtained from Statistics Canada's Regional Offices, its World Wide Web site at www.statcan.gc.ca, and its toll-
free access number 1-800-263-1136.

   2 3 4 5   14 13 12 11 10

Printed and bound in USA.

Contents

Chapter 3   Explaining Deviance: The Perception, Reaction, and Power   74

Chapter 4   "Deviant" and "Normal" Sexuality   103

Preface

Introduction

The sociology of deviance is a diverse field of study, and this diversity is reflected in the content of Canadian textbooks that are available. Some books are based on theory, with separate chapters on each category of deviance theory and specific deviance examples to illustrate components of those theories. These books provide a thorough description and critical analysis of a wide range of theories, but if there is one way to make a fascinating subject like deviance rather dull in the eyes of students (as they have repeatedly pointed out to me), it is to bombard them with theory for the sake of theory. In contrast, this textbook reviews theories of deviance in two chapters, but the remaining chapters focus on substantive issues, bringing in relevant theories when doing so can meaningfully contribute to the overall "story" being told within a particular section of the chapter, and within the chapter as a whole.

While some books address mainly theory, others have a criminological focus, containing extensive discussions of topics like prostitution, white-collar crime, police deviance, and sexual assault. These are all very important topics for students to be familiar with. However, students who take separate courses in criminology and in deviance frequently experience too much overlap between the course materials. In contrast, this textbook is specifically intended for courses in deviance or social control. There will still be a small amount of overlap for students taking both criminology courses and deviance courses, but that overlap is minimal. Furthermore, the material that might overlap is presented in a context very different from in a student's criminology course.

Some textbooks contain collections of readings that are based upon a similar theoretical approach, such as social constructionism. These collections have the benefit of providing students with original readings; however, they lack a cohesive context to enhance student learning. This book is the kind of single-authored textbook that many professors and students prefer.

Finally, some books are characterized by what Ben-Yehuda (1990, p. 5) calls "radical phenomenalism," where countless numbers of isolated, specific phenomena (e.g., call girls, transsexualism, and marijuana use) are described in tremendous detail, but without reference to a broader social and historical structure. These phenomena are usually quite interesting to read about, but without a wider context, the logic of including the various specific phenomena is unclear. To the reader, it can feel somewhat like randomly grabbing items in an all-you-can-eat buffet rather than sitting down to a four-course meal with different courses designed to complement each other. In contrast, in this textbook there is a method to the madness: the specific topics and issues addressed in each chapter have been selected as parts of a cohesive whole. Each individual topic covered is placed within a sociocultural context and contributes to a bigger picture.

Features

The features of this textbook include the following:

- *Pedagogical aids for students* appear throughout every chapter. Students are asked to engage with the material as they read it. *Ask Yourself* sections ask students to think about certain questions, their own lives, or their own points of view prior to reading the next body of material. *Exercise Your Mind* sections recommend that students go beyond the textbook material to explore particular issues in more detail, by looking for critiques of theories or renting certain movies that demonstrate a topic being discussed. An *Internet Moment* sections direct students to specific internet sites related to the material. These sections also indicate to students what they should be looking for or what questions they should keep in mind while on the recommended sites. *Time to Review* sections ask students to review questions at regular intervals throughout the chapters.
- *Objective and subjective approaches* to deviance are integrated in the textbook, rather than only one or the other being focused on. They are also presented as complementary rather than contradictory.
- *Two theory chapters* review those theories that are used in more objective approaches (Chapter 2) and more subjective approaches (Chapter 3).
- The topics of the substantive chapters are *relevant to students' lives*— i.e., sexuality, youth, voluntary and involuntary physical appearance, mental disorders, religious belief systems, and scientific belief systems. The topics have been selected to illustrate to students that the social typing and social control of deviance occurs everywhere around them each day of their lives. They illustrate that students have experienced these processes and participate in them.
- Each of the substantive chapters incorporates material on *social typing and social control.*
- Each of the substantive chapters reveals the *"deviance dance."* That is, each chapter demonstrates how the social typing of deviance is not a uniform process but is characterized by *disagreement, debate, and resistance,* even for the most taken-for-granted issues (e.g., pedophilia).
- Each of the substantive chapters *tells a cohesive story.* Students are not bombarded with an assortment of cafeteria-style facts and theories; rather, they learn about the sociocultural context within which particular forms of deviance are socially typed and socially controlled.

- In the narrative of each chapter, both *criminal and non-criminal* forms of deviance are explored in relation to the topic at hand.
- The vital role of *power* in determining and controlling deviance is discussed in each chapter.

Organization

The first three chapters in the book provide students with the foundation they need for a course in deviance. Chapter 1 looks at the various ways that academics, laypersons, and activists have defined deviance, and these definitions are embedded in a wider discussion of the objective/subjective dichotomy as it has traditionally been presented. From the objective perspective, various definitions are reviewed (i.e., statistical rarity, harm, normative violation, and negative societal reaction) and critiqued. From the subjective perspective, deviance is described as "anything that enough important people say it is," and is embedded in a discussion of social construction. After presenting the traditional objective and subjective points of view, this dichotomy or dualism is questioned, and material is presented showing how there is now more blending of the two perspectives in the work of many deviance scholars. Students are introduced to the concept of the social typing process, the different forms of social control, and the role of power in society. The notion of the "deviance dance"—that is, the negotiations over deviance (disagreement, debate, and resistance)—is introduced.

Chapter 2 explains that because scholars with more objective and subjective leanings shine their analytical spotlights on different aspects of deviance, different theories are more useful to each. The remainder of Chapter 2 reviews the positivist theories that are of most use to more objective researchers. This is not an exhaustive theoretical analysis, but rather a review of those theories that have been the most influential in the study of deviance. The section on functionalist theories includes Durkheim, Merton's anomie and strain theories, macro-level strain theory, differential opportunity theory, Agnew's general strain theory, and status frustration theory. The section on learning theories includes differential association theory, neutralization theory, and social learning theory. The section on social control theories reviews social bonds theory and the general theory of crime.

Chapter 3 reviews the interpretive and critical theories that are of most use to more subjective-leaning scholars. The section on symbolic interactionism addresses the perspective more generally, and then discusses the work of Tannenbaum, Becker, Lemert, and Goffman. The section on critical theories reviews conflict theories, power-reflexive (or critical poststructuralist) theories, feminist theories, and postmodern theories. In this third edition of the textbook, Chapter 2 and Chapter 3 include current cultural references and examples that illustrate the theories, such as digital piracy of software and music, the stigmatization of individuals of Middle-Eastern descent, the growth of government-sponsored public surveillance, and the aftermath of Hurricane Katrina.

The remaining chapters in the book focus on substantive issues. Chapter 4 explores sexuality. An historical and cross-cultural analysis of sexual cultures in Sambian society, fifth-century B.C. Athens, traditional and colonized Aboriginal cultures in North America, and Canadian/American society from the sixteenth century through the twentieth century is particularly effective in demonstrating how conceptions of sexual deviance vary. Moving into the present day, the criteria used for evaluating people's sexuality as deviant or normal are explored. In the third edition, new material on the legalization of same-sex marriage in Canada, California's Proposition 8 (regarding same-sex marriage), Canadian data on sexual orientation-related hate crimes, debates over how to define sexual consent, and the manner in which the marketing of sexual pharmaceuticals has emphasized the importance of sexual desire and frequency, have all been added.

Chapter 5 focuses on youth. The first section of the chapter addresses "deviant" youth—youth crime, gangs, and substance abuse (including binge drinking among college students). The concept of at-risk youth is then introduced and explored. The criticism that the concept of "at-risk" has rapidly expanded and now potentially includes all youth in society leads to the second half of the chapter. Here, the following question is asked: "Aren't all youth deviant?" That is, the issue of whether adolescence is an inherently deviant time in the life cycle is explored. In the third edition, there is coverage of Aboriginal gangs in Canada, expanded material on the origins of the concept of "moral panic," and the results of Reginald Bibby's most recent youth survey, which suggests that in many ways the current generation of youth are doing considerably better than prior generations he has surveyed (despite society's greater concerns about them).

In Chapter 6, voluntary and involuntary physical appearance is examined. The first half of the chapter explores body modification. Research from a more objectivist view analyzes tattoos and piercings in the context of what body modification tells us about individuals (i.e., risk and motivation). Research from a more subjectivist view explores what body modification tells us about social interaction (e.g., impression management) and about the larger society (e.g., structures of power). The second half of the chapter looks at body size—"too fat," "too thin," and "ideal." The way these criteria are determined medically is reviewed, as are medical forms of social control. Next, the social standards that define the "ideal" body are discussed; in the third edition, perceptions of hyper-muscular women (i.e., bodybuilders) are included, illustrating yet another way that a woman's body can stray from the ideal. Finally, the various means of controlling ideas of "too fat" and "too thin" through media, commercial industry, government, and medicine are reviewed, and resistance to that deviantization is addressed.

Chapter 7 is about mental illness. This chapter explores the nature and prevalence of mental illness, as well as its individual and societal costs. The contemporary and historical social control of mental illness is discussed, along with issues of mental health policy and funding and stigmatization. The impact of the deinstitutionalization movement is also presented. The chapter next moves to a more subjective look at how mental illness is determined. Criticisms of the *DSM* and the process by which it is created are presented. Rosenhan's study, "Being Sane in Insane Places," is reviewed, and finally, the social factors that influence diagnosis and treatment today are presented. The third edition includes a deeper level of analysis of various issues surrounding mental illness, such as the consequences of stigmatization and self-stigmatization, identity formation, psychiatric hospitals as total institutions, the hydraulic model of the relationship between the criminal justice and mental health care systems, and theoretical debates over the harm/benefits of stigmatization.

Chapter 8 addresses religious belief systems in two sections. The first explores "deviant" religions. Various churches, sects, and cults are defined and analyzed, as is the social control of sects and cults. The traditional distinction between churches, sects, and cults is then questioned, and students are presented with material demonstrating that all religious groups have been seen as deviant and made subject to social control at some time in some society. As well, the governmental barriers to religious freedom in various countries in the world are reviewed. The second section of the chapter, however, explores "religion as a social typer of deviance"—that is, the way that religious belief systems dictate what is deviant. Various instances of the blurring of boundaries between religious and political belief systems are presented—i.e., witch persecutions, residential schooling, and more contemporary concerns about the Christian Coalition's alleged control of the Republican Party in the United States. Important cultural events and shifts are addressed in the third edition, such as the federal government's resolution package for former students of residential schools, and the potential weakening of the political-religious right in the United States following George W. Bush's tenure as president.

Chapter 9 analyzes scientific belief systems. The first section looks at deviance in science—that is, various forms of scientific misconduct, as well as the extent of the problem of scientific misconduct and its relationship with the corporatization of science. The third edition includes a new section on the ways scientific misconduct is controlled, how the nature of control has changed from the 1970s to the present, and the factors that have contributed to these shifts. This chapter's second part explores "deviant" sciences, such as pseudo-sciences like astrology. The discussion covers the social control of such sciences and the historical changes in definitions of pseudo-science. The third section of the chapter looks at "science as a social typer of deviance"—i.e., how science may dictate to society who/what should be considered deviant, why, and what should be done to "fix" the problem. The chapter discusses how science can help address problems, but also reviews how "scientific" claims have had negative consequences in the past. Two examples are Social Darwinism, which influenced government policies regarding Aboriginal peoples, and the eugenics movement, which swept through the Western world and reached its apex in Nazi Germany. Today, some people suggest that the new science of genetic testing and manipulation is nothing more than eugenics in twenty-first-century clothing.

Chapter 10 brings students full circle by reminding readers of the key themes that were introduced in Chapter 1 and explored in each of the substantive chapters: the objective–subjective continuum; social typing, social control, and power; and the "deviance dance." Examples from the various chapters are reiterated to demonstrate these themes. Because of the role of subjectivity in determining and controlling deviance, some students may be left wondering if no one and nothing can ever be accurately socially typed as deviant. The notion of human rights is introduced as a possible starting point for thinking about when it is or is not appropriate to attach a deviant label and subject someone to measures of social control.

Supplements

Instructor supplements to this textbook include the following:

- Test Item File
- Instructor's Manual
- PowerPoint Presentations

These supplements can be downloaded from a password-protected section of Pearson Canada's online catalogue (**vig.pearsoned.ca**). Navigate to your book's catalogue page to view a list of those supplements that are available. See your local sales representative for details and access.

CourseSmart for Instructors

CourseSmart goes beyond traditional expectations—providing instant, online access to the textbooks and course materials you need at a lower cost for students. And even as students save money, you can save time and hassle with a digital eTextbook that allows you to search for the most relevant content at the very moment you need it. Whether it's evaluating textbooks or creating lecture notes to help students with difficult concepts, CourseSmart can make life a little easier. See how when you visit **www.coursesmart.com/instructors**.

CourseSmart for Students

CourseSmart goes beyond traditional expectations—providing instant, online access to the textbooks and course materials you need at an average savings of 50%. With instant access from any computer and the ability to search your text, you'll find the content you need quickly, no matter where you are. And with online tools like highlighting and note-taking, you can save time and study efficiently. See all the benefits at **www.coursesmart.com/students**.

PEARSON
mysearchlab

MySearchLab offers extensive help to students with their writing and research project and provides round-the-clock access to credible and reliable source material.

Research

Content on MySearchLab includes immediate access to thousands of full-text articles from leading Canadian and international academic journals, and daily news feeds from The Associated Press. Articles contain the full downloadable text—including abstract and citation information—and can be cut, pasted, emailed, or saved for later use.

Writing

MySearchLab also includes a step-by-step tutorial on writing a research paper. Included are sections on planning a research assignment, finding a topic, creating effective notes, and finding source material. Our exclusive online handbook provides grammar and usage support. Pearson SourceCheck™ offers an easy way to detect accidental plagiarism issues, and our exclusive tutorials teach how to avoid them in the future. And MySearchLab also contains AutoCite, which helps to correctly cite sources using MLA, APA, CMS, and CBE documentation styles for both endnotes and bibliographies.

To order this book with MySearchLab access at no extra charge, use ISBN 978-0-13-138377-7.

Take a tour at **www.mysearchlab.com**.

Acknowledgments

Not only does it take a village to raise a child; it also takes a village to write a book. I would like to take a moment to thank my "village." Special thanks must go to those who choose to work with academics, despite our peculiarities: Victoria Naik and Ben Zaporozan from Pearson Education provided welcome instruction, guidance, and tolerance, and demonstrated the ability to roll with the punches when the dark side of technology reared its ugly head. I would also like to express gratitude to my fellow academics, those reviewers whose thoughtful comments reinforce Adler and Adler's (2006b) assertion that the sociology of deviance is a field that is stronger and more relevant than ever:

Peter Doell, Ambrose University College; Norman Dubeski, University of Guelph; Jana Grekul, University of Alberta; Joan Harkness, University of Victoria; Jason Laurendeau, University of Lethbridge; John Martin, University of the Fraser Valley; Anthony Micucci, Memorial University of Newfoundland; Roksana Nazneen, Concordia University; Dorothy Pawluch, McMaster University; Vincent F. Sacco, Queen's University; Joanne Simister, Vancouver Island University.

And finally, there most certainly would not be a third edition of this book were it not for my husband's understanding and his skills as both a barista and, at times, a bartender.

CHAPTER 1

Determining Deviance

Learning Objectives

After reading this chapter, you should be able to

- Describe the objective/subjective dichotomy.
- Describe four definitions of deviance traditionally associated with the objective side of the objective/subjective dichotomy and explain their limitations.
- Describe the definitions of deviance traditionally associated with the subjective side of the objective/subjective dichotomy and summarize the concept of social construction.
- Explain how the study of deviance is influenced by how the researcher defines it. Depict the role of change, negotiation, opposition, and diversity in the "deviance dance" in Canadian society.
- Outline the three components of the social typing process through which someone is defined as "deviant."
- Explain the role of power, and identify who holds this power in Canadian society.

"Conformity makes everything easier, if you can still breathe." (Mason Cooley)[1]

"You have to be deviant if you're going to do anything new." (David Lee)[2]

The two above quotations both make some very pointed claims about the nature of **deviance** and **conformity**. The first quotation makes the claim that our lives will run more smoothly if we conform; however, it also makes the claim that conformity will constrict and limit us. The second quotation makes a related claim, that acting or thinking in a novel way is necessarily deviant; although "thinking outside the box" is a popular corporate phrase, the source of this quotation suggests that only "deviants" will actually do so.

Taken together, the claims made in these quotations raise questions about deviance and conformity. Who are the conformists in our society and in our world? Is life easier for them? Who are the deviants? Are they really the innovators of our world, or do they represent some sort of problem that we need to control? How can we distinguish between a "deviant" and a "conformist"? These are the kinds of questions that will guide us through this textbook.

Who Is Deviant?

Who is deviant? One way to try to answer this question is by looking at the topics covered in deviance textbooks and journals. Historically, certain themes have prevailed—what have been referred to as "nuts, sluts, [and] preverts [sic]" (Liazos, 1972, p. 103). Criminality has also dominated the topics covered in some deviance textbooks. However, a growing body of recent deviance research has moved away from these tendencies toward broader notions of deviance—the prenatal diets of women (Copelton, 2007), customers in adult novelty stores (Hefley, 2007), skydiving (Laurendeau & Van Brunschot, 2006), and people who are voluntarily childless (Park, 2002) have all been analyzed in the context of deviance. This shift in emphasis from the unusual to the mundane illustrates that "deviance is not marginal, it is central to what we do" (Adler & Adler, 2006b, p. 132). A second way to try to ascertain who is deviant is to ask people. As many other deviance professors have done (e.g., Goode, 1997; Herman, 1995), over several years of teaching I have conducted polls of students in my classes. Certain responses have predominated and may bear a striking resemblance to the list you created in the *Ask Yourself* exercise. People who commit crimes, especially violent crimes, are thought of as deviant by large numbers of students.

Ask Yourself

Before going on, make a list of types of people whom you consider to be deviant. We will come back to your list in a little while.

Ask Yourself

Go back to the list you made of people whom you consider to be deviant. Take a look at the list. What do all of the people on your list have in common? Is there a shared characteristic that might point to how deviance can be defined or how we can recognize a deviant when we see one? This issue will be addressed in the next section of the chapter.

There is also considerable consensus that those who perpetuate injustice, such as racists, are deviant as well, but once we go beyond the top three or four types of people listed, perceptions of deviance become as diverse as the students making those lists. Anyone the student dislikes or is annoyed by is added to the list—classmates who twirl their hair, people who drive SUVs, vegetarians, country singers, and professors who wear too much beige are just some of the hundreds of unique responses students have given. However, although using the term "deviance" in reference to our own individual pet peeves may be common practice, the concept of deviance transcends the individual level and instead exists at the societal level. That is, "deviance" does not describe people of whom I personally disapprove, but rather characteristics of the broader society and sociocultural processes.

Just because I might not like country singers does not mean that country singers are deviant in Canadian society. Although each of us (along with our individual opinions) is an important participant in the social processes that occur in Canadian society, social processes constitute more than the sum of their parts, and more than the sum of each of our personal points of view. Thus, studying deviance requires you to move beyond individual belief in order to analyze the broader social processes that occur in the society you live in, whether or not those processes correspond to your individual beliefs or challenge them. But how is it that some people are perceived and treated as deviant while others are not?

How Can We Recognize Deviance When We See It?

Asking how we are able to determine who is deviant brings us to the issue of definitions. The dictionary tells us the following:

Deviant: "deviating [straying] from an accepted norm." Synonyms: "abnormal, atypical, aberrant, unrepresentative." Contrasted words: "normal, natural." (Merriam-Webster, 2002)

At first glance, the dictionary seems to make the concept of deviance quite clear. Deviance involves violating norms that have been accepted in society, and apparently this is quite serious, because doing so makes one abnormal and unnatural. Clearly, breaking the rules has significant consequences. Perhaps Mason Cooley, quoted at the beginning of this chapter, was correct in saying that conformity makes one's life easier.

We could stop with the dictionary definition of deviance and let that serve as the foundation for our exploration through the remainder of this book. However, the ways that the word "deviance" is used in academic research and common usage often differ from the dictionary definition—defining deviance is not as straightforward as the dictionary implies. In the academic realm, deviance is studied by **deviance specialists** who analyze criminal and/or non-criminal forms of deviance; those who focus exclusively on criminal forms of deviance are more specifically known as **criminologists**. Among deviance specialists (including criminologists), the study of deviance has historically been characterized by considerable disagreement over the concept of deviance, and this "problem of definition" (Ben-Yehuda, 1990, p. 4) continues to the present day. Even deviance specialists cannot entirely agree on what deviance is.

Although contradictory definitions of deviance have co-existed for many decades, some researchers suggest that a broader shift in definitions has become evident over time (Hathaway & Atkinson, 2001). Older definitions, which suggested there is an *objective* way of determining what is deviant, have shifted to more recent definitions that deconstruct the notion of objectivity, and instead point out that deviance is necessarily *subjective*; in fact, some deviance specialists label the latter approach the "contemporary approach" (Herman, 1995, p.3). **Objective** views of deviance claim that the presence of certain characteristics defines deviance: behaviours or people with those characteristics are deviant, and those lacking such characteristics are normal (Rubington & Weinberg, 2008). By looking for these characteristics, we can all identify deviance. In contrast, **subjective** views of deviance claim that there is no shared, observable characteristic that can clearly tell us who or what is deviant, and who or what is normal—instead, someone must tell us who is deviant in Canadian society (Rubington & Weinberg, 2008). Both the objective and subjective ways of defining deviance will be outlined and explored in more detail as the chapter progresses.

Proposing that there has been a shift from objective to subjective ways of defining deviance implies certain underlying assumptions. The core underlying assumption is that there is an unmistakable distinction between objective and subjective definitions of deviance, so that an objective definition can be clearly differentiated from a subjective definition. The distinction between objective and subjective is typically described as a dualism, or dichotomy, wherein objective and subjective represent two oppositional and mutually exclusive categories (e.g., Adler & Adler, 2003; Ben-Yehuda, 1990). These categories are analogous to the two sides of a coin that, when tossed, will show *either* heads or tails, but not both. However, the recent shifts in definitions of deviance often go beyond this notion of objective and subjective as mutually exclusive categories, and instead combine aspects of both. And if it is possible to combine objective and subjective notions of deviance, this raises the question of whether the objective/subjective dichotomy that has been so frequently referred to is even a useful one to talk about in contemporary deviance research.

In the following sections, the traditional objective/subjective distinction will be explored. We will look at the different objective definitions of deviance that have been used in the academic arena as well as in common usage. Subjective definitions of deviance will also be reviewed. Finally, we will look at how these two different types of definitions may not be so different after all, and how many contemporary ways of looking at deviance are blends of both objective and subjective approaches. Although this section of the chapter began with what looked like a very clear dictionary definition of deviance, when you finish reading the chapter you will see that the subject of this book—deviance—is a far more complex and multi-faceted phenomenon than the dictionary definition suggests.

The Objective/Subjective Dichotomy
Objectivism: Deviance as an Act

The objective side of the dichotomy, as it has typically been depicted, emphasizes the assumption that there is something inherent in a person, behaviour, or characteristic that is necessarily deviant. All "deviants" have something in common that enables us to recognize them when we see them. However, the precise nature of that shared feature is a matter of debate. The characteristics that have been most frequently postulated include statistical rarity, harm, a negative societal reaction, and normative violation (e.g., Deutschmann, 2002; Sacco, 1992). Each of these features is emphasized by different deviance specialists, as well as by various laypersons. Each of these characteristics, when used as a defining characteristic of deviance, has also been subject to criticism by other deviance specialists, particularly those working from a subjective approach.

Statistical Rarity.   One of the definitions of deviance that has been associated with the objective side of the objective/subjective dualism is based on **statistical rarity**. Although this is a definition that is not commonly used in academic research, it is a definition that is "often heard in everyday conversation" (Clinard & Meier, 2001, p. 7); as a result of its popular usage, it is an important conception of deviance to analyze (Becker, 1963). According to this definition, if a behaviour or characteristic is not typical, it is deviant. Thus, smokers may be thought of as deviant in contemporary Canada, because only 16.5% of Canadians over the age of 12 smoke (Statistics Canada, 2007). Ex-cons may be thought of as deviant because most people have not been in prison. People with spiked green hair may be thought of as deviant because most people do not have spiked green hair.

While this definition of deviance has popular credibility, and although there are particular instances where statistical rarity can be observed, postulating statistical rarity as the defining characteristic of deviance has its limitations. First of all, how we define "rare" presents a problem. Is a behaviour rare if its prevalence is less than 50%? Or does it have to be less than 30%? Adlaf & Paglia-Boak (2007) have found that 47% of 18- and 19-year-olds have used marijuana within the past year, as have almost 31% of youth in Grade 10. A significant proportion (51.8%) of 18- to 19-year-olds who have consumed alcohol within the past 12 months have engaged in binge drinking on a monthly basis (Health Canada, 2008). Are these behaviours rare? The difficulty in determining the criteria for rarity illustrates one of the limitations of this definition of deviance.

A second limitation is that some behaviours are not statistically rare, but are still perceived as being unacceptable in the larger society and are subjected to control efforts. For example, 59% of Canadian youth in Grade 9 have consumed alcohol within the past 12 months (Adlaf & Paglia-Boak, 2007). Thus, alcohol consumption among young teenagers is statistically *common* rather than rare, and yet most of us would say that it is not acceptable for 12-year-olds to drink. Furthermore, extensive efforts to prevent this behaviour are found in the school curriculum, community programs, and families. A similar illustration of this limitation comes from the study of adolescent sexuality. It might surprise you that as many as 55% of students in Grade 9 and 74% of those in Grade 11 have participated in "heavy petting" (i.e., manual genital stimulation of a partner) (Boyce, Doherty, Fortin, & MacKinnon, 2003). Even though this behaviour is not statistically rare, as a society we still initiate efforts to control and reduce it through sex education programs in schools, religious teachings, and socialization in families.

Third, we must also consider that there are many rare behaviours or characteristics that are not considered deviant in Canadian society. Left-handed people are statistically rare, but they are not treated as deviant, although they were seen that way historically (Barsley, 1967). Sports prodigies (like Wayne Gretzky and Sidney Crosby) are statistically rare, but are respected and envied. Only 27% of Canadians over the age of 12 are physically active (Gilmour, 2007) but few of us would say that people who are physically active are considered deviant in our society. This limitation, along with the previous two, suggest that it is *more than* the statistical number of people who engage in a specific behaviour that determines what is considered deviant in our society. Some deviance specialists propose that the important factor is actually harmfulness.

Harm.   The second definition of deviance associated with the objective side of the objective/subjective dichotomy is based on the concept of **harm** (Deutschmann, 2002; Sacco, 1992). That is, if an action causes harm, then it is deviant. The most obvious type of harm is *physical harm*. Thus, if someone harms someone else—for example, through assault, drunk driving, or exposing others to secondhand smoke—then the perpetrator of that harm is deviant. Physical harm can also be done to oneself; for example, smoking may be considered deviant because of the harm caused to the smoker by increased risks of heart disease and various types of cancer. *Emotional harm* can be done to others (e.g., emotional abuse) and to oneself (e.g., repeatedly dating partners with addictions), as well.

Harm may also be directed not at a human being but at society itself: certain behaviours or people may constitute *social harm*, because they interfere with the smooth running of society as a whole. In this context, criminals can be considered

Exercise Your Mind

Since Al-Qaeda orchestrated the attacks on the World Trade Center and the Pentagon in 2001, "terrorism" has become a word we hear daily in the media. Within the context of "harm," terrorism can be perceived as causing all three types of harm, and in multiple ways. Identify the ways that terrorism causes (a) physical harm to others and/or to oneself, (b) emotional harm to others and/or to oneself, (c) harm to the social order and the smooth running of society, and (d) harm to the way people understand the world and their place in it.

deviant because they threaten the safety of the population at large and the social order as a whole. If everyone committed crimes, then anarchy would rule. In fact, implicit in criminal law is the assumption that certain acts must be prohibited because of their harmfulness. In Canada, *all* crimes are considered to harm society itself; the court case is between the Crown (i.e., the state) and the defendant, not the victim and the defendant.

Finally, harm may be directed at something far more abstract and ethereal than a person or society; harm may occur in the form of a *threat to the way we understand the world and our place in it*. Historically, religious belief systems have frequently provided us with this means of abstract understanding on a large scale. Even in contemporary societies, religious belief systems provide many people with a fundamental way of understanding existence. With the example of religion, we can see many instances of this more abstract notion of harm. For example, Joan of Arc was seen as deviant (Brower, 1999), in part because she claimed that she did not need the fathers of the church as a pipeline of communication to God, a claim that violated the dominant religion-based belief system of the time. In contemporary society, Muslim women who do not cover their heads may be seen by some other Muslims, who hold a particular interpretation of their religious doctrine, as threatening the fundamental assumptions upon which the religious belief system is based (Fernea, 1998; Todd, 2001).

At first glance, notions of physical or emotional harm to someone, harm to the social order, and harm to abstract world views appear to be useful in recognizing and defining deviance. Many different forms of deviance, from murder and smoking to the behaviour of persecuted historical figures such as Joan of Arc, can be seen as causing harm to someone or something. And perceptions of harm frequently do galvanize social action, such as the creation of non-smoking bylaws. However, a more critical look at the idea of harm is useful.

The very idea of physical harm is not as clear as it might initially appear, and has sometimes changed. Claims of physical harm can be, and have been, disputed. For many years, the tobacco industry claimed that smoking did not cause the harm that anti-smoking activists suggested it did. In the past, some claims of

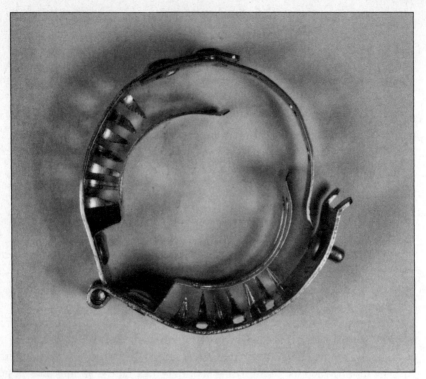

A variety of anti-masturbation devices were used on children during the Victorian era and the early twentieth century, because of the harm that the behaviour was thought to cause.

physical harm were greatly exaggerated. A century ago, doctors argued that masturbation caused hairy palms, acne, and outright insanity. For example, look at the following excerpt from a lecture by nineteenth-century health reformer Sylvester Graham: "This general mental decay . . . continues with the continued abuses [of masturbation], till the wretched transgressor sinks into a miserable fatuity, and finally becomes a confirmed and degraded idiot, whose deeply sunken and vacant glassy eye, and livid, shriveled countenance, and ulcerous, toothless gums, and fetid breath, and feeble broken voice, and emaciated and dwarfish and crooked body, and almost hairless head—covered, perhaps, with suppurating blisters and running sores—denote a premature old age—a blighted body—and a mined soul" (cited in Whorton, 2001, p. 3).

Elaborate measures were taken to curb children's masturbation in orphanages, hospitals, boarding schools, and middle-class homes. This included behavioural controls, such as cold baths, intense exercise, sleeping on hard beds, and moderate eating (Hunt, 1998). It also included a wide range of anti-masturbation devices (see photograph). Bondage would prevent children from touching themselves at night. The Stephenson Spermatic Truss prevented erections from occurring. The Bowen Device would pull on the wearer's pubic

Box 1.1   Emily Murphy's Marijuana Campaign

Emily Murphy, the first female judge in the British Empire and a leading Canadian suffragist in the early twentieth century, was dismayed at what she saw as the horrors of Canada's drug trade. After interviewing both drug users and law enforcement officials from across North America, in 1922 she wrote the book *The Black Candle* about drug use. One chapter focuses specifically on the harms caused by marijuana use, quoting police officials: "[Marijuana] has the effect of driving the [user] completely insane. The addict loses all sense of moral responsibility. Addicts to this drug, while under its influence, are immune to pain. . . . While in this condition they become raving maniacs and are liable to kill or indulge in any form of violence to other persons, using the most savage methods of cruelty. . . . They are dispossessed of their natural and normal will power, and their mentality is that of idiots. If this drug is indulged in to any great extent, it ends in the untimely death of its addict" (Murphy, 1973 [1922], pp. 332–333). These types of claims are somewhat humorous to today's reader, but had a significant influence on changing drug laws at the time.

hair if an erection occurred. Steel armour was padlocked shut at night, and a key was required to allow trips to the bathroom. Penis-cooling devices splashed cold water on the genitals if an erection occurred (Hunt, 1998).

Exaggerated claims about the dangers of marijuana use were also common in the past. In the years leading up to the criminalization of marijuana in 1923, social activists, community leaders, and law enforcement officials spoke out about the physical harm it caused. As can be seen in Box 1.1, marijuana use was alleged to cause horrific violent crimes, murder, idiocy, and ultimately complete insanity and even death. Today, such claims are perceived as greatly exaggerated; however, debates over the physical harm caused by marijuana use continue, as do debates over the physical *benefits* for medical purposes, both of which are fundamental to discussions of the issues of decriminalization and legalization.

When it comes to the idea of interfering with the current social order, or threatening a belief system or world view, the limitations of defining deviance by virtue of harm become more evident. First, whether or not society or a belief system is being *harmed* can be subjective. Are Muslim women who do not cover their heads actually a threat to the belief system contained in Islam? While some people would say so, these women themselves often say there is nothing in the belief system itself that requires it. What about Christian nuns who do not wear habits? Historically, the habit was considered an essential component of membership in a religious order, in part symbolizing the discarding of the worldly individual and becoming part of a communal whole, a sign of one's dedication to God (Kuhns, 2003). But in contemporary society, it is relatively uncommon to see a nun wearing a habit, a fact that causes some consternation among those religious orders that perceive this change as a threat to the order, the larger religion of which it is a part, and its doctrine.

During the twentieth century, there were several times when women in North America were accused of harming the social order or abstract belief systems or both. Early feminists who fought for the right of women to vote faced such accusations, as did later groups of women in the 1960s and 1970s when they questioned the "natural" role of women as homemakers and moved outside the home into paid employment. Were these women causing harm to society or to beliefs? Because the word *harm* implies a negative impact, many would say that these women were not *harming* society; they were simply changing society. Others would say that by *changing* society, they were having a negative impact on the social order of the time, and thus were technically causing harm, but that it was a social order that needed to be changed.

Indeed, there are times when the reactions cause more harm than the initial behaviours, characteristics, or people themselves. For instance, in 2007, Polish immigrant Robert Dziekanski arrived at the Vancouver airport. His mother was to pick him up; however, due to a series of procedural problems, he ended up wandering through the airport for 10 hours, unable to speak English. He became increasingly disoriented and his behaviour came to be perceived as potentially problematic. The RCMP were called, and following a confrontation in which officers say Dziekanski raised a stapler to them in an aggressive manner, they tasered him five times, which resulted in his death. Certainly in this case, the measures to control Dziekanski's behaviour were far more harmful than his behaviour was. Similarly, although Emily Murphy sought to control the "harms" of marijuana use (as well as other moral harms, such as opium use and prostitution), certain aspects of her efforts had racism as their foundation, and she was a supporter of the eugenics movement (see Chapter 9). Some would argue that both racism and the eugenics movement have caused more harm over the past century than marijuana use has.

All of the above limitations of defining deviance on the basis of harm illustrate the necessity of going beyond the idea of harm in seeking the defining characteristic of deviance. The nature of these limitations is such that this definition of deviance is rarely used in academic literature, although it does enjoy popular usage among laypersons, politicians, and social activists.

Despite the fact that academic literature rarely suggests that harm is *the* defining characteristic of deviance, some literature does acknowledge that harm, or a characteristic similar to harm (i.e., threat or dangerousness), is *one of* the characteristics of deviance. For example, Lianos (with Douglas, 2000) proposes that what is most significant to the study of deviance is not whether someone actually causes harm or is actually dangerous, but rather whether someone *seems* dangerous. Deviance specialists from the subjective side of the objective/subjective dualism suggest we look at the social processes that result in someone being seen as potentially dangerous, and not consider whether that person actually *is* dangerous. The *Ask Yourself* exercise has you further explore the concept of harm within the context of contemporary social debates.

Societal Reaction. Another one of the definitions of deviance that has been associated with the objective side of the objective/subjective dichotomy is based on

Ask Yourself

What are some of the controversial or hotly debated issues that are occurring in your community or in the larger society at the present time? Are claims of "harm" being made in any of these debates? In those instances, is harm (a) *actually* present, (b) a perception on the part of some groups of people but not others, and/or (c) merely being used as a justification for implementing particular actions?

the nature of **societal reaction**. People may respond to others in a number of different ways. If the responses of society's "masses" are primarily negative (such as dislike, anger, hatred, stigmatization, and teasing) rather than positive (such as liking, admiration, envy, or tolerance), then the person or act being responded to is deviant. Seeing this negative societal evaluation enables us to determine who or what is deviant.

However, focusing on a negative societal reaction as the defining characteristic of deviance raises many questions. Why does society react negatively to some actions, characteristics, or people, and not others? Whose reaction counts? Does my reaction, as a university professor and social scientist, count more than your reaction as a student? Does the prime minister's reaction count more than mine? How many individual negative reactions must exist before we can say that "society" is reacting negatively?

The gaps that emerge when defining deviance on the basis of societal reaction are revealed by numerous examples. For instance, Canadian surveys consistently find that "a strong majority . . . favour[s] a limited fine as the maximum penalty for cannabis possession" (i.e., decriminalization), and survey questions about full legalization reveal "an almost even split" (Fischer, Ala-Leppilampi, Single, & Robins, 2003, p. 277). However, despite this data on societal reaction, prior to winning the 2006 federal election, the Conservatives explicitly stated that they would "prevent the decriminalization of marijuana" (Conservative Party of Canada, 2006, p. 25). Since that time, they have successfully done so.

In contrast, the Conservative government's position on same-sex marriage was that it would "hold a truly free vote on the definition of marriage, [and] . . . if the resolution is passed, the government [would] introduce legislation to restore the traditional definition of marriage" (Conservative Party of Canada, 2006, p. 33). On December 7, 2006, parliamentarians voted on a motion against same-sex marriage; the motion failed 175 votes to 123 votes. Elected officials in Parliament presumably consider a free vote representative of Canadian public opinion—that is, a proxy for societal reaction. The comparison of these two issues shows that the legislative action regarding one issue (i.e., same-sex marriage) is to be based on a representation of societal reaction, while the legislative action on another issue (i.e., the decriminalization of marijuana) is to be independent of societal reaction, and in fact may directly oppose public opinion. These inconsistencies reveal that the law and, more broadly, determinations of who/what is deviant in Canadian society, are based upon processes that go beyond societal reaction.

Surveys of public opinion reveal diverse points of view; not everyone shares the same opinion. More than half of Canadians (54%) are in favour of marriage rights for same-sex couples (Matthews, 2005), but that means 46% are not in favour or have no opinion about those rights. A large majority of Canadians

(85 to 90%) support the full legalization of medicinal marijuana (Stein, cited in Fischer, Ala-Leppilampi, Single, & Robins, 2003), but that means 10 to 15% do not support it or are indifferent. These types of diverse survey results reveal that societal reactions are not uniform, and different groups of people react in various ways to the same behaviour or issue. Given the plurality of points of view on many issues, it appears that societal reaction alone does not determine how a particular behaviour is treated in Canadian society.

Normative Violation. The dictionary, as well as many deviance specialists, suggests that recognizing deviance is quite straightforward—a behaviour or characteristic is deviant if it violates norms. In fact, this is likely the definition of deviance that was included in your introductory sociology textbook. The "general statement that deviance is focused around the violation of norms" (Ben-Yehuda, 1990, p. 4) is shared extensively among deviance specialists from both the objective and subjective sides of the objective/subjective dichotomy, as well as those who transcend this traditional dualism. However, the manner in which **normative violation** is integrated into a definition of deviance varies among deviance specialists working in the various approaches.

Among deviance specialists working in the objective side of the dichotomy, the violation of norms has been proposed to be *the* defining characteristic of deviance. Indeed, the dictionary definition of deviance makes this point quite clearly as well. Yet even among those recognized as objectivists, the nature of the normative violation seen as constituting deviance has changed. Early objectivists used what may be considered an "absolutist" conception of normative violation, wherein a particular behaviour or characteristic was perceived as being inherently and universally deviant (Adler & Adler, 2006a, p. 3). According to this view, there are certain immutable norms and values that should be held in all cultures and at all times—norms and values that emerge from the word of God, the laws of nature, or some other unchangeable source. Because of that absolute moral order, what is considered wrong in one place should be considered wrong everywhere; cross-cultural and trans-historical norms prohibiting incest, murder, and lying are perceived as evidence of this absolute moral order.

The simplistic view of norms in the absolutist view led many objectivists to abandon the absolutist view. However, still on the objective side of the objective/subjective dualism, another view of normative violation has developed. Among these more modern objectivists, norms are perceived as being culturally specific rather than universal—based on a given society's moral code rather than on any type of absolute moral order. This perspective is still identified as objective, in that someone who violates the norms of the society they live in is seen as deviant. From birth, we are socialized into the norms that govern the society we live in, and we learn its standards and expectations. In Canadian society, as we grow up we are taught to share with others, to be polite, to work hard, to listen to our teachers—in essence, most of us are taught by our parents, teachers, community leaders, and religious leaders to follow the rules. We learn

Ask Yourself

List the norms that are being violated by each of the following people: an obese person; a student that plagiarizes by downloading a term paper from the internet; someone on social assistance; a drug addict or alcoholic; a thief. Remember, norms refer to standards or expectations of behaviour, so ask yourself what expectations each of these people is not living up to—what "rules" of society are they breaking?

what behaviours will be rewarded (like arriving at work on time) and what behaviours will be punished (like breaking the law). Knowing these expectations, if we then go on to violate the norms, we are "deviant." The *Ask Yourself* exercise requires you to take a closer look at some of the norms in Canadian society.

Looking at the examples in the *Ask Yourself* exercise, one can see that not all norms are the same. While violating some norms may result in prison (as for the thief), violating other norms has different (and some might say less severe) consequences. The obese person, alcoholic, social assistance recipient, or plagiarizing student will not be entered into the criminal justice system for their normative violations. These differential outcomes of normative violation emerge from the existence of various types of norms, ranging from *folkways* to *mores* to *laws* (Adler & Adler, 2006a; Kendall, Murray, & Linden, 2007; Sumner, 1906).

Norms, as standards or expectations of behaviour, can refer to informal, everyday behaviours, such as rules of etiquette, choice of clothing, and behaviour in the university classroom. These kinds of informal norms are called **folkways**, and if you violate these norms, you might be considered odd (Adler & Adler, 2006a), rude, or a troublemaker. Other norms are taken more seriously. **Mores** are those standards that are often seen as the foundation of morality in a culture, such as prohibitions against incest or homosexuality. If you violate these norms, you may be thought of as immoral (Adler & Adler, 2006a) or even evil. Finally, some norms are considered to be so central to the smooth running of society that they are enshrined within the legal system—for example, in Canada's Criminal Code. If you violate the Criminal Code you will be thought of as a criminal. At times, the legal system integrates mores (e.g., incest is included in the Criminal Code of Canada, and homosexual activities remain criminal offences in several American states); however, other acts that are not perceived as the foundation for morality in our culture (e.g., marijuana possession) are also integrated into the legal system.

AN INTERNET MOMENT

You can find a copy of the Criminal Code of Canada at http://laws.justice.gc.ca/en/C-46/. Look at the Table of Contents to see the kinds of normative violations that have been enshrined within Canada's legal system. You might find it particularly interesting to look at the behaviours that are prohibited in the section on Offences Against the Person (which include assault, hate crimes, and bigamy) and the section on Sexual Offences, Public Morals, and Disorderly Conduct. What, if anything, do all of the norms that are being supported in this document have in common, such that they are considered important enough to enshrine within our criminal justice system?

The way that norms are integrated into objectivist definitions of deviance presumes a certain level of consensus (McCaghy, Capron, & Jamieson, 2003; Miller, Wright, & Dannels, 2001; Rubington & Weinberg, 2008). Although cross-cultural variations in norms are acknowledged, it is assumed that, in a given society, the majority of citizens agree upon the norms. However, deviance specialists working in the subjective side of the objective/subjective dualism find this view of social norms problematic. Some have reservations about the presumption of normative consensus, and question the extent to which a given expectation must be shared in order to be considered a "norm" and then used as an objective standard against which deviance is judged (Ward, Carter, & Perrin, 1994).

Some even question whether it is possible to determine the level of consensus that does or does not exist for a given expectation. They point out that there are countless numbers of groups in society having innumerable different sets of rules; even a single individual belongs to multiple groups having varying sets of expectations. Given the multiplicity of individuals, groups, and sets of expectations that coexist in a society, normative consensus is difficult to determine (Adler & Adler, 2003; Becker, 1963). In fact, given all of these different sets of expectations that exist in society simultaneously, which expectations are the ones that constitute society's "norms" and are then used to judge deviance and normality?

In response to these critiques, some deviance specialists have elected to focus on those norms that they suggest are characterized by some consensus, "assuming that the agreed-upon norms of a society can be found in its criminal law" (McCaghy, Capron, & Jamieson, 2003, p. 8). Following this chain of logic, deviance becomes equated with criminality, and the forms of deviance studied include prostitution, drug use, white-collar crime, gang behaviour, and other forms of law-violating behaviour. The practice of equating deviance with criminality has resulted in an academic debate over the differences between the fields of criminology and the sociology of deviance, and whether the sociology of deviance has been subsumed under the umbrella of criminology (Miller, Wright, & Dannels, 2001). Whether focusing on criminal law violations is more illustrative of criminology or the sociology of deviance, the claim that agreed-upon norms can be found in a society's criminal law has itself been questioned.

Some criminologists and other deviance specialists working on the subjective side of the objective/subjective dichotomy draw our attention to the fact that law creation is a political activity, wherein those norms that are embodied in law do not necessarily reflect the opinion of the majority of citizens (Des Rosiers & Bittle, 2004). Indeed, the creation of a new law in Canada does not require the support of a majority, nor are the opinions of all Canadians sought prior to its creation. Marijuana possession remains illegal, even though since the late 1990s, the courts, the Senate Special Committee on Illegal Drugs, the Canadian Centre on Substance Abuse, the Centre for Addictions and Mental Health, the Canadian Association of Police Chiefs, and public opinion have all recommended its decriminalization (Fischer, Ala-Leppilampi, Single, & Robins, 2003). In this case, "consensus" seems to contradict the law rather than support it.

The **consensual view** of law, wherein the law is perceived as arising out of social consensus and is then equally applied to all, is only one of the possible views of crime and law (Siegel & McCormick, 2003).

Critiques of the consensual view of law point to conflict and interactionist views. Criminologists who use the **conflict view** (also known as the *social power perspective*) perceive the law as a tool used by the ruling class to serve its own interests, and believe that the law is more likely to be applied to members of the powerless classes in society.

For example, some research suggests that young offenders who belong to the lower classes are more likely to be drawn into the justice system than are youth of the middle and upper classes. In Canada, self-report surveys of youth crime show us that middle- and upper-class youth are underrepresented in official crime statistics; they are, in fact, committing more crimes than official statistics indicate (Bell, 2002). Why might this be the case? Howard Becker (1963), one of the first deviance specialists to critique objectivist views and propose a subjectivist view of deviance, suggested that even given similar behaviours by lower-class and middle-class youth, police are more likely to enter the former into the justice system, while letting middle-class youth go with a warning or into their parents' custody.

Another view of crime, the **interactionist view**, also presents a non-consensual view of criminal law. This view suggests that society's powerful define the law at the behest of interest groups, who appeal to those with power in order to rectify a perceived social ill. Again, the criminal law is not seen as emerging out of consensus, but rather out of the interests of certain groups in society. Finally, some criminologists portray a more complex view of criminal law, pointing out that the nation's law must attempt to strike some sort of a balance between the interests of the powerful, the opinion of the majority, and the views of special interest groups (Linden, 2000). Looking at these different views, we can see that criminal law is based on more than a simple consensus about what society's norms are.

The normative objectivity of the law has also been critiqued on the question of the situational applicability of broad social norms. For example, in a rather objective fashion we might say that legal prohibitions against murder reflect normative clarity in society—we know that murder is wrong. However, some deviance specialists point out the many situational characteristics that can modify this abstract norm. Depending upon the laws of a particular country, self-defence, capital punishment, military action in wartime, and euthanasia are all circumstances in which taking a human life may be considered acceptable.

So, is taking another human life deviant? Looking at the above, we see that the answer to that question is that taking another human life is deviant at some times but not at others. In fact, in situations where taking another human life is considered acceptable, the behaviour is not called "murder." For example, during wartime, the death of innocent civilians is not "murder," but "collateral damage." Consequently, given the situational variations in which even the most basic norms do or do not apply, some deviance specialists ask whether norms, as reflected in criminal law, are even useful in trying to define deviance (Ward, Carter, & Perrin, 1994).

Some deviance specialists step into this debate over the degree of consensus involved in social norms by proposing that there are some norms that do have higher levels of consensus. For example, despite the situational variations in prohibitions against taking another human life, it is likely that most (if not all) Canadians support the inclusion of homicide in the Criminal Code; the same can also likely be said for auto theft, sexual assault, and break-and-enter. Thio (1983) uses the concepts of **high-consensus deviance** and **low-consensus deviance** to distinguish between forms of deviance that have differential levels of support in the broader society. The norms reflected in criminal law are characterized by relatively more consensus than are society's non-legislative norms (such as norms governing physical appearance). And within the law, certain laws are characterized by relatively more consensus than are others.

Although the dictionary defines deviance on the basis of normative violation, the limitations of that definition make this definition problematic. In fact, limitations are associated with each of the objectivist definitions of deviance—not only normative violation, but also statistical rarity, harm, and a negative societal reaction. Some deviance specialists suggest that these limitations have caused a large-scale shift to the subjective side of the objective/subjective dichotomy (Hathaway & Atkinson, 2001).

TIME TO REVIEW

- What does the "problem of definition" refer to, and how is it related to the objective/subjective dichotomy?
- What is the core assumption underlying the objective side of the objective/subjective dichotomy?
- What are the four different objective definitions of deviance? Provide examples of each.
- What are the limitations of each of the objective definitions of deviance? Provide examples of each.

- What are the different types of harm that can occur, according to those who define deviance on the basis of harm?
- How has the objectivist notion of normative violation changed over time?
- What are the different views of the role of consensus in the development of criminal law text?

Subjectivism: Deviance as a Label

Having looked at the objective side of the traditional objective/subjective dichotomy, we now turn our attention to the subjective side. From this point of view, there is a very different answer to the question "How can we recognize deviance when we see it?" While objectivists suggest that deviance can be recognized by the presence of a particular characteristic, subjectivists say that we cannot recognize deviance when we see it; we have to be taught, through processes of socialization, that a person, behaviour, or characteristic is deviant. There is no singular trait or characteristic that is shared by all deviant people throughout history and across cultures, other than the fact that people with some influence on society have said they are deviant (Becker, 1963).

Just as objective conceptions of deviance have changed over time, so have subjective conceptions of deviance. Early subjectivism focused primarily on the process of labelling—deviance is anything that is labelled as such. This form of subjectivism has a negative reaction as its foundation, with Becker (1963) saying that if there is no negative reaction, there is no deviance; in other words, deviance lies in the reaction rather than in the act.

The distinction between the ways the concept of "negative reaction" is used by these early subjectivists and the way it is used by objectivists (as discussed earlier in the chapter) is somewhat hazy. The objective use of negative reaction focuses on a *societal* reaction—particular behaviours or characteristics *are* deviant in our society, and we can see that they are deviant because society's masses respond to them with hatred, dislike, or distrust.

In contrast, the early subjective use of negative reaction is more abstract, pointing to the reaction as being almost arbitrary—any behaviour may be reacted to negatively, such that we can never know how a particular act will be responded to. The abstract way that early subjectivists used the concept of negative reaction has been subject to criticism, particularly for ignoring the act that stimulated a negative reaction in the first place (Ward, Carter, & Perrin, 1994). The reaction itself does not create the initial act that people are reacting to; in other words, people are reacting to a specific act for a reason—their reactions do not arise out of a purely arbitrary process. It is the processes that contribute to that reaction, and the nature of the reaction itself, that must be analyzed.

Consequently, the **dominant moral codes** (Goode, 1997, p. 29) of a society serve as the foundation for determining who or what is deviant. These are the "lists" of right/wrong, appropriate/inappropriate, moral/immoral that predominate in a particular society at a given time in history and are enforced in multiple ways (e.g., by the criminal justice system, media, and education system). A society's dominant moral codes are shaped by the interests and the actions of groups that hold some level of power.

Contemporary subjective deviance specialists point to the complex nature of power relations. Social processes involve far more than simply the control and oppression of the powerless by the powerful. The use and legitimization of power interacts with negotiations about moral boundaries—negotiations in which less powerful groups in society are also able to participate. Consequently, "this process does mean that the powerless can resist deviantization" (Ben-Yehuda, 1990, p. 7) rather than simply being at the mercy of the interests of the powerful. Continual negotiations are occurring, such that the social construction of deviance and normality/conformity is in a constant state of flux (Ben-Yehuda, 1990).

Subjectivity and the "Social Construction" of Deviance

Referring to the subjective nature of deviance means focusing on deviance as a *social construction*. In other words, there is nothing inherent in a behaviour or characteristic that makes it deviant; a particular behaviour or characteristic is deviant only if the dominant moral codes of a specific society at a certain time in history say the behaviour is deviant. Consequently, Adler and Adler (2006a) label the subjectivist view the "relativist perspective" (p. 3).

The subjective view also recognizes that a society's dominant moral codes are influenced by powerful groups. Similarly, what is considered to be normal is also socially constructed, given that notions of deviance and normality exist only in relation to each other (Freud, 1999). **Social constructionism** refers to the perspective proposing that social characteristics (e.g., "thin," "delinquent") are creations or artifacts of a particular society at a specific time in history, just as objects (e.g., houses, cars) are artifacts of that society; consequently, a person, behaviour, or characteristic that is considered "deviant" in one society may be considered "normal" in another society or at another time in history.

Social constructionism has become a dominant force in the study of deviance today. In fact, more than a decade ago Goode (1997) suggested that "most deviance specialists [today] are *constructionists*" (p. 35). However, there are different levels or different types of constructionism. One type of constructionism is labelled **radical** (Goode, 1997) or **strict** (Best, cited in Rubington & Weinberg, 2002); the other type is labelled **soft** or **contextual** (Best, cited in Rubington & Weinberg, 2002).

Radical constructionists postulate a distinct theoretical perspective claiming that the world is characterized by endless relativism, that "there is no essential reality to the social world at all, that if everything and anything is simply looked at in a certain way, that is the way it is" (Goode, 1997, p. 35).

However, "most [contemporary deviance specialists] are not *radical* constructionists. What I mean by this is that most do *not* believe that *everything* is a matter of definition, that there is *no* essential reality to the social world at all. . . . Rather, most sociologists of deviance believe that there are limits to social constructionism" (Goode, 1997, p.35). Consequently, sociologists who are soft or contextual constructionists emphasize the processes by which certain social phenomena come to be perceived and reacted to in particular ways in a given society at a specific time in history. In such cases, social construction is addressed in terms of a process rather than a theory, and therefore can be combined with a number of different theoretical approaches, approaches that will be addressed in Chapter 3.

Viewing social constructionism as a process implies that what is of sociological significance is not the individual behaviour or characteristic itself, but rather: (a) its place in the social order; (b) the roles assigned to people who exhibit that behaviour or characteristic; and (c) the meanings attached to that behaviour or characteristic. For example, homosexuality is "universal" in the sense that it has existed across the world and throughout history. What varies is the way that homosexuality is perceived and reacted to in particular societies;

Figure 1.1   LEVELS OF SOCIAL CONSTRUCTION

thus, while homosexuality is a part of nature, and therefore "biological," it is also "socially constructed." The way deviance is socially constructed emerges from several ongoing interconnected processes, from the macro through the micro levels (see Figure 1.1) (Nelson & Robinson, 2002).

The first process to consider is the *sociocultural* level: beliefs, ideologies, values, and systems of meaning have an influence on the path of social construction. The second is the *institutional* level: the structures of our society, such as government, the education system, and religion (among others) that affect social construction. Third is the *interactional* level: our interactions with other people influence the way we think and feel about others, thereby determining the role that each of us plays in social construction. Fourth is the *individual* level: at this level our own identities, concepts of self, and ways of understanding our own existence in the world affect the path of social construction.

Transcending the Objective/Subjective Dichotomy

The objective and subjective sides of the objective/subjective dichotomy, as it has been traditionally expressed, appear to be considerably distinct. On the objective side of the dualism, deviance specialists claim that there is a shared characteristic that all deviants have in common, a feature that enables us to recognize deviance when we see it. Although statistical rarity, harm, and a negative societal reaction have each been identified as that shared characteristic (whether by academics, laypersons, or social activists), the defining feature of deviance that is most often

TIME TO REVIEW

■ What is the core assumption of definitions of deviance on the subjective side of the objective/subjective dichotomy?

■ What are the roles of *power* and *dominant moral codes* according to subjective definitions of deviance?

■ What does it mean when we say that deviance and normality are socially constructed?

■ What are the two types of social constructionism, and how do they differ?

■ What are the four levels at which the social construction of deviance and normality occurs?

identified is that of normative violation. On the subjective side of the dualism, deviance specialists claim that there is no shared feature among deviants; instead, a person, behaviour, or characteristic is deviant if enough important people say so. Through the processes of social construction, which are influenced by power, a dominant moral order emerges that then serves as the standard against which deviance and normality are judged.

The conception of the objective/subjective dichotomy serves as the foundation for the claim that a shift in definitions of deviance has recently occurred, from objective to subjective (e.g., Goode, 1997; Hathaway & Atkinson, 2001). In fact, some deviance specialists suggest that using the subjective, constructionist view in exploring both legal and illegal norm-violating behaviour defines the sociology of deviance as a discipline. However, recent shifts in the study of deviance may, in fact, transcend the objective/subjective dualism, with elements of objectivism and subjectivism being integrated to varying degrees.

We have already seen some evidence of this in the previous discussions of objective/subjective dualism. For example, we have seen that, over time, objective deviance specialists have changed their conceptions of norms from that of an absolute moral order to that of a culturally specific moral order. Similarly, over time, subjective deviance specialists have acknowledged the role of norms in defining deviance, but in terms of norms that may be socially constructed and determined by processes of power.

For example, Evans (2001) suggests that small group–specific normative systems can be identified. Evans delineates the set of norms that governs behaviour in Married Life chat rooms, which then serves as the standard against which certain types of chat room behaviour are judged deviant and made subject to a negative reaction by other group members. Tittle and Paternoster (2000) also propose that group-specific normative systems *can* be identified, and on a different level, they identify the normative system of middle-class America. Their discussion of norms goes a step further by suggesting that, although this is only one of countless numbers of normative systems in society, it is the one that has come to dominate American society as a whole, through the power that the middle class holds in processes of social construction: "[T]he middle class dominates U.S. society, both by imposing its standards through the schools, the mass media, and the law and by enjoying a degree of natural hegemony in behavior styles and thinking that flows from the admiration and emulation of those with higher status" (p. 29).

Many contemporary definitions of deviance combine normative violation, negative reaction, harm, power, and/or social construction (Hathaway & Atkinson, 2001; McCaghy, Capron, & Jamieson, 2003; Ward, Carter, & Perrin, 1994). For example, Stebbins (1996) defines deviance as normative violation, but goes on to say that the nature of society's response to that violation depends upon the level of perceived threat the normative violation entails, and that the structures and processes of power relations in society influence this entire process. A retrospective look at work by earlier deviance specialists reveals that the distinction between objective and subjective has always been somewhat blurred. Even Howard Becker (1963), one of the leading proponents of the subjective view of deviance, integrated the notion of harm into his definition of deviance. He stated that deviance is that which is so labelled, but that this process of labelling depends on who has committed the act and who feels harmed by it.

The boundaries of objective and subjective become further blurred when looking at the extent to which the objective traits that have been discussed are present within processes of social construction. For instance, interest groups that are opposed to same-sex rights sometimes argue that homosexuality is statistically rare, a violation of the laws of nature or the word of God, or a threat to "the family" and to any children being raised by gay or lesbian parents. People who work toward toughening young offender legislation bring arguments of harm into their work. Those trying to decriminalize marijuana possession often refer to changing public attitudes that reflect a positive societal reaction to the issue of marijuana use. All of these groups are involved in the process of social construction in that they are attempting to influence the meanings attached to a particular behaviour, its place in the larger social order, and the roles assigned to individuals who engage in that behaviour. Yet they also draw upon objectivist concepts as a foundation for their arguments, so that objectivist traits are embedded within the subjectivist process of social construction.

Examining the complexities of the work of both past and present deviance specialists indicates that perhaps the traditional objective/subjective dualism that has served as the foundation for discussing definitions of deviance in the field has always been an oversimplification. The actual nature of the work done by sociologists of deviance frequently transcends the dichotomy, blending aspects of both objective and subjective. Rather than being embedded in a dichotomy, definitions of deviance and research on deviance may actually fall along more of a continuum, with more objective assumptions lying at one end of the continuum and more subjective assumptions lying at the other (see Figure 1.2).

At the extreme objective end of the continuum are those deviance specialists who have proposed an absolute moral order as the standard for determining

Figure 1.2   THE OBJECTIVE–SUBJECTIVE CONTINUUM

Definitions of deviance fall along a continuum of objectivism and subjectivism, with most definitions integrating both objective and subjective elements.

deviance; at the extreme subjective end are the most radical constructionists, who suggest that there is no reality outside of perception. The definitions and analyses of each deviance specialist fall somewhere along this continuum, with some being more objective in nature and some being more subjective in nature. Those researchers who lean toward objectivism may be more likely to study those forms of deviance that Thio (1983) referred to as high-consensus forms of deviance, such as homicide, gang membership, white-collar crime, police corruption, and prostitution. Those researchers who lean toward subjectivism may be more likely to study those forms of deviance that Thio referred to as low-consensus forms of deviance, such as marijuana use, pornography, swinging, gambling, and aspects of physical appearance (e.g., tattoos, body piercing, punk rockers, goths, and being overweight).

Studying Deviance

The way that deviance is defined along the objective–subjective continuum has implications for the way deviance is studied. That is, deviance specialists who lean more toward objectivism will study deviance in ways that those who lean more toward subjectivism will not (and vice versa).

Studying the Act: Why People Behave the Way They Do

Those who perceive more objectivity in deviance shine their analytical spotlight on a particular act or characteristic. The deviant nature of these behaviours/ characteristics is, to some extent, taken for granted (because, after all, they *are* violating norms, or *are* causing harm, etc.), and then the details of the deviance are studied—who the people are, how they became deviant, what their lives are like (Adler & Adler, 2006a; Rubington & Weinberg, 2008). In essence, the interest lies in explaining the person, behaviour, or characteristic in question.

Studying Social Processes: The "Deviance Dance"

Deviance specialists who focus more on the subjective aspects of deviance are less interested in shining their analytical spotlight on the "deviant," and more interested in shining it on society and social processes—the perceptions of and reactions to the act, as well as the role of power in those perceptions and reactions. The focus becomes the "**deviance dance**"—the interactions, negotiations, and debates among groups with different perceptions of whether a behaviour or characteristic is deviant and needs to be socially controlled and, if so, how. The participants in this "dance" each take certain "steps" in order to move the dance in the direction they desire, whether that direction is the creation of a new law, the legalization of a behaviour that was previously illegal, achieving public recognition of a new social problem or one previously ignored, or changing public perceptions that will reduce the prejudices faced by certain groups.

In some cases, this "dance" may be characterized by considerable cooperation among the participants in achieving a consensual goal—analogous to a country line dance in which everyone does precisely the same steps. In other cases, it is characterized by participants taking opposing steps, but still moving together in their negotiation over the outcome—analogous to a waltz, where one partner moves backward and the other forward as they set their joint course across the dance floor. And in some cases the "dance" may look more like a mosh pit at a heavy metal or punk rock concert—with each participant moving independently of the others and in varying and often opposing directions, intentionally pushing, shoving, and ramming into other participants in order to move in his or her own individually desired direction.

The centrality of interactions, negotiations, debates, and resistance in the social construction and social control of deviance is illustrated by Hier (2002). In 1999, three young adults died at rave dances in Toronto following the consumption of the drug ecstasy. With widespread media attention, Toronto city council and rave organizers (i.e., the Toronto Dance Safety Committee, or TDSC) joined together in an effort to improve safety at raves; at the TDSC's request, Toronto city council passed legislation governing various safety-related measures at raves. However, as

---

Exercise Your Mind

List some current examples of each of these types of "dances": (a) groups who agree that a particular behaviour is deviant and work together to control that behaviour (a "country line dance"); (b) groups whose perceptions are somewhat different (they may agree that a behaviour is deviant, but disagree as to how to best control it) but who still cooperate in some way (a "waltz"); and (c) groups who have completely different perceptions (they disagree as to whether a behaviour is deviant at all) and try to impose those perceptions on others (a "mosh pit").

media attention continued over the next several months, some members of city council adopted a new goal—banning raves altogether. The deviance dance was played out within the media, as those in favour of banning raves used mainstream newspapers in an attempt to win public favour and achieve their goal, while rave organizers, who were more concerned about threats to safety that would emerge if raves were driven underground, used a wide range of media outlets (including MuchMusic) to communicate their message to the public. What began as a cooperative effort quickly became a debate between opposing sides.

Studying struggles and debates over deviance requires going beyond the problem of "radical phenomenalism" (Ben-Yehuda, 1990, p. 5) that some researchers see as plaguing the sociology of deviance, wherein countless numbers of specific phenomena (e.g., call girls, drug users, swingers) have been studied in tremendous detail but without paying attention to larger social structures. Ben-Yehuda (1990) suggests that the "study of deviance should be reframed . . . within general societal processes [of change and stability], in a dynamic historical and political perspective" (p. 5). In this vein, understanding an act of deviance requires understanding its larger context in a society's value systems and understanding the configuration of power relationships that influence the negotiation of moral boundaries among different groups of people.

Studying Acts and Social Processes

Both the more objective and the more subjective approaches help our understanding of deviance. The most comprehensive knowledge emerges from combining an analysis of the social processes involved in the "deviance dance" with an explication of the act or characteristic in question. For example, information about why people become overweight can be combined with knowledge of the processes by which certain people come to be perceived as "too fat" and are then made subject to various measures of social control.

Similarly, an understanding of why people engage in certain sexual behaviours can be combined with knowledge of the processes by which certain sexual behaviours are typed as deviant and made subject to measures of social control, while other sexual behaviours are labelled as conforming and thereby become the standard against which other behaviours are judged. Each of these levels of understanding paints an important part of the picture of deviance that will be integrated into this textbook—at various points we will analyze acts/characteristics, perceptions of and reactions to those acts, and the role played by power in these perceptions and reactions.

The Role of Powerful People

Who are the "important" people who are able to influence the dominant moral codes of society, from which emerge standards of deviance and normality? In Canadian society, some of the most powerful groups involved in this process are

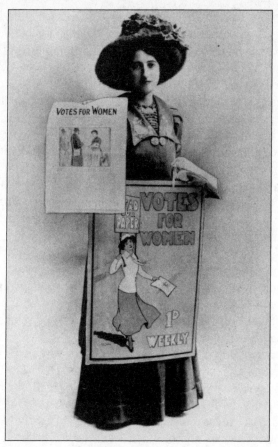

In the early twentieth century, groups of women in the United States and Canada acted as "moral entrepreneurs," and demanded the right to vote.

politicians/government, scientists, religious institutions, media, and commercial enterprise. Each of these groups of people may act as or have a relationship with **moral entrepreneurs** (Becker, 1963), those who "manufacture public morality" (Adler & Adler, 2006a, p. 136), first by bringing a problem to public awareness, and second by facilitating "moral conversion" (p. 136). For example, participants in the temperance movement, the abolitionist movement, and the "child-savers" movement all acted as moral entrepreneurs who worked to influence the development and enforcement of society's moral codes during the Victorian era.

In the temperance movement, members of church-based groups (frequently women's groups) throughout North America and Great Britain declared the "demon liquor" a social evil, and agitated for reduced alcohol consumption ("temperance"). In Canada and the United States, groups of people acting as moral entrepreneurs sought abolition (the eradication of slavery under the law) and demanded voting rights for women. And throughout North America and

Ask Yourself

Make a list of groups of people that you are aware of who try to influence society's dominant moral codes by seeking to influence our notions of right/wrong, bad/good, deviant/normal, acceptable/unacceptable. At its simplest level, these are groups that you feel are trying to change people's perceptions of a particular behaviour or group of people.

Western Europe, the "child-savers" influenced child labour laws, sought the criminalization of child abuse and neglect, and encouraged compulsory education for children. During the 1950s and 1960s, North America's civil rights activists acted as moral entrepreneurs in their efforts to end segregation and gain rights for African-Canadians and African-Americans. All of these groups had an influence on society's dominant moral codes, and thereby on perceptions of what was considered deviant and normal. In contemporary society, we continue to see groups of moral entrepreneurs, as illustrated in the *Ask Yourself* exercise.

Perhaps the most central group in society that acts as or has a relationship with moral entrepreneurs is composed of *politicians*. Politicians are the people in whom ultimate power has been vested in modern state systems: they have powers to invoke, revoke, and determine the enforcement of legislation and social policy. Interest groups, acting as moral entrepreneurs who have identified a social ill that they think must be solved in some way, often lobby the government to initiate change.

A second group, comprised of *scientists*, is able to effectively make claims that influence society's moral codes. The claims made by scientists are backed by the domain that is granted perhaps the highest level of credibility in our society—that of science. As we will see in the chapter on science and deviance later in the textbook, when scientists proclaim truths, many of us will believe those claims simply because scientists say so. When scientists tell us that smoking is harmful, or that having sex too frequently indicates an addiction, or that hearing voices indicates mental illness, they have a persuasive impact on what we see as "normal." When making such claims, scientists themselves may be acting as moral entrepreneurs; in addition, the claims made by scientists may be used as convincing support for the efforts of other moral entrepreneurs, such as anti-smoking activists.

Religious institutions have also played a central role in the creation of the dominant moral codes that determine deviance and normality. For example, during the Middle Ages and into the early Renaissance, the Christian church was the instigator of witch persecutions and the Spanish Inquisition, both of which resulted in countless numbers of people being tortured and killed for their deviance. In the present day, the power of religious institutions can be seen in the many nations in which religious-based governments are the source of social order. For instance, the displaced Taliban government imposed a particular and extreme interpretation of Islamic beliefs on the people of Afghanistan. Contemporary Canadian society is characterized by a separation of church and state; however, the influence of religion on perceptions of deviance and normality maintains its presence in many ways. Canadian society itself is built upon a Judeo-Christian foundation. Two of our national statutory holidays, those days when most businesses are closed, are Christian holidays—Christmas Day and Easter Sunday. Our criminal law is based on the Judeo-Christian ethic of free will—we are responsible for our own actions, and redemption can occur through punishment (Linden, 2000).

At a more individual level, many Canadians adhere to various religious belief systems. Their belief systems provide them with moral codes that subsequently affect the role individuals play in larger social processes. The Victorian prohibitionists, abolitionists, and child-savers described earlier were typically members of various Christian church-based groups. A later chapter in this book looks more closely at the relationship between religious institutions and the "deviance dance."

In our twenty-first-century world, the *media* serves as the central battleground in the struggles over moral codes. The media is a powerful tool used by a wide range of moral entrepreneurs. When politicians, medical doctors, or interest groups endeavour to raise awareness of an issue or sway public opinion, they turn to the media. Public service announcements, press conferences, and issue-driven advertisements all appear in the media. The media is not just a tool used by moral entrepreneurs, however; it also acts as a moral entrepreneur itself in terms of the choices made about what will and will not be included on a particular program or in a particular commercial segment. For example, when the television news program *Dateline* features child molesters being captured through sting operations, it contributes to the construction of pedophilia as a deviant (and criminal) activity.

Finally, in a modern capitalist economy, *commercial enterprise* has a significant level of power as well, frequently in conjunction with the use of the media; in fact, most components of the media itself are commercial enterprises driven by a profit motive. Ads, commercials, magazines, television programs, and movies tell us how we are and are not supposed to look: punk rock characters in a movie are the butt of the movie's jokes; magazine articles tell us we will be happier if we can just lose those 10 pounds by Labour Day; personalities on the reality show *The Hills* show us the right clothes to wear. They tell us how we are supposed to act: beer commercials show us that drinking is the best way to have fun with friends; a fictional television show tells us that "potheads" are losers; and a nighttime news program tells us that joining a cult is problematic.

Commercial enterprise has power outside of the media as well. For example, Giesbrecht (2000) discusses the power of the alcohol industry over the content and form of alcohol policies created by government. The manner in which alcohol production, marketing, and consumption is controlled in both Canada and the United States is determined, in part, by the influence of the alcohol industry itself. A similar example can be seen in the historical development of the institution of law in modern state systems. It is the law that delineates those actions considered to require the greatest level of control by society; historically, English law developed on the basis of merchant and commercial interests.

With the end of feudalism, kings had much to gain from the wealth of merchants involved in international trade. Feudal lords no longer had the means to finance the nation's warfare and colonial expansion, but merchants did. It was in the best financial interests of the king, as he oversaw the development and growth of a centralized state, to form it in accordance with commercial interests. These origins serve as the foundation for modern Canadian law, wherein most legal infractions by those involved in commercial enterprise are dealt with under the more lenient civil law rather than the more punitive criminal law (Linden, 2000).

This brief discussion of politicians, scientists, religion, media, and commercial enterprise demonstrates the complexity of the notion of power. People are powerful for many different reasons, and their power operates in diverse ways. The moral entrepreneurship of one group of powerful people may contradict or even oppose the moral entrepreneurship of another group of powerful people; for instance, the efforts of commercial enterprise might oppose the efforts of members of a religious-based group. But whether one group's involvement in social construction contradicts or, conversely, coincides with another group's involvement in social construction, the process through which they operate is the same—that of social typing.

The Social Typing Process

As moral entrepreneurs influence the content and enforcement of society's dominant moral codes, the foundation is laid for the standards that subsequently determine deviance and normality. A closer look at the process by which some people come to be seen as deviant and others come to be seen as normal reveals what Rubington and Weinberg (2008) label **social typing**. This three-component process has the end result of changing the way society treats people who are typed or categorized as deviant.

The first component of the social typing process is **description**, wherein a label is placed on an individual because of an observed or presumed behaviour or characteristic. The exact nature of the label that is applied is dependent on the culture in question (Rubington & Weinberg, 2008). For example, in contemporary Canada we are more likely to label someone a "terrorist" than a "heretic"; in contrast, in Europe during the sixteenth century, people were more likely to be labelled "heretics" than "terrorists." Terrorism is a social phenomenon that has become an integral part of our world view in the twenty-first century, while the concept of heresy reflected the religious foundations of the European world view in the sixteenth century.

The second component of the social typing process is **evaluation**. This occurs when a judgment is attached to the individual by virtue of the label that was previously attached or the category that individual was placed in under the description component. If someone is socially typed as deviant, this judgment is characteristically negative in nature.

The third component of the social typing process is **prescription**. This is where the processes of social control or regulation emerge. Because of the label that has been given and the resulting judgment that occurs, the individual is

Exercise Your Mind

Go through the three components of the social typing process, using the example of someone who is obese. What description or label is given to this person? What judgments or evaluations are attached to this person because of the label you have just given him or her? Finally, how is this person treated or socially controlled?

treated in a particular way—a way she or he would not be treated if the initial label had not been applied. In other words, individuals are made subject to a range of social treatments designed to regulate or control their deviance. Just as the larger culture determines the initial label that is used, it also shapes the nature of the prescription that is used (Rubington & Weinberg, 2002). For example, a Canadian woman who violates standards of female dress is likely to be teased or stared at rather than made subject to stoning, as women in Taliban-controlled Afghanistan were.

Forms of Social Control

As Newman (2008) points out, "all societies have ways of keeping deviants under control. . . . The ancient Greeks killed them; nineteenth-century societies hid them in their closets and attics, and twentieth-century societies rationalized this solution by building large institutions in which they were hidden" (p. xi). In contemporary society, we can see the regulation or social control of a person who has been subjected to the social typing process occurring at multiple levels. It may be *formal* or *informal* in nature (Becker, 1963; Edwards, 1988; Rubington & Weinberg, 2002). The informal aspect of the prescription component emerges at the level of patterns of informal social interaction—patterns of interaction with diverse people—such as family members, friends, acquaintances, colleagues, or strangers. As you go about your day seeing many different people, you react to them and interact with them in various ways. You may smile at, frown at, stare at, tease, laugh at, agree with, disagree with, talk to, avoid, ignore, criticize, applaud them, and more. These are all means by which **informal regulation or social control** can occur.

You can see one example if you think back to your adolescent years. Perhaps as you were leaving the house, your parents saw what you were wearing and clearly disapproved. They may have asked, "What do you think you're wearing?" They may have said, "In those baggy pants you look like a bum!" Or they may have even sent you back to your room to change. That is informal regulation. Alternatively, you may have noticed people staring at you and laughing when you walked down the street. Informal social controls can include staring, laughing, frowning, avoiding, shaming, and more (Braithwaite, 2000; Edwards, 1988; Goode, 1997). Informal regulation comprises much of our daily lives today, and prior to industrialization it served as the dominant way that deviance was controlled

Ask Yourself

As a student at the university you attend, how is your behaviour or appearance informally controlled? In other words, how is your behaviour or appearance controlled at the level of everyday social interaction? How is it formally regulated, at an organizational or institutional level?

(Spector, 1981). Take a moment to look at the first two questions in the *Ask Yourself* exercise, and consider how informal social control affects your life.

In answering the *Ask Yourself* questions, you may have referred to peer pressure; the desire to fit in with your classmates might have an effect on the clothes you wear to class, the way you style your hair, or whether you go to the library versus the bar after class. Maybe you recall a time when you were whispering to a friend during class and two of your classmates gave you a dirty look or even asked you to keep it down. When you first became a post-secondary student, perhaps an older sibling gave you advice on what it would be like and how you should act. These are all examples of informal control.

Formal social controls involve processing at some type of an organizational or institutional level. Prior to industrialization in the Western world, church prohibitions served as the central means of formal social control. With industrialization and the creation of a centralized government, there was a dramatic increase in organizations and agencies involved in regulation and social control (Spector, 1981). A wide range of types of formal regulation can serve as controls for deviant behaviour—a nation's laws (such as Canada's Criminal Code); a school or work dress code; regulations governing driver's licences or hunting permits; a teacher punishing a student for misbehaviour; or the psychiatrists' handbook that lists the symptoms of various forms of mental illness.

Look at the last *Ask Yourself* question regarding formal social controls in your life. In answering it, you could have referred to registration requirements—you are permitted to take Class B only if you have already passed Class A. You could have referred to the regulations governing student conduct at your university. What behaviours are considered unacceptable and what are the consequences for those behaviours? Perhaps you referred to a course syllabus, which tells you what exams and assignments you must complete in order to pass a particular course. Maybe you attend a university that has a student dress code. After an outburst in class, possibly the chair of the department gave you a written reprimand or made you see a student counsellor. These are all examples of **formal regulation**.

Social control may be *intentional* at times, such as through the creation of rules that must be followed by a child, student, employee, or citizen of the state. At other times, regulation might be the result of a more *general influence*; for instance, professionals such as doctors and lawyers have a general influence on their clients' lives (Edwards, 1988). Social control may be either **retroactive** (treating a known deviant in a certain way) or **preventative** (trying to prevent deviance in the first place—through socialization, for example) (Edwards, 1988). Social control may be directed at an individual by someone else (e.g., a doctor, a parent, or a judge), or may occur at the level of **self-regulation** or self-control, where people regulate their own behaviours (such as by dieting to try and conform to an idealized body image, by joining a self-help group to end an addiction, or by avoiding behaviours that they know will be stigmatized) (Foucault, 1995; Gottfredson & Hirschi, 1990).

Of course, because the social construction of deviance and normality are embedded within a bigger "dance," it means that a particular behaviour, characteristic, or person is subjected to only one social typing process at any given moment. Multiple social typing processes may be going on simultaneously, processes that may even contradict each other. One segment of society may socially type someone as "deviant," while another segment of society may claim that same person is "normal." In some arenas of society, for example, someone who is perceived as overweight is labelled "too fat," has negative judgments attached to them, and is then treated in particular ways as a result; however, in other arenas of society that person may be seen as "normal" or "healthy."

Even if there is some agreement that a person, behaviour, or characteristic is deviant, there may be differing views on what the appropriate forms of social control are. For example, while some people suggest that addiction is a disease and should be medically regulated, other people disagree and argue that another form of social control, such as punishment, should be instituted. Thus, within these multiple social typing processes, the claims made by one group often must compete with the claims made by another; claimsmakers compete with other claimsmakers "in a [deviance] marketplace" (Richardson, Best, & Bromley, 1991, p. 5). But the principal role of power in this process ultimately means that some people's claims count more than other people's, and that some people's claims have a greater bearing on the society at large—its norms, its structure, its institutions, and its people.

The consequences of the social typing process, whereby a person, behaviour, or characteristic becomes typed as deviant, or is **deviantized**, are far-reaching. Through this process " . . . description becomes prescription, which is then transformed into a desirable standard of normal behaviour to be upheld and maintained by the educational system, the religious system, the legal system, and of course the psychotherapeutic system, and to which every section of the population has to measure up or be found deficient" (Freud, 1999, p. 2).

TIME TO REVIEW

- Why is the notion of an objective-subjective *continuum* more accurate than that of a *dichotomy*?
- In what way do researchers' locations on the objective–subjective continuum influence their study of deviance?
- What is the "deviance dance," and why is it relevant to the study of deviance?
- What are moral entrepreneurs?

- What role do politicians, scientists, religion, media, and commercial enterprise play in the development of society's dominant moral codes?
- What are the three components of the social typing process?
- What are the different types of social control or regulation?

Our Journey through This Book

In the process of transcending the objective/subjective dualism and of integrating analyses of acts, perceptions/reactions, and power relations, many questions will serve as a guide in the remaining chapters of this book:

■ Where does a particular act or characteristic come from?

■ What is the nature of the social typing process? What are the descriptions, evaluations, and prescriptions that are being applied to this person, behaviour, or characteristic?

■ Who has done the social typing?

■ What is the foundation for their arguments?

■ Who benefits from the deviantizing of this behaviour, characteristic, or person?

■ What larger social conditions support the social typing process?

■ How is the "deviance dance" evident?

These kinds of questions will guide us in our understanding of deviance in relation to sexuality, youth, physical appearance, mental disorder, religion, and science. The choice of these topics is intended to provide you with critical insight into some of the core processes, as well as the people, that make up the foundation of our society. Such critical insight will be based on both specific structures and processes of deviance as described in the particular topics above, as well as at a level of theoretical understanding and explanations of deviance more generally. By the end of this book, you will see that you are not an outsider looking in at deviance in society, but instead will see that deviance is a part of *your* life every day. And you will see that although some sociologists decry the 'death of deviance' (e.g., Sumner, 1994), in the twenty-first century the field may be stronger and perhaps more relevant than ever (Adler & Adler, 2006b).

CHAPTER SUMMARY

■ We all can make a list of people we find annoying. However, the concept of deviance exists at the level of social processes, not personal opinion.

■ The study of deviance is characterized by disagreement about how deviance should be defined. Some deviance specialists suggest that there has been a general shift from *objective* to *subjective* definitions, drawing upon the notion of an objective/subjective dualism or dichotomy.

■ The *objective* side of the dualism suggests that there is a single characteristic that distinguishes "deviant" people from "normal" people. The four different defining traits that laypersons, social activists, politicians, or academics have mentioned are *normative violation, statistical rarity, societal reaction*, and *harm*.

■ According to the subjective side of the dichotomy, the only characteristic all deviant people have in common is that *enough important people have called them deviant*. In other words, deviance is a *social construction*.

■ Looking at deviance from a social constructionist point of view, what is of interest are a particular behaviour's place in the social order, the roles assigned to people who exhibit that behaviour, and the societal meanings attached to it.

■ Recent work in the study of deviance integrates both objective and subjective components. Thus, objectivism and subjectivism may be thought of as existing along a continuum, rather than as a dichotomy.

■ The way that deviance is defined has implications for the way it is studied. Some researchers focus their analyses on the deviant act without further contextualizing it, assuming that the act can be classified as a form of deviance, while others focus their analyses on the processes involved in the perception of and reaction to the act.

■ The perceptions of *powerful groups* play the central role in the creation of the *dominant moral codes* that underlie the construction of deviance. In our society, powerful groups include politicians, religious institutions, scientists, media, and commercial enterprise.

■ Central to issues of deviance are the processes of *social typing*, wherein someone is labelled in a particular way, judged on the basis of that label, and subjected to measures of social control. Such treatment can occur through various levels of regulation or social control—formal, informal, preventative, retroactive, and via the self.

DEVIANCE IN PRINT

Brandt, A. M. (2007). *The Cigarette Century: The Rise, Fall, and Deadly Persistence of the Product that Defined America*, New York: Basic Books.

Edwards, A. R. (1988). *Regulation and Repression: The Study of Social Control.* Sydney, Australia: Allen & Unwin.

DEVIANCE AT THE MOVIES

Read, D. (Director), Armstrong, M., Pettigrew, M., & Johansson, S. (Producers). (1990). *The Burning Times.* Available from the National Film Board of Canada. (56 minutes).

This documentary explores the European witch persecutions and is an excellent opportunity to apply the core concepts introduced in this chapter. Viewers can look for the objective characteristics of deviance, the three components of the social typing process, and the role of powerful groups.

Apatow, J. (Writer/Director), & Carell, S. (Writer). (2005). *The 40-Year-Old Virgin.* United States: Universal Pictures. (116 minutes).

    In this comedy, a man who is a virgin at the age of 40 is socially typed as deviant by his co-workers and subjected to various measures of social control as they attempt to "cure" him of this problem.

ENDNOTES

1 Mason Cooley [b.1927]. Columbia World of Quotations. City aphorisms, fourteenth selection. New York. Retrieved August 23, 2006, from **www.bartleby.com**

2 David Lee (producer of *Frasier*). Rand Lindsly's quotations from The Quotations Page. Retrieved August 23, 2006, from **www.quotationspage.com**

KEY TERMS

deviance, **p. 2**
conformity, **p. 2**
deviance specialists, **p. 4**
criminologists, **p. 4**
objective, **p. 4**
subjective, **p. 4**
statistical rarity, **p. 5**
harm, **p. 6**
societal reaction, **p. 11**
normative violation, **p. 12**
folkways, **p. 13**
mores, **p. 13**
consensual view of law, **p. 15**
conflict view of law, **p. 15**
interactionist view of law, **p. 15**
high-consensus deviance, **p. 16**
low-consensus deviance, **p. 16**

dominant moral codes, **p. 17**
social constructionism, **p. 18**
radical/strict constructionism, **p. 18**
soft/contextual constructionism, **p. 18**
deviance dance, **p. 23**
moral entrepreneurs, **p. 25**
social typing, **p. 28**
description, **p. 28**
evaluation, **p. 28**
prescription, **p. 28**
informal regulation/social control, **p. 29**
formal regulation/social control, **p. 30**
retroactive social control, **p. 30**
preventative social control, **p. 30**
self-regulation, **p. 30**
deviantized, **p. 31**

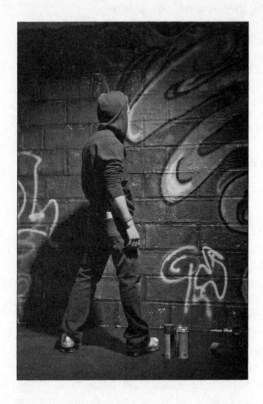

CHAPTER 2

Explaining Deviance: The Act

Learning Objectives

After reading this chapter, you should be able to

- Explain why different types of theory correspond to objective and subjective views of deviance, and describe the focus of positivist, interpretive, and critical theories in explaining deviance.
- Describe the core assumptions of positivist theories, as well as how deviance is explained by the three types of positivist theories presented in this chapter.
- Describe the core assumptions of functionalist theory, as well as how deviance is explained by (a) Durkheim's anomie theory, (b) Merton's strain

theory, (c) differential opportunity theory, (d) general strain theory, and
(e) Cohen's theory of status frustration.
- Describe the core assumptions of learning theories, as well as how
  deviance is explained by (a) differential association theory,
  (b) neutralization theory, and (c) social learning theory.
- Describe how Hirschi's social bonds theory explains deviance (and the
  absence of deviance). Describe Gottfredson and Hirschi's more recent
  general theory of crime.
- Outline the criticisms that have been directed at functionalist, learning, and
  social control theories, and identify any responses to those criticisms.

"There is nothing more practical than a good theory." (Leonid Ilyich Brezhnev)[1]

Theorizing Deviance

"Theory" is sometimes perceived as the flip side of the coin from "practice"; it is
seen as isolated from the "real world." But as the above quotation points out,
theory and practice are intimately intertwined and, in fact, theory is quite practical.
It is through theory that we come to understand the world we live in. It is through
past developments in theory that those of us living in the twenty-first century can
understand gravity, nuclear power, and child development. Similarly, it is through
theory that we are able to try to understand the way society works, the reasons
why some people are rich and some are poor, why the wives in most marriages
are still doing most of the housework while the husbands are doing most of the
breadwinning, why people commit crimes, why people get tattoos, and how an
underweight body has somehow come to represent the North American cultural
ideal. That is, theory provides us with the central means of explaining and
understanding deviance—what could be more practical than that?

Scientific theories of crime have existed for almost a century. The scientific
study of criminality is recognized as beginning in the early twentieth century with
the work of Cesare Lombroso, who explained criminality on the basis of
evolution. He suggested that criminals were **atavists**—evolutionary throwbacks
whose biology prevented them from conforming to society's rules (Lombroso,
1911). Other biological theories of crime soon followed, many of which explained
criminality on the basis of heredity. According to those theories, just as the colour
of one's eyes is biologically inherited, so is social behaviour, such as criminality
(e.g., Goring, 1919).

By mid-century, *social* theories of crime had largely replaced biological
theories, and theorizing about non-criminal forms of deviance gained prominence
as well. However, some deviance specialists suggest that since the mid-1970s, the
sociology of deviance has declined as a discipline in its own right because a
distinct body of theory is lacking (Sumner, 1994; Miller, Wright, & Dannels,
2001). Instead, they say, the sociology of deviance has been subsumed by the

discipline of criminology, and the overlap between the two areas of study can be seen in both research and theory. But it must be remembered that many of the theories utilized in criminology are, in reality, general sociological theories that are simply being applied to questions of crime—functionalism, interactionism, conflict theory, and social learning theory are all sociological theories rather than specifically criminological theories. Thus, specialists in *all* areas of sociology, and not just deviance and criminology, make use of these bodies of theory. Although the debate continues over whether there is a distinct body of deviance theory, there is no doubt that deviance specialists, whether they focus on criminal or non-criminal forms of deviance, use a wide range of theories: general sociological theories (e.g., conflict theory), specific criminological theories (e.g., strain theory), and interdisciplinary theories (e.g., feminist theories).

Numerous theories exist simultaneously in the social sciences, unlike in the natural sciences where more accurate theories replace older theories that have been disproven. This is frequently one of the first hurdles that students new to sociology must overcome—expanding their understanding of what "theory" means to include the possibility of multiple coexisting explanations for the very same phenomenon. The poem "The Blind Men and the Elephant" serves as an interesting analogy for this characteristic of sociological theory (see Box 2.1).

When American poet John Godfrey Saxe wrote this poem based on a Hindu fable more than a century ago, would he have predicted what a useful analogy it would be for sociological theory? What do blind men and elephants have to do with understanding society and explaining deviance?

Just as the blind men's explanations of the nature of the elephant depended wholly on what part of the elephant each focused on, sociologists' explanations of the nature of society depend on what aspect of society each sociological theory focuses on. There are diverse ways of looking at the world around us, and each theoretical perspective has a different view. Each of these ways of looking at society shines a spotlight on a different aspect of the social order—some theories focus on the stability of society, some focus on conflict, some focus on interaction. But when a spotlight is directed at one particular location, all other areas necessarily fall into the shadows, just as each blind man's hands resting on one part of the elephant mean that the rest of the elephant's body is going untouched. In other words, an area of focus within each sociological theory may be easily explainable, but areas outside of the focal range are explained to a lesser extent, if at all; and because of each theory's way of looking at the world, the explanations provided take a particular form. Thus, certain theories may be more useful than others in coming to understand a given issue or aspect of deviance.

For example, if you are interested in deviant *acts* (as those deviance specialists who lean toward the objective side of the objective–subjective continuum are), some of the theories of deviance will be more useful to you than others. In contrast, if you are more interested in the *perceptions* of and *reactions* to particular acts, as well as the role that power plays in those perceptions and

Box 2.1 The Blind Men and the Elephant

A Hindoo Fable

It was six men of Indostan
To learning much inclined
Who went to see the Elephant
(Though all of them were blind),
That each by observation
Might satisfy his mind.

The *First* approached the Elephant
And happening to fall
Against his broad and sturdy side
At once began to bawl:
"God bless me! but the Elephant
Is very like a wall!"

The *Second*, feeling of the tusk,
Cried, "Ho! What have we here
So very round and smooth and sharp?
To me 'tis mighty clear
This wonder of an Elephant
Is very like a spear!"

The *Third* approached the animal,
And happening to take
The squirming trunk within his hands
Thus boldly up and spake:
"I see," quoth he, "the Elephant
Is very like a snake!"

The *Fourth* reached out his eager hand,
And felt about the knee.
"What most this wondrous beast is like
Is mighty plain," quoth he;

"'Tis clear enough the Elephant
Is very like a tree!"

The *Fifth*, who chanced to touch the ear,
Said: "E'en the blindest man
Can tell what this resembles most;
Deny the fact who can,
This marvel of an Elephant
Is very like a fan!"

The *Sixth* no sooner had begun
About the beast to grope,
Then, seizing on the swinging tail
That fell within his scope,
"I see," quoth he, "the Elephant
Is very like a rope."

And so these men of Indostan
Disputed loud and long.
Each in his own opinion
Exceeding stiff and strong,
Though each was partly in the right,
And all were in the wrong!

MORAL

So oft in theologic wars,
The disputants, I ween,
Rail on in utter ignorance
Of what each other mean,
And prate about an Elephant
Not one of them has seen!

—John Godfrey Saxe (1816–1887)[2]

reactions (as those deviance specialists who lean toward the subjective side of the objective–subjective continuum are), other theories will be of more use to you.

In the previous chapter, more objective ways of recognizing deviance were addressed, including views based on normative violation, statistical rarity, harm, and societal reaction. Each of these definitions of deviance suggests that there is a trait that all deviant people share that differentiates deviants from those who are normal. Emerging from this core idea is an interest in finding out *why* people become deviant—why they violate norms, or engage in behaviours that are atypical, or cause harm, or act in ways that result in a negative societal reaction. This way of looking at deviance is intimately linked with theories of deviance that are labelled **positivist** (Ashley & Orenstein, 2001). Positivist theories will be the focus of the remainder of this chapter.

The more subjective ways of looking at deviance, which will be looked at in Chapter 3, suggest that the only characteristic all deviant people have in common is that enough important people have said they are deviant. Emerging from this core idea is an interest in exploring the social typing process—the process through which deviance and normality are socially constructed. Who becomes typed as deviant, how are they treated, and what rationales are offered? In what way does power influence societal perceptions of and reactions to particular behaviours? This way of looking at deviance and the concentration on these aspects are intimately linked with theories that are labelled **interpretive** and **critical** (Ashley & Orenstein, 2001). Interpretive and critical theories will be the focus of the next chapter. Because an exhaustive analysis of theories of deviance would require a virtual library of books, this book will focus on the core assumptions of the theories that have been the most commonly used, and/or those that have had the greatest impact, in the sociology of deviance.

Although positivist, interpretive, and critical theories will be discussed separately, a significant trend in theorizing is that of theoretical integration—combining aspects of different theories in order to explain a particular phenomenon. Consequently, positivist, interpretive, and critical theories may be integrated in multiple combinations (Ashley & Orenstein, 2001). Theoretical integration is not an entirely new phenomenon; even elements of positivist Émile Durkheim's work of more than a century ago have served as a foundation for some early interpretive and critical work. However, it is a growing trend in the sociology of deviance (Kubrin, Stucky, & Krohn, 2009). As you progress through the chapter, you will see some examples of how aspects of various theories have been combined in order to better explain a particular phenomenon.

Why Do People Become Deviant?

Using Positivist Theories

Positivist sociological theories are fundamentally interested in explaining why people act in particular ways. They are modelled after approaches to theorizing in the natural sciences, which "seek generalizable, universally applicable laws" (Ashley & Orenstein, 2001, p. 30) that govern the environment. In pursuing the rules that govern the *social* environment, positivist sociologists seek cause-and-effect relationships in the form of statistical relationships—they look for those variables that are associated with a particular behaviour or outcome (Ashley & Orenstein, 2001). Both positivist sociological theories and theories in the natural sciences are based on a technical interest in the mastery of the environment; in the case of positivist sociological theories, this technical interest is in pursuit of planning for a better society (Ashley & Orenstein, 2001).

Thus, seeking to understand why deviant people act that way triggers subsequent attempts to prevent other people from becoming deviant. Positivist explanations of deviance are inevitably coupled with efforts at social control, efforts you might personally agree with (such as with violent crime), or disagree with (such as with homosexuality). Individual theorists may not personally seek more effective social control of particular behaviours; their interest may lie solely in explaining the variability in people's behaviours. However, positivist theorizing lays the groundwork for those individuals who are seeking more effective social control or plans for a better society (Ashley & Orenstein, 2001).

The remainder of this chapter will review some of the positivist theories that have been the most commonly used in explaining deviant acts, and that have had significant influences on the sociology of deviance as a discipline. These include functionalist theories (including theories of anomie and strain), learning theories, and theories of social control.

TIME TO REVIEW

■ Why do multiple theories coexist in the sociology of deviance, and how can each theory be both "partly in the right" and "in the wrong" as well?

■ What is the nature of the link between particular types of theorizing (i.e., positivist, interpretive, and critical) and the objective–subjective continuum?

Functionalist Theories

Functionalist theories, which in the past were also called *structural functionalist theories*, have their origins in the birth of the discipline of sociology itself; in fact, this theoretical perspective dominated the discipline until the mid-twentieth century. In this perspective, society is seen as being comprised of various structures (e.g., the family, the education system, the political system), each of which fulfills necessary functions for the smooth running of the social order. Some are **manifest functions**, intended and recognized; others are **latent functions**, unintentional and unrecognized. For example, a manifest function of post-secondary education is to train young adults for employment, but post-secondary education does more than this: its latent functions may include providing individuals with social networks and facilitating the formation of romantic relationships. The *Ask Yourself* exercise addresses manifest and latent functions in the context of your own life.

Analogous to this functionalist view of society is a pyramidal stack of cans on display in the supermarket; each can is necessary for the display as a whole to keep standing. You may be stricken with fear at the idea of selecting one of those cans to place in your shopping cart, because if you move the wrong can, or if one of the cans is not perfectly in position, the entire display may collapse. Similarly, the smooth running of society is threatened if one of its structures has a poor fit with the other structures that make up society.

One of the core concerns in the functionalist perspective is the maintenance of the social order. This conservative focus is inherent in the perspective because of

Ask Yourself

One of the functions of families is the socialization of children, which is accomplished, in part, by parents providing their children with specific rules. Consider an example all of us are likely familiar with—your parents requiring you to clean your room. The overt, intended purpose of this rule (i.e., its manifest function) may be to keep the house looking nice and prevent vermin from invading. But what else were you learning by virtue of having to clean your room (i.e., latent functions)?

the assumption that the rules that make up the social order are consensual; in other words, the rules exist because we agree that they should exist. And we agree they should exist because they serve a useful function for society. For example, Parsons and Bales (1955) suggest that traditional gender roles—wherein men are responsible for instrumental tasks (e.g., breadwinning) and women are responsible for expressive tasks (e.g., nurturing the children)—are functional for society because they ensure that the division of labour in the family is done efficiently. Challenging traditional gender roles may threaten the equilibrium of society. Thus, if the rules are typically functional, and if rules exist because we agree they should, we need to figure out why some people do not follow those rules. It may be that breaking certain rules is dysfunctional for society, and we therefore need to determine the causes of such behaviour so that we can restore social order. Alternatively, it may be that a part of the structure of society has become dysfunctional, which is causing people to break the rules.

Within these broad assumptions that are part of the functionalist perspective, individual theorists have taken different paths in applying those assumptions to the study of deviance. In the remainder of this section on functionalist theories, we will look at the different ways that Émile Durkheim, Robert Merton, collaborators Cloward and Ohlin, Robert Agnew, and Albert Cohen have applied functionalist assumptions to an understanding of deviance.

Durkheim: Anomie Theory

Not only is Émile Durkheim (1933; 1951) recognized as one of the founders of the discipline of sociology, his work also defined the structural functionalist perspective itself. In his theory, the notion of deviance is addressed in two ways. First, Durkheim suggested that a certain level of deviance is actually functional for society: deviance serves a useful purpose in helping maintain society's balance or equilibrium. Second, Durkheim addressed deviance in the context of pathological levels of deviance that occur when society changes too quickly and **anomie** (normlessness) emerges.

Deviance is functional in that seeing someone break the rules leads the rest of us to realize how important the rules are and the necessity of following the rules. A certain level of deviance thereby enhances social order and *increases social solidarity* among those of us who join together in fighting back against those people who break the rules. Deviance is also functional in that it is through observing behaviour and its consequences that *a society determines what its moral boundaries are*, what its rules should be, and what is considered acceptable and unacceptable. Deviance can be functional in that it *tests society's boundaries* and may demonstrate when certain rules no longer work and need to be changed. Finally, deviance serves as a way of *reducing societal tensions*, which it can do in two ways. First, societal tensions can be reduced when there is some sort of scapegoat that can be blamed for a social problem, since blaming a scapegoat takes the pressure off society at large. The second way that societal tensions can be defused is when individuals engage in small acts of minor deviance that act as a safety valve and let off some steam.

Parsons and Smelser (1956) elaborate on this latter function, suggesting that letting off steam through minor acts of deviance subsequently activates social processes that return deviant actors to their acceptable roles in society. The social processes that return people to their acceptable roles include *socialization* (wherein deviant actors who are letting off steam have internalized society's rules sufficiently that they return themselves to their legitimate social roles), *profit* (which teaches citizens that there is a payoff or benefit accorded those who conform to society's rules), *persuasion* (through advertising, the sermons of religious leaders, psychologists' advice, etc.), and *coercion* (punishment for those who do not return to their legitimate social roles).

Several researchers have explored the functionality of deviance in reinforcing moral boundaries, testing social boundaries, increasing social solidarity, and reducing societal tensions. Kai Erikson's (1966) classic analysis of the Puritans of the Massachusetts Bay Colony reveals that acts of deviance helped to reinforce the moral boundaries of their community. As the needs of the community changed over time, the system of crimes and punishments changed as well, illustrating to citizens, for example, the power of the church (through the punishment of witchcraft) or the value of private property (through the punishment of theft). The nature of these punishments also reminded citizens about the norms and values that were considered important by authorities in that community.

When resident Anne Hutchinson began using Bible study classes held in her home as a forum for criticizing the minister's Sunday sermons, she was charged with heresy and disobedience to the church fathers. Her "crimes" under civil and religious law caused her to be banished from the colony and excommunicated from the Puritan church. Hutchinson's deviance reminded others of what the rules were. The severe consequences she faced by breaking those rules pointed to the importance of those rules. The entire situation reinforced the power of the civil and religious authorities in the community.

The role of deviance in testing society's boundaries and facilitating changes in outdated rules can be seen historically: Anne Hutchinson came to be seen as a champion of women's rights and religious freedom (and in the 1980s, the governor of Massachusetts granted her a pardon). More recently, the actions of activists on behalf of civil rights, women's rights, and disabled rights certainly changed society in significant ways. Their efforts demonstrated to the rest of society that some of its norms were outdated and needed to be changed. That is, certain norms had become dysfunctional for society and had to be modified in order to maintain social order.

Does deviance increase social solidarity? Victor's (1992) review of scapegoating in America illustrates the functionality of deviance both in reducing societal tensions and in enhancing social solidarity. He argues that directing hostility toward some type of external enemy temporarily helps to reduce tensions and increase social solidarity. When conflict emerges in society, "when moral values are in dispute, a witchhunt for moral subversives serves the purpose of clarifying, redefining, and strictly enforcing the limits of moral conduct" (Victor, 1992, para. 12). The collective manufacturing of an *evil enemy image* was directed at heretics and witches during the Middle Ages, Communist subversives in the 1950s, Satanists in the late 1980s and early 1990s, Jewish communities during various anti-Semitic pogroms from the twelfth through the twentieth centuries, citizens of Japanese extraction during World War II (Victor, 1992), and, since September 11, 2001, "terrorists" (Rapley, 2007). Each of these external "enemies" has served as a way of increasing social solidarity by allowing people to join together to fight that enemy and as a way of clearly illustrating to people the boundaries of acceptable behaviour or characteristics.

Although Durkheim proposed that deviance is functional for society, he pointed out that it remains functional only up to a particular point. Beyond a certain level, deviance no longer enhances the social order but rather interferes with it. Living in nineteenth-century Europe, Durkheim observed that the processes of industrialization and urbanization, with their growing emphasis on individuality, were causing more deviance—wherein deviance exceeded a functional level. He noted, for example, that suicide rates were higher in more individualistic communities characterized by less social integration (i.e., cohesion or social bonds) and lower levels of moral regulation (i.e., the enforcement of society's norms).

In explaining this apparent increase in deviance, Durkheim focused on the ways that society's structures had changed with industrialization and the impact this had on people's behaviour, including deviant behaviour. Before industrialization, he theorized, society's structure was held together by **mechanical solidarity**—i.e., society was bonded together by *likeness* or by a collective commitment to conformity. These societies were characterized by minimal specialization in the division of labour; people produced whatever they needed for their survival. Interactions between individuals in this type of society were quite personal and often kin-based; everyone knew and had a personal relationship with everyone else. Each person in this society had much in common with every other person.

With industrialization, the bonding mechanism for social structure was transformed into one of **organic solidarity**—society was bonded together by *difference* or interdependence through a highly specialized division of labour. In industrial society, the tasks that keep society running smoothly are divided among different institutions. The education system fulfills certain tasks while the political system and the medical system fulfill other tasks. Individuals employed in different parts of society are responsible for unique tasks as well. Interactions between people in this type of society are somewhat impersonal, based primarily on our dependence on others because of the degree of specialization in the division of labour. A collective way of thinking and interacting is replaced by individualism.

Under conditions of both mechanical and organic solidarity, social integration and moral regulation have the potential to keep deviance at a functional level and facilitate the degree of conformity necessary to maintain social order. However, when social change occurs at too rapid a pace, individualism gets out of control, and bonds between people become weaker than is necessary for the well-being of society. Traditional norms and means of social control deteriorate, creating a situation of *anomie*. The presence of anomie in modern societies opens the door for greater levels of deviance beyond the degree that is functional for society. Thus, it is the structure of society itself and its impact on individuals that contributes to harmful levels of deviance in society.

Durkeim's theory emerged during the process of industrialization, with its extensive social changes and the associated concerns about the stability of society itself. However, rapid social change is not limited to that era. The twentieth century brought possibly even greater transformation—the automobile, the airplane, immunization, the computer, the internet, and more. Massive political and economic change occurred throughout that century and into the twenty-first as well—change characterized by events such as World War I, World War II, the Cold War, the birth of the United Nations, the creation of human rights policy, the fall of the Iron Curtain, the "war against terrorism," various civil wars in Eastern Europe and in several countries in Africa, and the growth of multinational corporations with greater wealth than most nations. Some might say that ongoing, rapid social change has become a way of life, with significant consequences.

Davis (cited in Downes & Rock, 2003) describes Los Angeles, where outside of the protected communities of the wealthy, anomic disorder has created a "free-fire zone," a city characterized by "urban guerrilla warfare" (p. 113). Following the devastation of Hurricane Katrina in 2005, the news media constructed an image of an anomic New Orleans, characterized by violent crime, looting, and arson (Rodriguez, Trainor, & Quarantelli, 2006). McKee (2002) paints a similar picture of the consequences of anomie in 1930s Limerick, Ireland (as illustrated in Frank McCourt's autobiography, *Angela's Ashes*), in the outskirts of Edinburgh (as portrayed in Irvine Welsh's book *Trainspotting*), and in former Soviet-bloc countries throughout Eastern Europe:

"All are societies that have been fractured by changing circumstances, in which earlier values and meanings are no longer understood or accepted, and new ones have not developed. Traditional support networks have been disrupted. Expectations

have been raised, but with no obvious, legitimate means to fulfill them. These societies produce people, especially young men, but increasingly also young women, whose outlook is characterised by a sense of futility, lack of purpose, emotional emptiness and despair. . . ." (McKee, 2002, p. 456)

The societies or communities McKee describes are those in which injury, violence, infectious disease, and substance abuse are prevalent, with a corresponding increase in mortality. For example, Walberg and colleagues (cited in McKee, 2002) found that in 1990s Russia, communities with the most rapid and extensive socioeconomic change (a high number of job losses and gains in medium and large enterprises) had the highest crime rates and the largest decreases in life expectancy, presumably due to alcohol abuse. Anomic disorder creates a demand for alcohol and other substances due to weakened social cohesion; in addition, it improves the supply of such substances, due to diminished moral regulation in the form of police and government corruption (McKee, 2002). In those communities where people live more traditional lifestyles and have stronger family and social networks (e.g., rural areas and areas with large Muslim populations), addiction-related problems are less common (Walberg *et al.*, cited in McKee, 2002). The contemporary world, much like Europe of the nineteenth century, is rapidly changing. With these extensive changes, anomie is becoming more common, and, according to Durkheim's theory, the stage is being set for the emergence of dysfunctional levels of deviance.

Here we have seen one theorist's application of functionalist ideas to an explanation of why deviance occurs. Durkheim's approach exemplifies the central concern of both objective ways of defining deviance and the related positivist theoretical perspectives. Robert Merton, a twentieth-century functionalist theorist, both built upon and moved away from Durkheim's ideas. Looking at Merton's theory shows us another way that functionalist assumptions have been applied to the study of deviance.

TIME TO REVIEW

■ According to Durkheim's functionalist theory, in what way is deviance functional, and why does it become pathological? What past and current research supports his claims?

■ Can you think of other examples, real or fictional, that illustrate this functionalist theory?

Merton: Anomie and Strain Theories

Robert Merton (1938, 1968) applied functionalist assumptions to the study of deviance in different ways; however, he is best known for applying functionalist assumptions in the form of his anomie and **strain theories** (often labelled

> ### Ask Yourself
>
> As a member of Canadian society, what have you been taught that you are supposed to achieve in life in order to be considered "successful"? Who are the people considered the most "successful" in our society? What do you see in the society around you that reinforces your belief that these are, indeed, the criteria for success?

classic strain theory), which dominated "the area of deviance from the early 1950s until about 1970" (Collins, cited in Pfohl, 1994, p. 279). After two decades of being disregarded in favour of more micro-level theories, strain theories (along with other structural theories) once again came into favour (Kubrin, Stucky, & Krohn, 2009). In fact, Merton's theory of the linkage between anomie and strain "has been heralded as among the most significant of all major sociological theories" (Featherstone & Deflam, 2003, p. 471). Merton suggested that deviance originates not only from the individual, but also from the structure of society, which propels some people into deviance. What is it about the structure of society that creates a greater likelihood that some people, more than others, will become deviant? The *Ask Yourself* exercise will bring you closer to an answer to that question.

The *Ask Yourself* exercise asks you to think about what Merton referred to as **institutionalized goals**. In contemporary capitalist society, these are the goals that are culturally exalted, the ones that we are taught we are *supposed* to want to achieve. Merton said that in North America, the goals we are to aspire to include *wealth, status/power*, and *prestige*—the qualities that make up "success," or the "(North) American Dream." Almost everywhere we look we encounter the message that these qualities are what we should try to achieve in life. Who are the people who are admired and envied in society? We admire the wealthy: people who drive a Mercedes, Jaguar, or BMW, who live in houses with indoor swimming pools, and who travel to expensive and exotic places several times a year. We admire powerful people, such as Bill Gates. We admire professional athletes (like Sidney Crosby or Tiger Woods), famous actors (like Meryl Streep or Christian Bale), and famous singers and musicians (like Kanye West, Rihanna, or Gene Simmons)—people with prestige. Our society rewards those who attain wealth, power, or prestige; they have the nicest "toys," they win awards (such as the Grammy, the Oscar, or the Playoff MVP), they are interviewed endlessly to share their secrets for success, they have men and women throwing themselves at their feet offering sexual favours, and they have thousands of people wanting to be just like them. The fact that these characteristics are culturally exalted is evident even if you think back to your childhood—it is unlikely that you aspired to grow up to be poor, powerless, and unrecognized. Of course, as adults, some of you might not personally admire people who are wealthy or famous, and you might aspire to other goals. However, even if your personal goals differ from the institutionalized goals Merton referred to, the larger issue is that our society is structured in a way that gives benefit to or rewards those who have attained these institutionalized goals. The next *Ask Yourself* exercise addresses how these goals are achieved.

The (North) American dream serves as the foundation for deviance in society, according to Robert Merton.

Merton suggested that just as our culture is characterized by institutionalized goals, it is also characterized by **legitimate means** of attaining those goals. What are recognized as the legitimate ways of attaining wealth, power, and prestige? We are supposed to get a good education, find a high-paying job, and work hard; alternatively, perhaps you inherited wealth or were born into a powerful family. However, he pointed out that both *anomie* and *strain* have come to characterize American society (and presumably, North America more generally). A context of anomie has emerged, which Merton describes as an imbalance between culturally prescribed goals and legitimate means, whereby society's emphasis on the goals of wealth, power, and prestige exceeds the emphasis on the means of achieving those goals.

This has resulted in a "deinstitutionalization of the means" (Featherstone & Deflam, 2003, p. 478). That is, simply attaining the institutionalized goals has become more important than *how* one attains them. In their *institutional anomie theory,* Messner and Rosenfeld (2001) propose that it is because of the dominance of economic institutions (with their emphasis on competition and success) that anomie characterizes North American society; as economic institutions come to dominate other institutions (e.g., family, religion), economic values come to infiltrate those institutions as well.

In addition to this cultural context of anomie in which we all live, there are also structural constraints for some people. The normative social order is such that not everyone has equal access to legitimate opportunities. A child growing up in a middle- or upper-class neighbourhood—with the best teachers and well-equipped

Ask Yourself

Following Merton's assumption that our society's institutionalized goals include wealth, power, and prestige, think about how these goals are achieved. Living in Canadian society today, what do we learn about the ways in which we are supposed to try to achieve these goals? Are the means of achieving wealth, power, and prestige equally available to everyone?

schools, a wide range of extracurricular activities available, a home in a safe community, and middle- or upper-class parents—is likely to have assured access to the legitimate means of achieving institutionalized goals.

However, consider a child growing up in an impoverished neighbourhood. The dilapidated schools, devoid of library books, have trouble attracting teachers and offer few extracurricular activities. Home is a run-down house in a disordered community. The parents live in poverty or are chronically on social assistance. Although we often perceive Canadian society as a place of equal opportunity, does this child truly have the same access to legitimate opportunities in life as the middle-class child? The blocked opportunities that exist in some parts of the social structure create a *strain* between the goals and the means for people who live there. With this structural gap between institutionalized goals and the legitimate means of achieving those goals, individuals must find ways to adapt.

According to Merton, people can adapt to the gap between goals and means in five different ways, some of which result in deviance (see Table 2.1).

The first possible mode of adaptation is **conformity**. The individual continues to accept both society's institutionalized goals and the legitimate means; this person keeps pursuing wealth, power, or prestige by going to school, finding a good job, and working hard.

The second possible mode of adaptation, **innovation**, can result in deviance. The individual accepts the institutionalized goals, but rejects the legitimate means and instead seeks alternative means of achieving those goals. For example, if you want to become wealthy, you can do so in a conforming way by pursuing a higher education and training for a high-paying career, or you can do so in an innovative way by selling drugs.

Table 2.1   MERTON'S MODES OF ADAPTATION

Mode of Adaptation	Goals	Means
Conformity	Accept	Accept
Innovation	Accept	Reject
Ritualism	Reject	Accept
Retreatism	Reject	Reject
Rebellion	New	New

Adapted with the permission of The Free Press, a Division of Simon & Schuster Adult Publishing Group, from *Social Theory and Social Structure,* revised & enlarged edition by Robert K. Merton. Copyright ©1967, 1968 by Robert K. Merton. All rights reserved.

The third possible mode of adaptation is **ritualism**. The person engaging in ritualism has given up on or at least reduced the institutionalized goals, but continues to engage in the legitimate means. This is someone who thinks he or she will never get anywhere in life, but still keeps going through the motions—for example, never missing a day of work. With this mode of adaptation, people are unlikely to be looked upon as deviant because, to the outside world, they appear to reliably follow the rules.

Merton's fourth mode of adaptation is **retreatism**, wherein people reject both the institutionalized goals and the legitimate means. These are people who have given up on the goals, do not even go through the motions anymore, and instead retreat into their own isolated worlds, sometimes characterized by alcohol abuse or drug addiction.

The last mode of adaptation is **rebellion**. As with retreatism, people engaged in rebellion also reject both institutionalized goals and legitimate means; however, unlike retreatists, they substitute new goals and new means. These are people who have a "vision" of a different world and act to bring that vision to life.

For example, Louis Riel had a vision of a nation that would include Métis rights and culture; he fought for that vision in the Red River Rebellion (1869–70) and the North West Rebellion (1885), eventually being executed for high treason. In his famous "I Have a Dream" speech, American civil rights leader Martin Luther King Jr. described his dream for a society based on equality for all races, religions, and creeds; King was shot and killed by a man who did not share that vision. Nelson Mandela had a vision of a different South African society, one free of apartheid, and he fought for more than 20 years for that vision; although highly celebrated throughout the world (receiving the Nobel Peace Prize in 1993), even he continues to face social typing for his rebellion, being referred to by Calgary MP Rob Anders as a "communist and terrorist" (CBC News, 2001). In the 1960s and 1970s, the hippie counterculture envisioned a society in which everyone would give up material wealth—including money—and instead seek peace and love. In pursuit of these goals, many hippies stopped working, "made love, not war," consumed a wide range of mind-altering drugs, and moved into various types of commune-like settings.

AN INTERNET MOMENT

Go to the website for The King Center at www.thekingcenter.com. Emerging out of Martin Luther King Jr.'s vision and work, The King Center now carries on that "dream." On this website you can look at a biography of Martin Luther King Jr. (which demonstrates the many ways that he was socially typed as deviant and socially controlled, both formally and informally), hear some of his speeches, and see what impact King's "dream" has had not just on American society, but on the rest of the world.

These examples illustrate how Merton's five modes of adaptation allow people to adapt to the gap between institutionalized goals and legitimate means, and how some people are led into deviance—whether through rebellion, retreatism, or innovation. According to Merton, the current structure of society creates this gap, more so for some groups of people in society than for others. This is why some people engage in deviance.

Empirical research has directed its attention primarily toward innovation and retreatism by exploring the relationship between strain and criminal activity. Although early research yielded less-than-impressive results due to methodological weaknesses, more recent research finds that strain (measured by relative deprivation, perceptions of blocked opportunities, or dissatisfaction with monetary status) is associated with criminal activity (Agnew, Cullen, Burton, Evans, & Dunaway, 1996; Burton & Cullen, 1992; Burton & Dunaway, 1994). However, empirical research has largely disregarded the other modes of adaptation—conformity, ritualism, and rebellion (Kubrin, Stucky, & Krohn, 2009).

Thus far we have seen two diverse and highly influential ways that functionalist assumptions have been used to explain why people engage in deviance. As functionalist theories, both Durkheim's and Merton's approaches suggest that parts of the structure of society may become dysfunctional in some way and result in deviant behaviour on the part of some people. The next functionalist theorists we will be discussing are from collaborators Richard Cloward and Lloyd Ohlin, who also consider that the structure of society may lead to deviance for some people.

Cloward and Ohlin: Differential Opportunity Theory

Cloward and Ohlin's (1960) theory extends aspects of Merton's strain theory; although their theory has received relatively little empirical attention, it has served as a foundation for social action and policy (Kubrin, Stucky, & Krohn, 2009). Like Merton, they suggest that the way society is structured results in differential access to **legitimate opportunities**. However, Cloward and Ohlin go on to propose that the way society is structured also results in differential access to **illegitimate opportunities**—some people have more access to illegitimate opportunities than other people do by living in neighbourhoods that may have street gangs, drug dealers, or sex trade workers.

Due to the differential access to both legitimate and illegitimate opportunities that is created by the structure of society, Cloward and Ohlin suggest that some people are more likely to become participants in deviant subcultures. Some people in lower-class neighbourhoods may become part of **criminal gangs**, in which criminal behaviour is akin to a small business (e.g., the Fresh-off-the-Boat, or FOB, gang in Calgary, which formed in the late 1990s for the purpose of selling drugs). Other people may become part of **retreatist gangs**, which, reflecting Merton's concept of the retreatist mode of adaptation, consist of groups of people who retreat into substantial drug or alcohol use. Finally, people in these neighbourhoods may join **conflict gangs**, which fight for status and power in the neighbourhood via the use of violence against competitive gangs.

For instance, although FOB formed as a criminal gang in the 1990s, a falling out among some of its members led to the creation of a new gang, the Fresh-off-the-Boat Killers (FK); extreme violence has now broken out between the two groups, "motivated not by battles over drug turf, but mutual hatred" (Van Rassel, 2009), resulting in more than 25 deaths since 2002.

All three of these instances are a consequence of the opportunities that are available in the community. As children grow up in these neighbourhoods, they may see people making their livings through criminal involvement with similar others, people drinking and taking drugs to excess (and perhaps even trying to sell drugs and alcohol to neighbourhood children), or gang violence. Being a part of this environment makes certain illegitimate opportunities easily available. As with Durkheim's and Merton's theories, Cloward and Ohlin see society's structure as the impetus for deviant behaviour. Robert Agnew, the next theorist to be addressed, also focuses on the roles played by structure and strain in creating deviance, but suggests that they interact with social psychological factors.

Agnew: General Strain Theory

Robert Agnew (1992, 1998) has expanded upon the notion of strain by identifying a number of possible sources for this strain. Merton stated that strain emerges when the social structure places limitations on people's access to the means of achieving positively valued goals. However, Agnew proposes that strain can be produced by a variety of processes. While it can occur when we are unable to achieve goals (e.g., failing a course), it may also arise when valued stimuli are removed (the loss of a job or the dissolution of a marriage), or when negative stimuli are presented (being teased at school or living in a conflict-ridden family). But strain is not sufficient in itself to produce deviance; deviance emerges only when strain is accompanied by **negative affect** (negative emotions) such as anger, depression, or fear. If someone has the economic, interpersonal, or psychological resources to deal effectively with strain-producing situations, deviance is unlikely to occur.

Agnew's general strain theory has been analyzed for its applicability with different forms of deviance, both criminal and non-criminal, and with different populations. In these analyses, anger and depression emerge as the two most salient types of negative affect that are related to deviance when faced with strain-producing situations (Mazerolle, Piquero, & Capowich, 2003; Ostrowsky & Messner, 2005). There is some disagreement, however, as to the precise link between deviance, depression, and anger, as illustrated by two seemingly contradictory studies on criminal behaviour. In one study, White and Agnew (cited by Broidy and Agnew, 1997) found that anger combined with low levels of depression was associated with criminal behaviour among male adolescents. In contrast, Ostrowsky and Messner (2005) found that high levels of depression independent of anger were associated with both property and violent offences among male young adults.

Among university students, high levels of academic strain are associated with depression, which is related to a greater likelihood of using "homework drugs."

Although most of the research on general strain theory has focused on criminal behaviour, particularly among adolescents and young adults, some research has explored the application of general strain theory to non-criminal forms of deviance as well. These studies further illustrate the complex relationship between strain, anger, and depression. For instance, Ford & Schroeder (2009) found that university students who experience the highest levels of academic strain (those who place a high value on academic work, yet have grade point averages below 3.0) are the most likely to use stimulants as a "homework drug," with the intervening variable being depression.

Purging behaviour among young women has also been analyzed using this theory (Sharp, Terling-Watt, Atkins, & Gilliam, 2001). A negative correlation was found between purging behaviour and the successful achievement of goals; women who were less successful at goal achievement were more likely to engage in purging. Anger and depression mediated this relationship: women who had high levels of anger and depression engaged in purging behaviour in response to strain. Sharp and colleagues conclude that anger accompanied by high levels of depression may result in internalized forms of deviance, such as purging. In contrast, anger that is accompanied by low levels of depression (as found by White and Agnew) may result in externalized forms of deviance, such as delinquency.

The addition of negative emotions to notions of strain is what distinguishes Agnew's general strain theory from Merton's strain theory and from Cloward and Ohlin's differential opportunity theory. More recently, Agnew (2006) has developed a more macro-level strain theory, which postulates that the principles of general strain theory can be integrated with structural factors. Here he suggests deviance will be more prevalent in certain locations within the social structure (e.g., low-income neighbourhoods) because of the large number of people who are experiencing strain (due to unemployment, low wages, or low education).

The last functionalist theorist we will be addressing is Albert Cohen, whose subcultural theory also integrates structured inequalities as the impetus for deviance.

Cohen: Theory of Status Frustration

Albert Cohen (1955) claims that the inequalities in the structure of society are reproduced in the classroom, resulting in delinquent subcultures among lower-class boys. Consequently, Cohen's theory is sometimes categorized as a **subcultural theory** rather than a functionalist theory. The middle-class foundation of the school system creates a **middle-class measuring rod** that lower-class boys find difficult to live up to. The school's emphasis on delayed gratification, politeness, and the value of hard work does not correspond well with the lives of lower-class boys. In their homes and communities, delaying gratification may result in the object of the gratification disappearing or being taken away. Politeness may compromise safety, and instead toughness is emphasized. They may see their own parents working very hard, perhaps at two or three jobs, and yet not making any progress; thus, the value of hard work may be unapparent. When they are unable to succeed according to the standards in the classroom, they experience a situation similar to strain—**status frustration**. As a result, they join together with other lower-class boys who are having the same experience (**mutual conversion**) and develop a set of oppositional standards at which they are able to succeed (**reaction formation**). If the middle-class standard is to delay gratification, the oppositional standard is to be hedonistic. Non-utilitarian, malicious, negativistic youth gangs are the result. In support of Cohen's theory, many empirical studies have found poor school performance or early school leaving to be associated with criminal behaviour (e.g., Gomme, 1985).

TIME TO REVIEW

- According to Merton's concepts of anomie and strain, why does deviance emerge and what are the different modes of adaptation to strain? Is everyone in society equally likely to engage in deviance? Is deviance equally likely in all societies?
- According to Cloward and Ohlin's differential opportunity theory, how does the structure of society contribute to deviance and what different forms does deviance take?

- According to Agnew's general strain theory, what causes strain and what role do emotions play?
- According to Cohen's theory of status frustration, why do lower-class boys become deviant, and what form does their deviance take?

A Closing Look at Functionalist Theories of Deviance

Émile Durkheim, Robert Merton, collaborators Richard Cloward and Lloyd Ohlin, Robert Agnew, and Albert Cohen have each applied functionalist assumptions to an explanation of deviance, although in slightly different ways. Durkheim's theory of society includes discussions of how deviance can be functional for society but can reach pathological levels when social change occurs too rapidly and anomie is created. Merton's theory, which focuses more explicitly on explaining deviance, describes with greater specificity what it is about the normative social order that leads some people into deviance. For Merton, this is the gap between institutionalized goals and legitimate means of achieving those goals, which is experienced more by people located in certain parts of the social structure. Like Merton, Cloward and Ohlin suggest that the structure of society creates differential access to legitimate opportunities, but they extend the notion of differential access in showing how it applies to illegitimate opportunities as well. Agnew goes a step further by saying that strain must be accompanied by negative emotions for deviance to be the result. Finally, Cohen suggests the reproduction of structured inequalities in the school system serves as the impetus for deviance among groups of lower-class boys.

Despite the slightly different paths that are taken by these various theories, they all make use of functionalist assumptions—that society is comprised of structures that fulfill important functions for the maintenance of the social order, that the structure of society contributes to deviance in some way, and that deviance is a threat to society's equilibrium (at least at certain levels).

Functionalist theories have been subject to considerable criticism. In fact, Martins (cited in Downes & Rock, 2003) states that "every Autumn term . . . [functionalism] is ritually executed for introductory teaching purposes . . . the demolition of functionalism is almost an initiation rite of passage into sociological adulthood" (p. 81). Functionalism has been criticized on both logical and ideological or political bases. Critiques of functionalist logic suggest it is teleological (i.e., related to goals) and tautological. It is **teleological** in that "the grounds for the existence of [a] phenomenon are simply read into the alleged function it serves" for society as a whole (Downes & Rock, 2003, p. 98).

Functionalism proposes that since society has specific needs, particular institutions are created in order to meet those needs. However, functionalism is not able to explain *why* that specific institution, at the exclusion of others, is required to achieve particular societal goals (Ritzer & Goodman, 2004). For example, because society requires that children be socialized, the institution of family emerged; the existence of family is explained in terms of the functions it fulfills. But critics suggest that family is not *necessary* for the socialization of children; many other institutions can and do fulfill that function as well (e.g., the education system). If other institutions are able to fulfill that same function, then functionalism really has not explained the need for the family at all (Turner & Maryanski, cited in Ritzer & Goodman, 2004).

Functionalist arguments are also **tautological** (i.e., circular), where the whole is described in terms of its parts, and the parts are described in terms of the whole (Ritzer & Goodman, 2004). In a tautological argument, we would say that because we see families socializing children, the socialization of children is one of the functions of the family. The latter part of the argument merely restates the information in the former part of the argument.

Functionalist theories are also criticized at an ideological or political level: critics claim that by determining the functions of almost any aspect of social life, functionalists ignore the social and historical circumstances from which those aspects emerge. The presumption of functionality (the idea that deviance is somehow useful) also contributes to the critique of functionalism's conservative bias (Cohen, cited in Downes & Rock, 2003; Deutschmann, 2002; Pfohl, 1994; Ritzer & Goodman, 2004). Racial inequalities, gender inequalities, and low wages for the working class can all be justified on the basis of being "functional" for society in some way. For example, while strain theorists point out the influence of structural inequalities on deviance, they do not explicitly state that society's structure should be modified in order to reduce inequalities in the distribution of opportunities.

Finally, it has been suggested that functionalist theories have an **androcentric bias**, meaning that women have been addressed in functionalist theories only to a limited extent. When women's experiences have been addressed in functionalist theories, a conservative bias once again becomes evident; for instance, traditional gender roles have been identified as serving important functions for society (e.g., Parsons & Bales, 1955).

Each of the specific theories reviewed thus far has also been subject to particular criticisms. As a result of their emphasis on criminal behaviour and reliance on official crime statistics, the various strain theories—such as Merton's theory of anomie and strain, Cloward and Ohlin's differential opportunity theory, and Cohen's theory of status frustration—have all been criticized for identifying deviance and criminality as lower-class phenomena. If criminal behaviour is acknowledged to be a middle- and upper-class phenomenon as well, and non-criminal forms of deviance are also analyzed (e.g., "swinging"), then it becomes clear that these theorists' explanations of deviance are limited (Kitsuse & Dietrick, 1979). In that case, the very foundation of their explanations—the assumption that deviance originates from differentially structured opportunities—comes into question (Ritzer & Goodman, 2004; Downes & Rock, 2003; Ward, Carter, & Perrin 1994; Hackler, 2000; Siegel & McCormick, 2003).

However, Agnew and colleagues (1996) claim that strain theory does not necessarily implicate the lower-class; if strain is operationalized as dissatisfaction with one's monetary status, the concept can be applied to all levels of socioeconomic status. Similarly, the theory of status frustration and differential opportunity theory have been criticized for not being able to explain why youth who are located in the same lower-class position in the social structure have different outcomes. Most lower-class youth grow up to be contributing, conforming members of society, with diplomas or degrees and gainful employment (Downes & Rock, 2003).

In response to criticisms of strain theories' emphasis on deviance as a lower-class phenomenon, some deviance specialists have used expanded notions of deviance, exploring non-criminal forms. For example, Parnaby and Sacco (2004) apply Merton's strain theory to what they identify as a newly emerged institutionalized goal: that of the pursuit of fame and celebrity (see Box 2.2). This change eradicates the inherent linkage between deviance and the lower socioeconomic strata.

Strain theories have also been criticized for failing to recognize individual differences, such as gender and cultural differences, in response to strain (Deutschmann, 2002). More recently, however, a growing body of research has been investigating strain theories within the context of gender and race. For example, Konty (2005) analyzes gender differences in deviant behaviour using the concept of **microanomie**, a state wherein an individual's self-transcendence values (value placed on qualities such as honesty, helpfulness, equality, and social justice) are exceeded by self-enhancement values (value placed on authority, ambition, competition, social power, and beating the system). Because females (when compared to males) are less socialized into accepting *self-enhancement values*, and because those values are associated with attitudes that support deviant behaviours (physical fights, stealing, marijuana use), males are more likely than females to engage in those behaviours.

Several studies have looked at whether there are gender differences in the effects of strain on criminal behaviour among youth and young adults (Hoffman & Su, 1997; Agnew & Brezina, 1997; Mazerolle, 1998; Ostrowsky & Messner, 2005). For example, Ostrowsky and Messner's (2005) analysis of general strain theory finds that young adult males are less likely than females to respond to strain with depression; however, depression is more likely to be associated with criminal offending in males than females.

Lauritsen (1994) looks at both gender and race in a form of non-criminal deviance, namely, sexual activity (and especially unprotected sexual activity) among adolescents. Lauritsen does not apply any specific strain theory, but rather uses the concept of strain as a variable in the analysis, with strain operationalized as neighbourhood disorder and educational disappointment (i.e., having educational expectations that are lower than one's aspirations). The research finds that strain increases the frequency of sexual activity among African-American females but not African-American males or Caucasian males and females. Lauritsen suggests that for African-American girls, the structure of opportunities in their neighbourhoods reduces their expectations, creating strain and resulting in an alternative "success" goal—that of pregnancy and motherhood.

Cohen's theory of status frustration has been criticized for failing to recognize nonutilitarian, negativistic, malicious acts of deviance among middle-class suburban gangs (Kitsuse & Dietrick, 1979). This brings into question Cohen's assumption that failing to live up to the middle-class measuring rod in schools is the

Box 2.2 The "Strain" of Fame and Celebrity

Although Merton initially emphasized material or economic success in his theory of the relationship between anomie and strain, his more recent work uses the broader concept of *opportunity structures*, which can be generalized to goals outside of the economic realm (Merton, 1995). Using Merton's revised theoretical formulation, Parnaby and Sacco (2004) suggest that in our "mass mediated society" (p. 2), fame and celebrity status have become institutionalized goals. We have only to look at the popularity of reality shows on television, the opportunity for everyday people to become superstars on *American Idol*, or *Nashville Star*, and the rapidly increasing sales figures of celebrity-following magazines like *Us Weekly* or *People* to see the pedestal upon which celebrity has been placed. Legitimate means of achieving this institutionalized goal include "individual struggle (or hard work), personal accomplishment and/or a rare talent, and . . . 'dumb luck'" (Parnaby & Sacco, 2004, p. 5). However, the opportunity structure is such that not everyone has equal access to these legitimate means. Thus, individuals who experience the strain between goals and means may use one of the four deviant *modes of adaptation* proposed by Merton.

Innovation involves continuing to pursue institutionalized goals, but rejecting the legitimate means of doing so. Innovative means of pursuing fame or celebrity include the gangster celebrities of the past (e.g., Al Capone) and their contemporary equivalents—those living the "gangsta lifestyle" (p. 13). Gangsters (and gangstas) cross the line between media celebrity and criminal, a fact that has been integrated into the lyrics of rappers themselves. The merging of fame and criminal behaviour is also evident

in the news media's creation of the "killer as celebrity" (p. 14), whose picture is placed on the front page of every newspaper and news magazine and whose life is dissected and sometimes emulated. Graffiti artists use the innovative mode of adaptation as well, wherein their "tagging" is intended to both bring them recognition as artists and mark their territories.

Ritualism brings a diminishing of goals but an adherence to legitimate means. The ritualistic pursuit of celebrity is found in the workers who dress up as characters at amusement parks and people who detail every aspect of their daily lives on personal web pages or blogs. Ritualism is also evident in "the struggling actor . . . who abandons his or her dreams of mainstream Hollywood for the pornography industry" and "the cover band that dedicates itself to the remaking of songs when the multi-million dollar record deal becomes more fiction than fact . . ." (p. 16).

Retreatism leads individuals to reject both goals and means and retreat into isolation. Although somewhat difficult to apply to those in the public eye, Parnaby and Sacco suggest that this mode of adaptation is evident in those who experience extreme stage fright and people who have already achieved fame yet avoid all of its trappings by leading relatively isolated lives (e.g., Marlon Brando, who died in 2004; Johnny Depp).

Rebellion involves replacing existing goals and means with a new vision. "Culture jamming" (Adbusters, cited in Parnaby & Sacco, 2004, p. 20) works toward changing the way that the culture and consumer industries set their agendas. It is linked with critiques of globalization and resistance to corporate-driven global inequality and exploitation.

cause of gang behaviour (Downes & Rock, 2003). His weak treatment of female deviance has also been critiqued; without any supporting empirical data, Cohen suggested that female deviance emerges from interpersonal strain rather than economic strain and is therefore more likely to be of a sexual nature.

The theorists we have discussed are certainly not the only functionalist theorists who have sought explanations for deviance. They are, however, among the most influential. Although functionalist theories no longer dominate the study of deviance, they do continue to maintain a presence (Agnew, 1992; Sharp *et al.*, 2001; Victor, 1992).

In addition to functionalist theories, other perspectives originate from a positivist understanding of why people act in deviant ways. The next set of positivist theories we will be addressing are learning theories.

TIME TO REVIEW

- What are the logical and ideological/political criticisms of functionalist theories?

- What criticisms have been directed at strain theories and status frustration theory, and how has empirical research responded to these critiques?

Learning Theories

Learning theories, like functionalist theories, have been widely used as explanations of deviance. As the label suggests, these theories explain deviant behaviour as a result of the learning process. In other words, someone has taught deviant people to be deviant. The precise nature of this learning process is outlined in various learning theories. In this section of the chapter, we will focus on differential association theory, neutralization theory, and social learning theory—all of which have had considerable influence on the way deviance has been understood over the last several decades.

Sutherland: Differential Association Theory

Our exploration of learning theories begins with an influential theorist whose work is recognized by some people as one of the dominant explanations of deviance today (Erickson, Crosnoe, & Dornbusch, 2000; Cullen & Agnew, 1998). Edwin Sutherland (1947), beginning with the assumption that deviant behaviour is learned, developed a theory that focuses on explaining the nature of the learning process—a process he labelled **differential association**.

Although Sutherland's theory was initially proposed as a theory of crime, it has since been successfully applied to other forms of deviance, particularly adolescent substance use (Aseltine, 1995; Elliot, Huizinga, & Ageton, 1985). Sutherland proposed that deviant behaviour is learned through the very same process by which conforming behaviour is learned. Central to the learning process is the direct interaction and communication that occurs in small, intimate groups.

Deviant people act that way because that is what they learn through communication within the intimate groups of which they are a part. Intimacy is crucial to the learning of deviance, such that impersonal agents like music, television, and movies are relatively inconsequential. Within these personal groups, individuals learn both **techniques** (skills) and **motives** (reasons) for

Ask Yourself

Think about the various groups that you interacted with as a child or adolescent. For each group, consider the types of techniques and motives you were exposed to. Did you learn ways to engage in what might be seen as deviant behaviour and reasons for doing so? Did you learn ways to engage in conforming behaviour and reasons for doing so? If you consider your childhood and adolescence as a whole, do you think you were exposed to more deviant definitions than conforming definitions, or vice versa?

particular kinds of behaviour. If people are exposed to more deviant definitions than conforming definitions overall, they are likely to become deviant themselves; in other words, if they are learning techniques for how to engage in deviance and motives for engaging in deviance more than they are learning techniques for how to be conforming and motives for conforming, they are more likely to engage in deviant behaviour.

This differential exposure to deviant and conforming definitions is further complicated by the fact that not all group interactions have the same impact on our learning processes. First, the extent of group influence varies by *frequency*, in that those groups we interact with more frequently will have more of an influence on our learning. Second, interactions that are of longer *duration* have more of an influence than those of shorter duration. Third, there is a *priority* to our small group interactions: those intimate groups with which we interact earlier in life have a greater influence on our learning. Finally, interactions vary in *intensity* or in how important a particular group is to us; the more important a particular group is to us, the greater its influence on our learning processes. The frequency, duration, priority, and intensity of exposure to group interactions determine how influential the definitions of behaviour are on our learning processes.

Research finds that it is the definitions provided by *in-group* members that are especially important in influencing behaviour. Piquero, Tibbets, & Blankenship (2005) presented MBA students with a vignette in which they were responsible for making a decision as to whether the company for which they worked would continue to distribute a drug discovered to be harmful. They were also asked the extent to which they believed their co-workers, friends, business professors, and board of directors would support that decision. Some support for differential association theory was found in that the employees' decisions were associated with the corporate climate—that is, the extent to which they believed the board of directors and their closest co-workers would support that decision. Their decisions were also *negatively* associated with the extent to which they believed their business professors and friends would support those decisions. The researchers conclude that it is "somewhat disturbing" that "many of the respondents . . . essentially reported that they would take actions that would lead to injuring or killing innocent people, while knowingly disregarding the ethical responsibilities they learned from their professors and defying moral values of their closest friends" (p. 181). In this case, "the corporate environment can subvert the other associations and normative values that the individual has learned [in life]" (p. 181).

Sutherland's explanation of the learning process that leads to deviance had a substantial impact on subsequent theorizing about deviance. Gresham Sykes and David Matza's neutralization theory later highlighted and expanded upon one aspect of differential association theory.

Sykes and Matza: Neutralization Theory

Sykes and Matza (1957), like Sutherland, focused on criminal behaviour in the formulation of their theory, which was later appropriated for understanding the broader issue of deviance. They agreed with Edwin Sutherland's suggestion that deviance emerges as the result of a learning process in group interactions. However, the particular focus of their theory is on the nature of some of the *motives* that Sutherland referred to. According to Sykes and Matza, the most important motives that are learned, which subsequently open the door for deviant behaviour, are **techniques of neutralization**. Part of what deviant people learn is the rationalizations for the behaviour they engage in; by rationalizing their behaviour, they can convince themselves that what they are doing is not *really* wrong.

One of the techniques of neutralization is the **denial of responsibility**, which shifts the blame or responsibility off the individual, directing it elsewhere. The blame may be directed at other people, situations, or environments. Statements illustrating this technique of neutralization include "It's not my fault," "I didn't know there would be drugs there," "My father was never there for me when I was growing up," and "There's nothing else to do in a small town!"

The second technique of neutralization is the **denial of injury**. In this situation, the accused deviants express the perception that what they have done hurts or harms no one. For example, some people refer to "victimless crimes," such as drug use or prostitution. Similarly, a male cross-dresser or someone who dresses in "rave" style may also say that what they do does not hurt anyone.

The **denial of the victim** is the third neutralization technique, where the perception is that the victim of the deviant's behaviour was somehow deserving of their fate. For example, Robin Hood was seen as a hero for robbing from the rich, who were perceived as corrupt and immoral and therefore deserved to be robbed. When Matthew Shepard, a young gay man, was murdered simply for being homosexual, protesters at his funeral carried signs saying "God hates fags." Matthew Shepard was perceived by some people as deserving his fate.

The fourth neutralization technique that Sykes and Matza refer to is **condemnation of the condemners**. This technique shifts the focus from the deviant's own behaviour to the deviant behaviour of others, especially people from the social groups that have pointed to this person's deviance. The condemners are accused of being hypocrites who are engaging in other forms of deviance, perhaps secretly. For example, although hippies in the 1960s were frequently accused of being deviant, they turned the tables on their accusers by pointing to all of the negative actions of "the establishment," such as destroying the environment for profit and being party to the Vietnam War. The condemners are thereby perceived as hypocrites who have no right to be criticizing anyone else's behaviours.

The final technique of neutralization is **appealing to higher loyalties**, where the deviant behaviour is justified as serving a higher purpose. In this situation, people acknowledge that they have violated norms, but in service of other more important norms. Someone might get into a violent fight in order to protect a friend. Someone might dress in goth attire in the name of individuality and freedom. A suicide bomber might walk into a shopping mall in order to punish evildoers and achieve spiritual salvation in the afterlife.

These five techniques of neutralization (since expanded to include a number of additional techniques), adopted through the kind of learning processes described earlier in differential association theory, are central to explaining why people engage in deviance. Only by being able to rationalize their actions do people become deviant. Techniques of neutralization have most commonly been explored in the context of minor forms of law breaking. For example, Ingram and Hinduja (2008) found widespread use of neutralization in an analysis of digital music piracy among university students. They deny *responsibility* for their actions, shifting the blame to ambiguous laws or a lack of money with which to purchase music. They *deny injury*, claiming that most authorities do not really care about music piracy and that it does not hurt anybody. They *deny the victim*, stating that the music industry makes more than enough profit from the pockets of customers. By explaining the downloading of music as being for friends/family or for a project at school/work, university students make an *appeal to higher loyalties*.

Techniques of neutralization have also been explored to some extent within the context of other forms of deviance. For example, exotic dancers have been found to make use of three techniques of neutralization (Thompson, Harred, & Burks, 2003). They *deny injury*, saying that it is "harmless fun," "doesn't hurt anybody," and "is perfectly legal" (p. 562). They *condemn the condemners* by saying, "You should see the cops when they come in. They watch us dance for an hour or two before they bust anybody . . . there's usually a half dozen of 'em at a time. How many cops does it take to write a ticket for lewd dancing to one or two harmless girls?" (p. 564). They also *appeal to higher loyalties*, particularly in terms of providing for their children.

Techniques of neutralization have been found among numerous other groups as well, such as pregnant women who violate the nutritional norms of "good mothers" (Copelton, 2007); male high-school students who engage in fighting, truancy, vandalism, and drug use (Teevan & Dryburgh, 2000); people who use illegal fireworks (Buzzell, 2005); and the mothers of child beauty pageant contestants (Heltsley & Calhoun, 2003) (see Box 2.3).

Box 2.3   Beauty Pageant Moms

Following the 1996 murder of child beauty queen JonBenet Ramsey (which remains unsolved), child beauty pageants were suddenly in the spotlight. The pageants were criticized as dangerous events that sexualize little girls and attract pedophiles. Mothers of child beauty pageant contestants were especially singled out for criticism for bringing their daughters into that "deviant" world that attracts a sexually "deviant" audience. Taking a closer look at the world of child beauty pageants, Heltsley and Calhoun (2003) interviewed 43 mothers of child beauty pageant contestants to determine whether they used any of the techniques of neutralization suggested by Sykes and Matza (1957). The researchers found that these mothers used four out of five neutralization techniques.

The most commonly used technique (46.5% of the mothers) was *condemnation of the condemners*. In using this neutralization technique, mothers expressed outrage at the accusation that pageants attract pedophiles. They turned the tables on their accusers, stating that only someone who was really "sick" themselves would suggest that anyone would find these little girls "sexy."

The second neutralization technique used by the pageant mothers was *denial of injury* (25.6% of the mothers). In this way they claimed that not only were beauty pageants not *harming* their daughters, pageants were actually *benefiting* them. Mothers pointed to characteristics like increased confidence and an enhanced ability to concentrate in school as arising from the experience of competing in pageants.

The third technique used was *denial of responsibility* (13.9% of mothers). With this technique, mothers indicated that they really did not have any choice but to enter their daughters in these pageants. In some cases, the mothers claimed that pageants were their daughters' ideas in the first place, and that their daughters insisted on continuing in the competitions. In other cases, the mothers stated that pageants were the only way to improve their daughters' delicate self-esteem, and to prove to them that they were beautiful, smart, and charming.

The last technique of neutralization used was *appealing to higher loyalties* (13.9% of mothers). Mothers using this technique frequently acknowledged that there were problems with the structure of child beauty pageants and their competition requirements. At the same time, however, they remained committed to the pageant world for their daughters' sakes or because their daughters were still interested in competing.

Social Learning Theory

Social learning theory highlights the role of learning processes not only in deviant behaviour but in behaviour more generally; according to these theorists (e.g., Bandura, 1986; Burgess & Akers, 1966), all of our behaviours can be explained in the same way.

> ### Ask Yourself
>
> As a child, how did your parents respond when you broke the rules, like when you stole a cookie from the cookie jar before dinner or broke curfew as a teenager? How did they respond when you did something they approved of, like cleaning your room or receiving a high grade on a report card?

In social learning theory, it is suggested that all behaviour is the result of *definitions* (attitudes about the acceptability of specific behaviours), *differential association* (with whom one associates), *imitation*, and *differential reinforcement* (rewards and punishments). It is related to the behaviourist theory of *instrumental conditioning*, which suggests that we are more likely to engage in behaviours we have been rewarded for (or that have been reinforced) in the past, and we are less likely to engage in behaviours that we have not been rewarded for or that we have been punished for in the past.

We can see principles of instrumental conditioning being used in parenting all the time: a child who misbehaves is spanked, is given a time out, has telephone privileges taken away, or is grounded, while a child who acts in accordance with the parents' wishes is given praise, attention, or perhaps an increase in allowance. In school, children are rewarded for behaving well and studying by getting good grades and perhaps special privileges (such as getting to help the teacher clean the blackboard after school).

Social learning theory goes a step further by saying that not only are our behaviours influenced by what we personally have been rewarded and punished for in the past, they are influenced by what we see other people being rewarded and punished for, through the process of imitation or modelling. For example, if we hear Dad make a racist joke and see his friends laugh and show approval, we are more likely to act in similar ways and develop similar views. If Mom is bulimic and we see her rewarded with compliments on how beautiful she is, we are more likely to act in similar ways. Thus, people engage in deviance because they either have been rewarded for it in the past or have seen other people being rewarded for it (Bandura, 1986; Akers, 1977).

The role of social learning, and especially differential reinforcement, has been found with a wide range of deviant behaviours. This includes adolescent alcohol use (Benda, 1994), academic dishonesty among university students (Vowell & Chen, 1994), and property crime (Bruinsma, 1992). Most empirical research has directed its attention to these relatively more minor acts of deviance and crime; research on more severe behaviours (e.g., violent crime) is less common and more inconsistent (Kubrin, Stucky, & Krohn, 2009).

Akers (1998, 2000, 2006) has recently modified his version of social learning theory to integrate structural factors as well, factors that learning theorists have been criticized for ignoring. He suggests that dimensions of the social structure create the differential contexts in which learning occurs for different people. These dimensions include *differential social organization* (a community's demographic characteristics), *differential location in the social structure* (an individual's defining characteristics such as ethnicity, gender, and educational attainment), *theoretically defined structural variables* (e.g., anomie, conflict, social disorganization), and *differential social location* (an individual's membership in different social groups, such as peer groups). He goes a step further, stating that social learning theory should be integrated with other theories that focus primarily on structural factors (Kubrin, Stucky, & Krohn, 2009). Akers's social learning theory has been extensively applied to adult and youth crime, police misconduct, and more (Chappell & Piquero, 2004).

A Closing Look at Learning Theories

The principles of social learning theory appeal to most of us at a common sense level; it is fairly easy for us to see reinforcement, punishment, and modelling everywhere around us and in our own lives. Like neutralization theory and differential association theory, social learning theory draws attention to processes of learning as key to explaining why people engage in deviance. Despite the differences in the way each of these theories explains the learning process that leads to deviance, they all point to learning as the answer to the question of why people act the way they do—why people become deviant.

However, learning theories have also been subjected to critique. Methodological criticisms have been directed at differential association theory, with critics pointing to the difficulties in arriving at a "tally" of the number of deviant and non-deviant associations in an individual's life. Furthermore, critics suggest that "the theory is riddled with escape clauses and qualifications that diminish its power to predict" (Downes & Rock, 2003, p. 74). Priority, intensity, frequency, and duration each have an influence on deviant or conforming outcomes. But which takes precedence—the parenting an individual received in early childhood (i.e., priority), which may have involved more "conforming" definitions, or the emotional attachment that a police officer has to the police subculture in which "deviant" definitions may contribute to police misconduct (Chappell & Piquero, 2004)?

Neutralization theory has been criticized for what it *hasn't* explored—how techniques of neutralization may vary across different types of deviant behaviours or across different normative contexts. Research using neutralization theory has responded to these critiques, finding variations in the specific neutralization techniques used by different types of white-collar or workplace criminals (Benson, 1985; Hollinger, 1991), as well as the influence of normative context on neutralization techniques. For instance, Buzzell (2005) compared the use of specific techniques of neutralization among two groups of people purchasing fireworks for Independence Day in the United States. One group lived in an area where fireworks were legal, and a second group lived in an area where fireworks were recently banned. Those living in the area where fireworks had been banned were more likely to agree with statements like, "most fireworks people use really don't hurt anyone" (denial of injury), and "if people in my neighbourhood are worried about noise or harm from fireworks they should take responsibility to protect themselves or be out of town that evening" (p. 35) (denial of the victim).

Neutralization theory has also been critiqued on the basis of its reasoning and methodology. Although the theory states that techniques of neutralization are used *prior* to committing an act, most research has looked at the techniques being used by people *after* an act has occurred (e.g., convicted shoplifters). Thus, the only conclusions that can be legitimately made are that these are post-act techniques of justification rather than techniques of neutralization that contribute to the act in the first place (Piquero, Tibbets, & Blankenship, 2005; Lyman, 2000). However, Hirschi (cited in Cromwell & Thurman, 2003) suggests that a post-act technique of justification may become a pre-act technique of neutralization in the future, such that the two are not necessarily mutually exclusive. Other research attempts to overcome this critique using a vignette design: participants read about a hypothetical situation and then identify how they would act in that situation and why. For example, MBA students referred to several neutralization techniques when explaining why they would take a particular action in a hypothetical situation that involved distributing/recalling a drug being investigated by the FDA for causing harm to consumers (Piquero, Tibbets, & Blankenship, 2005). Participants who said they would continue to distribute that drug claimed that the government exaggerates the dangers (denial of injury), suggested that government regulations impede business (condemnation of the condemners), and subscribed to the expression "let the buyer beware" (denial of the victim).

The final set of positivist theories that have been frequently used to explain deviance—*social control theories*—provide yet another way of understanding the origins of deviance based on the objectivist conceptualization of the nature of deviance.

TIME TO REVIEW

- What are the core assumptions of learning theories?
- How is deviance learned according to (a) differential association theory, (b) neutralization theory, and (c) social learning theory?
- What type of empirical support exists for each of the learning theories?

- What criticisms have been directed at Sutherland's differential association theory, and Sykes and Matza's neutralization theory?
- How have empirical researchers using these theories responded to critiques?

Social Control Theories

Social control theories focus on a different type of question than other positivist theories. While other positivist theorists direct their attention to why some people become deviant, social control theorists direct their attention to why not all people become deviant. They suggest that deviant behaviour is inherently attractive, exciting, and appealing. Given the appeal of deviant behaviour, it is only through higher levels of social controls that some of us do not become deviant.

Hirschi: Social Bonds Theory

The most widely used social control theory in explanations of deviance has been Travis Hirschi's (1969) **social bonds theory**. His argument is that four different types of social bonds rein most of us in, restraining us from deviance.

The first bond is that of **attachment** to parents, teachers, and peers. Hirschi suggested that the greater our level of emotional attachment to others, the more bound we are to conformity. Conversely, a lack of emotional attachments leaves us freer to engage in deviance. The *type* of person to whom we are attached is not important; rather it is the mere fact of having an emotional attachment itself that restrains us from deviance.

The second bond is **commitment** to conformity. Being committed to conventional activities like school, work, organized sports, or childrearing gives us more of a stake in the conventional world; if we were to engage in deviance, we would threaten our investments in conventionality and have too much to lose. In contrast, people who have little invested in conventional activities have less to lose by engaging in deviance.

The third social bond is **involvement** in conventional activities. In other words, people who are so highly involved in such activities that the activities take up much of their time simply do not have any time for deviance. People who have substantial unused time on their hands are more likely to be drawn to the appeal of deviance—"idle hands are the devil's workshop."

The last bond is **belief** in the norms, values, and assumptions that comprise the conventional world. Holding such beliefs bonds people to the conventional world, while not holding such beliefs loosens the restraints from deviance. The interaction of these four types of social bonds determines the extent to which individuals will be restrained, or fail to be restrained, from the appeal of the deviant world.

Social bonds theory was initially applied to the study of delinquency. However, it has been successfully applied to other behaviours as well, such as the use of marijuana, cigarettes, and alcohol (Hawdon, 1996; Massey & Krohn, 1986; Marcos, Bahr, & Johnson, 1986), as well as sexual behaviours. Lauritsen (1994) finds some support for social bonds theory in the sexual behaviour of Caucasian adolescents. Caucasian females who have high educational aspirations (commitment) and who place a high value on marriage and parenthood in the future (belief) are less likely to be sexually active. Caucasian males who say they are close to their families (attachment) and who place a high value on marriage and parenthood in the future (belief) are also less likely to be sexually active. Social bonds have less of an effect on the sexual activity of African-American females (for whom *strain* has a greater influence), and no effect at all on the sexual activity of African-American males.

Gottfredson and Hirschi: General Theory of Crime

Ask Yourself

Try to apply social bonds theory to your own life. How many people would you say you have an emotional attachment to? What might you lose from your life if you engaged in deviance? How much of your time is spent engaging in conventional activities?

Although Hirschi initially focused on the relationship between social control and deviance, more recently he has collaborated with Michael Gottfredson on a general theory of crime (Gottfredson & Hirschi, 1990). Here they suggest that **self-control** is central to explaining why some people are predisposed to deviant acts while others are not; in fact, the theory has since come to be commonly known as *self-control theory*.

Low self-control is characterized by impulsivity, a preference for simple tasks, risk-seeking, a preference for physical tasks, self-centeredness, and a quick temper (Grasmick, Tittle, Bursik, & Arneklev (1993). It is the result of ineffective parenting—an absence of attachment, weak supervision, and a lack of discipline when deviant behaviours occur. Although it may be ameliorated to some extent by other influences in a child's life, it remains relatively stable throughout life. Whether in childhood, adolescence, or mid-adulthood, individuals with low self-control are more likely to engage in deviant behaviours when the opportunity presents itself than are individuals with higher levels of self-control. Gottfredson and Hirschi suggest that low self-control can explain white-collar crime, street crime, cheating on exams, and risky sexual behaviours equally well.

Although self-control theory is relatively recent, a considerable amount of research has been done testing its propositions, with mixed results (Nakhaie, Silverman, & LaGrange, 2000). Research has directed its attention primarily to criminal behaviours, as well as "analogous behaviours" (Kubrin, Stucky, & Krohn, 2009) such as substance use, risky driving, truancy/resistance to school, and adolescent sexual activity (Stylianou, 2002; Nakhaie, Silverman, & LaGrange, 2000; Hope & Chapple, 2005). More recently, some empirical research has expanded its focus to other types of behaviours, such as binging/purging, relational aggression (e.g., spreading rumours about someone), and criminal victimization (Harrison, Jones, & Sullivan, 2008; Schreck, Stewart, & Fisher, 2006).

However, some research suggests that certain forms of deviance are actually an attempt to lose self-control rather than a result of low self-control. These researchers claim that in a modern capitalist society, people are surrounded by restrictions and regulations; modern life requires that we constantly control and regulate our own behaviour. Consequently, behaviours like fist fighting, drug use, and "flashing" during events like Mardi Gras "are statements against the ways people are expected to have 'enough' self-control to govern their everyday lives in a capitalist society" (Redmon, 2003, p. 384), rather than acts that reflect a lack of self-control (Presdee, 2001).

Jones and Quisenberry (2004) have found that low self-control is related to a wide range of antisocial deviant behaviours connected to risky driving (driving above the speed limit, following vehicles closely, driving without a seatbelt, driving while drinking), and risky sex (sex with unfamiliar partners, sex without condoms, sex without any contraception, number of sexual partners). They also found that it is related to the experience of and/or the intention to engage in thrill/adventure-seeking behaviours, such as rock climbing, skydiving, whitewater rafting, and more. However, they found that the same individuals did not engage in both antisocial deviant behaviours *and* thrill-seeking behaviours. Rather, low self-control led some people into risky driving and risky sex, but led others into socially acceptable forms of risk taking, which the general theory of crime is unable to explain. Jones and Quisenberry suggest that it is necessary to integrate self-control theory with other theories in order to explain this phenomenon. For example, certain social bonds, such as attachment to family or commitment to conventionality, may translate low self-control into socially acceptable forms of thrill-seeking behaviour.

Other research has also integrated self-control theory with social bonds theory. Higgins, Wolfe, and Marcum (2008) found that both social bonds (in terms of commitment to school and attachment to parents) and self-control were associated with the illegal downloading of music and/or software among university students. Similarly, Li (2004) found that low self-control was associated with delinquency, as were each of the four social bonds. Low self-control had more of an effect on delinquency than did any of the individual social bonds, but when the four social bonds were combined into a single measure, they had more of an influence than low self-control. Furthermore, Li found an interaction effect as well. The bonds of belief and involvement had the greatest effects at the lowest level of self-control, and as self-control increased, the effects of the social bonds declined. Similarly, low self-control had the greatest influence on delinquency at the lowest levels of belief and involvement, and as belief and involvement increased, low self-control had less of an influence.

A Closing Look at Social Control Theories

Social control theories, by asking why we do not all engage in deviance instead of asking only why some people do engage in deviance, provide us with a unique standpoint from which to study deviance. However, social control theories have been subject to criticism. Self-control theory has been criticized for the manner in which self-control is defined and measured. First, it is perceived as tautological (Akers, 1991).

The origins of the tautology lie within the development of the concept itself. That is, in defining low self-control, Gottfredson and Hirschi (1990) looked to the characteristics of criminal behaviour. For instance, because they considered most criminal acts to be impulsive and resulting in some type of gain for the criminal, they concluded that low self-control includes impulsivity and self-centredness.

Particular pieces of research have since been critiqued for tautology at the empirical level as well, by measuring self-control behaviourally. In one study that applied self-control theory to impaired driving (a form of "risky" driving), self-control was measured by the occurrence of other forms of risky driving (driving without a seatbelt, having driven after drinking in the past). They found that people who engage in other forms of risky driving (and who therefore are low in self-control) are more likely to drive while impaired; risky driving behaviours are treated as both the cause and the effect (Keane, Maxim, & Teevan, cited in Kubrin, Stucky, & Krohn, 2009).

In response to these perceived problems in measurement, others have measured self-control psychologically. Using this approach, low self-control is treated as a personality trait and is determined via personality inventories (e.g., Grasmick, Tittle, Bursik, & Arneklev, 1993). This has become the dominant means of defining and measuring self-control in contemporary research, although Hirschi has expressed objections about the movement away from a sociological paradigm towards a more psychological paradigm. However, the results of research applying self-control theory are similar, regardless of which type of measure is used (Kubrin, Stucky, & Krohn, 2009).

Self-control theory's proposition that self-control remains stable throughout life has also been questioned. Individuals' life course trajectories and life events (such as employment and marriage) are related to a reduction in criminal behaviour (Farrington, cited in Nakhaie, Silverman, & LaGrange, 2000) and appear to enhance self-control (Sampson & Laub, cited in Nakhaie, Silverman, & LaGrange, 2000).

Both self-control theory and social bonds theory have been criticized for ignoring the role of peer associations in deviant outcomes. Looking at peer associations within the context of social bonds theory, Erickson, Crosnoe, and Dornbusch (2000) try to explain adolescent delinquency and substance use. They conclude that social bonds influence these behaviours via deviant peer associations and susceptibility to deviant peers; that is, adolescents who have strong social bonds are less likely to associate with deviant peers, and are less susceptible to influence even if they do associate with deviant peers. Looking at peer associations within the context of self-control theory, Jones and Quisenberry (2004) suggest that associating with deviant peers may explain why some people with low self-control commit antisocial acts (e.g., risky driving), while others engage in adventure-seeking behaviours (e.g., skydiving). Longshore, Chang, Hsieh, and Messina (2004) propose a more complex relationship between self-control, social bonds, peer associations, and drug use among adults. In their final model, they conclude that low self-control results in associations with deviant peers and weakened social bonds, which result in drug use.

Although social bonds theory and self-control theory have been subjected to critique, research that integrates these theories with each other and/or with additional theories (e.g., differential association) has had some explanatory success, illustrating the role that theoretical integration can play in better explaining deviant behaviour and enhancing our understanding of deviance.

TIME TO REVIEW

- What are the core assumptions of Hirschi's social bonds theory, and what type of support does it have?
- What are the core assumptions of Gottfredson and Hirschi's self-control theory/general theory of crime, and what type of support does it have?

- What criticisms have been directed at social control theories, and how have researchers responded?

Summarizing Positivist Theories

The diverse positivist theories of deviance that have been addressed in this chapter share one goal—trying to explain why people act in particular ways. Functionalist theories, such as Durkheim's anomie theory, Merton's strain theory, Cloward and Ohlin's differential opportunity theory, Agnew's general strain theory, and Cohen's status frustration theory direct their attention to the role that the structure of society itself plays in the emergence of deviance. Learning theories, such as Sutherland's differential association theory, Sykes and Matza's neutralization theory, and social learning theory point to the centrality of learning processes in the emergence of deviance. In other words, people learn to be deviant from others around them. Social control theories, such as Hirschi's social bonds theory, explain why not all of us become deviant. They point to social bonds that restrain us from giving in to the appeal of deviance. Gottfredson and Hirschi's general theory of crime addresses the influence that parenting patterns have on the development of self-control.

Functional, learning, and social control theories each shine a light on a particular aspect of social life in their efforts to explain deviance. Despite their differential areas of focus, and despite the diversity within each of these bodies of theory, there is a commonality. They are all positivist theories that seek to explain why some people act in deviant ways and others do not.

Positivist theories dominated academic understandings of deviance for many years. However, as more subjective views of deviance developed and become more widespread, different types of theories became useful. Just as certain types of theory correspond with more objective views of deviance, certain kinds of theory correspond with more subjective ways of looking at deviance—i.e., interpretive and critical theories. These theories will be addressed in the next chapter.

Exercise Your Mind

How would each of the theories in this chapter explain deviance/conformity as it exists in your own life (or the life of someone you know)? What facets of your experience are left unexplained by each theory? If you had to select the one theory that best explains deviance/conformity in your own life, which would it be?

CHAPTER SUMMARY

- Many different theories are used in the sociology of deviance, corresponding to the various ways one can look at deviance. Each theory shines a spotlight on a particular aspect of deviance and provides one way of understanding it.

- People with more *objective* views of deviance, who are interested in why deviant people become that way, find positivist theories to be the most useful. Positivist sociological theories are modelled after theories in the natural sciences as tools for mastering the natural or social environment.

- People with more *subjective* views of deviance find *interpretive* and *critical* theories to be the most useful for understanding societal perceptions of and reactions to particular acts, as well as the role played by power in these perceptions and reactions.

- *Functionalist theories* dominated positivist understandings of deviance for many years, suggesting that problems with the social structure cause some people to become deviant. Durkheim directed his attention to *anomie* as the root cause of deviance, Merton suggested a strain between *institutionalized goals* and *legitimate means* as the cause, Cloward and Ohlin pointed to differential access to *legitimate* and *illegitimate opportunities*, Robert Agnew emphasized the relationship between strain and *negative affect*, and Albert Cohen focused on *status frustration*.

- Functionalist theories have been criticized for their tautological and teleological logic, their conservative ideology, and their androcentric bias. A number of functionalist theories have also been criticized for treating deviance as a lower-class phenomenon and ignoring gender and race. Empirical and theoretical research has responded to these criticisms, exploring non-criminal forms of deviance across classes and analyzing gender and race in a variety of situations.

- *Learning theories* explain deviance as a result of individual learning processes. *Differential association theory* suggests that we learn techniques and motives within intimate groups that lead us either into deviance or into conformity. According to *neutralization theory*, the key process is the learning of rationalizations that enable people to think that what they are doing is not *really* wrong. *Social learning theory* points to the importance of differential reinforcement in particular.

■ Some empirical research supports learning theories, and the principles of learning theories are easily visible to the layperson. However, learning theories have been critiqued as well. Methodological critiques are the most common, but recent empirical and theoretical research has responded to these criticisms, particularly with neutralization theory.

■ *Social control theories* include Hirschi's *social bonds theory*, which asks why not all of us become deviant rather than why some people do become deviant. He suggests that people with strong social bonds are restrained from deviant behaviour. Gottfredson and Hirschi's *general theory of crime* or *self-control theory* emphasizes the role of ineffective parenting in the development of low levels of *self-control*.

■ As the most recently developed social control theory, self-control theory has been subjected to the most criticism. It has been criticized for its measurement of self-control and its assumption that self-control remains stable throughout life. Both control theories have been criticized for ignoring the importance of peer associations, but recent research has responded to this critique by integrating social control theories with learning theories.

DEVIANCE IN PRINT

Akers, R. L. (1998). *Social Learning and Social Structure: A General Theory of Crime and Deviance.* Boston: Northeastern University Press.

Gottfredson, M. R., & Hirschi, T. (1990). *A General Theory of Crime.* Stanford: Stanford University Press.

Rapley, R. (2007). *Witch Hunts: From Salem to Guantanamo Bay.* Montreal: McGill-Queen's University Press.

DEVIANCE AT THE MOVIES

Hook, H. (Director), Golding, W. (Writer), & Schiff, S. (Screenplay). (1990). *Lord of the Flies.* United States: Metro Goldwyn Mayer. (90 minutes).

In this feature film, a group of boys is left on a deserted island with no adults, no structure, and no society—an environment of complete anomie. As they struggle through each day, deviance emerges, threatening the group as well as the life of each boy.

Polak, H., & Celinski, A. (Directors & Producers). (2004). *The Children of Leningradsky.* Available from the National Film Board of Canada. (34 minutes).

In this chapter, the anomie that characterizes many former Soviet Bloc countries was addressed. This documentary illustrates one of its consequences: more than 30 000 children homeless and living in the sewers of Moscow.

ENDNOTES

1 Leonid Ilyich Brezhnev [b.1906]. Retrieved August 24, 2006, from **www.quotationspage.com**

2 Saxe, J. G. (1873). *The Poems of John Godfrey Saxe*. Boston: James R. Osgood and Company. pp. 135–36. Retrieved August 24, 2006, from **http://rack1.ul.cs.cmu.edu/is/saxe/**

KEY TERMS

atavists, **p. 36**
positivist, **p. 38**
interpretive, **p. 39**
critical, **p. 39**
functionalist theories, **p. 40**
manifest functions, **p. 40**
latent functions, **p. 40**
anomie, **p. 41**
mechanical solidarity, **p. 43**
organic solidarity, **p. 43**
strain theories, **p. 45**
institutionalized goals, **p. 46**
legitimate means, **p. 47**
conformity, **p. 48**
innovation, **p. 48**
ritualism, **p. 49**
retreatism, **p. 49**
rebellion, **p. 49**
legitimate opportunities, **p. 50**
illegitimate opportunities, **p. 50**
criminal gangs, **p. 50**
retreatist gangs, **p. 50**
conflict gangs, **p. 50**
negative affect, **p. 51**
subcultural theory, **p. 53**

middle-class measuring rod, **p. 53**
status frustration, **p. 53**
mutual conversion, **p. 53**
reaction formation, **p. 53**
teleological, **p. 54**
tautological, **p. 55**
androcentric bias, **p. 55**
microanomie, **p. 56**
learning theories, **p. 58**
differential association, **p. 58**
techniques, **p. 58**
motives, **p. 58**
techniques of neutralization, **p. 60**
denial of responsibility, **p. 60**
denial of injury, **p. 60**
denial of the victim, **p. 60**
condemnation of the condemners, **p. 60**
appealing to higher loyalties, **p. 61**
social learning theory, **p. 62**
social bonds theory, **p. 66**
attachment, **p. 66**
commitment, **p. 66**
involvement, **p. 66**
belief, **p. 66**
self-control, **p. 67**

CHAPTER 3

Explaining Deviance: The Perception, Reaction, and Power

Learning Objectives

After reading this chapter, you should be able to

- Explain how interpretive theories approach the topic of deviance, and describe how symbolic interactionism gave rise to other interpretive theories of deviance.
- Describe such concepts as labelling, stigmatization, transition from primary to secondary deviance, the dramatization of evil, deviance as a master status, and the deviant career. Tie each concept to its roots in symbolic interactionist theory, and contrast it with the other concepts.
- Explain how critical theories approach the topic of deviance.
- Describe critical theories like Marxist and pluralist conflict theories, power-reflexive theories, feminist theories, and postmodern theories. Explain what they all share as critical theories and how they differ from each other.

"There are no moral phenomenon [sic] at all, but only a moral interpretation of phenomena." (Friedrich Nietzsche)[1]

Non-Positivist Theorizing

The above quotation emphasizes *interpretation* as the source of understanding, suggesting that moral codes emerge from a process of interpretation rather than from any type of absolute morality. This signals a substantial shift away from the positivist approach to theorizing that was addressed in Chapter 2. Positivist theories shine their spotlights on the actor or the act and try to explain why some people behave in deviant ways while others do not. Affiliated with more objective ways of understanding deviance, positivist theories are based on the assumption that deviance can be identified in some clear-cut way, and once identified, an explanation for that outcome can be sought. The strengths of positivist theories of deviance lie in their search for causation, which facilitates identification of the most effective means of achieving fixed ends (Ashley & Orenstein, 2001). For instance, preventing youth crime or treating alcoholism is most effective when based on an understanding of how people enter criminal activity or begin to abuse alcohol.

However, deviance specialists affiliated with more subjective ways of understanding deviance are critical of positivist theories. They suggest that trying to understand why some people act in ways that the rest of us do not takes the concept of deviance for granted. Focusing on individual deviance implies assumptions about what the world *should* be like and how people *should* act, and tries to explain deviations from normative behaviour more than the normative behaviour itself.

In contrast, more subjective deviance specialists suggest that we should not assume that normative behaviour is necessarily indicative of the way people *should* act. According to some researchers, "nearly all positivist attempts to explain deviance have been disappointing. The expected differences between deviants and nondeviants rarely materialize when the evidence is carefully examined" (McCaghy, Capron, & Jamieson, 2003, p. 17). A more moderate critique of positivist theories of deviance claims that positivism has not resulted in the level of predictive value that might be hoped for.

Because the more subjective views of deviance claim that we cannot know deviance when we see it and instead must be told that a behaviour or characteristic is deviant, the associated theories do not look at the violation of social expectations, but rather at the nature of the social expectations themselves (McCaghy, Capron, & Jamieson, 2003). The interest is not in the act, but in the perceptions of and reactions to the act, as well as in the role of power in influencing these perceptions and reactions. Deviance is seen as constructed through the social typing process, whereby people have descriptive labels attached to them, are evaluated or judged on the basis of those labels, and then are treated in certain ways because of prior descriptions and evaluations (Rubington & Weinberg, 2008). When society, rather than deviant people, is held under a microscope—when the interest is in understanding social processes rather than specific people—the positivist interest in explaining the acquisition of deviant behaviour becomes less relevant. In its place, those theories that are often categorized as *interpretive* or *critical* are the ones that can best explain the social construction of deviance.

Most interpretive and critical theories reject the claim that there are certain standards of objectivity that can be recognized in the study of society, and that it is the role of the sociologist to discover what those standards are. Rather, they propose that social processes are the result of culturally and historically specific human social interaction. Social interaction creates bodies of social rules that then influence our lives. These rules influence all members of society, even though people may frequently be unaware of what those rules are. The role of the sociologist is to examine the processes by which these social rules are created and the impact those rules subsequently have on individuals.

Interpretive theories explain "something that might be unique and unrepeatable" (Ashley & Orenstein, 2001, p. 31). This stands in contrast to positivist theories that seek to identify generalizable, immutable laws that govern the environment. Interpretive theorists claim that the only "reality" is that which emerges through reciprocal, intersubjective understanding between people, and as such their focus becomes the meanings that emerge from interactions between people who are engaged in symbolic dialogue. In other words, interpretive theories emphasize how people develop understandings of the world around them, other people, and themselves. **Critical theories** have a self-reflective **value-orienting** foundation (Ashley & Orenstein, 2001), that is, an underlying interest in emancipation and working toward social justice. Their focus is on the power relations that underlie the creation of social rules. Taken together, critical and interpretive theories are useful in explaining those aspects of deviance that more subjective-oriented deviance specialists are interested in—the social construction of deviance.

A combination of several interpretive and critical theories is associated with the contextual social constructionism that informs more subjective understandings of deviance. One of the most well-known deviance constructionists, Joel Best (2003), claims that labelling theory (which he equates with interpretive theory more generally) and conflict theory (one of the core critical theories) make up the approach referred to as "constructionism." Other researchers suggest that elements of social learning theory (discussed in the previous chapter), symbolic interactionism, ethnomethodology, feminist theories, and postmodernist theories constitute the constructionist approach as well, even though they are all considered distinct theoretical perspectives in their own rights (Nelson & Robinson, 2002; Beaman, 2000; Peace, Beaman, & Sneddon, 2000). The boundaries among these various interpretive and critical theories are certainly somewhat more ambiguous than is the case with positivist theories, and they can be quite complementary to each other as well.

Many contemporary deviance specialists use combinations of these theories in their analyses of various aspects of deviance and normality (e.g., McCaghy, Capron, & Jamieson, 2003; Rossol, 2001). It should also be noted that some level of theoretical integration exists beyond interpretive and critical theories. That is, there are some theorists who have combined elements of interpretive or critical theories with positivist theory as well, as will be illustrated at a later point in the chapter.

Why Are Some Acts Considered Deviant? Using Interpretive and Critical Theories

As we have already noted, a wide range of specific theories is used to explain the social construction of deviance and normality. In the remainder of this chapter, the interpretive and critical theories that will be reviewed are those most commonly used in explaining the construction of deviance, and those that have had significant influences on the sociology of deviance as a discipline.

Interpretive Theories

Symbolic Interactionism

Symbolic interactionism, or what some people simply refer to as *interactionism*, is the foundation for the range of interpretive theories used to study deviance; in fact, some deviance specialists (e.g., Deutschmann, 2002) equate interactionism with interpretive theories and with constructionism. This section of the chapter will begin with a broad discussion of the core assumptions of symbolic interactionism and will then progress to some of the more specific components of interpretive theories of deviance—the dramatization of evil, labelling, and stigmatization.

From a symbolic interactionist perspective (Blumer, 1986), society is created by social interaction, which occurs via communication through symbols. In other words, society is made up of people in constant communication with each other, and this is the source of all meaning and understanding. All communication is symbolic in nature. The symbols that constitute the English alphabet serve as the foundation for written and verbal communication in English. For example, in English, we use the symbols C-A-T to refer to a small furry creature that meows and grabs your toes under the covers when you are trying to sleep. Nonverbal communication, through avenues such as gestures and facial expressions, is symbolic as well. For example, when you have cut someone off in traffic and you are subsequently shown that person's middle finger, you know precisely what message that person is communicating to you. Clothing serves as a form of symbolic communication as well. For instance, when you are going to a job interview, do you wear sweatpants and a stained T-shirt? Why not? Do you think that would communicate the wrong message to the interviewer? All of these forms of symbolic communication constitute the basic foundation of society, according to symbolic interactionists.

However, symbolic communication is complex and nuanced, such that the same symbols may have different meanings in different contexts. The symbols C-A-T, within the context of a construction site where a new parking lot is being built, is more likely to refer to a piece of equipment that moves piles of dirt than a furry animal that meows. Add the symbols T-Y onto the end, and the message changes once again—referring to someone who says nasty things about others behind their backs, and interacting with gender stereotypes, is more likely to be used in reference to a woman than a man.

Via these avenues of communication, we create meaning in our lives and an understanding of the world around us, of other people, and of ourselves. Because each of us has a distinct set of interactions during the course of our lives, the way each of us understands the world varies to some extent. Thus, for example, my interpretation of a particular movie or novel may be different from your interpretation of that same movie or novel. Both of us may watch the same movie and, because of our different interpretations, engage in a resounding debate afterward. The way you choose to act as a student in a university classroom may be different than the way someone else chooses to act in that same environment.

Various processes contribute to the meanings and understandings each of us creates. One of these processes is that of **role taking**. By vicariously placing ourselves in the roles of others, we try to see the world from their points of view and determine our own attitudes and actions accordingly. In that regard, when you are going for a job interview, you try to imagine the position of the interviewers and what they are looking for in a job candidate when you are deciding what to wear and how to answer their questions.

A second process that contributes to the way we develop meaning is through the role of the **looking-glass self**. When determining how to look or act and how we feel about ourselves, we imagine how we appear to other people. What we imagine other people think of us influences what we think about ourselves and how we look or act. These "others" may be *significant others* or a *generalized other*. **Significant others** are those people who are important to us—those people whose perceptions and reactions matter to us. What these significant others think about you has a substantial impact on your actions—you might think, "What would my grandmother/husband/boss/favourite professor say if I did that?!" The **generalized other** refers to "other people" more generally, almost as a generic person—"What would people think if I dressed like that?!"

Through the influences of role taking, the looking-glass self, significant others, and the generalized other, we come to understand the world in particular ways, understand our places in that world, and choose our appearances and actions. The next *Ask Yourself* exercise further explores these processes.

As applied to the concepts of deviance and normality, these processes contribute to our understanding of the "rules" in society, our perceptions of and

Ask Yourself

Think for a few moments about the roles that these processes have played in your own life. In what situations have you tried to understand the world from someone else's point of view? When have you looked to other people to figure out how you should be looking or acting? Have there been times when other people's opinions of you have affected your own opinion about yourself? Who are the specific people in your life whose opinions matter the most to you? How much does what others think about you matter to you?

reactions to ourselves and others on the basis of those rules, and whether we identify ourselves as followers or flouters of those rules. It is also through these processes that individuals who share some perceptions come together and form groups based on those shared perceptions. These groups may then attempt to influence the perceptions of deviance and normality held by others. And because meanings and understandings vary among people based on their own interactions and communications, the "deviance dance" emerges—some individuals or groups will try to socially type certain people as deviant, while other individuals or groups will argue that those same people are normal.

Deviance specialists who hold an interactionist view may focus on many different aspects of this deviance dance. What sociocultural and individual forces influence people's understandings of deviance? What leads some people to join groups that consist of others with similar understandings? How do participants in the deviance dance understand and attribute meaning to their roles in the social construction process? How do people and groups try to influence the perceptions of other people and groups? The specific questions that can be asked from within this approach are almost endless. However, what they have in common is the foundational assumption of the symbolic interactionist perspective—we develop understanding and attribute meaning to the world around us and to ourselves on the basis of interactions we have had with other people in our lives.

Labelling and Stigmatization.   Arising from these core assumptions are a number of specific concepts and theories used to understand the social construction of deviance. One of the most widely used interpretive or interactionist theories in the study of deviance is **labelling theory**. According to labelling theory, deviance is a label that is attached to some people, which then has consequences for how they are treated by others and how they come to identify themselves; this then has consequences for their subsequent actions in life. This view of deviance is most often associated with Howard Becker (1963), but other scholars who preceded him also used notions of labelling.

Tannenbaum (1938) spoke of the role that **tagging** plays in the **dramatization of evil**. He suggested that as observers in society, we may initially identify a particular act as deviant or "evil," but soon come to generalize that judgment to the person as a whole—in other words, we identify the actor as deviant or "evil." This act of *tagging* the individual results in changes in that person's self-image and identity, whereby the identity comes to be built around the label and subsequent behaviours correspond to that label and new identity.

Box 3.1 The Meaning of Being Straightedge

The emphasis on interpretation and meaning that underlies the interactionist approach is vital to researchers who study various subcultures or lifestyle groups. Research on groups such as nudists (Weinberg, 1967), gangs (Jankowski, 1991), and people with tattoos (DeMello, 2000) uses interviews with members of those groups to explore what that lifestyle means to them. Recently, the straightedge lifestyle has been the focus of this type of research attention as well (Atkinson, 2003a, 2003b; Irwin, 1999; Wood, 2001).

To the outside observer, a straightedger may look like any other punk rocker—Doc Martens boots, shaved heads, Mohawk hairstyles, torn clothing. And, indeed, the straightedge movement did emerge from the punk rock scene. However, there are distinct characteristics of straightedgers that make them very different from other punk rockers and from mainstream society. The lifestyle is referred to as *straight*edge because of its ideological epicentre: a clean, straight, physically pure life. Disturbed by the hedonistic, self-indulgent nature of modern life, straightedgers developed an oppositional value system based on abstaining from alcohol, drugs, and casual (or even premarital) sex. Some members of this lifestyle group abstain from caffeine, prescription drugs, and over-the-counter medication as well. This value system does not come out of any strongly held religious belief system, as you might expect, but rather from their personal observations of where self-indulgence leads people. Straightedgers have seen how one night of "fun" can ruin people's lives—from drug overdoses, drunk driving, sexually transmitted diseases, and unwanted pregnancies to the many other "stupid" things people frequently do while intoxicated. In addition to ruining people's lives, these hedonistic behaviours are perceived by them as holding people back from personal fulfillment and self-awareness, as well as having a negative impact on society. Controlling their bodies through physical purity and body modification (such as tattooing) is a form of resistance to the self-indulgent wider society.

There is, however, diversity within straightedge; the meaning of being straightedge varies somewhat among individuals and among subgroups. In the broader pursuit of physical purity and resistance to mainstream society, some individuals incorporate other behaviours—vegetarianism, anti-racist activism, militant animal rights activism, or violence directed at people who are engaging in the behaviours seen as "deviant" by straightedgers (e.g., consuming drugs). Those straightedgers who engage in violence against others in order to spread their message, or violence in pursuit of militant animal rights activism, face the disdain of other straightedgers—within the straightedge lifestyle itself they are socially typed as "deviant" by those who wish to distance themselves (and the larger straightedge lifestyle) from extremists. Being straightedge has different meanings for different people, and symbolic interactionist ideas allow us to understand why.

Lemert (1951) used the term "labelling" rather than "tagging" in what is perhaps the most well-known version of labelling theory. Lemert distinguished between **primary deviance** and **secondary deviance**. He suggested that we all engage in little acts of rule breaking that are seldom noticed and rarely caught by others (primary deviance). Even though we all engage in occasional rule breaking, few of us build a lifestyle around it (secondary deviance). Getting caught sets into motion a series of processes that result in the transition from primary deviance to secondary deviance. Someone who is not caught in an act of deviance may eventually just move on.

For instance, as a child or a teenager you may have shoplifted an item of low value from a neighbourhood convenience store, but it is likely that most of you did that only once or twice and eventually grew out of that "phase." However, Lemert suggested that the mere act of being caught changes the way others see you and subsequently changes the way you see yourself. That is, if you were caught shoplifting and then arrested, the police saw you as a "thief." If convicted in youth court, you were officially labelled a "thief" and a "delinquent." Your parents may have then considered you to be a "thief." As a result of this process of labelling, you come to understand and identify yourself as a "thief" or a "delinquent"—one who commits crimes.

Howard Becker (1963) elaborated upon the processes involved in the transition to secondary deviance. He suggested that once a person is labelled deviant, that label becomes that person's **master status**. A master status is a characteristic by which others identify you. For example, you may immediately identify others on the basis of age ("teenager"), sex ("girl"), or class ("rich"). A deviant label assumes the level of master status; if you have been officially given the label of "thief," others will identify you as "that thief" rather than as "Sam."

Once a deviant label becomes a master status, implications for a person's daily life emerge. Certain life opportunities will be blocked, in that the legitimate, "normal" world will no longer be as accepting. With the conforming world no longer as accepting, the only place to turn may be the deviant world. For example, if you were convicted of theft as a youth, the way you were treated at school may have changed. Perhaps certain peer groups began to exclude you because they did not want to hang out with a "thief." Maybe the girl you were dating broke up with you because she did not want to tarnish her own reputation. The teacher who had offered you a babysitting job on Wednesday nights with her children may have revoked the offer. Soon, you began to feel like an "outsider" (which happens to be the title of Becker's 1963 book).

At that point, it may have been that only other kids who had been labelled "troublemakers" or "delinquents" were willing to spend time with you, and that became the only world in which you felt accepted. And before long, you began to see yourself as a "troublemaker"—your identity gradually changed and your behaviour soon followed. This process of exclusion from the conforming world and acceptance in the deviant world is what Becker suggested led to a lifestyle built around deviance—and what Lemert (1951) called *secondary deviance*.

Other deviance specialists have referred to this process of exclusion, of becoming an outsider, as **stigmatization** (Goffman, 1963). A proponent of the sociological school of thought known as **dramaturgy**, Goffman (1959) suggested that social life is analogous to being in the theatre. In our lives, we are all assigned or assume particular "roles" to play—university student, daughter, soccer player, homosexual, smoker. When we are in front of certain groups of people, we play our roles in certain ways; we control the images that we present, and the messages that we convey to the audience by bringing out our **front-stage selves**. When we leave the front stage and retreat with select groups of people who are a part of our private lives, we allow our **back-stage selves** to emerge; that is, we no longer feel like we have to play a particular role, but instead can be our true selves. If the role we have assumed is deviant in nature (i.e., we have had a deviant label attached to us), managing the impressions others have of us is that much more difficult. No matter what we try to do, others will still perceive us as deviant because we have been stigmatized—we have a **spoiled identity**.

There are a number of ways we can respond to that spoiled identity (i.e., engage in **identity management** or **impression management**). For instance, topless dancers **divide their social worlds**, carefully managing who is and is not aware of what they do for a living (Thompson, Harred, & Burks, 2003). Since 9/11, people of Middle-Eastern descent living in the United States have had to engage in greater stigma management than previously (Marvasti, 2008). Some individuals use *humour*, such as when they are asked about their names. (When a woman named Ladan was seriously asked by a customer about whether she was related to Bin Laden, she joked that he was, in fact, coming to dinner.) Others use *educational* techniques, such as explaining to others the ways in which Islamic doctrine actually promotes peace, or answering questions about clothing. When subjected to negative treatment, some engage in *defiance*, standing up to the perpetrator. In similar situations, others will engage in *cowering*, such as agreeing to leave the elevator when challenged by a fellow passenger. Finally, Marvasti finds that many try to *pass* as non-Muslims (e.g., by changing clothing, accessories, or hair), or even as non-Middle-Eastern (e.g., by getting a license plate with an Italian flag). A stigma must be managed on a daily basis, and different individuals will use diverse techniques to carry that out. The next *Ask Yourself* exercise addresses the ways that you may have responded to stigmatization in your own life.

Although Goffman's work on stigmatization emphasizes the negative impact of stigma, there are potentially positive consequences of stigmatization in certain situations. Braithwaite (2000) postulates that unlike **disintegrative shaming** (wherein deviantized persons are rejected by the community), **reintegrative shaming** is an effective treatment for criminal behaviour. With reintegrative shaming, the criminal is stigmatized, or shamed, for the criminal act, but it is a temporary stigma; the criminal is shown that leaving criminality behind will result in being fully accepted back into the community. Research with former psychiatric patients has also found that being labelled can have a wide range of

Ask Yourself

In your own life, has there ever been anything about yourself that you have tried to hide from the outside world because of your fear of stigmatization (such as a criminal past, substance abuse problem, or learning disability)? Have you ever restricted your interactions to people you knew would be accepting of you, people you knew would be able to understand you? Have you ever proudly displayed an aspect of yourself that you know many people in society consider to be deviant? What are the implications of these different approaches to stigma management?

positive consequences, including enhancing personal growth, bringing families closer together, and exempting such individuals from some of the demands and responsibilities of daily life (Herman & Miall, 1990).

Early interactionists, and particularly early labelling theorists, frequently painted a picture of the labelled deviant as a powerless, passive recipient of a socially constructed label that subsequently had irreversible consequences for the deviant's life. However, some deviance specialists have emphasized the possibility of resistance to a deviant label.

Kitsuse (1980) refers to **tertiary deviance** as a stage that can potentially emerge after the transition from primary to secondary deviance. Some people who have been labelled and who then develop an identity and a lifestyle based on that label may resist the idea that the label is a "deviant" one. They may go on to try to change social norms, to show society that the behaviour they have engaged in or the characteristic they have is not "deviant" at all. They seek to redefine "normal" to include that act or characteristic. For example, some groups of gay and bisexual men who are HIV positive engage in activism to remove the stigma associated with their illness and to increase acceptance in society (Siegel, Lune, & Meyer, 1998). Similarly, some customers in an adult novelty store engaged in tertiary deviance by providing legal advice to store owners, or by recruiting participants to resist conservative efforts to close down such stores in other communities (Hefley, 2007).

Whether we use the terminology of "the dramatization of evil," "tagging," "labelling," or "stigmatization," the processes of deviance being referred to are similar. Being perceived as "deviant" affects the way people treat us, which affects the way we see ourselves, which then affects the way we act in the future. But in addition to studying the processes that occur after being "caught" at deviance, some interactionists are also interested in the process of living a deviant life—the **deviant career**.

The Deviant Career. In addition to the work already discussed, Howard Becker (1963) used the concept of the "deviant career" to study deviance. He postulated that deviance emerges, progresses, and changes over time, and there are stages to involvement in deviance just as there are stages in the development of a career. Thus, the concept of the "deviant career" refers not to those who make a living out of deviance, but rather the way that deviance unfolds in people's lives. Just as in the traditional notion of a "career," people enter deviance, manage their experiences of deviance, and may quit (or exit) deviance, all of which are

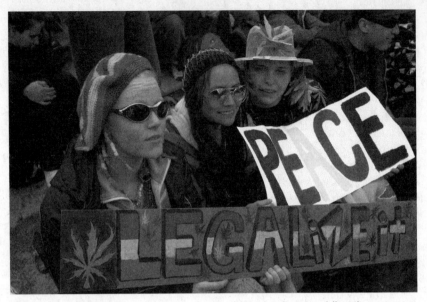

Why do some people become part of cannabis subcultures, while others remain casual smokers or do not use marijuana at all?

intertwined with changes in their identities and understandings of self. Becker illustrated this sequential model of deviance with marijuana users, exploring the stages of meaning and understanding by which they became marijuana users, acted as marijuana users, and stopped using marijuana at some point. He identified three "stages" in this career—the beginner user, the occasional user, and the regular user.

A number of factors are involved in "becoming a marijuana user," such as having access to the drug, learning how to smoke correctly, and coming to perceive the effects of the drug as pleasurable. Various **career contingencies**, or what may be seen as significant *turning points*, influence the directions that people take at various points in the deviant career. For example, a lack of access to a steady supply of marijuana may lead some people to drop the habit, while leading others into associations with organized groups that have a stable supply of the drug. While Becker applied the deviant career to marijuana users, other deviance specialists have used the concept to analyze the transition from pre-mental patient to ex-mental patient (Goffman, 1959), and becoming a cocaine dealer (Murphy, Waldorf, & Reinarman, 1990). Particular deviance specialists may focus specifically on the entrance phases, management phases, or exit phases of the deviant career. The interactionist concepts and assumptions discussed earlier in the chapter, such as role taking, meaning, understanding, and communication, lie at the core of the processes involved in deviant careers.

A Closing Look at Interpretive Theories

Interpretive theories focus on the construction of meaning and understanding in interpersonal interactions, as well as the consequences of people's understandings for how they treat others and how they perceive themselves. These theories draw our attention to various aspects of deviance, such as the processes by which understandings of deviance and normality develop in people's lives and the processes by which variation in these understandings among individuals and groups materializes.

Interpretive theories give us insight into the emergence of the "deviance dance," wherein some people will say that Group X is deviant and can be fixed in a certain way, other people will agree that Group X is deviant but can be fixed in a different way, and other people will say that Group X is not deviant at all. These theories shine a spotlight on how someone's lifestyle and identity may come to be based on deviance, on the different ways that individuals may react once they are identified as deviant by others, and on how some people may exit deviance.

The primary criticism of interpretive theories as a whole is that they fail to address the social structure and its role in the processes surrounding deviance and normality (Dennis & Martin, 2005; Downes & Rock, 2003). In order to deal with this issue, interpretive assumptions have been combined with structural approaches. A growing body of theoretical and empirical work acknowledges that the social structure provides a context in which people engage in interaction. This research suggests that interaction can result in social change (changes to the social structure), but says that the structure also places limitations on people's interactions.

For example, Solivetti (2003) found that the growing problem of drug addiction in Italy can be explained by combining functionalist and interactionist variables. Drug addiction (measured by the number of deaths due to drug use and the number of people in drug treatment) shows considerable regional variation based on structural factors. That is, drug addiction is more prevalent in urban areas that have higher incomes and levels of education, a "reduced and fragile family" (p. 45) (higher rates of separation and smaller family size), and higher levels of individualism (e.g., more independent, unmarried women).

Although functionalist theories frequently associate deviance with lower socioeconomic classes, Solivetti points out that in these more affluent communities in Italy, the people who are addicted to drugs are those who experience chronic unemployment or underemployment and who have lower levels of education; thus, there is a considerable gap between their own achievements and the broader characteristics of the communities in which they live. The structural aspects of their communities (e.g., affluent) combined with the social traits of the addicted individuals (e.g., unemployed) leads those individuals into particular kinds of social interactions, where they "experiment with drugs, . . . interact with other people, . . . accept [their] own dealings with drugs, . . . [and] build up the role of addict" (p. 57). Thus, the social structure influences interactions.

Labelling theory in particular has faced a number of criticisms as well. Just as interpretive theories have been criticized for ignoring the role of the social structure, so has labelling theory. But in addition to that overarching critique, three other specific criticisms have also been made. First, labelling theory has been criticized for focusing most of its attention on adolescents and not exploring the long-term effects of labelling. Second, much of the research on labelling theory has looked only at those who have been formally labelled in some way (e.g., through the criminal justice system), rather than comparing those who have been labelled with those who have not. Third, the specific processes involved in the transition from primary to secondary deviance have not been sufficiently addressed.

Research by Bernberg and Krohn (2003) takes all four of these criticisms into account in their analysis of crime, which integrates the assumptions of labelling theory with structural variables. They found that labelling does have a long-term effect, but the effect varies to some extent on the basis of race, which is one factor that determines an individual's location in the social structure. Bernberg and Krohn looked at young adult males who had been a part of the longitudinal Rochester Youth Development Study, and compared youths who had experienced official intervention during adolescence with youths who had not. Two types of official intervention were included: *police intervention* (arrest or other contact with the police) and *juvenile justice system intervention* (formal sanctions, such as detention, probation, or community service).

The effects of both types of intervention on drug selling and other criminal behaviours at ages 19–20 were analyzed. Bernberg and Krohn found that males who had experienced police intervention during adolescence were more likely to have sold drugs or engaged in criminal behaviour in early adulthood. Intervention by the juvenile justice system had a similar effect; however, that effect was greater for African-American males than for Caucasian or Hispanic males. The long-term effects of intervention by the juvenile justice system were partially mediated by educational attainment and employment. That is, high school graduation was less likely in those who were formally labelled, due to either time away from school (because of incarceration) or the harsher discipline they faced in school after being officially labelled. Those who faced official intervention were also more likely to be unemployed in early adulthood, partially due to lesser educational attainment. Thus, the authors concluded that an individual's location in the larger social structure (e.g., as influenced by race) shapes the short- and long-term effects of formal labelling, and that individuals at some locations in the social structure will have more resources to resist formal labelling than will individuals at other locations.

Research has integrated interpretive theories with other non-structural positivist theories as well, in an effort to explain particular phenomena more effectively. For instance, research on exotic dancers finds that in addition to carefully managing who is and is not aware of what they do for a living (*dividing the social world*, one of Goffman's responses to stigmatization), they also use several *techniques of neutralization* (addressed in Chapter 2) to manage the stigma. They engage in *denial of injury*, claiming that what they do is harmless and does not hurt anybody. They *appeal to higher loyalties*, talking about the importance of being able to provide for their children. Finally, they *condemn the condemners* by pointing out that when the police come to give tickets to some of the dancers, they first watch the performances for an hour or two (Thompson, Harred, & Burks, 2003).

Labelling theory has been integrated with self-control theory (Gottfredson & Hirschi, 1990) and differential association theory (Sutherland, 1947) in an analysis of teenage girls who engage in high-risk sexual activity (Victor, 2004). In interviews, these girls talk about being labelled in junior high on the basis of their sexual activity (i.e., as "sluts," p. 74) and their socioeconomic status (i.e., as "welfare kids" and "white trash," p. 74). After being ostracized by their peers, those girls who had experienced inadequate parenting and subsequently developed low levels of self-control began associating with similar others. By high school, they had internalized the labels, referring to themselves as "ghetto kids" or "wiggers" (p. 76). They became part of the "marginal teen subculture" of their city, which consisted of teenagers who lived in apartments with other teenagers much or all of the time. In this environment, they learned definitions that supported risky sexual behaviours, such as unprotected sex with a high number of unfamiliar partners (see Figure 3.1).

The manner in which interpretive theories have been extensively integrated with a wide range of positivist theories and critical theories (to be addressed later in this chapter) provides support to those who suggest that interactionism, labelling, and stigmatization are *processes* more than they are formal *theories*. Each of the interpretive theories has, at some point, been criticized for not meeting the criteria for a formal theory, such as having concepts that can be

Figure 3.1   ADOLESCENT SEXUAL BEHAVIOUR: THE EFFECTS OF LABELLING THEORY, THE GENERAL THEORY OF CRIME, AND DIFFERENTIAL ASSOCIATION THEORY

Victor, 2004.

operationalized and propositions that can be empirically tested and falsified (e.g., Downes & Rock, 2003; Ritzer & Goodman, 2004; Reid, 2003). Despite these "theoretical" shortcomings, the integration of interpretive assumptions into other theories has improved the explanatory value of those theories when analyzing particular phenomena. Interpretive concepts may be questioned as valid theories, but they nevertheless can be looked on as meaningful processes (Downes & Rock, 2003; Ritzer & Goodman, 2004).

Although interpretive assumptions provide insight into how our perceptions of and reactions to particular acts develop (including our self-perceptions and identity formation), they do not help us understand how some people are more able than others to influence what will and will not be labelled as deviant in a particular society at a particular time in history. Some interpretive theorists (e.g., Becker, 1963) have pointed out that the meanings and understandings held by some groups may be imposed on others. However, interpretive theories do not explain the precise mechanisms by which some people are more able than others to determine the direction that the "deviance dance" will take. Although different people will have varying perceptions of deviance and normality, some people's perceptions have more of an impact on the larger society; in other words, some people's perceptions count more than others. This is where critical theories of deviance step in—exploring the role of *power* in the social construction of deviance.

TIME TO REVIEW

■ Why are interpretive and critical theories particularly useful to more subjectivist deviance specialists?

■ How can the processes described in the symbolic interactionist approach help us understand our perceptions of and reactions to particular behaviours and people?

■ What are the core assumptions of "labelling theory"? What are some of the different ways that various interpretive deviance specialists have discussed the process of labelling and responses to being labelled?

■ What do the concepts of "dramaturgy" and the "deviant career" add to our understanding of deviance?

■ What criticisms have been directed at interpretive theories, and what have been the theoretical and/or empirical responses to these criticisms?

Critical Theories

The range of theories that have been categorized as **critical theories** of deviance is quite substantial—Marxist theories, non-Marxist conflict theories, non-conflict critical theories, feminist theories, postmodernist theories, discourse theories, anarchist theories, peacemaking theories, radical multicultural theories, and more

(Kubrin, Stucky, & Krohn, 2009; Pfohl, 1994; Deutschmann, 2002). These theories are all both theoretical and practical in nature. At a theoretical level, they analyze "the relationship between human struggles for power in history and the ritual construction, deconstruction, and reconstruction of normative social boundaries" (Pfohl, 1994, p. 404).

At a practical level, these are all theories that have an emancipatory interest—that is, an interest in working toward social justice for society's powerless. In fact, conflict theorist Karl Marx stated that social scientists have a *responsibility* to use their work in pursuit of practical, emancipatory goals, which he referred to as **praxis**. In the remainder of this chapter, a range of critical theories that have been definitive for the study of deviance will be reviewed— conflict theories, power-reflexive theories, feminist theories, and postmodern theories.

Conflict Theories

Although **conflict theories** themselves are of considerable diversity, they do share some core assumptions (McCaghy, Capron, & Jamieson, 2003). First, they presume that social rules do not emerge out of consensus but rather out of conflict, and serve the interests of the most influential groups in society. Second, they suggest that members of powerful groups are less likely to break the rules because the rules were created to serve their interests in the first place. Third, conflict theories propose that members of less powerful groups are more likely to act in ways that violate social rules, either because (a) their sense of oppression and alienation causes them to act out in rule-breaking ways, or (b) because social rules have defined the acts of the powerless as deviant in the first place. Precisely which groups are perceived as being in conflict varies among specific conflict theories, but all conflict theories integrate propositions about the structures of societal inequality with views about the ideologies that are used to maintain the status quo and reproduce the existing structures of inequality (Beaman, 2000).

The origins of conflict theory are typically attributed to Karl Marx, who proposed that society consists of a small group of powerful people at the top and a large group of powerless people at the bottom. He ascribed these power differentials to economic factors, specifically the relationship to the means of production. Society's powerful (the **bourgeoisie**) are those who own the means of production; society's powerless (the **proletariat**) are the wage earners who work for the people who own the means of production. The sense of alienation experienced by the proletariat due to their working conditions gives rise to deviant behaviour among some people.

Later Marxists fell into two general camps, **instrumental Marxists** and **structural Marxists**. Instrumental Marxists (e.g., Quinney, 1977) propose that institutionalized social rules, such as the law, are created by the powerful in order to serve the interests of the powerful—the owners of the means of production. A deviant label thereby becomes an instrument used to control the proletariat and maintain the economic structure in society. Structural Marxists (e.g., Chambliss & Seidman, 1982) propose that institutionalized social rules are created by the powerful in order to protect the capitalist economic system rather than to protect individual capitalists. The need to maintain the power of the economic system as a whole means that even members of the bourgeoisie may be subject to a deviant label if their behaviour threatens the fundamental principles of capitalism.

AN INTERNET MOMENT

A number of contemporary political and social activism groups in Canada have Marxist theory as their foundation. For example, you can go to the website of the Communist Party of Canada (Marxist-Leninist) at www.cpcml.ca to learn more about how Marxist ideas are being applied in Canadian society today. This website will tell you about the political party itself and provide information on a number of social issues in provinces across the country, such as educational funding cuts. The way these issues are addressed on the website will show you how a Marxist theoretical framework influences the way social issues and events are interpreted.

Although Marxist conflict theories are based upon the presumption of economic structures of inequality, **pluralist conflict theory** focuses on multiple axes of inequality that make up the structure of society based on conflicts between various economic, religious, ethnic, political, and social groups. Sellin's (1938) **culture conflict theory** claims that in societies having multiple, diverse cultural groups, there will be multiple sets of norms that may conflict with each other. Dominant cultural groups have the power to impose the norms that comprise their culture on all other cultural groups in society, labelling the norms of conflicting cultural groups as "deviant" and in need of measures of social control.

For example, some years ago, Sikh RCMP officers were not permitted to wear turbans (even those with the same patterns of coloration and having the same RCMP insignia as the hats that were a part of the uniform). Turbans are a central component of the Sikh religious and cultural belief system; however, the norms of Euro-Canadian cultural groups had been the ones integrated into the rules governing dress in the RCMP. Tremendous debate emerged among different groups of Canadians. Some groups claimed that the hat that was part of the RCMP uniform was a fundamental symbol of Canadian identity that "foreigners" had no right to tamper with. This side of the debate illustrates the notion of cultural conflict quite nicely. Other groups countered that the RCMP uniform had changed multiple times over the past century and the hat that was part of the current uniform could not be considered a fundamental part of Canadian identity. Furthermore, they pointed out that the Canadian government had no problem with Sikh men wearing turbans when they were laying their lives on the line as Canadian soldiers during World War II. This counterargument illustrates the idea that rules are constructed by the powerful to serve their own needs at a particular time.

In **group conflict theory**, George Vold (1958) extended conflict assumptions beyond cultural groups to a wide range of other groups as well. He suggested that multiple groups are always manoeuvring for more power in society, and clash with each other as a result of their simultaneous struggles for power. The norms or social rules of certain groups gain more legitimacy in society because these groups are able to get authorities on their side more effectively. In situations of conflict, crime and deviance emerge because people will commit acts they do not normally engage in (e.g., vandalism, assault) in pursuit of their higher goal—trying to attain more power for their social groups.

Austin Turk (1969) stated that the core struggle in society is more broadly between *those who are in positions of authority* and *those who are subject to authority*. Those who are in authority try to maintain their authority by convincing society's less powerful groups of the validity of the existing social rules, using as much coercion as necessary if the less powerful groups refuse to be "convinced." Socially typing the norms or actions of conflicting groups as deviant is one of the ways that positions of authority can be maintained.

Whether referring to Marxist theories, other conflict theories described above, or one of the many additional criminological conflict theories that have been proposed (e.g., Richard Quinney's radical conflict theory; Left Realism), the theoretical interest in exploring the struggle for power and its role in defining social norms, and the practical interest in emancipation, together define critical theories of deviance. In essence, the various conflict theories postulate that different groups in society have different interests and perceptions of what the rules should be; however, having more power and resources enables groups to pursue their own interests more effectively. Thus, the "rules" as perceived by powerful groups are imposed on all of the groups that make up society as a whole.

In this regard, it is society's powerful who are able to construct the dominant moral code by which deviance and normality are defined. Powerful groups are able to maintain their power by socially typing the interests and the perceptions of other social groups as deviant; they are able to quash the competition simply by creating rules that deviantize the competitors' behaviours. Of course, in contemporary democratic societies, powerful groups cannot act in ways that would make them look oppressive or authoritarian. Instead, they maintain their power by convincing enough of the populace that they are responsive to the interests of the people and are working in everyone's best interests. Consequently, powerful groups must strike a balance between pursuing their own interests, integrating some of the interests of society's masses, and integrating the desires of vocal interest groups. In the end, "deviance" is a label that justifies the control efforts of powerful groups and thereby helps them to maintain their power.

Convincing society's masses that those in positions of authority in society are working in everyone's best interests involves manufacturing a world view within which the actions of the powerful seem logical. Marx and other conflict theorists use the term **ideology**, in its broad sense, to refer to the world view, a way of seeing and understanding the world, held by society's powerful groups—a world view based on the interests and needs of the powerful.

Because the powerful control society's institutions, such as schools and the media, their ideology is taught to citizens as "common sense" via those institutions, thereby achieving what Antonio Gramsci called **hegemony** (i.e., becoming the dominant way of seeing and understanding the world). However, a later school of critical theorists that grew out of the conflict perspective, the Frankfurt School, explained that society's masses develop a **false consciousness** (originally a Marxian concept). Even though the hegemonic ideology is one that serves the interests and needs of the powerful, and is imposed upon everyone else through society's institutions, people come to perceive it as rational and acceptable. Consequently, they do not realize that they have been duped, and come to believe that they have more freedom than they actually do. The roles of ideology, hegemony, and false consciousness are to render any alternative ways of seeing and understanding the world as outside of the realm of possibility in most people's minds, and thus the dominant view becomes "common sense."

Once a particular world view is perceived as "common sense" by society's masses, there are implications for the structure and functioning of society. This is illustrated by Kent and Jacobs's (2004) application of conflict theory to a cross-national analysis of police presence. Economic-based conflict theory postulates a relationship between economic stratification and the need for social control. Of course, the most overt form of social control is the criminal justice system, including law enforcement. In a capitalist society, the role of law enforcement is to protect the property of the wealthy; thus, more economic stratification should be associated with greater police presence.

Kent and Jacobs compared the ratio of the number of law enforcement officers to the national population from 1975 to 1994 in 11 countries—Australia, Belgium, Canada, Denmark, France, the Republic of Ireland, Italy, Norway, Sweden, the United Kingdom, and the United States. In accordance with conflict theory, they found that nations with higher levels of economic inequality had a greater number of law enforcement officers per 100 000 people in the population. They also found that countries with higher crime rates had a higher ratio of police officers to national population—but only in recent years, once crime had become more politicized in these nations. Kent and Jacobs concluded that the economically powerful play the central role in the politicization of street crime and the corresponding public demand for more police officers; economic inequality gives "economic elites greater control over public values" (p. 357) through ownership and control of the media.

Despite the rather gloomy picture of power and control that conflict theorists paint, they do suggest that change is possible. That is, there will always be some people in society who are able to see the ideological nature of "common sense" and the hidden interests operating in the institutionalized knowledge of society. The goal of theory and action, they suggest, is to enlighten society's masses, so that they too become aware of ideology, false consciousness, or hegemony. Only then can hierarchal structures of power be changed in order to create social justice.

Power-Reflexive Theories

Power-reflexive theories, or what Pfohl (1994) calls **critical poststructuralist theories**, are built on a foundation that emphasizes the intertwining of knowledge and power. Within these theories it is proposed that all claims to knowledge are socially situated, embedded within relations of power. Multiple **discourses** (bodies of knowledge, or all that is "known" about a particular phenomenon) coexist in society; relations of power determine which claims to knowledge come to be institutionalized or perceived as "truth" within society as a whole (Foucault, 1980). For example, during the Middle Ages in Europe, the claims made by the Christian church (as a quasi-governing body in most European nations) were seen as the "truth." With the Enlightenment and the related development and growth of science, the claims made by "science" were accorded more "truth" than the claims of the Christian church. As we will address in a later chapter, in contemporary society, the claims made by science are granted more legitimacy in the eyes of the public than any other claims to truth being made.

Poststructuralist Michel Foucault discussed the linkages between power and knowledge (Foucault, 1980), as well as analyzing mechanisms of social control (Foucault, 1995) through his discussion of the **Panopticon**. Philosopher Jeremy Bentham designed a panoptical prison, a design that enabled guards to observe all prisoners at all times. However, the design did not allow prisoners to know for a fact whether they were currently being observed or not. They therefore lived in an environment in which they knew that the guards *might* be observing them at any given moment. The potential for constant surveillance eventually led the prisoners to regulate their own behaviour all the time, even when they were not actually being observed.

Foucault proposed that the processes of industrialization and bureaucratization had created a panoptical society as well. He suggested that bureaucratization results in the development of numerous mechanisms of social control that ensure "normal" behaviour and punish or prevent "deviant" behaviour. We accept government-sponsored surveillance because it is presented as being for our own good, or with the increased surveillance since 9/11, as for our safety and survival (Staples, cited in Robinson, 2008).

Indeed, in the twenty-first century, panoptical surveillance is not only figurative but literal—a massive increase in the number of closed-circuit television monitoring systems (CCTVs) in private (e.g., convenience stores) and public (e.g., parking lots, city intersections, freeways) means that people can be "watched" by others at various points throughout the day. As part of a broader crime reduction strategy, the United Kingdom has implemented more public-space CCTVs than anywhere else in the world, covering more than 1 000 towns and cities in the U.K.; estimates of the number of public-space cameras range from 1.5 to 4.5 million (the latter figure representing approximately one camera for every 14 people) (CCTV User Group, 2008).

Because of the pervasiveness of social control in modern society—and of the potential for constant surveillance—most of us do not need to be watched for normative transgressions; we engage in self-surveillance and regulate our own behaviours (e.g., weighing ourselves; stopping our cars when encountering a four-way stop on an abandoned road in the middle of the night). This is what Robinson (2008) refers to as "imprinting the panoptic eye in the consciousness of individuals" (p. 235). The more control becomes internalized in the form of self-control or self-regulation, the more effective it becomes.

However, Foucault pointed out that power always goes hand-in-hand with resistance. For instance, anarchist groups (which have been labelled terrorist threats since the nineteenth century) have created a "security culture" to resist their surveillance by law enforcement and other authorities. The security culture controls speech (what information can be shared, with whom, and in what settings), forbids speaking to the authorities, results in the wearing of black masks at demonstrations, and triggers the use of aliases (Robinson, 2008).

Feminist Theories

Rather than there being a "feminist theory," there are in fact multiple forms of **feminist theories** and practice, often quite distinct from each other (Nelson

In what ways are you monitored?

& Robinson, 2002), ranging from those that emphasize women's experiences to those that focus upon the negative impacts that patriarchy has had on both women and men. Historically, the discipline of sociology has largely been a male-oriented enterprise—male sociologists studying and theorizing about male social experiences. Mainstream sociological theories, particularly those dating from the emergence of the discipline until the mid- to late twentieth century, have often been guilty of ignoring women altogether, implicitly or explicitly assuming that the male experience can be generalized to understand the female experience, or explaining female behaviour in terms of the inherent qualities of women. Mainstream theories may also treat women in a peripheral fashion—as the Other that stands in contrast to the normative male standard. For example, some social theorists have first developed a "theory of society," and then (usually much later) a separate "theory of women" as though women were somehow separate from or outside of "society."

In studying deviance, feminist theories in general underscore the fact that the bodies of knowledge and the norms by which we judge deviance and normality vary for women and men. That is, what are considered "normal" behaviours, appearances, or characteristics for women are quite different than for men. For example, a woman who wants to work in a daycare centre will be viewed very differently than a man who wants to work in a daycare centre; she is far more likely to be perceived as "normal," while he is far more likely to be perceived as "deviant." Similarly, a woman who dislikes being around children is more likely to be seen as abnormal than is a man who dislikes being around children. In relation to power, most feminist theories also share the assumption that historically, society has been structured in ways that serve the interests of males.

But outside of these shared basic assumptions, the feminist analyses of and theories about deviance vary tremendously. For example, prostitution is addressed in very different ways by radical feminists and liberal feminists. While radical feminists see prostitution as one more example of the sexual oppression of women in patriarchy, liberal feminists are more likely to see it as an occupation in which women need to be given more control over working conditions (Larsen, 2000; Peace, Beaman, & Sneddon, 2000). The even wider range of feminist perspectives (e.g., socialist and postmodern) means there are even more varying perceptions of prostitution and ways of addressing the topic.

Feminist theorizing about deviance is perhaps most developed in the area of criminal forms of deviance. Downes and Rock (2003) suggest that feminist theorizing is so successful in this area that one can speak of *feminist criminology*. On the other hand, Reid (2003) claims that "feminist scholars are not clear on what constitutes a feminist theory in criminology" (p. 149), other than looking at how power differentials affect female crime, female victimization, and the treatment of women in the criminal justice system.

The complexities of feminist theories about deviance are further magnified when we consider the fact that not only is there a wide range of distinct "feminist theories" (such as radical feminism, cultural feminism, liberal feminism, and maternal feminism), but feminist theorizing is also done from within virtually every theoretical perspective addressed in this book. That is, there are feminist interactionist theories, Marxist feminist theories, feminist functionalist theories, feminist learning theories, and feminist social control theories. Feminist theorizing, in its diversity, is becoming fully integrated into the study of deviance as a whole. Despite the fact that feminist theorizing has been incorporated into the positivist and interpretive theories reviewed in this book (as well as into other types of critical theories), feminist theories are often categorized as inherently critical theories. This is because of their foundation in the theoretical interest in exploring power relations in society and the practical interest in emancipation— achieving equality for women in society.

Postmodern Theories

If discussing "feminist theories" as a cohesive category is difficult and somewhat artificial, discussing **postmodern theories** as a cohesive category is perhaps even more so (Downes & Rock, 2003). In fact, there is limited agreement about precisely what constitutes "postmodern" theorizing and whether or not it can be included in the category of "critical theories." For instance, postmodernism is sometimes equated with the power-reflexive or critical poststructuralist theories addressed earlier, such as the work of Foucault (e.g., Deutschmann, 2002; Peace, Beaman, & Sneddon, 2000). Postmodern theories are broadly based on the notion of *rejection*—rejection of overarching theories of society (such as structural functionalism or symbolic interactionism), rejection of social categorization (e.g., "man," "Black," "Christian"), and rejection of the possibility of "truth." In its **skeptical** form (Rosenau, 1992), postmodern theory is solipsistic, postulating that knowledge is not possible and that only chaos and meaninglessness exist. In its **affirmative** form, postmodernism deconstructs what are seen as "knowledge," master narratives, or overarching theories, and focuses analysis on the local and specific. This form is sometimes associated with social movements, such as environmental activism.

Postmodernists claim that advanced capitalist societies faced rapid social change following the end of World War II. Such societies can no longer be considered "industrial" societies, because symbols and culture (rather than products) have taken centre stage in the economy. Capitalism now exists primarily "by selling consumers new needs, new experiences, and new forms of meaning, all of which are defined exclusively by the marketplace" (Ashley & Orenstein, 2001, p. 475). Commercialism is the defining feature of society, with people pursuing "style over substance" (p. 475)—even politics has become a commercial activity. People are "consumers" rather than "citizens," becoming politically indifferent, self-absorbed, and hedonistic in their endless pursuit of personal style.

Postmodernists speak of the "end of the individual" for this very reason; the individual is no more than the style or image being pursued at a given moment in time, an image that is disjointed and constantly changing. Any notion of a dominant moral code by which we can judge deviance and normality is gradually being eroded. "The postmodern subject is besieged by an endless jumble of messages, codes, and ideas, most of which are incompatible, inconsistent, and quite infantile. Many people respond to the current cacophony of mostly commercial messages that bombard them daily by abandoning all hope that they ever could attain some kind of rational understanding of the world," becoming "an empty shell that is incapable of exercising any kind of critical judgment" (Ashley & Orenstein, 2001, p. 476).

Although postmodern assumptions in their skeptical forms are rarely used in analyses of deviance, it is interesting to ponder the implications of the lack of a moral code and the creation of subjects that are incapable of critical judgment. Is "deviance" possible if there is no moral code that serves as the foundation for its social construction? Can anyone be socially typed as deviant if people become incapable of critical judgment? Is a populace that is incapable of critical judgment simply more susceptible to the interests and whims of those who are in authority?

In the study of deviance, postmodernism raises more questions than it answers, which some say is the point of postmodern theories. These critical theoretical approaches do not pretend to answer questions; their goal is largely to problematize and raise questions about knowledge creation and human behaviour.

A Closing Look at Critical Theories

Critical theories are defined by a theoretical interest in the power struggles by which normative social boundaries are created, as well as a practical interest in the pursuit of social justice. Through their analyses, critical theorists try to determine the processes by which the views of certain groups of people come to be applied to society as a whole—how some people's "rules" become society's "rules," and thereby serve as the standard against which deviance and normality are judged.

Conflict theories focus on social structures that create an opposition between the powerful and the powerless. Power-reflexive theories emphasize the intertwining of power relations and claims to knowledge (including their own). Feminist theories focus on the gender bias embedded in most sociological knowledge claims of the past and the historical oppression of women in society. Postmodern theories, which are still rather amorphous and hard to pin down, focus on the "end of the individual" and a rejection of the possibility of "truth." They represent an important layer of recent theoretical development, although their usefulness for understanding the social construction of deviance is yet to be determined.

Each of the different bodies of critical theory has faced particular criticisms. For example, in the study of criminal forms of deviance, conflict theories have been criticized on the basis of inconsistent empirical support for the relationship between economic factors and crime, and for structural bias in the criminal justice system. More broadly, conflict theories have been criticized for failing to recognize the consensus that does exist in society regarding many laws and rules (e.g., prohibitions against theft and murder). Critics suggest that a more complete theory should be able to deal with both conflict and consensus (Ritzer & Goodman, 2004).

Critical theories as a whole face an accusation similar to that levelled at interpretive theories: some theorists suggest that conflict, poststructuralist, feminist, and postmodernist assumptions may be more appropriately considered processes, perspectives, or ideologies, rather than formal theories with empirically verifiable propositions. Siegel and McCormick (2003) state that research on conflict theories "places less emphasis on testing the hypotheses of a particular theory and instead attempts to show that conflict principles hold up under empirical scrutiny" (p. 238). Although they are referring specifically to conflict theories, other critical theories have been discussed in similar ways (Downes & Rock, 2003).

Some of that "empirical scrutiny" has integrated different bodies of critical theory. For example, feminist and poststructuralist perspectives have been applied to the study of Aboriginal women living in Vancouver's downtown Eastside, in conjunction with an analysis of the drug education film *Through a Blue Lens*, which was filmed there (England, 2004). England explored how these women's real-world experiences are characterized by considerably more racism and sexism than is depicted in the film, particularly in the relationship between addicts and police officers.

The perspectives or assumptions of critical theories have also been combined with interpretive theories. One example of this is found in analyses of racial profiling in the criminal justice system. Many Canadians have become more aware of this topic in recent years, following extensive media attention to accusations of racial profiling by the Toronto Police Service (Wortley & Tanner, 2003; Roberts, 2003); however, the problem of racial profiling has been recognized in cities throughout North America. Gabbidon (2003) analyzes the issue of racial profiling in an American context, applying interactionist and conflict theories to shoplifting-related false arrest cases. Gabbidon's finding that members of visible minority groups are less likely than Caucasians to obtain clear victories in court illustrates the conflict assumption that the law is a tool used by the powerful to oppress the powerless. Gabbidon's finding that African-Americans are more likely to be falsely accused of shoplifting than are members of other visible minority groups illustrates interactionist assumptions about the effects of labelling and stigmatization. Stereotypes associate the master status of "Black" with the auxiliary trait of "criminal," hence the greater likelihood of false accusations. Independently, interactionist and conflict theories are unable to explain the complete phenomenon, but when integrated, they are able to explain both why African-Americans are more likely than other minorities to be falsely accused of shoplifting and why members of minorities as a whole are less likely to secure clear court victories.

Taken together, critical and interpretive theories paint a picture of the social construction of deviance. Interpretive theories address the interactions between people by which diverse and even contradictory understandings of deviance and normality emerge. They also explore what happens to people once they have been labelled deviant and how people who are considered deviant attribute meaning to their own life experiences. Interpretive theories draw our attention to the many steps involved in the deviance dance.

On the other hand, critical theories address the role that power plays in the social construction of deviance, whereby the understandings of deviance held by more powerful groups in society are the understandings that become institutionalized. They draw our attention to the fact that some people are better able to determine the direction of the deviance dance—are allowed to "lead" the dance—those of a particular sex, those with more wealth, those who control the media, or those whom we consider "scientists." Critical theorists look closely at various aspects of power relations, depending upon the particular theory in question, and assess their relationship to how deviance is socially constructed in a particular culture at a certain time in history.

At this point in the book, we have explored what "deviance" is, as well as changing conceptions of deviance. We have also reviewed the dominant theoretical perspectives used by deviance specialists who have more objective understandings of deviance (positivist theories), and by deviance specialists who have more subjective understandings (interpretive and critical theories). Having established this foundation of knowledge about the discipline and how deviance may be studied, in the next section of the book we will turn our attention to an exploration of several substantive topics of deviance and normality—sexuality, youth, voluntary and involuntary physical appearance, mental disorder, science, and religion. As you progress through these substantive topics, the concepts, ideas, and theories that have been reviewed in the first three chapters of the book—for example, normative violation or social typing—will repeatedly emerge. The application of particular concepts and theories in the discussion of concrete situations will clarify these concepts and theories.

TIME TO REVIEW

■ What are the theoretical and practical interests shared among critical theories?

■ What are the similarities and differences between the different conflict theories addressed in the chapter?

■ What do power-reflexive theories tell us about *knowledge* and *social control*?

■ What do feminist theories have in common, and why is it difficult to draw conclusions about what "feminist theory" tells us about deviance?

■ What are the core assumptions of postmodern theory, and what questions does the theory raise about the study of deviance?

■ What criticisms have been directed at critical theories, and what have been some of the theoretical and/or empirical responses?

■ In what ways have various critical theories been integrated with other theories?

Exercise Your Mind

How would each of the theories in this chapter explain deviance/conformity as it exists in your own life (or the life of someone you know)? What facets of your experience are left unexplained by each theory? If you had to select the one theory that best explains deviance/conformity in your own life, which would it be?

CHAPTER SUMMARY

■ Deviance specialists who have more subjective understandings of deviance are interested in the way particular acts are socially constructed and socially typed as deviant. *Interpretive* and *critical* theories are the most useful in understanding the social construction of deviance and normality.

■ *Interpretive theories*, with their emphasis on how meaning is created through social interaction and symbolic communication, draw our attention to how each of us comes to understand that certain acts are "deviant" while others are "normal." They also draw our attention to how different people develop contrasting understandings of deviance.

■ *Labelling theory* explains how the process of getting caught in a deviant act and subsequently labelled serves as the impetus for the transition from *primary* to *secondary* deviance. A deviant label becomes a *master status* that limits opportunities in the "normal" world, opens up opportunities in the "deviant" world, and changes a person's self-perception and identity.

■ Different people may react to being *stigmatized* in various ways, such as by trying to hide the stigma, immersing themselves in a world of similarly stigmatized others, or proudly displaying the stigma.

■ The notion of the *deviant career* is another interpretive strategy for exploring people's entrance into, management of, and possible exit from deviant activities.

■ *Critical theories* share a theoretical interest in the power struggles that define normative social boundaries and a practical interest in emancipation. Diverse critical theories exist, including conflict theories, power-reflexive theories, feminist theories, and postmodern theories.

■ *Conflict theories* originated with the economic deterministic model of Karl Marx, but have since expanded to include alternative models of power wherein powerful groups are able to impose their moral order on powerless groups.

■ *Power-reflexive theories* emphasize the intertwining of power relations and claims to knowledge. Some power-reflexive theorists also analyze structures of surveillance and the creation of self-surveillance, by which we regulate our own behaviours even if no one else is doing so.

■   *Feminist theories* suggest that deviance and normality are socially constructed in different ways for males and females in society.

■   *Postmodern theories* represent a recent theoretical development arising out of the social changes following the end of World War II. Their proponents propose the notion of the "end of the individual" and posit that people have become consumers rather than citizens. These theorists reject overarching theories of society, and claim that the moral codes that would enable people to rationally understand society have eroded.

DEVIANCE IN PRINT

Goffman, E. (1963). *Stigma: Notes on the Management of Spoiled Identity*. Englewood Cliffs, NJ: Prentice Hall.

McHoul, A., & Grace, W. (2000). *A Foucault Primer: Discourse, Power, and the Subject*. Washington Square, NY: New York University Press.

DEVIANCE AT THE MOVIES

Luhovy, Y. (Director & Producer). (1994). *Freedom Had a Price*. Available from the National Film Board of Canada. (55 minutes).

This documentary illustrates the complex social processes by which Ukrainian Canadians were socially constructed as "enemy aliens" during World War I. More than 5 000 were placed in internment camps, and 80 000 were forced to register with the government. The roles of social interaction, labelling, and structures of power are reflected.

Radford, M. (Director & Writer), Orwell, G. (Writer). (1984). *Nineteen Eighty-Four*. United States: Metro-Goldwyn-Mayer. (113 minutes).

The movie adaptation of the George Orwell novel is a fascinating portrayal of social control and its consequences—Big Brother is always watching.

ENDNOTE

1   Friedrich Nietzsche. (2004, Sept 23 [1886]). *Beyond Good and Evil*. I. Johnston. (Translator). Retrieved August 28, 2006, from **www.mala.bc.ca/~Johnstoi/Nietzsche/beyondgoodandevil4.htm**

KEY TERMS

interpretive theories, **p. 76**
critical theories, **p. 76**
value-orienting, **p. 76**
symbolic interactionism, **p. 77**
role taking, **p. 78**
looking-glass self, **p. 78**
significant others, **p. 78**
generalized other, **p. 78**
labelling theory, **p. 79**
tagging, **p. 79**
dramatization of evil, **p. 79**
primary deviance, **p. 81**
secondary deviance, **p. 81**
master status, **p. 81**
stigmatization, **p. 82**
dramaturgy, **p. 82**
front-stage selves, **p. 82**
back-stage selves, **p. 82**
spoiled identity, **p. 82**
impression/identity management, **p. 82**
dividing social worlds, **p. 82**
disintegrative shaming, **p. 82**
reintegrative shaming, **p. 82**
tertiary deviance, **p. 83**

deviant career, **p. 83**
career contingencies, **p. 84**
critical theories, **p. 88**
praxis, **p. 89**
conflict theories, **p. 89**
bourgeoisie, **p. 89**
proletariat, **p. 89**
instrumental Marxists, **p. 89**
structural Marxists, **p. 89**
pluralist conflict theory, **p. 90**
culture conflict theory, **p. 90**
group conflict theory, **p. 90**
ideology, **p. 91**
hegemony, **p. 92**
false consciousness, **p. 92**
power-reflexive theories, **p. 93**
critical poststructuralist theories, **p. 93**
discourses, **p. 93**
Panopticon, **p. 93**
feminist theories, **p. 94**
postmodern theories, **p. 96**
skeptical postmodernism, **p. 96**
affirmative postmodernism, **p. 96**

CHAPTER 4

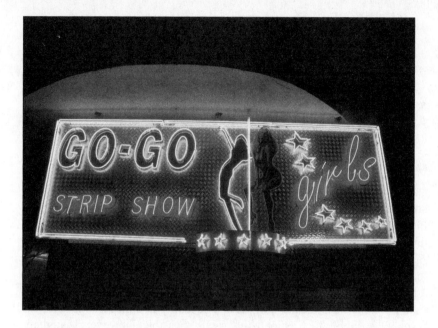

"Deviant" and "Normal" Sexuality

Learning Objectives

After reading this chapter, you should be able to

- Describe the sexual culture of Sambian society, contrasting the dominant meaning of sexuality in that culture with that of Canadian society. Explain how the concepts of heterosexuality, homosexuality, and pedophilia are (or are not) recognized by Sambian sexual culture.
- Describe "deviant" and "normal" aristocratic male sexuality in ancient Athens, and explain the role of the hierarchy of power in shaping those judgments.
- Contrast the sexual cultures of traditional Aboriginal societies with that of the colonizing Europeans, and explain how colonization affected Aboriginal sexual cultures.
- Describe how deviant sexuality was defined and regulated from the seventeenth century through the twentieth century, explaining how the changing sexual cultures reinforced class, gender, and racial hierarchies of the times.

■ Describe the criteria that we use in determining "deviant" and "normal" sexuality, and describe how the "deviance dance" is evident in sexual cultures both past and present.

"The only unnatural sexual act is that which you cannot perform." (Alfred Kinsey)[1]

"There is hardly anyone whose sexual life, if it were broadcast, would not fill the world at large with surprise and horror." (W. Somerset Maugham)[2]

What Is Deviant Sexuality?

At first glance, the two quotations above seem contradictory. If, as Alfred Kinsey claims, "the only unnatural sexual act is that which you cannot perform," then why would people's sexual lives fill us "with surprise and horror," as suggested by W. Somerset Maugham?

In fact, these two quotations demonstrate the complexity of sexuality in human societies, and point to the different ways sexuality can be perceived—biologically and sociologically. Kinsey's view of sexuality draws on biology as the foundation upon which normal and deviant sexuality is defined, and says that normal sexuality is simply that which is physically possible. However, Maugham suggests that we all judge people's sexuality, and that most people's sexual lives, if known, would be judged negatively. Evidently, something more than biology plays a role in how sexuality is perceived, and in the aspects of sexuality that are defined as deviant or normal. There appears to be a substantial difference between what is biologically possible and what is considered socially acceptable.

> **Ask Yourself**
>
> In your opinion, what is "normal" sexuality? What is "deviant" sexuality? In your response, you might refer to fantasies, behaviours, identities, or more abstract ideals. Now answer a slightly different question: In Canadian society, what do you think is considered to be "normal" and "deviant" sexuality? How similar is this list to the one you made of your own opinions?

If you compared the list you made in response to the *Ask Yourself* questions to the list that someone else made, you would see some differences. You might be shocked by something that someone else is not shocked by and vice versa. In other words, what is considered acceptable varies between individuals. However, as pointed out in the first chapter, a deviant label is not a product of individual perceptions but rather of social processes, processes that you were referring to in the *Ask Yourself* exercise.

Social processes determine what is considered deviant and normal sexuality in society. More objective deviance specialists refer to cultural and historical variations in the norms that are used as the standard against which deviance is judged, and more subjective deviance specialists refer to processes of social construction. Social processes determine who is socially typed as deviant through the processes of *description* (placed in a category because of their sexuality), *evaluation* (judged on the basis of the category into which they have been placed), and *prescription* (made subject to particular measures of regulation or social control). Thus, although similar sexual activities and characteristics may be found throughout much if not all of the world, there is variation across cultures and time as to where those characteristics fit within the social hierarchy, in the roles assigned to people who exhibit those characteristics, and in the meanings attached to those characteristics.

In the contemporary sociology of sexuality, the constructionist perspective predominates. Consequently, the interactionist and critical theoretical perspectives presented in Chapter 3 are the lenses through which sexuality is most often studied.

Interactionist perspectives address the processes by which people come to understand and attribute meaning to their own sexuality, and the sexuality of others. For instance, Seidman (2002) interviews gays and lesbians to determine what *the closet* means to them. Similarly, Shirpak, Maticka-Tyndale, and Chinichian (2007) explore how Iranian immigrants understand Canadian sexuality, and find that what these immigrants see as the sexual permissiveness of Canadian society is interpreted as a potential threat to their own family lives.

Critical perspectives analyze the ways that power influences people's understandings and attributions of meaning. From this perspective, the power-reflexive work of Foucault is emphasized, to the extent that it is considered by many to be at the core of contemporary sociological studies of sexuality (Moon, 2008). Foucault (1978) and the many sociologists of sexuality who have followed in his footsteps emphasize the role of *elite discourse*—that is, the knowledge about sexuality that is conveyed by those in authority, and that subsequently comes to be perceived as truth. For example, Foucault draws attention to the distinction between sexual behaviour and sexual identity, pointing out that the two do not necessarily correspond; one can engage in a particular behaviour and yet not perceive that behaviour to be an essential component of one's self. He claims that although homosexual activities have always existed, it was only when the science of psychology began to propose the existence of the "self" in the late-nineteenth century that homosexual *identities* (and indeed, identities of any type) became possible.

In the present day, Foucauldian sociologists who study sexuality analyze the ways that scientific, political, legal, religious, and media discourses of sexuality "shape the ways audience members can imagine organizing their lives" (Moon, 2008, p. 193). Elite discourses place limits on "what kinds of persons it is acceptable or even possible to be" (p. 194) at a particular sociohistorical moment, such that individuals cannot even imagine possibilities that lie outside of those limits.

As you progress through the remainder of the chapter, which addresses the social construction of sexuality cross-culturally, historically, and in contemporary

Canadian society, you will see that even when interactionist and critical theories are not being explicitly addressed in research on sexuality, their core assumptions still serve as the implicit framework for such research.

The Cultural and Historical Construction of Sexuality

Even a brief look at cultural and historical variations in sexuality reveals how the perceptions, meanings, and control of sexuality in contemporary Canada represent only a small portion of that which is found throughout the world. Your own perceptions and meanings of sexuality, as revealed in the list you made near the beginning of this chapter, are an even smaller segment of what people in the world think and feel about sexuality.

Cross-cultural variations in sexuality have been studied for a century, particularly by anthropologists. One anthropologist who has had a substantial influence on understandings of the normative variation or social construction of sexuality is Gilbert Herdt (1984). His research on the Sambia of New Guinea has become what is perhaps the most cited cross-cultural research on sexuality to be found in deviance books today. His analysis reveals cross-cultural variations in what are seen as "normal" sexual behaviours, but even more significantly leads us to question the very categories of "heterosexual" and "homosexual" that we take for granted in contemporary Canadian society.

The Sambia of New Guinea

Sambian society, at the time that Herdt studied it, was characterized by both **patriarchy** (social power was embedded in the males) and **misogyny** (extreme distrust and even hatred of women). It was believed that the presence of females polluted boys and, if uncontrolled, would prevent the development of masculinity, which was seen as the ability to engage in warfare. In a culture based on a long history of tribal warfare, the masculinity of its potential warriors was considered crucial.

To ensure the development of "normal" manhood, when a sufficient number of boys reached the ages of approximately 7 to 10, they were removed from daily contact with the females in the village and separated into an all-male enclave for the next 10 to 15 years. However, removing boys from the "contamination" of the female presence was not perceived as sufficient for the full development of masculinity. Lacking certain biological and scientific knowledge, Sambians presumed that semen (a fluid that only males—and therefore warriors—have) was the source of masculinity and that it had to be transmitted to boys so that they could also become warriors. Thus, within the all-male enclave in which boys were isolated, acts of fellatio occurred between the older males and the boys.

As boys progressed through adolescence and were seen as having accumulated sufficient masculine essence, they would move from being the fellator to the fellatee. At marriage, they would move out of the male enclave and begin having sexual intercourse with their wives while continuing same-sex activities with the segregated younger males. When a man's first child was born, he would no longer participate in the same-sex activities except for a short, ritualized period of time when a new group of boys would be moved into the all-male enclave.

As North Americans learning about Sambian society, we would place these males into categories—homosexual when they are boys, bisexual when they are young men, and heterosexual when they are adults. Furthermore, we also would interpret sexual activities between adult men and boys as "pedophilia." However, there are no similar types of categories in Sambian language or perception. Males are not categorized on the basis of these sexual activities for the simple reason that all of these activities, in the temporal order described above, are a "normal" part of the life-cycle for every male, without exception. The behaviours are simply characteristic of being "male," and not of being a particular type of male.

In Canadian society, many of the activities described above would be perceived as "deviant" and both formally and informally socially controlled. For example, a man who participated in sexual activities with a boy would be dealt with by the criminal justice system, and adults who participate in same-sex activities with other adults are stigmatized in everyday social interaction. But what is considered "deviant" sexuality—subject to formal and informal social control—in Sambia is quite different: a male who does not participate in these rituals; an older male performing fellatio on a younger male rather than vice versa; a father who continues to participate in same-sex activities in the all-male enclave outside of the short, ritualized periods of time defined within the culture; and the spilling of semen on the ground.

These Sambian practices of **ritualized homosexuality** have social and religious purposes. They are intended to reproduce and perpetuate the society they live in (the strictly distinct roles of men and women, the patriarchy that characterizes Sambian society, and the ability of males to be effective warriors if it becomes necessary) as they believe is prescribed in their spiritual belief system.

Gilbert Herdt's research on sexuality in Sambian culture raises significant questions for those of us living in Canadian society about the way we perceive and categorize particular sexual behaviours. It also raises important ethical questions. Because sexual activity between boys and adult men is perceived as "normal" in Sambian society, does that mean it is an "acceptable" behaviour in the world at large? Should all cultures be accepted for what they are, or are there certain standards that can and should be applied universally? These kinds of complex questions will be addressed in the final chapter of this book, where we will explore the issue of whether the fact that deviance is "socially constructed" means that "anything goes."

The example from Sambian society illustrates normative variation (from a more objectivist perspective) or the social construction of sexuality (from a more subjectivist perspective) in a rather dramatic fashion. However, the dramatic nature of this example can result in the perception of Sambian society as a very "foreign" Other, which can contribute to **ethnocentrism** (the belief that one's own culture is better than or superior to another culture) and to misperceptions about the influence of social processes on norms and perceptions of sexuality. In fact, the social construction of sexuality is everywhere around us, which we can see more clearly by looking at some less sensational examples of cross-cultural variations. We will look at the nature of the sexual cultures among the ancient Greeks, the traditional Aboriginal cultures of North America, and during the process of industrialization.

Ancient Athens

The ancient Greeks are typically looked upon as having created the foundation upon which Western societies are built. Their technology, medicine, philosophy, and political systems each continue to have extensive influence on the lives we live today. Yet despite the similarities between contemporary Canadian society and ancient Greek society, there are also considerable differences, including in the meanings and structures of sexuality. The latter varied even across regions in Greece; thus, we will focus on one area in Greece at one particular time in history—fifth-century B.C. Athens (Arkins, 1994).

The relationship between *power* and both "normal" and "deviant" sexuality is quite clear in fifth-century B.C. Athens. Aristocratic men were at the highest level in the hierarchy of power. Indeed, they were the only people considered to be citizens in Athenian society. Slaves, people from outside of Greece, and women were not considered citizens of the state. Thus, the sexual culture of the time was structured such that the needs of these powerful male citizens were satisfied. A wide range of sexual relationships and behaviours was permitted for aristocratic males. They would have sexual relationships with the aristocratic women they married for the purpose of producing male heirs. They could have sexual relationships with other women, slaves, and foreigners, who were expected to sexually service male citizens. Aristocratic males could also form sexual relationships with adolescent aristocratic boys. Thus, "normal" sexuality for male citizens included sexual relationships with a wide range of people, both male and female. There was no distinction made between heterosexual and homosexual; rather, these diverse sexual relationships and activities represented "a single state available to [all] adult male [citizens]" (Arkins, 1994, para. 13). Normality was of considerable range in Athens at this time.

Looking at the flip side of normality, controlling deviance in the realm of sexuality was an important part of Athenian culture as well, and the social typing process was evident. For example, sex was expected to be a unidirectional relationship between a superior and an inferior, not a mutual relationship between two equals, as illustrated in the following quotation: "In Athens a man would have been regarded as perverted if he sought a relationship with another person

Ask Yourself

What are the similarities and differences between the way sexuality was socially constructed in fifth-century B.C. Athens and Canadian society today? For example, does the way sexuality is constructed in contemporary Canada serve the needs of adult males in particular, or not? Does it serve the needs or interests of any other powerful groups, or does our sexual culture serve the interests of everyone in society equally?

equal to him in age and status. For his sexual needs he could use women, slaves, prostitutes, and boys, in any combination, but not another adult male citizen" (Bloch, 2001, para. 6).

Even though sexual activities between male citizens and adolescent boys were viewed as acceptable, there were guidelines to prevent deviance. The state acknowledged that there was the potential for some type of harm to come to adolescent males in their relationships with the more powerful adult citizens; thus, certain laws were instituted, such as prohibiting such sexual activities between dusk and dawn, when the greater level of isolation might enable deviant sexual behaviours to occur.

Changes in sexual behaviours were expected during the lifespan. Boys who had been passive partners with adult males during their youth were expected to make the transition to the dominant sexual role as they grew up, and "if they persisted in sexually passive ways they were . . . subject to deep humiliation and shame" (Bloch, 2001, para. 18). Anal intercourse between males was perceived as unacceptable, because it meant that a man was acting like a woman—only women were to be recipients of insertion. If, in his relationship with an adult male, an aristocratic adolescent boy allowed anal intercourse to occur, and furthered that deviant behaviour by taking some type of compensation for it (prostituted himself), he was forbidden to ever become a citizen of the state. Upon reaching adulthood he could not vote or participate in politics. If he attempted to act as a citizen, he would be dealt with by the justice system and possibly lose his life. In fifth-century B.C. Athens, the formal and informal social controls of sexuality were widespread in order to prevent and punish deviance.

Thus, by looking at the ways in which sexuality was socially typed in Athens, we can see that although ancient Greece created the foundation upon which Canadian and other Western societies are built, it had a distinctive sexual culture. What was perceived as "normal" sexuality was of considerable range—marital sex for the purpose of producing male heirs and sexual relationships with other women, slaves, foreigners, and aristocratic adolescent boys for the purposes of pleasure. But "normal" and "deviant" sexuality were defined on the basis of power—focusing on the needs and desires of aristocratic males (Athens's only "citizens"), and reproducing the existing social structure.

Although we could explore the sexual cultures of countless numbers of other cultures around the world and at different points in history, looking at the Sambia of New Guinea and Athens in the fifth century B.C. already demonstrates how sexuality varies across time and place. But if we narrow our focus even further by moving geographically much closer to home, we can see the power of normative variation even more clearly.

Traditional Aboriginal Cultures of North America

The arrival of Europeans in what is now the Americas and their subsequent colonization of that land and its indigenous peoples had a massive impact on all aspects of Aboriginal societies. For hundreds of years, various facets of Aboriginal cultures were suppressed, facing potential eradication at the hands of political and religious authorities. It has been only in the last few decades that scholars and historians have begun to bring the norms, values, beliefs, and practices of traditional Aboriginal cultures to widespread attention. Within this growing body of knowledge, the distinct sexual cultures of these societies are being addressed.

Although there were many different Aboriginal societies in what is now Canada, at the time of European colonization, many did share some similarities in cultural beliefs and practices when contrasted with the beliefs and practices of the colonizing European cultures. The different constructions of sexuality in Aboriginal and European cultures were so distinct that sexuality became a nexus of conflict and subsequent social control as colonization progressed (Mandell & Momirov, 2000).

In traditional Aboriginal cultures, sexuality was inextricably interwoven with all other aspects of social life (Newhouse, 1998). Life was viewed as consisting of four components—physical, intellectual, emotional, and spiritual. Because life was seen as consisting of these components, so was sexuality; the physical, intellectual, emotional, and spiritual were perceived as existing in sexuality, and sexuality was thought to enhance these four components in the rest of a person's life. As with all else in the world, sexuality was perceived as being a sacred gift from the Creator, intended to be pleasurable—"having sex was to touch the life force within us, and . . . to touch the life force meant to touch Creation" (Newhouse, 1998, para. 12). In fact, a 1998 survey of more than 600 Aboriginal people across Ontario reveals that more than half describe sex as "magical" (Newhouse, 1998, para. 10). Sexuality was incorporated into myths and stories, and although all cultures have their own myths and historical stories, the following tale illustrates the pleasure-oriented view of sexuality in many traditional Aboriginal cultures:

"One of the Anishnabe teachings tells of the way in which sex is introduced into the world. Men and women lived separately for a long time. The Creator, in his efforts to increase the population of humans, made sex pleasurable so that men and women would desire it, and hence, through acting upon their desire, increase the population. Sex was to be an act of pleasure." (Newhouse, 1998, para. 12)

In many Aboriginal cultures, this pleasure was acceptable between members of the same sex as well. Recognizing more than two sexes and more than two genders, many cultures perceived a wider range of sexualities (and genders) as "normal" (Nelson, 2006). Sexuality/gender variants in biological males have been recognized in 110 to 150 Aboriginal cultures, variants in biological females in 55 to 75 cultures (Nanda, 2000). For instance, the Navajo used the term *nadleeh* to refer to both masculine female-bodied and feminine male-bodied members of the community. European explorers used the derogatory term *berdache* ("male prostitute") to refer to biological males who assumed female roles, including sexual relationships with men, in various Aboriginal cultures; sexual relationships between two biological males was acceptable, as long as they were of different genders.

But not only were people who were attracted to members of the same sex accepted in these cultures and given specific roles in the social structure, they were perceived as "normal" and even "necessary." As Newhouse (1998, para. 16) points out, "Mojaves believed that 'from the beginning of the world, it was meant that there should be homosexuals.'" The moral codes of these cultures did not regulate particular types of sexual behaviours specifically, but rather proper types of relationships between people—ones that, within the spiritual belief systems, were necessary to maintain harmony and balance in social life and in the larger society (Newhouse, 1998).

For the colonizing European cultures of the time, sexuality had a very different meaning. Sex was for the sole purpose of reproduction, and even then, notions of pleasure were frowned upon; sexuality was sinful, requiring careful and stringent control. Sexuality was not integrated in social life, but rather isolated from it, almost as a necessary evil, and infused with guilt (Newhouse, 1998; D'Emilio & Freedman, 1997). The only non-deviant sexuality was that which occurred between husband and wife, and even then, only if their sole sexual behaviour was intercourse, if it took place in the "missionary" position, and if they did not enjoy it too much or do it too often. Same-sex activities were unacceptable, and subject to both informal sanction (e.g., by the community) and formal sanction (e.g., excommunication from the church) (D'Emilio & Freedman, 1997).

Of course, with these considerably divergent sexual cultures, conflict between European and Aboriginal peoples became inevitable. However, during the early years of colonization in Canada, sexual unions between white men and Aboriginal women were common due to a relative scarcity of white women as well as the usefulness of Aboriginal women because of their skills in trapping, languages, diplomacy, and other areas (Mandell & Momirov, 2000; Das Gupta, 2000; Razack, 2002). The Aboriginal women with whom early European settlers formed relationships were called *les femmes du pays*, or "country wives" (Mandell & Momirov, 2000, p. 22). Such pragmatic concerns led to the Hudson's Bay Company to not only allow but encourage these interracial relationships among employees. Even missionaries during the early years did not actively discourage the unions (Razack, 2002). However, as colonization progressed, Aboriginal sexuality became one of the things that the emerging authorities felt the need to regulate: " . . . missionaries attempted to eradicate 'devilish' practices such as polygamy and cross-dressing, and condemned the 'heathen friskiness' of the natives" (D'Emilio & Freedman, 1997, p. 6).

Conflicts grew between religious authorities and many Aboriginal women, because of the women's rejection of the European ideals of male authority, monogamy, premarital chastity, and marital fidelity (Mandell & Momirov, 2000). Changes in the social perceptions of sexual relationships between Aboriginals and Euro-Canadians occurred as settlement progressed and as the fur trade was slowly replaced by agriculture as Canada's primary economic activity. Relationships between Euro-Canadian men and Aboriginal women were discouraged as the population of mixed-race women, such as Métis, grew. Being of mixed ancestry, these women were perceived as more acceptable partners (Das Gupta, 2000; Mandell & Momirov, 2000). Even in Western Canada (which was settled considerably later), by the mid-nineteenth century "colonial officials and religious authorities began to fear the consequences of this widespread 'race-mixing'" (Razack, 2002, p. 52). Laws were instituted at various times in various parts of Canada as well as the rest of the Americas, prohibiting white/Aboriginal relationships.

Thus, over time, we can see Aboriginal sexuality being socially typed—it was described as "heathen friskiness," judged as being "devilish," and made subject to a wide range of prescriptions, including Aboriginals being taught by church fathers the "right" way to have sexual intercourse (hence the phrase "missionary position"). With such overt attempts to regulate and control Aboriginal sexuality, substantial changes occurred in the sexual cultures of Aboriginal societies as they adopted and integrated many aspects of European sexual culture (Newhouse, 1998).

Sexual cultures are comprised of dynamic and ever-changing processes, whether we are speaking of Aboriginal cultures or other cultures of the world. As cultures continuously evolve and transform, so does sexuality, as we can see by looking at how the meanings and place of sexuality in the social structure have changed in the dominant culture of North America over the last few centuries. It is by looking at transhistorical changes—that is, changes over time in a single society—that the powerful role of social processes in the creation of sexual cultures and sexual identities becomes acutely evident.

North America: From the Seventeenth Century to the Twentieth Century

The past few hundred years have been a time of immense social change in North America. And as economic, religious, familial, scientific, and other cultural changes have occurred, sexuality has changed as well. Looking at social changes in both Canadian and American history reveals that the meaning of sexuality, its place in the social order, how it is judged, and the agents of its regulation have all

Figure 4.1   CHANGES IN THE DOMINANT MEANING OF SEXUALITY

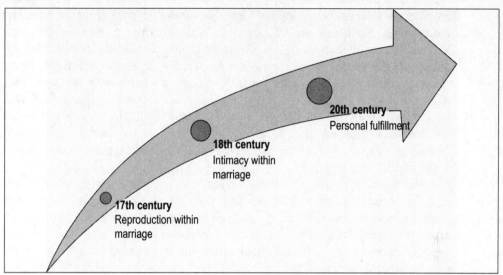

20th century
Personal fulfillment

18th century
Intimacy within
marriage

17th century
Reproduction within
marriage

fluctuated over time and been intertwined with racial, class, and gender hierarchies of the broader society (D'Emilio & Freedman, 1997; Valverde, 1991).

There is a particular wealth of historical analyses of American sexuality (more so than for Canadian sexuality) that visibly conveys these ideas to us. During the progression from the seventeenth century (referred to as the *colonial era* in American society) to the end of the twentieth century, the meaning of sexuality transformed from a primary association with reproduction within a powerful structure of kinship, to a primary association with emotional intimacy in marriage, and then to an association with personal fulfillment for individuals (see Figure 4.1).

The seventeenth century in Canada was a time of early exploration and settlement, and economic activities revolved around the fur trade. As described previously, sexual relationships between Aboriginal women and white men were common and accepted during this time, despite broad differences between Aboriginal and European sexual cultures. Meanwhile, among the small number of European families who had settled in Eastern Canada, ownership of Black slaves also sprang up during this era and continued until the early nineteenth century (Das Gupta, 2000). The practice of slavery was closely intertwined with the control of sexuality. Slave owners frequently determined who was permitted to mate with whom for the purposes of reproduction (and when). Female slaves were valued in part for their reproductive capacities and certain male slaves were selected as "studs" to impregnate these females (Das Gupta, 2000). Female slaves were also expected to be continually sexually available for male members of the owner's family. Even the sexuality of free Blacks came to be socially controlled, as laws were instituted prohibiting Blacks from marrying outside their race (Das Gupta, 2000).

In the more urbanized United States, sexuality during the colonial era was channeled into marriage for the purpose of reproduction, although some sexual activity was tolerated in courtship. Sexuality outside of the arenas of courtship and marriage was considered unacceptable, and sexuality was both formally and informally controlled by the local Christian church, the courts, family, and the community. Premarital pregnancy would usually result in marriage being enforced, often at the insistence of the young woman's father—the phrase "shotgun wedding" refers to those weddings that occurred, figuratively and sometimes literally, at the barrel end of the father's shotgun once a premarital pregnancy was detected. The young couple usually respected the father's directive because the kinship system was perceived as a legitimate regulator of sexuality and reproduction.

The community was also seen as a legitimate regulator of deviance, and it was not uncommon for neighbours to report sexual improprieties to relevant family members, or community and church leaders. Individuals could be excommunicated from the local church for deviant sexuality and, in fact, in some regions certain forms of sexual deviance were considered criminal and sometimes even punishable by death. However, during the colonial era, deviating individuals were more often seen as having made an error in judgment—it was the behaviour that was viewed as deviant rather than the person. Thus, some form of punishment for the unacceptable behaviour was dispensed in order for individuals to learn the error of their ways (e.g., via public whipping or sitting in the stocks) and thereby be accepted back into the family, the community, and the church.

The specific nature of the punishment dispensed often depended on the social characteristics of the person involved. For example, the higher the socioeconomic status of the sexual transgressors, the less severe their punishments were likely to be. In the case of rape, upper-class men were less likely to go to trial and usually received milder penalties if they did, while more severe penalties were dispensed to lower-class men. Women and men regularly received different types of punishment. Men, who often owned property, were more likely to be fined, while women, who did not own property, were more likely to be physically punished. Women were also more likely than men to be punished for sexual deviance such as adultery. Racial hierarchies embedded in the social structure of the time were also reflected in colonial society's sexual culture and its definition and regulation of deviant sexuality. In many American colonies, Black men convicted of raping white women (but not Black women) were castrated. In contrast, white men convicted of raping either white or Black women were not castrated; in most regions, it was even unlikely that a white man could be considered as having "raped" a Black woman.

The various ways that deviant sexuality was controlled and defined revolved around dominant meanings of sexuality during the seventeenth century, meanings which incorporated both pragmatic considerations as well as cultural ideals. In the growing Euro-Canadian and Euro-American cultures, the nature of the definition and control of sexual deviance "served the larger function of reminding the community at large that sexuality belonged in marriage [or in Canada, marriage-like relationships between European men and Aboriginal women] for the purpose of producing legitimate children" (D'Emilio & Freedman, 1997, p. 28). The definition and control of sexual deviance also reinforced socioeconomic class, gender, and racial hierarchies through which society was constructed.

Near the end of the eighteenth century and throughout the nineteenth century, Canadian and American society underwent significant changes that affected the way sexuality was perceived (Valverde, 1991; D'Emilio & Freedman, 1997). Urbanization and wage labour outside of the kinship system took hold and progressed at a rapid pace, creating more anonymous lives distanced from extended family members and community surveillance. Religious shifts transferred the responsibility for salvation onto the individual, reducing the role of the church and subsequently the state as regulator of morality.

In the United States, the Revolutionary War (1775–1783) and the expansion of commerce spread the ideology of the "pursuit of happiness," which subsequently infused sexual culture as well. Although the "pursuit of happiness" was explicitly voiced in American discourse, similar ideals came to characterize Canadian and British societies as well (Mandell & Momirov, 2000; D'Emilio & Freedman, 1997). Economically based and arranged marriages declined, people were more likely to be marrying for "love," and more open expression of affection emerged.

Enlightenment ideology within philosophy and science identified nature (including sexuality) as inherently good. These changes permeated the sexual culture of the time, such that the language of sexuality was no longer reproductive, but based on *emotional intimacy* in marriage. The role of the church in regulating sexuality declined, as did the role of the state. The family was becoming more of an isolated unit in society, recognized as a *private* realm outside of the surveying gaze of many others. However, the role of other social control agents grew: women, the medical profession, social reformers, and culture industries (D'Emilio & Freedman, 1997; Valverde, 1991).

Women played a larger role in regulating sexuality through their efforts at reducing pregnancy rates. Previously, high infant mortality rates meant that women would have many babies simply to ensure that a sufficient number of them survived into childhood to contribute to the maintenance of the family. During the nineteenth century, infant mortality rates declined, but perinatal and postnatal mortality rates of women did not. With the tremendous health risks associated with pregnancy and childbirth, and less need for large numbers of children, middle- and upper-class women acted to reduce pregnancy by abstaining from sex with their husbands for extended periods of time and by using contraception.

The use of contraception was aided by the medical profession, which was growing in size, knowledge, and legitimized power. The medical profession came to have a more encompassing role in the regulation of sexuality by "scientifically" defining sexual deviance (such as the "disease" of sodomy), and by conveying medical knowledge to the broader community. For example, medical knowledge at the time described the body as a closed energy system, wherein overindulgence in any activity (including sexual) could be a danger to physical health—*self-control* became a dominant theme in the contributions of science to the sexual culture of the time.

Self-control as a means to avoid illness and energy depletion was perceived as particularly important during this era because of its relevance to commercial expansion. The "self-made man" was idealized in politics, religion, and popular culture; in order to achieve such success in this new industrial and capitalist economy, he had to ensure that he did not waste too much of his bodily energy elsewhere. Thus, controlling his sexual passions would enable him to focus his energies on economic success.

The economic changes that were occurring in society at this time included the emergence of a powerful culture industry—newspapers, magazines, mass-produced books, and more. On one hand, the culture industry contributed to the sexual culture of the era in terms of the spread of the sex industry, such as in pornography (in the form of stories, books, drawings, burlesque shows, and early photography). But other facets of the culture industry also contributed to sexual culture in terms of the role it played in the regulation of sexual deviance. For example, young women were viewed as being extremely vulnerable to the sexual appetites of unsavoury young men in growing cities. In response to this problem, poems and stories in popular publications warned young women of these dangers, and these stories frequently ended with the untimely death of the young woman who had been led astray.

The perceived vulnerability of young women contributed to the emergence of **social purity** or **sex hygiene movements**, which believed that this susceptibility drew women into the sex industry. At a broader level, social purity was equated with sexual purity for females and males of all ages; sexuality was seen as the heart of morality, which was defined as the cornerstone of society as a whole. Social purity activism was well established by the late 1800s in Canada, the northeast United States, and Britain, and included a number of alcohol temperance groups, such as the Women's Christian Temperance Union (Valverde, 1991). The concerns of these groups included "prostitution, divorce, illegitimacy, 'Indian and Chinese [male immigrants],' public education, suppression of obscene literature, prevention (of prostitution) and rescue of fallen women, and shelters for women and children" (Valverde, 1991, p. 17). Social purity efforts were directed particularly at the lower classes, which by virtue of simply being lower class were presumed sexually depraved as well.

The specific ways in which sexual deviance was defined and regulated depended on social characteristics, just as it had in earlier eras. Racial ideologies continued to infuse sexual culture. Black men were defined as being passionate and incapable of self-control, sexual regulation included laws against sexual relations with white women, and lynching by angry mobs occurred if those laws were broken. American perceptions and panic over Black men's sexuality were having a considerable influence on Canadian society as well. Portrayals of Black men's sexuality as dangerous and uncontrollable, making them liable to rape white women, were being

Ask Yourself

Reflecting on what you have learned about the way sexuality was socially constructed in Canadian and American culture during the nineteenth century and into the early twentieth century, consider the following questions. Who was doing the social typing of deviant sexuality? What was the foundation for their arguments—that is, did they type certain sexual behaviours as deviant because they thought those behaviours were statistically rare, harmful, violated norms, or engendered a negative societal reaction? How did the social typers and/or the larger society benefit?

spread by Canadian media. In the early twentieth century such attitudes would serve as a rationale for Emily Murphy's efforts to regulate immigration (Valverde, 1991).

Not only was Black men's sexuality suspect by the end of the nineteenth century in Canadian society, but so was that of Chinese men. Chinese men, brought to Canada as labourers for the building of the railway, were also perceived as a threat to young white women, who might be easily lured by what was perceived as the men's innocent, less "masculine" countenance, and by the opium they might supply. It was thought that opium had strong sexual qualities, which would result in "the amazing phenomenon of an educated gentlewoman, reared in a refined atmosphere, consorting with the lowest classes of yellow and black men" (Emily Murphy, cited in Valverde, 1991, p. 184).

The nineteenth century, then, brought considerable transformation to Western sexual culture. The meaning of sexuality changed, and responsibility for controlling sexual deviance shifted to individuals and their own self-control. The role of the state in regulating sexual deviance declined somewhat in the early part of the nineteenth century. However, as moral entrepreneurs identified and drew attention to sexual "diseases" (e.g., sodomy, homosexuality), the sex industry, and female sexual exploitation, the state's role in controlling sexual deviance and regulating morality grew once again.

With the dawn of the twentieth century, the sexual culture of American society continued to transform. The dominant meaning of sexuality eventually shifted from a focus on emotional intimacy in marriage to a focus on *personal fulfillment*, regardless of marriage (D'Emilio & Freedman, 1997). In other words, sexual activity came to be accepted not only in marriage, but also in courtship, casual dating, and even much briefer relationships; pleasure and "fun" were considered sufficient reasons for sexual activity. Sexuality continues to be controlled in many arenas, including the criminal justice system and the culture industry. In the realm of criminal justice, criminal codes regulate sexual deviance by criminalizing particular aspects of sexuality, such as sexual assault and public indecency.

 ## AN INTERNET MOMENT

Find a copy of the Criminal Code of Canada at the Department of Justice website (http://laws.justice.gc.ca/en/C-46/index.html) and go to the section on sexual offences (located in Part V). Here you can see the aspects of sexuality that are defined as deviant in a criminal sense in Canadian society at the present time. Look at the range of sexual offences that are included, and think about what aspects of sexuality are being regulated in each case. For example, is a particular behaviour being regulated? Is the nature of the relationship the issue being controlled? Is a broader issue, such as age, involved? Looking at this material will provide you with a more informed background for the upcoming section on sexuality in contemporary society.

The culture industry grew rapidly during the twentieth century to become the dominant force it is today. In contemporary North America, the culture industry, through the sex industry (see Box 4.1) and integration of sexuality into mainstream culture (television, movies, music, advertising, etc.), is perhaps the predominant contributor to sexual culture. At the same time, moral entrepreneurs and special interest groups also use the media as a tool for communicating their positions in the deviance dance. For example, public service campaigns promote "safer sex" in magazines, the pharmaceutical industry creates television commercials for the drug Viagra, and gay rights organizations send out press releases about their organizations' activities.

If you have engaged in the above exercise, you now have some additional insight into the media as one facet of sexual culture, and into how, even when focusing solely on mass media, there have been considerable changes in the way sexuality has been socially constructed during the twentieth century. The ways that sexuality is constructed have a tremendous impact on how we, as people living in a given society at a precise moment in history, think and act, and how we are treated by others in terms of sexuality. This realization brings us to the present moment and the sexual culture of *our* time. In the following sections of the chapter, we will more closely examine the sexual culture of contemporary Canadian society.

Exercise Your Mind

For this exercise, I want you to watch television, go to the movie theatre, and/or rent movies. And yes, you can tell everyone that you are doing this as an exercise in learning for your deviance class. Spending a night watching television or movies is a good way to see the role played by the culture industry in the way sexuality is socially constructed in modern society. As you watch these television shows or movies, think about the broader sexual culture involved. What are these shows or movies saying about sexuality? What meanings of sexuality are they communicating to the audience? What is "acceptable" and "deviant" sexuality according to whatever shows or movies you are watching? Are there conflicting or opposing messages about sexuality being conveyed? You may want to rent some movies or watch reruns from different time periods to see the ways in which the sexual culture has changed or stayed the same. Movies you might want to choose from include *Gone with the Wind* (1930s), *The Philadelphia Story* (1940s), *The Graduate* (1960s), *Animal House* (1970s), *Porky's* (1980s), and *American Pie* (1990s). Easily found television shows from different eras include *I Love Lucy*, *Petticoat Junction*, *All in the Family*, *M*A*S*H*, *Seinfeld*, and *Two and a Half Men*.

Box 4.1   The Sex Industry

What is the "sex industry" worth? It is difficult to say for certain. The "sex industry" includes internet pornography, adult video sales and rentals, strip clubs, peep shows, pornographic magazines, telephone sex, and adult on-demand or pay-per-view movies. Although there is some debate over specific numbers, there is consensus that the industry's worth is almost beyond imagination, both within and outside of Canada.

The pornographic video industry alone has a substantial economic worth, earning more than $57 billion worldwide in 2002—and more than $12 billion in the United States alone (Simpson, 2004). Simpson states that "North American statistics indicate that porn makes more money than Hollywood at the box office, more than the sum of NBC, CBS, and ABC's revenues, more than the music industry generates from record sales, and more than all major professional sports in the United States *combined* [italics added]" (p. 635). The profit that emerges from these revenues is staggering; estimates are that the porn video industry has profit margins of 50 to 200% (*Contemporary Sexuality*, 2001). Internet pornography itself is a billion-dollar industry worldwide, and online components of the sex industry generate more income than any other income-generating websites (Cooper, 2002). There are more online searches for sex-related sites than for sites devoted to education, government, or fine arts (*Network World Canada*, 2002). In the last few years, adult video-on-demand or pay-per-view has expanded as well, and by 2010 is projected to earn $600 million annually (Hall, 2005). Clearly, the economic power of the sex industry makes it a significant contributor to our sexual culture today.

TIME TO REVIEW

- Which theoretical perspectives underlie contemporary sociological research about sexuality?
- What is the process of *ritualized homosexuality* in Sambian society? How does the fundamental meaning of sexuality, as well as the language used to categorize sexuality, differ in Sambian and Canadian society?
- What constituted "normal" and "deviant" sexuality in ancient Athens, and how was it related to power?
- How was sexuality embedded in the holistic Aboriginal view of life, and how did that contrast with the Euro-Canadian view of sexuality?
- How did the prevalence of sexual relationships between Aboriginal women and Euro-Canadian men change over time, and why?
- How did the dominant meaning of sexuality change in North America from the seventeenth through the twentieth centuries, and how was sexuality regulated? How was it integrated with hierarchies of race, class, and gender?
- What roles have the criminal justice system and culture industry played in the creation of the sexual culture of the twentieth and twenty-first centuries?

Sexual Culture Today

If you participated in the last exercise, you spent some time watching television and/or movies to learn something about sexuality in contemporary society. In watching television or movies, you have been able to observe the construction of deviance and normality in those arenas—what is considered acceptable, what is considered deviant, what happens to those who are deviant. These are precisely the issues we will direct our attention to in this section of the chapter. We will explore some of the criteria by which sexual deviance and normality are determined in the sexual culture of our time, and some of the contrasting viewpoints in this deviance dance.

Criteria for Determining Deviance

A closer look at our contemporary sexual culture reveals a number of criteria that are used to evaluate sexuality as either "deviant" or "normal." Dimensions that have been explored by other deviance specialists include the degree of consent, nature of the sexual partner, nature of the sexual act, setting, frequency, time, age, and number of partners (Wheeler, 1960; Goode, 1997). We will explore consent, nature of the partner, and nature of the act as core criteria by which we determine "deviant" sexuality, and setting and frequency as two of the more peripheral criteria.

Consent

One of the criteria we use to determine deviance in the realm of sexuality is that of **consent** (Wheeler, 1960; Goode, 1997), and some researchers (e.g., Mackay, 2000) use the concept of consent as the defining characteristic of "normal" sex. Although the notion of consent is commonly used within legal and social discourse, conceptually there is some disagreement regarding how consent can be defined (Beres, 2007). Is "consent" an attitude (based on the intention to engage in certain sexual activities)? If that is the case, then determining whether consent is present in a particular situation requires access to a person's thoughts and state of mind. Or is it a behaviour (based on particular actions)? If that is the case, then determining whether consent is present in a certain situation requires comparing actions that have (or have not) occurred to some type of agreed-upon list of precise behaviours that constitute "consent."

Despite different conceptions of now consent is to be defined, there is some consensus that at its broadest level, "consent represents some form of agreement to engage in sexual activity" (Beres, 2007, p. 97). Is consent involved in the sexual act in question? Is it even possible for consent to be involved in this act? The most obvious use of this criterion is by the criminal justice system in cases of sexual assault; if there is no consent involved, then the act is a criminal one, making it necessarily deviant.

Ask Yourself

How can you determine whether someone's sexuality is "deviant" or "normal"? Make a list of the criteria that you use when you make your judgments about other people's sexuality or your own.

In fact, the complete lack of consent leads many people to interpret sexual assault as more of an act of violence than a sexual act. In court cases involving "date rape"—that is, a victim sexually assaulted by a date—the issue of consent is usually central to the case. The defence attorney will argue that the victim did consent, or at least that the defendant reasonably thought that consent had been given, and the prosecutor will argue that the victim did not consent. In the courtroom, the way date rape cases are argued elicits the question of whose story is more believable—the defendant's or the victim's.

The question of whether it is possible for consent to be involved is another aspect of this criterion for judging sexual deviance. Beginning in the late 1990s, the use of **date rape drugs** escalated. These drugs, such as Rohypnol (also known as "roofies" or "roopies") and GHB (also known as "G" or "Liquid X"), are odourless and tasteless, and when mixed with alcohol cause intense drowsiness and memory impairment. If one of these drugs is slipped into someone's drink, that person will not know it is there and may not be able to remember anything that happens in the ensuing hours. These drugs are referred to as "date rape drugs" because they have been used in order to have sex with someone without having to get consent.

These consequences of the drugs have caused them to be labelled as a danger, and formal and informal regulation have emerged. It is likely that the student services organization at your university has had campaigns to raise people's awareness of these drugs and the way they are used. For example, you may have seen posters displayed on your campus that provide information about how to avoid being a victim. When you and friends go to bars or nightclubs, perhaps you do not accept drinks being brought to you by anyone other than the bar server. The legal system has determined that having sex with someone after giving them these drugs constitutes sexual assault, arguing that in these situations the person is not of a state of mind where giving consent is possible.

Courts have also argued that consent is not possible in situations involving sexual acts between children and adults. Due to the level of cognitive development as well as significant power differentials, a child is not considered capable of giving consent, especially to an adult. Thus, sexual acts between children and adults are defined as crimes on the part of the adult. You can see a description of Canada's age-of-consent laws—and their complexities—in Box 4.2.

Although sexual interaction between adults and children is necessarily deviant because it is forbidden by the Criminal Code, social characteristics of the child and the adult may play a role in public perceptions of deviance or normality. The age of the child and the age of the adult may influence public perceptions of whether consent is possible. For example, an 8-year-old may be perceived as much less capable of giving consent than a 13-year-old is. And if a 13-year-old is having sex with her 16-year-old boyfriend, in contrast to her 37-year-old boyfriend, the public may view it as a consensual relationship (even if they disapprove of 13-year-olds being sexually active in general). The interaction of gender with age may affect public perceptions of deviance or normality as well.

Box 4.2 Canada's Age-of-Consent Laws

What is the age of consent for sexual activity in Canada? The answer to that question is not as straightforward as one might initially think. Canada's age-of-consent laws are multi-faceted and complex. Under current legislation, the laws governing sexual behaviour, in which age of consent is an issue, are as follows:

Sexual Assault: A common defence in sexual assault trials is that the accused believed there was consent involved in the sexual activity. However, if the complainant is under the age of 16, the accused cannot make the claim of consent; consent is perceived as not being possible in that instance.

Sexual Interference: This is a crime defined by the sexual touching of a body of someone under the age of 16. The lack of the possibility of consent is what defines this crime.

Invitation to Sexual Touching: This is a crime defined by requesting someone under the age of 16 to sexually touch the accused. Again, the lack of the possibility of consent is what defines this crime.

The above age-of-consent laws are further complicated by the question of the age of the accused. That is, consent *is* considered possible in regard to the above behaviours if the complainant is 12 or 13, if the accused is no more than 2 years older than the complainant, *and* if the accused is not in a position of trust and authority over the complainant. Consent is also considered possible if the complainant is 14 or 15, and if the accused is less than 5 years older and is not in a position of trust or authority over the complainant. In these instances, legislation prevents the criminalization of sexual activity between youth of similar ages who are in a dating relationship.

Bestiality in the Presence of a Child: Bestiality (sexual activity with an animal) is itself a crime. However, committing an act of bestiality in front of a child under the age of 16, or inciting a child under the age of 16 to commit an act of bestiality, is a specific subsection of that same law.

Sexual Exploitation: Although the age of 16 is highlighted in the age-of-consent laws described above, sexual exploitation involves sexually touching (or inviting sexual touching from) someone under the age of 18, if the accused is in a position of trust or authority over the complainant.

That is, teenage boys are often seen as being more capable of giving consent to adults than teenage girls are.

This gender discrepancy became evident in the state of Washington in 1997, when Mary Kay Letourneau, a 35-year-old schoolteacher, was convicted of having a sexual relationship with a 12-year-old boy—her former student. When arrested, she was pregnant with the boy's child and subsequently became pregnant a second time after receiving a suspended sentence. Continuing to see the boy was a violation of her suspended sentence, so she was subsequently sentenced to more than seven years in prison.

An intense debate ensued in the media. On one side of the debate, people suggested that while what she had done was rather "odd," she and the boy (who had said he did consent to the sexual relationship) were in love and wanted to spend the rest of their lives together. On the other side of the debate, people pointed out that both as a child and as a former student of Letourneau's, the boy was incapable of giving consent. They argued that if this were the case of a 12-year-old girl who became pregnant as a result of her relationship with a 35-year-old male teacher, there would be no debate over the possibility of consent—everyone would be outraged.

Letourneau and the man were married in 2005. Letourneau's former husband (who originally found out about the relationship and reported it to the police) divorced her and moved to Alaska with their four children. This case has since been treated as humour in the popular media, used as a comedic reference on television shows such as *Gilmore Girls* and *30 Rock*. More recently, a number of similar cases involving female schoolteachers and young males in Canada and Britain have received media attention as well.

Issues of consent are perceived differently across place and time. Although "no means no" even within marriage in Canadian society, in many countries, consent is not considered necessary between husband and wife; sexual relations are prescribed as required in the marital relationship. In fact, it was only in 1983 that the Canadian legal system defined sexual assault as possible in marriage. Similarly, it was only in 1987 that our legal system made sexual assault laws gender-neutral, recognizing that it is possible for a man to be raped by either another man or a woman (Nelson & Robinson, 2002); many societies today continue to define the crime of sexual assault only in terms of a male perpetrator and a female victim. In the historical section of this chapter, we saw that from the seventeenth century through most of the nineteenth century, Black women were expected to be sexually available to white men (Das Gupta, 2000; Mandell & Momirov, 2000; D'Emilio & Freedman, 1997). Because of this expectation, white men were unlikely to be charged with raping Black women if there was no consent. In fact, if the Black woman was a slave and the white man a member of the slave-owner's family, then consent was a non-issue because she was considered a piece of the family's property, to do with as they pleased.

Today, divergent points of view exist even on the issue of the age at which consent is possible, not only across cultures, but within North America itself. Historically we saw that in ancient Athens, male youth were perceived as capable of consenting to sexual relationships with adult aristocratic males. Cross-culturally we saw that among the Sambia of New Guinea, adult male sexual activities with male children and adolescents is normative, and that the question of consent itself is non-existent. In contemporary North America, the North America Man/Boy Love Association (NAMBLA) argues that teenagers are capable of giving consent in sexual relationships with adults, and some members of NAMBLA suggest that even younger children are capable of giving consent (NAMBLA, 2002). Of course, as you may have expected, tremendous opposition exists to NAMBLA's message and to the organization itself. Afraid of being associated with this organization, gay rights organizations have been especially vocal in their opposition, "deploring NAMBLA and everything it advocates which basically amounts to a push to legitimize child molestation," and arguing that the organization "has no legitimate place in society, Queer or Straight" (The NAMBLA Controversy, para. 1). Obviously, the debate over age-of-consent laws is a highly contentious one. By challenging one of society's most firmly held beliefs, members of organizations like NAMBLA have been socially typed as deviant—they are described as "pedophiles," evaluated in an extremely negative light, and face intense public outcry.

AN INTERNET MOMENT

The NAMBLA website can be found at www.nambla.org. Use interactionist and critical perspectives in exploring this site. How do members of NAMBLA understand and attribute meaning to sexuality? How are scientific, political, religious, and media discourses used to support this group's efforts?

Nature of the Sexual Partner

The historical and cross-cultural variations that were presented earlier in this chapter pointed to the role that the **nature of the sexual partner** plays in determining sexual deviance. In Sambian society, the appropriate sexual partner varies during a male's life, from older males to younger males, to younger males and wives, and finally to wives alone. In Athens, during the fifth century B.C., acceptable sexual partners for aristocratic men included wives, prostitutes, slaves, foreigners, and adolescent males; men of equal social status were defined as inappropriate sexual partners. In the dominant Europeanized culture of North America from the seventeenth century to the twentieth century, marriage gradually lost its monopoly as the only legitimate outlet for sexual behaviour, and a wider range of sexual partners came to be deemed appropriate. However, despite this transition to more freedom in the selection of a sexual partner, there still is not *complete* freedom in the choice of a sexual partner in contemporary North America.

Beginning with the law, we can see particular people being defined as unacceptable sexual partners. We already addressed the issue of age-of-consent laws, making individuals who are under the age of consent inappropriate sexual partners. The Criminal Code also prohibits sexual relationships between close family members—parents, children, grandparents, grandchildren, siblings, and half-siblings. Violating this prohibition between close family members constitutes the crime of *incest*. Bestiality is a crime in Canada, making animals unacceptable sexual partners. Finally, several sexual laws in the Criminal Code (such as "sexual exploitation") define as inappropriate sexual partners anyone over whom the individual is in a position of trust or authority, or anyone who is in a relationship of dependency with the individual.

The nature of the sexual partner is also controlled outside the legal system. The choice of sexual partners is formally regulated in some places of business, where company policies may prohibit intimate relationships between bosses and employees or between co-workers. Some schools, and universities prohibit sexual relationships between teachers and students. Within the psychiatric and psychological communities, professional organizations define sexual relationships between therapists and clients as a violation of the professional code of ethics.

Additionally, if the sexual partner in question is not a person but an object necessary for sexual stimulation to occur, the psychiatric community labels the sexual activity a *fetish,* for which treatment can be obtained.

At an informal level, particular sexual partners may be perceived as socially unacceptable. For example, although the law does not prohibit sexual relations between first cousins, such relations would still push the boundaries of social acceptability (although, in other cultures, it is quite common for marriages to be arranged between first cousins). And even though many universities do not have policies prohibiting intimate relationships between students and professors, within the cultural climates of those institutions, professors who engage in such relationships may still be stigmatized.

At both formal and informal levels, members of the same sex continue to be defined as inappropriate sexual partners to some extent. We have come a long way since Everett Klippert was sent to prison as a dangerous sex offender in 1967, for having admitted that he was gay. There have been significant changes in social attitudes regarding homosexuality over the past several decades as a result of social activism and education, and these changes have increased individual freedom to choose a member of the same sex as a sexual partner.

Even within the Catholic Church, which has historically strongly condemned homosexuality as an abomination, there is a deviance dance regarding homosexuality. Catholic doctrine continues to prohibit homosexuality. However, there are some priests and bishops who have overtly expressed disagreement with this position. For instance, several U.S. Catholic bishops wrote a pastoral letter that "advised parents to put love and support for their gay sons and daughters before church doctrine" (Hone-McMahan & Schleis, 1998, para. 3), saying that science tells people homosexuality is not a choice, and since it is not a choice, it is not a sin.

However, despite some changes in prevailing social attitudes, gays and lesbians continue to be deviantized due to their choice of sexual partners. Of course, the stigmatization experienced by gays and lesbians in North America may not be as formal and as overt as in some other cultures in the world, where homosexuality is a crime punishable by the death penalty—such as Iran, Mauritania, Pakistan, Saudi Arabia, Sudan, United Arab Emirates, and Yemen (Mackay, 2000). But even in the United States, several states continued to define homosexual acts as crimes.

In Canada, it wasn't until 1996 that Parliament voted to add sexual orientation to the *Canadian Human Rights Act*. Same-sex common-law couples did not receive the same benefits as opposite-sex common-law couples until 2000, and same-sex couples did not receive the right to legally marry across Canada until 2005 (Canadian Broadcasting Corporation, 2007). Although the state of California legalized same-sex marriage early in 2008, in November of that year voters supported Proposition 8, which removed that right; an appeal is currently in front of the Supreme Court of California (Judicial Council of California, 2009). Throughout North America, various organizations and helping professionals claim that through therapy or prayer they can help people to become "ex-gay."

In the informal realm of everyday interaction, the stigmatization of gays and lesbians is evident as well. A brief search of the internet reveals thousands of "anti-gay" websites, many of which express support of physical violence directed at people who are homosexual. Franklin (2000) found in a survey of university students that 10% admitted to acts of physical violence or threats of physical violence directed at people whom they *thought* were homosexual.

Verbal stigmatization is even more common. Franklin's (2000) survey found that approximately one-quarter of young adults admitted to calling people whom they thought were gay various derogatory names. High-school students report that they hear anti-gay comments or name-calling an average of 25 times a day (PFLAG, 2004). Gays and lesbians face a greater risk of criminal victimization than does the general population not only in North America (Herek, Gillis, Cogan, & Glunt, 1997; Bochenek & Brown, 2001) but also in the United Kingdom (Mason & Palmer, 1996), and Australia (Mason & Tomsen, 1997). For example, one California study found that 41% of homosexuals and bisexuals had been victims of a hate-related crime at some time since the age of 16 (Herek, Gillis, Cogan, & Glunt, 1997). In Canada, approximately 10% of all police-reported hate crimes are committed on the basis of sexual orientation, placing it in the top three motivations for hate crimes, following race/ethnicity and religion (Walsh & Dauvergne, 2009).

Overall, Western cultures are characterized by considerably more freedom in the choice of sexual partners today than in the past. However, freedom is not unlimited. The choice of sexual partners is still regulated by the law and other formal processes, as well as informal means such as social stigmatization. The nature of the sexual partner is an important criterion in our evaluations of people's sexuality as either deviant or normal (Goode, 1997; Wheeler, 1960). However, even if the sexual partner is considered acceptable and "normal," other criteria become involved in our evaluations as well, such as the nature of the sexual act.

Nature of the Sexual Act

Even if your choice of sexual partner is defined as normal and acceptable, is what you are doing with that partner considered "kinky" (Goode, 1997, p. 208)? That is, are you engaging in "normal" or "deviant" acts? The answer to that question is both culturally and historically specific, and at times is tied in with the nature of the partner. In Sambian society, oral sex between males is considered acceptable, but only if the younger male is performing the act on the older male, and only if the older male has not yet become a father. In fifth-century B.C. Athens, oral sex between males was perceived as appropriate, but only if the males were not of equal social status, and only if the younger male was not paid for the act. Following European colonization of the Americas, sexual intercourse between husbands and wives was the only acceptable sexual act, and only if in the "missionary" position.

Even over the last century there have been significant changes in the way that sexual acts are perceived as being "deviant" or "normal." For example, in Chapter 1 there was a discussion of the extreme measures taken in the early twentieth century to prevent masturbation in children, based on medical discourses of the time, which claimed a wide range of physical, mental, and social harms as consequences of masturbation. Now, in the early twenty-first century, the same stigma is no longer attached to masturbation. The growing sexual freedom of the last century has allowed a range of sexual acts to be seen as more acceptable. Walk into any bookstore or public library, and you will find books that present information on various new sexual positions to try and new techniques to use. Retail stores that sell a variety of "sex toys" to incorporate into sexual acts abound, both on the streets of any city as well as on the internet

Due to the rapid growth in sexual freedom during the twentieth century, greater subjectivity has emerged in precisely which sexual acts are perceived as "kinky." In other words, what is considered a sexually deviant act is now more in the eye of the beholder than was true in the past. Our sexual culture has come to be infused with an ideology of privacy; as long as a particular sexual activity is performed by consenting adults outside the view of others, we define it as being nobody else's business. And although each of us individually might perceive particular sexual acts as "kinky," the ideology of privacy limits contemporary social controls on sexual behaviours, particularly at a formal level. In the late 1960s, Justice Minister Pierre Trudeau suggested that the government had no place in the bedrooms of adult Canadians, monitoring their sexual behaviours. Today, we not only continue to accept that perception, but also think that none of us as individuals has a place in the bedrooms of others, monitoring their sexual behaviours, either.

The issue of consent, the nature of the sexual partner, and the **nature of the sexual act** are three of the core criteria by which we evaluate sexuality and subsequently judge it as deviant or normal. In addition to these three core criteria, there are also a number of more peripheral criteria that are used for judgment in contemporary sexual culture (Goode, 1997). For example, sexual activities in certain locations are considered deviant.

An episode of the popular TV show *Seinfeld* highlights the issue of location in determining deviance. In this episode, George Costanza has a sexual encounter with the cleaning lady in his office cubicle. The next day he is called in to his boss's office and fired for that encounter, despite his protests that he had never been warned that the company frowned upon having sex in the office. This *Seinfeld* episode points out that the workplace is seen as an inappropriate setting for sexual activity in North American society. In Canada, the law defines certain locations (i.e., public places) as unacceptable for sexual activities. People who enjoy having sex in places where others might see them are labelled **exhibitionists**.

The frequency of sex is another one of the more peripheral criteria used to evaluate sexuality. Is someone having sex too often, not often enough, or just the right amount? This is a common question asked of advice columnists, sex therapists, and marriage counsellors. One issue of the women's magazine *First for Women* (August 6, 2001) devotes an entire article to what constitutes "normal" sex, including a table that readers can refer to in order to determine the "normal" frequency of sex based on age at marriage and number of years married. In fact, this table is titled "How Much Sex is Normal?"—implying that frequency outside of the numbers listed is "abnormal." This magazine article also addresses the previous criterion mentioned, that of the nature of the sexual act, explaining to the hundreds of thousands of monthly readers which particular acts are "normal." Our collective interest in the question of frequency even results in its inclusion on the annual *Durex Global Sex Survey*. Durex surveys tens of thousands of people in countries around the world every year, providing data on which nation has the most sex (Greece, at 138 times per person per year in 2005) and the least sex (Japan, at 45 times per person per year in 2005). Canadians have sex an average of 108 times per year.

Those who have sex too frequently may be labelled "nymphomaniacs" or may even be diagnosed with a sexual "addiction." In the recent past, people who had sex too infrequently were often perceived as "frigid" (Goode, 1997). However, in the twenty-first century, infrequent sexual activity may be considered a sexual dysfunction.

Contemporary society is one in which sexuality has become highly medicalized (and commercialized). Drugs like Viagra, which were initially marketed to aging men with erectile dysfunction, are now used by increasingly younger men as part of a demonstration of sexual prowess and masculinity (Marshall, 2006; Tiefer, 2006); on the popular television sitcom *Two and a Half Men*, even Charlie and Alan (two characters in their early 40s), have each used 'the little blue pill' during nighttime marathons. Low sexual desire in women is now being similarly medicalized, and its solution being found not in changing relationships and gendered responsibilities, but rather in the search to develop the "Pink Viagra" (Marshall, 2006, p. 287). And in the world of email spam, pills, lotions, and gels designed for improved sexual performance are common. In our current "Viagra culture" (Potts & Tiefer, 2006, p. 267), where sexual desire (for women) and sexual prowess (for men) are essential components of the discourses of sexuality, masculinity, and femininity, frequency has assumed a whole new level of importance.

Discussions of frequency, location, nature of the act, nature of the partner, and the issue of consent point to both the increasing freedom that has come to characterize our sexual culture, and the formal and informal limitations that continue to be placed on that freedom. As a society, we perceive a narrower range of behaviours as sexually deviant than we did in the past, but through the use of various criteria, sexual deviance continues to be defined, identified, and controlled. However, the processes of defining, identifying, and controlling sexual deviance are not uniform; they are part of the "deviance dance."

Sexuality and the "Deviance Dance"

In any given culture at any particular time in history, certain trends or characteristics can be identified in sexual culture. However, a multiplicity of perceptions, reactions, and social controls are also intertwined with those broader trends. For example, Herdt's (1984, 1993) description of *ritualized homosexuality* among the Sambians includes some description of the mixed feelings about the practice, particularly as the boys were being separated from their mothers. Sexual relationships between aristocratic adult and adolescent males, although common in fifth-century B.C. Athens, were not uniformly accepted. Segments of Athenian society were critical of such relationships, and often sought to initiate levels of control for the purposes of protecting these "exploited" adolescent males (Bloch, 2001). The discussion of Canadian and American history presented earlier in the chapter captured some of the diversity entwined within sexual culture, wherein class, race, and gender variations were central to the ways that sexuality was constructed and controlled. During the Victorian era, considerable restrictions on sexual behaviour were countered with the expansion of the sex industry—photographs, books, and sexually oriented live performances (D'Emilio & Freedman, 1997; Ullman, 1997).

In contemporary North America, considerable debate exists over many aspects of sexual culture. The large numbers of shops selling sexual "toys" coexist with organizations that condemn TV programs that include explicit sexual references (Parents Television Council, 2009) like masturbation, oral sex, and partial nudity. Gay, lesbian, and bisexual activist groups and changing human rights legislation coexist with segments of society that continue to stigmatize and condemn homosexual practices. Widespread efforts to eliminate the sexual abuse and exploitation of children even coexist with organizations trying to place limits on those controls, such as NAMBLA. University tours by sex educator Sue Johanson occur even while administrators attempt to censor the publication of a student sex survey in a university newspaper (e.g., *Intercamp*, 2001). Rapidly changing technologies are raising additional questions and debates about "deviant" sexuality—popular psychologist Dr. Phil McGraw answers the question of whether using internet pornography constitutes "cheating" on one's spouse (he says it does), and others are asking the question of whether sexually explicit conversations with strangers in internet chat rooms constitute adultery (Mulgrew, 2001).

There are even different points of view regarding precisely what constitutes a "sexual act." Is oral sex still "sex"? Former American President Bill Clinton did not think so when he was asked whether he "had sex" with a female intern. Is exotic dancing a "sexual act"? The research that has been done on exotic dancing reveals that the situation is far too complex to be able to give a simple answer to the question.

Exotic Dancing.   Is exotic dancing a "sexual act"? The vast majority of customers say they go to men's clubs for a "voyeuristic/pornographic experience" (Erickson & Tewkesbury, cited in Wesely, 2003, p. 290). They are seeking a sexual experience, even if there is no intercourse or physical contact at all (Mestemacher & Roberti, 2004). The specific nature of that experience varies across different groups of customers. Some are "cursory customers" (Egan, 2003, p. 109) who go to men's clubs for special occasions, such as a bachelor party or a night out with the guys. Others are "regular customers" (Egan, 2003, p. 109) who form emotional and erotic relationships with particular dancers and buy them gifts. These men frequently want to form a personal relationship with that dancer outside the club environment, and may become upset when repeated attempts are refused. However, not all customers may be seeking a sexual experience. Mestemacher and Roberti (2004) found that in one club, most of the men were not even watching the dancers, but were playing pool or carrying on conversations in a group. For these men, some other motivation brought them into the club.

The question of whether exotic dancing is a "sexual act" for women is even more complex. Ongoing debates in feminism question whether dancers are "victims of violence" in a patriarchal system or "businesswomen" who deserve the same freedoms, rights, and protections as other businesswomen. Some research does find support for the victimization hypothesis: substance abuse, life histories of physical/sexual/emotional abuse, low self-esteem, and backgrounds characterized by risky sexual behaviours are common among exotic dancers (Mestemacher & Roberti, 2004). Furthermore, many women enter the occupation because of financial desperation (Sloan & Wahab, 2004; Wesely, 2003).

However, Sloan and Wahab (2004) find that a "continuum of work and life experience" (p. 19) is characteristic of the exotic dancing subculture. They describe four different types of female exotic dancers. First, there are **survivors**, who have extensive histories of childhood abuse and who felt forced into the industry because of few available alternatives. Second, there are **non-conformists**, rebels who come from privileged, educated backgrounds and who have the freedom to enter and leave the industry as they wish. When dancing is no longer "fun," they change careers (by going to medical school, for example). Third, there are **dancers** who have considerable training in dance and who enjoy the artistic and creative expression of the industry. Finally, there are **workers**, women primarily from working-class backgrounds who become exotic dancers because of the money they can earn.

Although it appears that some exotic dancers might be perceived as "victims," it is important to point out that these women do not consider themselves as such. Even those women who enter the industry because of financial desperation, and who may have hated it in the beginning, say that over time "the money makes it worth it" (Wesely, 2003, p. 490). Sloan and Wahab (2004, p. 42) say the following about the women they interviewed: "These were intelligent women who had considered their own lives and their own realities. Many of them simply disagreed with the abolitionist perspective that they were victims. Others were too busy surviving to care what white, upper socioeconomic status women had to say about whether or not they were exploited."

Regardless of what type of exotic dancer a particular individual is, all dancers must negotiate relationships with customers, as well as their own identities, within a structure of power inside the industry. The dancers are objects of the customers' desire, and must interact with them socially off stage in order to make the customers stay for longer periods of time and spend more money on drinks. They must create a fantasy relationship based on "counterfeit intimacy" (Mestemacher & Roberti, 2004, p. 49), or face being fired by their employers. As one dancer says, there are times when she really wants to say to the customer, "'. . . shit I don't wear these heels at home! I am a regular girl. I wear flannel pajamas and you are ugly!'" (p. 113).

But even though the dancers are subjected to the power of their employers and customers, they are also active agents of their own power. They perceive their male customers as "'lonely and . . . want[ing] somebody to make them feel better'" (Egan, 2003, p. 114). The women use their bodies to manipulate customers and earn more money. For example, in the fantasy relationship they create, they may secretly "confess" to a customer what their "real" names and life stories are—however, it is all a lie designed to "'hook a regular customer'" and "'keep him coming back'" (Egan, 2003, p. 112).

As each dancer negotiates her relationship with customers, she must make decisions about her own boundaries—what she will and will not do for money. Will she give a lap dance? Go to a private room? Leave the club with a customer if he offers enough money? A dancer's boundaries frequently change over time as she becomes more embedded in the industry (Wesely, 2003). As the boundaries change and become more flexible, many dancers end up feeling violated, not by customers but by themselves; the gap grows between their *ideal selves* (who they want to be) and their *perceived selves* (who they see themselves as being currently) (Wesely, 2003). As a result, some dancers talk about loosening boundaries as characterizing not only their work lives but their personal lives as well, through exhibitionism and promiscuity: "'. . . you've given yourself up to so many situations, it really doesn't matter anymore'" (p. 498). One dancer says, "'About a year and a half into it, it was hard to separate the stage Julie from the real-life Julie'" (p. 499). Others speak of becoming numb and losing their sense of self over time—'"there is no real identity there'" (p. 500).

In the exotic dancing subculture, a "dance" surrounds the question of whether exotic dancing is a "sexual act." Differing points of view and differing behaviours are found among the various types of customers, among the various types of dancers, and even in individual dancers' lives and careers as they change and as there are shifts in their identities.

Although the "deviance dance" is evident in many issues related to sexuality, including exotic dancing, it may be most evident in contemporary society when considering the issue of pornography. Anti-pornography activism exists alongside anti-censorship groups seeking to control the influences of such activism, and the question of whether pornography is "harmful" continues to be a nexus of passionate debate. Even the question of what pornography *is* remains subject to debate.

Pornography

What is **pornography**? Is it harmful? Should it be controlled, and if so, how? These questions represent continuing discrepancies of opinion when the topic of pornography arises. Many definitions of pornography incorporate some notion of *explicit sex*, which at the surface seems a common-sense assumption. However, even this common-sense assumption is more ambiguous than it may initially appear (Childress, 1991).

A certain level of subjectivity is involved when trying to determine precisely what constitutes "explicit" sex—whether it can be found in mainstream media like *Sex and the City* or solely in those videotapes and magazines that only adults may purchase. The often-cited words of U.S. Supreme Court Justice Potter Stewart (e.g., Childress, 1991) suggest that despite the difficulties in defining pornography, we all know it when we see it. However, as Childress (1991, p. 178) points out, "Although everyone knows hard-core pornography when they see it, they see it in strikingly different places, and so no one really knows it at all."

Academics, politicians, and social activists have tried to define pornography, resulting in several different types of definitions. Some are **functional definitions** that suggest pornography is anything used by an individual for the purposes of sexual arousal (Goode, 1997)—pornography is "in the groin of the beholder" (McKeen, 2002, p. D6). The broad nature of this definition means that the women's undergarment section of the Eaton's catalogue of the early twentieth century (which boys would sneak peeks at), the Victoria's Secret catalogue today (which many boys and men sneak peeks at), and women's romance novels (e.g., Silhouette Desire) could all be considered "pornography" if they are used by people to become aroused.

Other definitions are **genre definitions** (Goode, 1997), which propose that products created for the purposes of arousing the consumer constitute "pornography." Even the definition of pornography offered in the Merriam-Webster dictionary (2002) adheres to this principle; pornography is "the depiction of erotic behavior (as in pictures and writing) intended to cause sexual excitement." Of course, this type of definition leads us to try to infer what the producer's intentions were, in some cases. Are Harlequin romance novels trying to cause sexual excitement? How about the publishers of *Maxim* magazine or the *Sports Illustrated* swimsuit issue?

Labelling definitions of pornography focus on community standards— anything that community members deem obscene (Goode, 1997). The notions of obscenity and community standards are central to Canadian law. Section 163 of the Criminal Code defines an obscene publication as "any publication a dominant characteristic of which is the undue exploitation of sex, or of sex and any one or more of the following subjects, namely, crime, horror, [or] cruelty and violence. . . ." Exceptions to this definition include publications that have artistic/literary merit or that are for educational or medical purposes. The "community standards test" has traditionally been one way of determining whether a publication can be considered obscene. The question here is what a majority of Canadians would not tolerate other people seeing (rather than what they might find personally distasteful).

The legal definition of **child pornography** is considerably clearer. Section 163 of the Criminal Code defines child pornography as any representation of someone under the age of 18 engaged in explicit sexual activity or any representation of someone under the age of 18, "the dominant characteristic of which is the depiction, for a sexual purpose, of a sexual organ or the anal region." Again, materials having artistic/literary merit or those that are for educational or medical purposes are excluded from this definition, as are personal writings that are kept private (such as a diary or short story) and self-photographs that are kept private. However, even though the legal definition of child pornography has greater clarity than the legal definition of obscenity (not involving children), both have been subject to social and legal debate.

In 1992, the Supreme Court of Canada reviewed the Butler case (*R. v. Butler,* 1992), in which a store owner had been convicted of selling obscene materials portraying homosexual acts. The defence claimed that prohibiting the possession and/or selling of obscene materials was a violation of the freedom of expression, guaranteed in the Canadian Charter of Rights and Freedoms. The Supreme Court agreed that it was a violation of this right, but that the violation was reasonable in pursuit of the protection and greater good of society.

Debate over this issue extended beyond the criminal justice system as well. In the ensuing years, some Canadian feminist groups protested that the Butler decision had resulted in the biased suppression of the sexual expression of minorities, such as materials portraying gay and lesbian sexuality. They argued that because homophobia pervades society, those "community standards" that are used as a test for obscenity integrate homophobia and result in discrimination based on sexual orientation within the criminal justice system (Bell *et al.,* 1998).

More recently, the Supreme Court has moved away from the concept of "community standards" of tolerance in favour of the concept of "harm" when

Box 4.3 Obscenity, Community Standards, and Harm

Although obscenity laws are more frequently referred to in the context of pornography, they apply to other aspects of sexual culture as well. In 2005, the Supreme Court heard the case of a man who had been convicted of "keeping a common bawdy house" under the Criminal Code. He was the owner of a swinger's club, *L'Orage*, in Montreal. This was a private club open to members and guests, and for which members had to pay an annual fee. The first floor of the club consisted of a bar, the second floor a salon, and the third floor the "owner's apartment," which was a locked room in which members (who had the passcode to the lock) could engage in sexual activities with other members. In the first trial, the judge ruled that the business was "degrading and dehumanizing, was calculated to induce anti-social behaviour in its disregard for moral values, and raised the risk of sexually transmitted diseases" (*R. v. Labaye*, 2005, para. 10); thus, it violated community standards of tolerance.

However, upon reaching the Supreme Court (*R. v. Labaye*, 2005), the court claimed that rulings based on community standards of tolerance were inherently subjective, reflecting the ruling judge's own standards rather than any objective standards.

Furthermore, the court claimed that defining "community" was problematic as well—which particular community's standards are to be used? Consequently, the Supreme Court ruled that obscenity must be based on *harm*, which must be objectively proven in court beyond a reasonable doubt. Harm can refer to (a) the loss of autonomy and liberty when members of the public are forced to view an act, (b) harm caused to society by an act predisposing others to commit further antisocial acts, or (c) harm to the individuals engaging in the act (e.g., through lack of consent or through victimization).

The Supreme Court ruled that in this particular case, no harm was caused by *L'Orage*. A doorman ensured that only adult members and guests entered the establishment, only members had the numerical code to unlock the room on the third floor where sexual activity occurred, and interviews with potential new members clearly outlined the purpose of the club and ensured that only individuals who shared an interest in that lifestyle were given membership. Thus, the obscenity ruling was overturned. However, it is important to point out that there was a "deviance dance" surrounding the ruling itself, with two of the Supreme Court judges dissenting.

determining whether obscenity laws have been violated (see Box 4.3). Even the prohibition against possessing child pornography has been challenged. In 2001, the Supreme Court of Canada (*R. v. Sharpe*) once again agreed that the law does violate freedom of expression, but that it is a reasonable violation of that freedom in the name of the protection of children's rights. They ruled that although scientific research could not definitively prove that people who possess child pornography will subsequently sexually harm particular children, the possessors of child pornography create a demand that results in the production of child pornography, which does harm the children represented in that pornography.

The question of whether pornography that includes only adults is harmful has been a matter of considerable debate as well, both inside and outside the legal realm (Childress, 1991; Greco, 1995; Stark, 1997; Davies, 1997). Some participants in this debate focus on the question of physical harm—whether male consumers of pornography will be driven to sexually victimize women. Other participants in this debate focus on the question of a broader harm to the functioning of society—that is, whether pornography affects attitudes toward and perceptions of women in society. Still other participants direct their attention at questions of ontological harm. Such questions may address religious issues or concerns about the moral fibre of society. Regardless of the particular type of harm being addressed, research results are similar in that they are contradictory and inconclusive (Davies, 1997), and are often confounded with the moral or social agendas of specific researchers or sponsors of such research (Stebbins, 1996). The issue of pornography is characterized by the "deviance dance"— disagreement, debate, resistance, and plurality—just as are other issues related to sexuality.

AN INTERNET MOMENT

The *Universal Declaration of Sexual Rights* can be found on the website for the World Association for Sexology, at www.worldsexology.org/about_sexualrights.asp.

Amidst the plurality of views of sexuality in our society and others, there have been attempts to create cross-cultural standards for evaluating sexuality. For example, in 1999, the World Association for Sexology adopted a *Universal Declaration of Sexual Rights*, trying to strike a balance between sexual freedoms and sexual protections.

Sexual culture is of considerable complexity, integrating sexual, scientific, religious, political, family, and popular discourses. What is considered sexually deviant varies among cultures on the basis of these varying discourses; however, all cultures do differentiate between deviant and normal sexuality, and all cultures formally and informally regulate sexuality.

TIME TO REVIEW

■ How is sexuality involved in the "deviance dance"? Give cross-cultural, historical, and/or contemporary examples.

■ What debates and issues surround the topic of pornography in society?

■ How does the Universal Declaration of Sexual Rights fit into the "deviance dance"?

CHAPTER SUMMARY

■ Perceptions of "deviant" and "normal" sexuality vary cross-culturally and historically, but also vary among different social groups in a particular culture at a particular time in history.

- The practice of what Western anthropologists have called *ritualized homosexuality* in Sambian society illustrates cross-cultural variations in the very concepts used to categorize sexuality, as well as the fundamental meaning of sexuality in society.

- In fifth-century B.C. Athens, *power* was linked to the sexual culture of the time, which revolved around the location of aristocratic males in society.

- Traditional Aboriginal societies had very different sexual cultures than those of the colonizing Europeans. With European colonization, the sexual cultures of Aboriginal societies were made subject to significant measures of social control.

- In North America from the seventeenth century to the twentieth century, meanings of sexuality shifted from focusing on *reproductive ideals*, to *intimacy in marriage*, to *personal fulfillment*; agents of social control changed during this time as well. During all eras, hierarchies of race, class, and gender influenced the complexities of sexual culture.

- In North America today, although sexual freedom has increased considerably since previous eras, judgments of "deviant" and "normal" sexuality continue to be made. Criteria we use to make these judgments include *consent, nature of the sexual partner, nature of the sexual act, location*, and *frequency*.

- In any given culture at any given time, there is also a multiplicity of perceptions, reactions, and social control measures.

- In contemporary society, the deviance dance is particularly evident when considering issues such as whether exotic dancing is a "sexual act" in the eyes of customers and dancers, and the definitions and harms of pornography.

DEVIANCE IN PRINT

Valverde, M. (1993). *The Age of Light, Soap, and Water: Moral Reform in English Canada, 1885–1925*. Toronto: McClelland & Stewart.

D'Emilio, J., & Freedman, E. B. (1997). *Intimate Matters: A History of Sexuality in America* (2nd ed.). Chicago: University of Chicago Press.

Marshall, B. L. (2006). The new virility: Viagra, male aging, and sexual function. *Sexualities, 9*(3), 345–362.

DEVIANCE AT THE MOVIES

Cowan, P. (Director). (2000). *Give Me Your Soul. . . .* Available from the National Film Board of Canada. (81 minutes).

This documentary takes an inside look at the porn industry, including interviews with directors, aspiring and experienced actors, and journalists who follow the industry.

Condon, B. (Director). (2004). *Kinsey*. United States: Fox Searchlight Pictures. (113 minutes).

   This fictional film portrays the life of Alfred Kinsey, a groundbreaker in the scientific study of sexuality. The film explores his work, people's reactions (e.g., withdrawing of funding), and his own personal life.

ENDNOTES

1 Alfred Kinsey. Rand Lindsly's quotations, from The Quotations Page. Retrieved August 31, 2006, from **www.quotationspage.com**

2 W. Somerset Maugham [b. 1874]. In "W. Somerset Maugham's birthday: January 25, 1874." (January 25, 1998). Retrieved August 31, 2006, from **www.quotationspage.com/special.php3?file=w980125**

KEY TERMS

patriarchy, **p. 106**
misogyny, **p. 106**
ritualized homosexuality, **p. 107**
ethnocentrism, **p. 108**
nadleeh, **p. 111**
berdache, **p. 111**
les femmes du pays, **p. 111**
social purity/sex hygiene
movements, **p. 116**
consent, **p. 120**
date rape drugs, **p. 121**
nature of the sexual partner, **p. 124**

nature of the sexual act, **p. 127**
exhibitionists, **p. 127**
survivors, **p. 130**
non-conformists, **p. 130**
dancers, **p. 130**
workers, **p. 130**
pornography, **p. 132**
functional definitions, **p. 132**
genre definitions, **p. 132**
labelling definitions, **p. 133**
child pornography, **p. 133**

CHAPTER 5

The Troubling and Troubled World of Youth

Learning Objectives

After reading this chapter, you should be able to

- Compare popular images of youth crime with statistics on the nature and prevalence of youth crime, and explain why a gap exists between the perceptions and realities.
- Describe theoretical and empirical research on (a) youth crime and (b) gang involvement.
- Explain how gangs and youth crime are socially controlled.
- Describe the extent and patterns of use of tobacco, drugs, and alcohol among youth, as well as how their usage is socially controlled.
- Explain what the concept of "at-risk youth" means, and what the "science of risk" does.

- Describe how *all* teenagers are perceived as deviant in society, and explain the nature of the generation gap in the past, present, and future.

"Our concern with the deviant nature of youth is most evident in headlines that warn us about escalating rates of juvenile crime and in political rhetoric that sees the solution to the problem of crime in the reform of the juvenile justice system. Public views of the troublesome character of youth, however, extend beyond any narrow conceptualization of criminal conduct. Many elements of contemporary youth culture, including hip-hop or heavy metal music, raves, video arcades, and spectacular styles of dress are widely seen as reflecting, stimulating, or resulting from the social problems that plague adolescents." (Tanner, 2001, preface)[1]

As the opening quotation suggests, "youth" and "deviance" go hand in hand in the public mind. More than any other age group, it is youth who are perceived as having lifestyles built around deviance. They are seen as being both "troubling" and "troubled"—and "troubling *because* they are troubled" (Tanner, 2001, p. 2). **"Troubling" youth**, such as young offenders, gang members, and street youth, are seen as threats to society. **"Troubled" youth** are perceived first and foremost as threats to themselves—for example, through substance abuse; they are also seen as potential threats to society as well, likely to become "troubling" if their problems are not solved early enough. However, at some level *all* youth are viewed as potential threats to both themselves and the larger society. It is not just *some* youth who are seen as being deviant; rather, youth culture, and indeed this period in the life-cycle itself, is deemed to be deviant and in need of social control.

But precisely what time in life is captured by the term "youth"? **Youth** generally refers to a transitional time in life between childhood and maturity; one is no longer a "child," but is not yet an "adult." However, what this actually means varies across cultures, over time, and even across contexts within a particular culture at a specific point in time; in other words, the concept of "youth" is socially constructed (Tyyskä, 2001). Some constructions define it on the basis of age. For instance, in the criminal justice system, youth refers to a particular age group governed by distinct legislation. In Canada, 12- to 17-year-olds are regulated by the Youth Criminal Justice Act (YCJA). The United Nations has also defined youth on the basis of age, referring to those aged 15–25. However, others define youth on the basis of social status rather than age; for them, youth refers to anyone who has not achieved full economic and social independence. In everyday conversation, the meaning of the term can be much more diverse, referring to adolescents or teenagers, university-age adults, and even individuals in their mid-twenties (Tyyskä, 2001). As you progress through the chapter, you will see that this diversity in definition is reflected in research on various subjects—i.e., crime, substance use, and those perceived as responsible for the "generation gap."

Deviant Youth: "Troubling" Youth

Youth Crime

Before continuing, take a moment to look at the *Ask Yourself* exercise. As indicated by the opening quotation of the chapter, when we think of deviant youth, those who are criminals are likely to come to mind first. Indeed, when the search terms "youth and deviance" are inserted into numerous academic and popular databases, the majority of articles retrieved are about youth crime in particular. Comparing these articles brings forward a central theme: there are significant differences between the *perceptions* of youth crime and *patterns* of youth crime. Your responses to the *Ask Yourself* questions may reflect perceptions of youth crime and images and information contained in popular discourse that illustrate "the singular collective perception that kids are out of control, are more dangerous now than ever, and that youth crime is expanding at an alarming rate" (Schissel, 2001, p. 86). Calls for a "crackdown" on youth crime can be heard on the news, in politicians' comments to the press, and from victims of youth crime. But to what extent is this perception of youth crime accurate? Are kids out of control? Is youth crime expanding at an alarming rate?

Schissel (2001) points out that there is a vast "gulf between reality and perception" (p. 86). The extent and nature of youth crime is far from approximating the frightening picture painted in the popular mind. Official statistics gathered through the Uniform Crime Reporting System reveal that there was an increase in youth crime rates (ages 12–17) between 1962 and 1990 (Statistics Canada, 1992). However, analysts point out that some of this increase is due to factors *other than* actual increases in youth crime, such as changing policing and administrative practices, changes in legislation, and greater public pressure to control youth crime, all of which may have resulted in more youth being brought into the criminal justice system over that period of time (Schissel, 1997). Furthermore, adult crime rates, not just youth crime rates, also increased during this period (Statistics Canada, 1992).

Following this period of increasing crime rates, youth crime declined each year during the 1990s (Savoie, 2002). After that decade, youth crime rates increased slightly (Wallace, 2003), followed by a decline (see Figure 5.1). It continued to decline through 2005, but then increased again (by 3%) in 2006; despite this increase, the rate was still lower than a decade earlier, and was 25% lower than the peak of youth crime in 1991 (Taylor-Butts & Bressan, 2008). One year later, there was another slight decrease. Although 12- to 17-year-olds are overrepresented in the criminal justice system, 18- to 24-year-olds are the most overrepresented age group in the criminal justice system, and adults are responsible for the majority of crimes in every

Ask Yourself

When you think of "youth crime," what images and information come to mind? Is youth crime a problem in Canadian society? How big a problem is it? Where do those images and pieces of information come from?

Figure 5.1   CHANGES IN YOUTH CRIME RATES (CHARGED) IN CANADA
(AGES 12 TO 17), 1977–2007

Adapted from: Statistics Canada, CANSIM, Table 25220014.

criminal offence category, including almost 85% of violent crimes (Statistics Canada, n.d.). In fact, if we look at the most violent of crimes, homicide, the largest proportion of male offenders is in the 18–24 age group (37%) and the largest proportion of female offenders is in the 30–39 age group (32%). Only 14% of male offenders and 15% of female offenders are ages 12–17 (Statistics Canada, 2008). There is no criminal offence category for which youth constitute the majority of offenders.

Looking at this data, you may find the answer to the question of whether youth crime is a problem for society to be somewhat different from the answer you gave to that question earlier. Of course, any level of crime is a problem for society, and for those victimized by such crimes. But youth crime is no more of a problem—and indeed may be less of a problem—than adult crime. One area where issues of youth and crime are certainly more problematic than issues of adults and crime is that of victimization. Children and youth are far more likely to be the *victims* of crime than adults are. For example, those aged 18 and under comprise 61% of sexual assault victims, and although 14- to 17-year-olds constitute 5% of the population, they comprise 17% of robbery victims (AuCoin, 2005). These are likely surprising statistics for those who rely primarily on popular or media images as their source of information about crime in Canada.

Where does this gap between the perceptions and patterns of youth crime come from? Many criminologists attribute the gap in part to **moral panics**. This concept was popularized by Cohen (1973), based upon his analysis of the aftermath of a minor altercation between two groups of youth ("Mods" and "Rockers") at a British seaside resort in 1964. Although the incident itself was relatively minor, in the following days (and in fact, for the next three years) the media exaggerated and distorted the magnitude of the events, with headlines such as "Day of Terror by Scooter Groups" and "Seaside Resorts Prepare for Hooligans' Invasion." Public fear grew, and pressure was placed on law enforcement and politicians to crack down on the youth-inspired terror that was gripping the nation.

The concept of moral panic referred to exaggerated and sensationalized concerns of a particular phenomenon. Goode and Ben-Yehuda (1994) list five elements of a moral panic: heightened concern; hostility toward the offending group; a certain level of consensus that there is a real threat; disproportionality (the attention given to the phenomenon is far greater than the level of objective threat that the phenomenon presents); and volatility (they erupt suddenly and then may just as suddenly disappear, although some may become institutionalized and therefore reappear time and again). This concept has since been applied to the analysis of diverse youth cultural phenomenon (e.g., concerns over youth-oriented media), and has been used to explain the gap between the perceptions and patterns of youth crime.

Moral panics are constructed within the media, wherein youth crime is overrepresented, portrayed as a new problem for society, and consistently linked to particular ethnic groups and classes (Tanner, 2001; Bortner, 1988; Pearson, 1983). But as Pearson's (1983) analysis of British media illustrates, this portrait of youth crime has been repeatedly painted throughout the twentieth century; public concerns about youth crime today are quite similar to public concerns about youth crime during the last one hundred years. Even a century ago, there were gaps between the perceptions and realities of youth crime, and moral panics about youth crime were conveyed in popular discourse, creating a distorted view of youth crime in the eyes of the public. Moral panics about youth crime are not limited to contemporary North American society; they have also been found in Austria, Germany, and other European societies as far back as the late nineteenth and early twentieth centuries (Wegs, 1999).

Even though the nature and extent of youth crime diverges considerably from public perceptions and media portrayals, concerns about those youth who *are* involved in criminal activity have stimulated a significant body of research over the past several decades. Thus, research on the causes of youth crime abound. Many of the theories of deviance that lean toward the more objective end of the objective–subjective continuum, and were addressed in Chapter 2, are used to explain youth crime. Its existence (or its absence) has been variously explained as resulting from the following: learning deviant techniques and motives from peers (differential association theory); bonds with others that restrain most of us from crime (social bonds theory); the level of self-control developed early in life (general theory of crime); structural inequalities in access to legitimate opportunities (Merton's strain theory) and to illegitimate opportunities (differential opportunity theory); and the system of rewards, punishments, and role models we have been exposed to in life (social learning theory).

Empirical research has also tried to establish the causes of youth crime, and has investigated the roles of intelligence (Liska & Reid, 1985); family structure

Parenting styles combining control, supervision, and high levels of affection are associated with a wide range of positive child outcomes, including a lower risk of criminal behaviour.

and processes (Baumrind, 1991; Thornberry *et al.*, 1991); school performance (Davies, 1994); and peer influences (Regioli & Hewitt, 1994). Parent and peer influences have been the particular subject of many analyses of the causes of youth crime. Various aspects of family life have been studied, such as family structure (i.e., single-parent versus two-parent homes) and parenting style. Early research suggested a link between single motherhood and delinquent behaviour in children, but that link has subsequently been shown to be relatively weak, and to be due to the quality and effectiveness of parenting rather than the structure of the household itself (Milan, 2000; Wells & Rankin, 1991).

Parenting style incorporates several characteristics, including supervision, parental control, and emotional ties between parent and child. Although different researchers label parenting styles in various ways, their conclusions about parenting characteristics that improve child outcomes are quite similar. Moderate control of the child's behaviour, combined with moderate levels of supervision and strong, positive, emotional ties between parent and child are effective means of influencing child behaviour in both the short and long term, as the children develop their own internal moral standards and higher levels of self-control. This parenting style involves having high expectations for children, knowledge of and interest in who the children are socializing with and what they are doing, as well as clearly explained rules and consequences for breaking those rules.

In addition to high expectations, there is also some flexibility (e.g., parents are willing to listen to the children's point of view), and substantial levels of warmth and affection. This kind of parenting reduces the risk of negative outcomes in children, including criminal activity, substance use, poor school performance, low self-esteem, and susceptibility to negative peer influence. In contrast, both lax and extremely strict parental controls, as well as weak or non-existent emotional ties, are associated with negative child outcomes (Baumrind, 1991; Thornberry *et al.*, 1991; Jang & Smith, 1997; Brook *et al.*, 1999).

Not only do family variables influence child outcomes themselves, they also affect peer influence. Effective parenting styles are associated with children who select higher quality peers as friends, who have stronger, more emotionally intimate and trusting relationships with those friends, and who are less susceptible to negative peer influences. These relationships have been found in a number of societies in the world, including Columbia, where, despite extremely high societal levels of drug use and violence, parenting variables improve child outcomes and mediate negative peer influences such as criminal behaviour and marijuana use (Milan, 2000; Brook *et al.*, 1999).

The single most effective predictor of criminal activity among youth is criminal activity among friends (Zeman & Bressan, 2008); consequently, the role that parenting plays in peer selection and influence is significant. Parenting is central in reducing the likelihood of the initial association with criminally involved peers and the likelihood of adopting criminal behaviour if a relationship with a criminally involved peer does form. However, neither parenting styles nor peer influence exist in a vacuum. The most recent version of the International Youth Survey (administered in more than 30 countries, and in Toronto for the Canadian version) finds that a complex set of factors is associated with criminal behavior among youth (Zeman & Bressan, 2008) (see Box 5.1).

Although the crime problem, and in particular the youth crime problem, is nowhere near the level that public images convey, crime is a social issue in need

Box 5.1   Factors Influencing Youth Crime

Property Crime
- single-parent or blended family
- no university aspirations
- skipping school
- perceive school environment as unsafe
- have been stolen from
- going out at night without adult supervision
- spending time alone rather than with family
- spending time with friends rather than with family
- peer acceptance of illegal acts

Violent Crime
- male
- no university aspirations
- skipping school
- have been discriminated against on the basis of race, language, or religion
- have been stolen from
- have been threatened
- perceive school as unsafe
- negative relationship with father and/or mother
- going out at night without adult supervision
- spending time with friends rather than with family
- peer acceptance of illegal acts

of control. In recent years, a particular form of youth criminal behaviour has come to predominate in the public mind: gangs (Schissel, 2001).

Youth Gangs

Youth street **gangs** are a popular topic for newspaper articles, politicians' speeches, movies, and both fictional and non-fictional television. Youth gangs can be found throughout much of the world; however, the prevalence of youth gangs in the United States, combined with the emphasis placed on youth gangs in the American media, means that much of the research done on gangs is American. In fact, Canadian research on youth gangs continues to be comparatively sparse, and American research has dominated Canadian academic, public, and governmental policy discussions (Grekul & Laboucane-Benson, 2007; Chatterjee, 2006; Gordon, 2001). The American-centric nature of gang research is problematic when one considers Canadian–American differences in gun control legislation, drug laws, government policies, ethnic/cultural composition, and social supports (Grekul & Laboucane-Benson, 2007).

Two broad streams of research can be identified. One of those streams focuses on causation or motivation—why gangs form, why youth join gangs, and why gangs engage in particular behaviours. The second stream of research focuses on various aspects of the social construction of the "gang problem," such as how and why moral panics about gangs emerge, and even the problems involved in the very definition of "gang" itself.

The "How" and "Why" of Gangs

What has been labelled "traditional criminology" has dominated theorizing about gang emergence and gang membership (Hagedorn, 2007), bringing us back to a number of the theories reviewed in Chapter 2. For instance, the underlying proposition of strain theories is that gangs will emerge in socially and economically disadvantaged communities. In such communities, where legitimate opportunities to achieve social status and economic success are limited, gangs form as an alternative way of achieving status, social acceptance, and economic success (e.g., Merton's strain theory).

The status and economic success to be gained via gang activity is not to be underestimated, given the amount of money to be made in the drug trade. However, the pursuit of economic success is not central to the activities of all youth gangs. Other theorists have asserted that different types of gangs have different types of activities as their foundation. Status frustration theory suggests that lower-class boys, if unable to live up to the middle-class measuring rod that pervades the education system, would join with other similar boys in forming gangs that engage in expressive, destructive, non-utilitarian behaviours (e.g., vandalism, violence) rather than economically-driven activities (Cohen, 1955).

Differential opportunity theory proposes that the nature of the illegitimate opportunities present in the community determines the nature of gang behaviour;

particular illegitimate opportunities result in the formation of gangs that may be economically enterprising, violent, or drug-using and retreatist (Cloward & Ohlin, 1960). Although the pursuit of economic success is not a component of all youth gangs, the pursuit of status is—but the type of status that can be achieved through gang membership depends on the gang in question.

Although positivist theories dominate the area, research on gangs does also come from more subjective theoretical orientations. For instance, drawing upon the critical Marxist perspective of the Birmingham Centre for Contemporary Cultural Studies, Bourgois (1995) analyzes youth gangs as sources of identity and expressions of resistance among youth who are structurally marginalized. Pointing to the interactionist perspective, Venkatesh (2003) discusses the fact that within a gang, individual members have different interests, motivations for gang membership, and understandings of what it means to be in a gang member.

Ethnographic research, emerging from the interactionist perspective, involves researchers embedding themselves in gangs for extended periods of time, interviewing gang members, and observing their daily activities. For example, Jankowski (1991) conducted an ethnographic study that is one of the few pieces of research to explore the relationships between gangs, other people, and other organizations within the community (Venkatesh, 2003). He concluded that individuals join gangs for a variety of different reasons rather than for any one reason (such as blocked opportunities).

The various reasons for joining a gang are based on a rational calculation of what is in the best interests of the individual at a particular time. First, Jankowski (1991) suggests that one reason for gang membership is **material incentives**. Some people join gangs based on the belief that the gang will provide an environment that increases the chances of making money—more regular money, and with less individual effort, than if pursuing economic success individually. Jankowski found that material incentives also include financial security for gang members and their families during difficult times, as well as networking for future economic endeavours.

Recreation serves as another reason for gang membership. That is, gangs provide entertainment and a social life, and in some communities may serve as the primary social institution in the neighbourhood, promoting social events and supplying drugs and alcohol. The comments of one gang member illustrate the recreational aspect of gang membership: "'Man, it [the gang] was a great source of dope and women. Hell, they were the kings of the community so I wanted to get in on some of the action'" (Jankowski, 1991, p. 283). Gangs may serve as **a place of refuge and camouflage**, motivating some individuals to seek gang membership. Being just "one of the gang" provides a level of anonymity, removing a sense of personal responsibility for illegal activities—"'the gang is going to provide me with some cover'" (p. 283).

Other people are drawn to gangs for the **physical protection** they provide from known dangers in the neighbourhood. As gang member Cory points out, "'Now that I got some business things going I can concentrate on them and not worry so much. I don't always have to be looking over my shoulder'" (p. 284). For some people, joining a gang may serve as a **time to resist** living the kinds of lives their parents lived. In this vein, becoming a gang member is a statement of rejection to society, a rejection of the type of lives being offered. At the same time, the economic prospects of gang membership may be a way of avoiding just that type of life—"'Hey, I just might make some money from our dealings. . . . If I don't [make it, at least] I told those fuckers in Beverly Hills what I think of the jobs they left for us'" (p. 284).

In some neighbourhoods, certain gangs have existed for generations, so that individuals whose fathers, uncles, and grandfathers have been members of the gang at some point in their lives feel a **commitment to the community** and join the gang in order to continue a tradition. As Pepe states, "'A lot of people from the community have been in [the gang]. . . . I felt it's kind of my duty to join 'cause everybody expects it'" (p. 285). Feeling a commitment to the community, along with the other possible motivations for gang membership, leads individuals to conclude that joining a gang is currently in their best interests. Both the more objective and more subjective theorizing on gangs frequently point to gang formation and gang membership as a rational alternative for the individuals involved, given their current sociocultural surroundings and their networks of social interaction.

Grekul and LaBoucane-Benson (2007) combine positivist (social bonds), critical (conflict) and interactionist (labelling) theories in their analysis of Aboriginal gangs in Canada. Interviews with former gang members, police officers, and corrections workers reveal that weak bonds of attachment, commitment to conventional society, involvement in conventional society, and beliefs that support conventional society play a significant role in gang membership. The legacy of colonization and residential schooling (which will be discussed further in Chapter 8) has had a lasting effect on Aboriginal families, such as those in the Edmonton area. Aboriginal children are six times more likely to be involved with child protection services; it is these children who are prime targets for gang recruitment efforts.

Although there have been considerable increases in high-school completion and post-secondary education, dropout rates continue to considerably higher among Aboriginal youth, with higher unemployment rates as a consequence. Ongoing discrimination continues to be a problem as well: "One of our respondents recalled being called a 'dumb little Indian who would never amount to anything' by one of his school teachers" (p. 33). The negative effects of being labelled have an impact; one respondent states, "'police called them a gang so they began to act that way and identify themselves that way'" (p. 42). All of these factors have an interactive effect, and gangs are able to step in and "fill the gap for disenfranchised and marginalized" (p. 2) Aboriginal youth.

A number of different variables, including personal, family, community, and educational factors increase the likelihood of gang involvement (e.g., Gordon, 1995; Flannery, Huff, & Manos, 2001; Edmonton Police Service, 2009). In

Exercise Your Mind

In order to further explore the linkages between theory and empirical research, identify which of the risk factors in Box 5.1 might fit within (a) Merton's Strain Theory; (b) Cloward and Ohlin's Differential Opportunity Theory; (c) Sutherland's Differential Association Theory; (d) Social Learning Theory; (e) Hirschi's Social Bonds Theory; and (f) Gottfredson and Hirschi's General Theory of Crime.

Box 5.2, you will find a summary of these factors, illustrating that gang involvement emerges in part from unhealthy personalities, unhealthy relationships, unhealthy families, and unhealthy communities.

The Construction of the "Gang Problem"

While the first stream of gang research explores the causes of or motivations for gang emergence, membership, and behaviour, the second stream concentrates on a different set of issues, related to social construction. Within the latter stream, some emphasize the social construction of "gangs" themselves. For instance, Sanday (cited in Vankatesh, 2003) asks why fraternities are not considered to be gangs. One of the more commonly used definitions of "gang" (albeit far from being agreed upon) is "any denotable . . . group [of adolescents or young adults] who (a) are generally perceived as a distinct aggregation by others in the neighbourhood, (b) recognize themselves as a denotable group (almost invariably with a group name), and (c) have been involved in a sufficient number of [illegal]

Box 5.2 Factors Influencing Gang Involvement

Family Indicators

- excessive parental controls
- lax parental controls
- low parental nurturance
- abuse/neglect
- low parental educational level
- criminality among other family members

Personal Indicators

- low self-control
- low motivation
- truancy
- failing grades
- low aspirations or goals in life
- substance abuse

Community Indicators

- community disorganization
- high crime rate
- high population turnover
- lack of cultural resources
- lack of recreational resources
- gang presence

School Indicators

- negative school environment
- violence in the school
- low expectations for students
- inadequate funding for school resources (e.g., library books, extracurricular activities)
- lax controls over students

incidents . . ." (cited in Chatterjee, 2006). Fraternities are most certainly perceived as a distinct group, both by others and themselves, and Sanday points out that "theft, vandalism, sexual conquest (read: harassment), and the imbibing of alcohol (read: underage drinking)" (Vanketesh, 2003, p. 5) are common, and are even explicitly included in some fraternity charters or manifestos.

Others who are embedded within the latter stream of research focus more on the social construction of the "**gang problem**." Discussions of media representations of gangs have been central to research from this perspective. The way youth gangs are represented in the media and other forms of public discourse is similar to the portrayal of youth crime more generally. Gangs are portrayed as a new and growing problem for society, one that is out of control (Fasiolo & Leckie, 1993; Tanner, 2001; Gordon, 1993, 2001).

Just as with images of youth crime more generally, public images of gangs surpass their actual existence. Not only are stories about gangs found on television news and in newspapers, they can also be easily found in the fictional media—on television shows like *Law & Order* and *CSI: Crime Scene Investigation*, in movies, and in the glamourized images of gangs within some rap and hip hop music lyrics/videos (Delaney, 2005). The involvement of particular ethnic and age groups is a significant component of public images of gangs.

Canadian newspapers **racialize** the "gang problem" (Bell, 2002). In other words, stories about gangs frequently include references to specific racial or ethnic groups, Grekul & LaBoucane-Benson, 2007; Gordon, 2001). This is problematic on two fronts. First, a distorted picture of Canadian gangs is presented to the audience, when the reality is that gangs are not associated with any single racial or ethnic group, but are ethnically diverse (Tanner, 2001; Gordon, 2001; Chatterjee, 2006). Second, race and ethnicity are only overtly linked in the media to gang activity when it is non-whites that are involved. "We read and hear of the 'Asian' gang problem, the problem of Jamaican Blacks in the east, and 'Aboriginal gangs.' We don't often hear of 'Caucasian' or 'White' gangs. Racial and ethnic stereotyping leads to processes such as racial profiling and creates misunderstanding, labelling, mistrust, and hostility between groups" (Grekul & LaBoucane-Benson, 2007, p. 25).

Media representations of the gang problem vary in different parts of Canada, particularly in Quebec as compared with the other provinces and territories. In Quebec, the racialization of gangs is less common. Instead, age is one of the areas of focus in the media: gangs are most commonly referred to as "youth gangs" (Fasiolo & Leckie, 1993). Just as with race and ethnicity, the linking of "youth" and "gangs" is inaccurate in that most Canadian gangs have considerable age diversity. The 2002 Canadian Police Survey found that the age range in gangs is from 8 to over 50, and that fewer than half of street gang members are under the age of 18 (Chatterjee, 2006). Thus, although calls from politicians and the general public to strengthen young offender legislation often follow publicized gang incidents, it is adults who predominate in Canada's gang landscape. When combined, the media's overrepresentation of gangs, its racialization of gangs, and its distortion of the age composition of gangs all contribute to a view of Canada's gangs that is quite different from the reality—showing that a "moral panic" has been created.

Certain groups may benefit from the creation of a moral panic about street gangs. Drawing on the conflict and critical theoretical perspectives addressed in Chapter 3, a number of researchers suggest that not only do the media benefit from the creation of moral panics, so do some politicians, interest groups, and law enforcement agencies (Bell, 2002; Tanner, 2001; Gordon, 2001; Schissel, 2001; Cohen, 1973). By presenting sensationalistic and fear-provoking stories, the media draws an audience, and thereby increases profit.

Some politicians may similarly engage in fear mongering, and then vow to toughen legislation and enforcement if elected. By contributing to moral panic and then promising to reduce the social problem, they are able to obtain more votes.

Interest groups and community agencies who want legislation strengthened or who provide social programs may receive more funding by exaggerating the nature of the problem. Law enforcement agencies may benefit in some communities by also receiving more funding to hire more officers or create specialized gang units if they are able to convince municipal, provincial, and federal politicians that the "gang problem" is out of control. Some researchers suggest that even gangs themselves may benefit from this moral panic, which provides them with free publicity and may thereby increase their membership and power in the community. Youth who are currently not involved in gangs may form new gangs in order to protect themselves from the perceived threat (Tanner, 2001).

However, although the gang research done in this second stream suggests that the moral panic surrounding youth gangs surpasses what is actually going on and that various groups benefit from this moral panic, it does not claim that gangs are a figment of the social imagination or that gangs are nothing to worry about. Indeed, the gangs that do exist must be socially controlled.

Controlling Youth Gangs and Youth Crime

"How do you deal with youth crime? 'Toughen up' the Youth Criminal Justice Act, send 'bad guys' (and girls) to jail for a very long time, make parole eligibility criteria more restrictive and keep the problem away from our homes and families. Easy. Simple. Quick fix." (Grekul & LaBoucane-Benson, 2007, p. 24)

In fact, as Grekul and LaBoucane-Benson go on to point out, the effective control of gangs, and of youth crime more generally, is far from an easy, quick fix. Throughout North America, street gangs are socially controlled at multiple levels—formal and informal, retroactive and preventative. These social control efforts occur in families, communities (schools, community agencies, community organizations, businesses, and religious institutions), and the criminal justice system (government, courts, and law enforcement).

At a formal level of regulation, many schools have integrated gang awareness programs to teach children about the dangers of gangs and the consequences of gang membership. These programs are intended to prevent children from joining gangs. Community agencies, particularly those operating in gang-ridden neighbourhoods, frequently have both retroactive and preventative programs. Retroactive programs are designed to try to persuade existing gang members to leave that lifestyle. They may offer educational upgrading, job training, assistance in finding employment, free tattoo removal, and various types of counselling.

Preventative programs in communities may operate in conjunction with schools, teaching young children basic life skills (e.g., nutrition, grooming) and social skills (e.g., problem solving, anger management), or providing organized community activities. Many police departments in North America have specialized gang units who become familiar with and closely monitor known gang members, as well as deal with gang issues and events that arise. Governments provide gang-related legislation and social programs (e.g., job-training programs).

The Community Solution to Gang Violence (CSGV) in Edmonton is a large-scale formal effort that integrates all of the groups listed above. Administered through Native Counselling Services of Alberta, this program combines intervention and prevention, bringing together 40 community organizations, the Edmonton Police Service, and all levels of government (municipal, provincial, and federal). Informal social controls occur at the level of everyday social interaction, typically focusing on preventative efforts. This includes parenting efforts (e.g., parenting style, talking to your children about gangs) and community involvement with neighbourhood children (e.g., becoming a soccer coach, helping the neighbourhood children organize a food drive).

Coordinated efforts at gang control at multiple levels are the most effective means of prevention and response to the gang problem. However, the regulation of gangs is even more complex in that different types of specific controls may be required in cities with varying levels of gang activity. A community that currently has no signs of gang presence requires a basic foundation of control, which can be provided by community parenting programs, teaching children multicultural sensitivity, and reinforcing codes of conduct. In contrast, a community with the highest level of gang activity—i.e., one where gangs dominate the neigbourhood—will require the assistance of anti-gang professionals and intense efforts to reclaim the neighbourhood (Edmonton Police Service, 2003).

Measures to control youth gangs are intertwined with the regulation of youth crime in general. Many of the formal and informal social controls that were discussed in the context of gangs are also utilized in relation to youth crime—it is presumed that the prevention of gang involvement is also the prevention of crime at a broader level. For instance, effective parenting, community involvement in children's lives, and effective classrooms will reduce not only the likelihood of gang involvement, but also the likelihood of all types of criminal activity.

Over the past century, there have been considerable changes in the way youth crime has been formally controlled or regulated. Public concerns about youth crime gained force during the late nineteenth century. This was a period of tremendous social and economic change in Canadian society. The process of industrialization was well underway, cities were growing, and an identifiable working class was present. Because of the long hours that working-class parents had to spend at work simply to ensure the survival of their family, their children were left unsupervised more than the children of middle-class parents. Social reformers during that era were concerned with the lack of supervision these children faced as well as the subsequent danger they presented to middle-class personhood and property (Leon, 1977; Sutherland, 1976).

Various small pieces of legislation encompassed the control of youth crime, neglected children, and abandoned children. Children under the age of 7 were presumed not to know the difference between right and wrong, and so could not be charged with criminal offences. If it was proven that a child between the ages of 7 and 14 knew the difference between right and wrong, the child could be subject to the same sentence as an adult; thus, it was possible for a 7-year-old child who had committed a crime to be sentenced to life in prison or even death. Youth over the age of 14 were considered equal to adults in criminal law.

In 1908, the Canadian juvenile justice system was created with the implementation of the Juvenile Delinquents Act. Its foundation was the principle of *parens patriae* ("parent of the country"), meaning that the state would act in the best interests of children under the age of 16 if it became clear that their own parents were unwilling or unable to—and both neglected and delinquent children were presumed to need such legislative attention. Although it controlled youth criminals, the Juvenile Delinquents Act was more a *child welfare* piece of legislation, since it was believed that with the right assistance and correct teaching, young criminals could be set on the right path in life. Separate detention facilities and jail facilities were created for youth, based on the belief that integrating juvenile delinquents with adult criminals would simply further juvenile delinquency (Reitsma-Street, 1989–90).

The Juvenile Delinquents Act was amended several times over the ensuing decades, and in 1984 was replaced by the Young Offenders Act. This new piece of legislation was based on *justice* principles rather than child welfare principles. It extended the legal rights of adult offenders (e.g., due process, the right to an attorney) to youth as well, who were not guaranteed such protections under the Juvenile Delinquents Act. Youth who committed crimes were no longer perceived as juvenile delinquents but as **young offenders**; an offending youth was now seen as a *criminal* rather than a child gone astray (West, 1984; West, 1991). After a number of amendments throughout the 1990s, the Youth Criminal Justice Act replaced the Young Offenders Act on April 1, 2003.

Under this new legislation, chronic and/or violent young offenders are treated more stringently, while first-time and non-violent young offenders are more likely to be treated via community and alternative measures. The Youth Criminal Justice Act is one component of the federal government's Youth Justice Renewal Initiative, a multi-faceted initiative involving the criminal justice system, schools, community agencies, and more. Its underlying principles are prevention, meaningful consequences for youth crime, and intensified rehabilitation and reintegration.

AN INTERNET MOMENT

On the website for the Department of Justice, www.canada.justice.gc.ca, select "Programs & Initiatives" along the top of the page. At the bottom of the next page, you will find "Youth Justice Renewal." This extensive site reviews all the components of the Youth Justice Renewal Initiative, including an overview of the differences between the old Young Offenders Act and the new Youth Criminal Justice Act.

The social control of youth crime has been modified in substantial ways over the past century, and more recently has included efforts to control gangs. Although legislation, criminal justice programs, and social programs are continually changing, the desire to control "troubling" youth is as old as civilization itself. However, youth who are perceived as threats to society because of their criminal activities are not the only ones considered deviant and in need of social control; "troubled" youth are a focus of concern as well.

TIME TO REVIEW

- In what ways are youth perceived as both "troubling" and "troubled"?
- What are the broader patterns of youth crime, and how do these compare with common perceptions of youth crime? Is the "moral panic" over youth crime unique to the twenty-first century?
- Which theories have been used to explain youth crime, and what has empirical research found about the roles of family structure, parenting style, and peers?
- In what way do positivist, interpretive, and critical theories contribute to our understanding of gang emergence, membership, and behaviour?

- How does the media represent the "gang problem," and who potentially benefits from the moral panic about gangs?
- In what way is the social control of gangs intertwined with the control of youth crime more generally, and how are gangs controlled within families, schools, community agencies, and the criminal justice system?
- How has legislation governing youth crime changed over the past century?

Deviant Youth: "Troubled" Youth

Some youth are considered deviant and are made subject to measures of social control not because they are "troubling," and therefore currently a danger to society, but because they are "troubled." "Troubled" youth are first and foremost a danger to themselves; their behaviour threatens their own well-being, physical or mental health, and future. But "troubled" youth are also perceived as potentially "troubling"—if they are uncontrolled, or if their problems are not effectively dealt with, they may become not only a danger to themselves, but a danger to society as well. Youth who abuse drugs or alcohol, engage in premature sexual activity, become teenage parents, or live on the streets are just some of those youth who are considered "troubled." When considering "troubled" youth, one of the areas of greatest public concern is substance abuse, due to its potential effects on the substance abusers themselves, others, and the larger community.

Substance Use among Youth

We live in a culture where substance use, in some form, is often widely evident. Step outside the doorway of office buildings, shopping malls, and even hospitals, and you will see groups of people gathered, a haze of cigarette smoke hovering over their heads. Attend a wedding, retirement party, or dinner party, and alcohol will likely be served. Prior to New Year's Eve, liquor stores sell out of bottles of champagne. Some single people who are searching for Mr./Ms. Right (or Mr./Ms. Right-Now) carry out those searches in bars—bars that likely have a happy hour (when drinks are less expensive) or even a ladies' night, where schoolgirl attire buys five drinks for five dollars. Attend certain concerts (e.g., Kid Rock, Snoop Dogg, Bob Dylan), and although cameras may be confiscated, marijuana will not, and even those members of the audience who are not drug users will find themselves getting a secondhand high. On television and in movies, characters may be smoking, drinking, or using drugs. For example, on *Friends*, when "Fun Bobby" became sober, he was no longer fun, and despite everyone's best efforts to support his sobriety, they eventually found themselves trying to convince him to start drinking again.

The related social controls we see around us are further evidence of substance use. Walk into your university's student resource centre, and you will find pamphlets about alcohol abuse, smoking, and "club drugs." Prior to reading week (or spring break), abuse prevention campaigns might be displayed throughout your campus. If you tell someone you are going to a club, they may warn you about the dangers of "date rape" drugs. In school, you may have been exposed to educational programs about smoking, alcohol use, and drug use, often beginning in early elementary school. Rarely does a day go by when each of us does not see someone using such a substance (whether in person or in the media) or see some type of substance control efforts.

The most commonly used substances among Canadian adolescents and young adults have traditionally been, in order of use, alcohol, tobacco, cannabis (marijuana and hashish), and hallucinogens (e.g., LSD). However, the most recent version of the biennial *Ontario Student Drug Use*

Ask Yourself

Estimate how many youth use the following substances: alcohol, tobacco, marijuana, other illegal drugs. On what did you base your estimates—youth whom you know personally, your own observations, media portrayals, or public information campaigns? How do your estimates compare to your own levels of usage of these substances?

and Health Survey asked students in Grades 7 through 12, for the first time, about their non-medical use of opioid pain relievers (e.g., Percocet, Percodan, Tylenol 3), with surprising results. The survey found that the three most commonly used substances are now alcohol (61.2% use in the past year), cannabis (25.6% use in the past year), and opioid pain relievers (20.6% use in the past year); tobacco was a distant fourth (11.9% use in the past year) (Adlaf & Paglia-Boak, 2007). Of those adolescents who used opioid pain relievers, 72% obtained them from home.

Substance use among youth peaked in 1979, and then steadily declined until the early 1990s. Usage increased throughout the 1990s (Roberts *et al.*, 2001), but has since declined, such that drug use overall is lower today than it was in 1979 (although the use of some specific drugs, such as hallucinogens, is higher) (Adlaf & Paglia-Boak, 2007). More than one-quarter of students in Grades 7 through 12 are substance free, a lower proportion than in the early 1990s, but still a higher proportion than in the 1970s.

Tobacco

The health risks associated with smoking and secondhand smoke exposure have now been well established by medical research. When those risks were first publicized during the 1970s, smoking rates among youth began a steady decline that lasted until 1990. But beginning in 1990, youth smoking increased once again, and continued to grow throughout the decade (Health Canada, 1999). Another shift has occurred since that time, such that from 2000 through 2005, smoking among 12- to 17-year-olds declined from 14% to 8% (Statistics Canada, 2006b). Smoking has also declined among university students, from 17% in 1998 to 13% in 2004 (Adlaf, Demers, & Gliksman, 2005).

However, there are significant gender differences in youth smoking. Smoking has historically been more prevalent among males; but beginning in 1990, that pattern reversed, with more adolescent girls than boys becoming smokers. That pattern was still evident in 2005, when although 8% of all 12- to 17-year-olds were smokers, only 8% of boys smoked compared to 10% of girls (Statistics Canada, 2006b) (see Figure 5.2). The pattern of adolescent girls being more likely than boys to smoke occurs in most Western countries in the world, including Canada, Germany, France, England, Norway, Denmark, and Sweden (Health Canada, 1999). Youth say that the primary motivation for smoking comes from friends or peer pressure (Health Canada, 2005a), but research also shows that the likelihood of smoking is correlated with family income, highest level of education in the household, and parental smoking behaviour (Shields, 2005a)

Youth smoking is socially controlled in a variety of ways. The Federal Tobacco Act prohibits the sale of cigarettes to those under the age of 18, although provincial legislation can increase the minimum age requirement to 19. This kind of legislation has existed for many years, but enforcement has been lax for much of that time. In the 1970s, it was not uncommon for children as young as six or seven to be sent to the corner store to buy cigarettes for a parent or an older

Figure 5.2   PROPORTION OF MALE AND FEMALE SMOKERS (AGES 12 TO 17), 2000, 2003, AND 2005

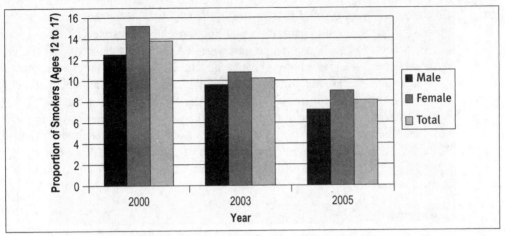

Adapted from "Percentage of Current Smokers, by Sex and Age Group, Household Population aged 12 or older, Canada, 2005," Statistics Canada, *Smoking and Diabetes Care: Results from the CCHS Cycle 3.1 (2005),* Catalogue 82-621, No. 02, (June 13, 2006): 15.

sibling. More recently, enforcement has become more stringent, and penalties for selling cigarettes to minors have become more severe. For example, Alberta retailers risk a $3 000 fine for a first offence and up to a $50 000 fine for a second offence (Gregoire, 2003).

And most retailers in Canada are complying. Health Canada conducts regular investigations of retail outlets in 30 cities across Canada. A research team of one youth and one adult go into a retail outlet (although not as an identifiable pair), and the youth requests a package of cigarettes. The youth lies about his/her age, if asked, but does not carry any identification. Using this methodology, Health Canada (2005b) found that 80% of retailers complied with legislation, refusing to sell cigarettes to the youth. Alberta has taken an additional step, and is the first province to create legislation targeting underage smokers themselves, wherein anyone under the age of 18 who is caught smoking in "public" is subject to a $100 fine (Gregoire, 2003). However, the enforcement of this legislation is another issue; as one police officer states, "'It's not something we're going to devote a lot of time to—trolling food courts and arresting kids'" (para. 6). The Alberta legislation does not operate in isolation, but rather is just one piece of a larger $11.7 million strategy that also involves school education packages, websites, and seminars.

Social control efforts specifically aimed at curtailing youth smoking are part of broader forms of regulation for smoking. We have come a long way from the days when cigarette commercials appeared on television, people smoked anywhere they wished (including university classrooms and hospitals), and doctors prescribed smoking as a weight-loss tool. Today, cigarette commercials cannot be shown on television, and cigarette advertising is in fact widely restricted. The media is now a central source for public service campaigns to reduce smoking.

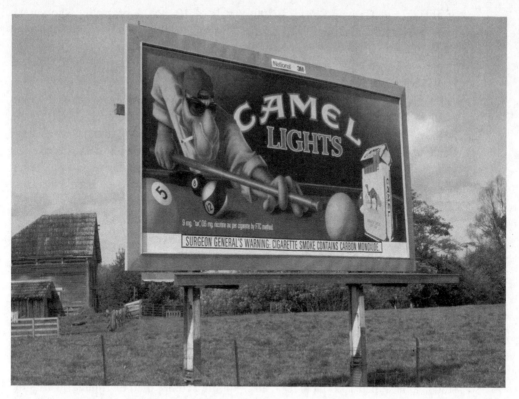

The use of this animated character in cigarette advertising was highly criticized for its apparent attempts to attract the attention of children.

In many communities, recent laws have banned smoking in many workplaces, shopping malls, hospitals, and restaurants. Other communities have taken this legislation a step further, prohibiting smoking in all public buildings including bars (e.g., New York, Victoria, San Francisco, and Edmonton). And, of course, instead of prescribing smoking as a weight-loss tool, contemporary doctors try to convince their patients to stop smoking and provide resources to help them quit (e.g., nicotine patches, support groups). A growing proportion of households are smoke-free. The Canadian Community Health Survey (Statistics Canada, 2006b) found that smoking is banned in 64% of households, an increase from 57% in 2003. This relatively simple act has a significant impact on youth, who are less likely to smoke if they live in households where smoking is prohibited. This is the case even if parents are smokers themselves (Shields, 2005a).

The health dangers of smoking are well known and have led to comprehensive anti-smoking efforts for people of all ages. However, smoking among youth is a public concern not only because of the health dangers, but also because of its association with other forms of substance use. Youth who smoke are also more likely to use other drugs, particularly marijuana (U.S. Department of Health and Human Services, 2000); half of 12- to 17-year-olds who smoke have used marijuana, compared to only 4% of those who do not smoke (Health Canada, 2005a).

Drug Use

Cannabis is the most widely used psychoactive drug among Canadian youth (excluding alcohol) (Adlaf & Paglia-Boak, 2007; Adlaf, Demers, & Gliksman, 2005). The National Longitudinal Survey on Youth has found that 3% of Canadian youth have tried marijuana by age 12, and by age 15 the proportion increases to 38% (Hotton & Haans, 2004). This is a significant increase from 1990, when only one quarter of youth in Grade 10 had ever tried marijuana (Health Canada, 1999). However, although a considerable proportion of youth have tried marijuana, they do not use it regularly. Data from Ontario shows that only 14% of adolescents who have used marijuana within the past year have used it six or more times (Adlaf & Paglia-Boak, 2007).

Among university students, the prevalence of marijuana use is slightly higher. Fifty-one percent have used it at some point in their lives, 32% have used it within the last year, and 17% have used it over the last month (Adlaf, Demers, & Gliksman, 2005) (see Figure 5.3).

Other psychoactive drugs have lower rates of usage than cannabis, although rates did increase during the 1990s (Health Canada, 1999). University-age youth have higher rates of illicit drug usage than adolescents, but even among university students, less than 10% have used an illicit drug (other than marijuana) within the previous year, and only 2% have used one within the last month (Adlaf, Demers, & Gliksman, 2005). Canadian youth are more likely to use psychoactive drugs (including marijuana) than are European youth, even those European youth who

Figure 5.3   SELF-REPORTED MARIJUANA USE AMONG UNIVERSITY STUDENTS, 2004

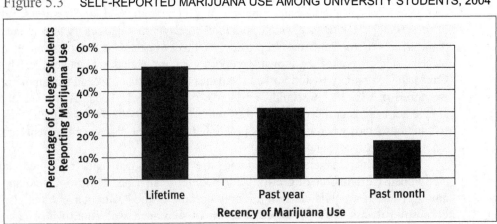

Source: Adlaf, E. M., Demers, A., & Gliksman, L. (Eds.) (2005). Canadian Campus Survey 2004. Toronto, ON: Centre for Addiction and Mental Health. Reproduced with permission.

live in nations with more lenient marijuana laws (Harkin, Anderson, & Goos, 1997; Health Canada, 1999).

Although the regular use of psychoactive drugs is fairly uncommon among Canadian youth, those who do regularly use psychoactive drugs tend to do so problematically, increasing their risk of negative life consequences. In Quebec, of those adolescents who have used an illegal substance more than five times, more than half have gone to school stoned, or used an illegal substance in the morning or while participating in a competitive sport (Roberts *et al.*, 2001).

The reasons for drug use vary among different groups of Canadian youth. Some may use drugs for reasons similar to adult drug users—to relieve stress, as a form of escapism, or as a social activity. However, youth may also have distinctive motivations for drug use as well, such as to satisfy their curiosity, show their independence, or become part of a peer group (Roberts *et al.*, 2001). The relationship between an individual's drug use and drug use among peers is especially strong. Among youth who report having friends who use drugs, 80% also use drugs themselves; in comparison, only 7% of youth whose friends do not use drugs use drugs themselves (Hotton & Haans, 2004).

Whether drug use becomes problematic depends on individual, community, family, and school factors (Roberts *et al.*, 2001)—all factors that also influence youth crime or gang membership. *Individual* factors that influence whether substance use becomes problematic include the following: genetic and environmental predispositions, degree of personal competence (e.g., extent to which the individual feels in control of life and optimistic about the future), connection with violent behaviour, and gang involvement. *Community* factors include norms about substance use, prevalence of crime, price and availability of substances, economic conditions, and nature of peers. At the level of the *family*, parenting style, degree of parent–child emotional attachment, and family history in relation to substance use play significant roles. Finally, within the *school*, academic success, reading skills, problem-solving abilities, participation in extracurricular activities, and feelings of belonging influence the nature and extent of drug use (Brounstein & Zweig, 1999; Benard, 1991).

Due to the multiple factors operating at different levels that influence youth drug use, effective programs are comprehensive, targeting factors at all levels and thus involving families, communities, schools, and youth themselves (Roberts *et al.*, 2001; Health Canada, 1999). Programs must be age-appropriate and occur *prior to* the child's likely exposure to particular types of drugs. Effective programs integrate youth's own perceptions of drugs and drug use, and realistically take their lifestyles into consideration. For example, the "Just Say No" campaign is seen by many adolescents as being unrealistic, not providing them with the tools they really need to deal with the situations they will encounter in their lives.

The problematic nature of drug use among regular users makes the reduction of drug use an important goal for these comprehensive programs. However, it is important to keep in mind that only a small percentage of youth use drugs and an even smaller percentage use them regularly. In contrast, the use of alcohol is far more prevalent among Canadian youth.

Alcohol Use

Alcohol use is a normative behaviour for contemporary youth in Canadian society. By Grade 7, more than one-quarter of youth have used alcohol within the past year and that proportion increases to 83% by Grade 12, with 13.5 as the average age of first use and 14.0 as the average age of first drunkenness (Adlaf & Paglia-Boak, 2007). The problem of youth alcohol use is not just Canadian or North American—in Europe, the frequency of adolescent drunkenness has increased as well (Hagmann, 2001).

The alcohol industry has been widely criticized for its role in facilitating or even promoting this phenomenon by targeting adolescents with the creation of "alcopops" (low-alcohol beverages intended to taste like soda) and other fruit-flavoured alcoholic beverages (Mosher & Johnsson, 2005). These types of drinks are frequently promoted in conjunction with music that is particularly popular with adolescents (e.g., providing a free CD or music download with purchase) and in venues frequented by adolescents (e.g., youth-oriented websites) (Center on Alcohol Marketing and Youth, 2004). As a result of these commercial efforts, research in the United Kingdom has found that 13- to 16-year-olds are the largest group of consumers of this kind of beverage (Health Education Authority, cited in Jernigan, 2001). Although drinking is common in youth of all ages, more recently, one particular aspect of problematic alcohol use has garnered public attention: binge drinking among university students.

Binge Drinking among University Students.   Research on **binge drinking** (five drinks in one sitting for males and four drinks in one sitting for females) among university students has found it to be a rather unique pattern of behaviour, different from alcohol use in younger youth or even among youth the same age who are not university students. The unique nature and pattern of university binge drinking necessitates distinct social control measures.

In many people's minds, "university" and "parties" go hand in hand. In fact, the 2004 Canadian Campus Survey found that 86% of undergraduates have used alcohol within the past year, and 77% within the past month (Adlaf, Demers, & Gliksman, 2005). Popular university rating guides often rate universities not only on academic factors but also social factors, such as the best "party universities." Picture yourself at a university party such as a fraternity party. The images that come to mind likely contain large numbers of people present and loud music playing. Some of you might picture a few party attendees smoking marijuana or using other types of drugs, but in all likelihood it is images of alcohol that prevail—kegs of beer, drinking contests, and large punch bowls of brightly coloured and highly potent beverages. You might

Ask Yourself

How do you define "binge drinking"? What proportion of students at your university do you think engage in binge drinking?

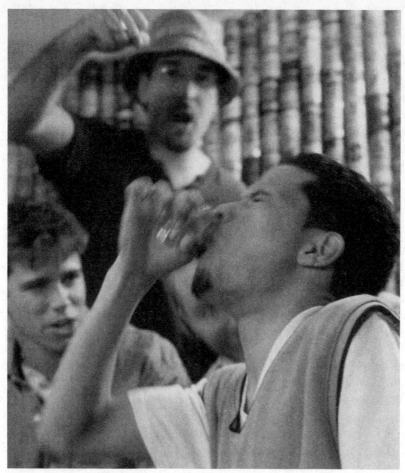

Binge drinking and the university lifestyle go hand in hand in the popular imagination.

imagine people at these parties consuming five, six, or even more drinks in one evening, perhaps even passing out. These kinds of images reflect the "binge-drinking problem" on university campuses.

Most of our knowledge about university binge drinking comes from the United States, where research shows that approximately 40% of university students are binge drinkers (have engaged in binge drinking within the past two weeks), a proportion that has remained consistent since 1993 (Wechsler & Nelson, 2008; Wechsler, Seibring, Liu, & Ahl, 2004; Weitzman & Nelson, 2004; Adlaf, Demers, & Gliksman, 2005). However, the prevalence of binge drinking varies across various subgroups of students. The "traditional" university student (aged 18 to 23 and living away from parents) is much more likely to binge drink. Among this group of students, 51% report having engaged in binge drinking within the past two weeks. In this specific student population, we can look at further subgroups as well.

For example, binge drinking is more common among members of fraternities, sororities, and university athletic groups (Wechsler *et al.*, 2002).

Although the proportion of binge drinkers has remained consistent since the early 1990s, some important changes in binge-drinking patterns have emerged. Alcohol use among university students has become more polarized: the proportion of abstainers (people who do not drink alcohol) has grown to 20% of university students, but the proportion of "frequent" binge drinkers (three or more binge drinking episodes within the past two weeks) has grown to 23% of university students (Wechsler *et al.*, 2002). Another change in binge drinking is that it has increasingly moved off campus (Keeling, 2000, 2002).

It has been suggested that more stringent university alcohol policies that emerged during the 1990s may have created a more supportive environment for abstainers, contributing to the increase in the proportion of non-drinkers. However, for heavier drinkers and for student subcultures in which drinking is more common, the more stringent policies may have facilitated resistance and rebellion. As these subcultures isolate themselves within their more accepting social networks and move their drinking activities to less-supervised off-campus areas, bingers' social contact with non-drinkers declines. Bingers are increasingly surrounded by heavier drinkers, subsequently raising the proportion of university students who are "frequent" binge drinkers (Keeling, 2000, 2002).

Individual binge drinking is correlated with the rate of binge drinking among peers, particularly close friends; that is, binge drinkers associate with other binge drinkers, and non–binge drinkers associate with other non–binge drinkers (Weschler & Kuo, 2000). Patterns of binge drinking change during the academic year. There is a significant amount of binge drinking at the beginning of the year, but as class demands increase during the middle portion of the academic year and students become entrenched in their study routines, binge drinking declines. However, it increases once again following exams. It is especially prevalent during students' first year at university and then declines during subsequent years (Brower, 2002).

When university binge drinking first came to widespread public awareness, a common concern was that the current cohort of binge drinkers would turn into the alcoholics of the future. However, the research conducted over the last decade finds no evidence that binge drinking in university is associated with alcohol abuse or alcoholism in later life; in fact, binge drinking usually ceases following graduation (Brower, 2002).

But even though university binge drinking is not associated with problem drinking in later life, there is no doubt that it does create problems. Of students who are binge drinkers, approximately 30% have experienced each of the following consequences: missed classes, regretted actions while drunk, driving while drunk, forgotten where they had been or what they had done the night before (Wechsler *et al.*, 2002).

People who are exposed to binge drinkers experience negative consequences as well—study or sleep interruptions, having to "babysit" a drunken peer, being insulted (Wechsler *et al.*, 2002). At a community level, binge drinking rates among this age group are associated with the rates of automobile accidents, deaths in automobile accidents, drownings, falls, suicides, and homicides. This association has been found not only in Canada and the United States, but in numerous other countries as well (Jernigan, 2001). Thus, a wide range of preventative and retroactive social control measures have been implemented on campuses throughout North America to curb the problematic consequences of binge drinking.

The majority of students in the Harvard College Alcohol Study report that they have been exposed to the following preventative controls: being informed of the university's alcohol rules and penalties for violating those rules, being targeted by educational campaigns about the dangers of consuming too much alcohol, and being informed of where they can seek help for alcohol problems (Wechsler *et al.*, 2002). For students who have violated university alcohol policies or who have been otherwise identified as problem drinkers, a wide range of retroactive controls are utilized—written reprimands, fines, mandatory attendance at alcohol education programs, community service, and referral to alcohol treatment programs (Wechsler *et al.*, 2002).

Preventative and retroactive social controls that target the individual and attempt to motivate them to refrain from problematic drinking are the most common social controls found at universities. In other words, the most prevalent university controls are efforts at stimulating self-control or self-regulation. However, the effectiveness of these efforts is questionable, as illustrated by the fact that despite increasing control efforts, the prevalence of binge drinking has remained unchanged for at least the last 15 years. And although there are more abstainers than in the past, there are also more "frequent" binge drinkers.

Brower (2002) proposes that the shortcoming of many traditional social control efforts is that they mirror approaches for controlling alcohol abuse in society at large, which is based on the presumption that university binge drinking is the same as any other type of "problem drinking." However, the fact that binge drinking usually stops following graduation suggests that it is a product of the university environment rather than being associated with alcoholism or other types of "problem drinking." Treating alcoholism (or other types of problem drinking) effectively typically means using individual treatments that are based on complete abstinence from alcohol. But if binge drinking is a product of the university environment, then control efforts must modify the role that alcohol plays in that environment.

"Most school responses to student binge drinking have involved alcohol-demand reduction strategies. These are educational and motivational programs aimed at reducing students' alcohol consumption. However, we know of no published evidence that educational and motivational efforts have decreased student drinking levels, binge drinking, alcohol-related problems, or secondhand effects of alcohol use. . . ." (Wechsler *et al.*, 2004, p. 159)

A growing body of evidence from countries around the world suggests that the only effective means of control may be changes to regulatory environments, i.e., changes in the university environment and the larger societal environment. At a societal level, a considerable amount of research, including research done by the World Health Organization, has found that the harmful consequences associated with binge drinking are significantly lower in communities that have higher alcohol taxes, a higher minimum drinking age, and stricter legislation or policies regarding accessibility, availability, and driving while intoxicated (Wechsler & Nelson, 2008; Jernigan, 2001).

In the university environment, there is a **prevention paradox** (Weitzman & Nelson, 2004); the growing efforts to help "problem" drinkers on campus have not reduced the extent of harm caused by alcohol consumption, because, in fact, most of the harm comes from the larger number of low- to moderate-risk drinkers rather than the smaller number of high-risk drinkers (Weitzman & Nelson, 2004).

Thus, a *population prevention* approach has been found to be most effective in reducing harm (Wechsler & Nelson, 2008). This type of approach targets the university environment as a whole, rather than trying to change the behaviour of particular individuals. It includes regulating the prices of alcohol in university venues (e.g., policies governing drink specials, promotions, and alcohol advertising on campus), mandatory responsible beverage service (e.g., policies requiring employees at university venues to refuse further service to intoxicated people), limitations on the number of campus outlets that sell alcohol, and policies governing the overall accessibility and availability of alcohol (Weitzman & Nelson, 2004).

However, it is also the case that taking extreme measures in which students are not consulted (e.g., "dry" campuses) is ineffective as well, because "students—like most of us—will react defensively and angrily to actions taken 'against' them" (Keeling, 2002, para. 29). What controls *do* students approve of? Wechsler and colleagues (2002) found that students approve of the following measures: making the rules clear, providing more alcohol-free recreational and cultural activities, offering more alcohol-free residences, prohibiting kegs on campus, and banning alcohol advertising on campus.

Binge drinking among university students, teenage alcohol use, drug use, and teen smoking are harmful to the individual consuming those substances, but are also perceived as dangerous to society. Youth who engage in these behaviours are therefore seen as both "troubled" and "troubling." Young offenders, youth gang members, and young people who engage in substance use are just some of those youth who are considered deviant in our society and made subject to various measures of social control. However, other youth are also considered "troubled" and/or "troubling," such as street kids, runaways, and those who

Ask Yourself

What is your university doing to curb binge drinking? Your Student Resource Centre may have information on the various aspects of your university's social control efforts—education programs, peer support, services for students with serious drinking problems, and university policies.

are prematurely sexually active. More recently, the concept of "at-risk youth" has emerged, which is able to encompass all of these groups of deviant youth—and even more.

TIME TO REVIEW

■ How have the patterns of youth tobacco use changed since 1970, and in what ways is youth smoking formally and informally controlled?

■ What are the patterns of marijuana use and other illicit drug use among youth, and what problems do regular users of drugs experience?

■ Why do youth use drugs, and what factors determine whether drug use becomes problematic?

■ What are the patterns of alcohol use among adolescents, and why has the commercial industry been criticized?

■ What proportion of university students engage in binge drinking, and how does this proportion vary over time and across different groups of students? What are the consequences of binge drinking?

■ How is binge drinking among university students most commonly controlled, and why have these controls been criticized? What are the implications of the "prevention paradox" for effectively controlling the harm caused by alcohol use?

Youth "At Risk"

The concept of "**at-risk youth**" has come to permeate many sectors, including health, social services, education, policing, and even industry (Bessant, 2001; Ericson & Haggerty, 2001). This concept emerges from the broader notion of a **risk society**, which Beck (1992, 1999) suggests has emerged over the last several decades—a society in which knowledge experts warn us that risks are everywhere around us. It is the job of professionals to then identify those populations that are "at risk" of various negative outcomes, and implement programming that will manage those risks. The precise nature of those risks and their potential negative consequences depend on the particular social group in question. For youth, the risks and consequences are seen as many: "It has become part of the contemporary common sense that leaving school 'early,' living in certain family arrangements and having a particular socio-economic or ethnic background put a young person 'at risk' of various other social ills like unemployment, crime, suicide, homelessness, substance abuse and pregnancy" (Bessant, 2001, p. 31).

Particular groups of youth are labelled "at risk" because of numerous personal, family, community, and educational factors, similar to those we addressed in looking at youth crime, gang involvement, and substance use. Those particular outcomes are just some of the possible consequences when risks remain unmanaged; thus, "at-risk youth" has become a label that replaces "troubling," "troubled," "delinquent," and "maladjusted." It is an encompassing category into which those youth who are threats to the social order or threats to themselves can be placed and then subsequently controlled through the **science of risk** (Bessant, 2001; Ericson & Haggerty, 2001).

The science of risk, constructed by those experts and professionals who are presumed to have the necessary knowledge in that area, enables management of young criminals, gang members, substance users, street kids, teenagers who are prematurely sexually active, runaways, and even those youth whom the science of risk identifies as having a higher probability of any of those outcomes *in the future*.

Via the social typing process, "at-risk" youth are identified in schools, community agencies, or by the police, and they are then subjected to particular risk management strategies. For example, schools in "high-risk" neighbourhoods may have their own police officers to provide drug education, interact with students to create more favourable perceptions of the police, help resolve conflicts so that they do not escalate, and liaise with other individuals or agencies that can help individual youth whom the police have identified as facing more "risks" than others (Ericson & Haggerty, 2001). High-risk youth will find themselves on the receiving end of an array of risk management strategies. They may be entered into special educational programs in their school to increase their commitment to education and grades, they may be provided with necessary types of counselling or personal programs (e.g., anger management), or their families may be provided with needed resources or counselling.

In practice, professionals in the numerous sectors permeated by the science of risk frequently implement risk management strategies with *all* youth, rather than distinguishing between those who are and are not "at risk"; the implication is that all youth are "at risk" (Bessant, 2001; Ericson & Haggerty, 2001). Bessant (2001) suggests that although the label "at risk" has replaced older categories of troubled and troubling youth, ". . . the youth-at-risk categories are different from the older categories in terms of their capacity to incorporate the entire population of young people" (p. 32). All youth are perceived as being potential threats to the social order, or threats to themselves and their own futures. The very nature of youth itself is seen as being deviant and in need of social control. "The wider culture constitutes youth as a symbolic threat. Disorderly youth are an expression of 'respectable fears' . . . about disorder and decline in general" (Ericson & Haggerty, 2001, p. 107).

Aren't All Youth Deviant?

"It was about the fourth time my daughter Katie had made cookies on her own. She was 12, which is precariously close to 13, which in humans is not an age but a serious mental disorder." (Beck, 2001, p. 69)

The above statement, although intended to be humorous, reflects the perception that youth are problematic—not just *some* youth, but *all* youth. The popular image of the teenager is imbued with both "troubled" and "troubling" facets. Most of us have heard (or even participated in) conversations about the problems of adolescents. Themes in these conversations typically include phrases like the following: "They have no respect for authority anymore!" "Back in my day, things were different!" These kinds of laments portray adolescents as a very distinct and separate group, a group that is at the very least an annoyance, and that may even pose a danger to themselves, to society, and to the future of civilization. As the title of Patricia Hersch's (1998) book suggests, they are "a tribe apart."

As we look around, it does appear that teenagers might be "a tribe apart." We often see a separation of the world of adults and the world of adolescents, suggesting that there may be a separate youth subculture, one that many members of the adult world perceive as breaking all of the rules—a subculture that is deviant and in need of intense control. We see youths congregating in groups that are all roughly the same age; 12- and 13-year-olds are usually with others of the same age, not with 20-year-olds and not with 9-year-olds.

We see teenagers attending concerts that few adults are attending (e.g., Rihanna) and listening to music their parents often describe as "noise." In the family room, those watching certain television shows (e.g., *The Hills, Gossip Girl*) are predominantly junior-high and high-school students. Particular sub-groups of teenagers are often seen wearing similar clothes, a teenage "uniform" that will most certainly be different at the time you are reading this than at the time it was written. If we go into a shopping mall—*the* hangout for contemporary adolescents—teenagers are shopping at particular clothing stores that carry the "uniform" and that have certain types of music playing in the background. In these stores, parents and their teenage children can be heard arguing over the clothes being too revealing, too expensive, or too sloppy. Continuing a journey through the mall, if we enter a bookstore we can see that family conflicts are becoming too much for some parents, who are in the "Parenting" section of the bookstore perusing titles like *How to Talk so Your Teen Will Listen*, or *How to Survive Your Child's Adolescence*.

The problematic nature of adolescence began receiving widespread public attention not long after the "teenager" was labelled in the 1950s. At that time, articles about how to parent teenagers could be found in women's magazines such as *Ladies' Home Journal* and *Good Housekeeping*, and parenting manuals were written that focused specifically on teenagers. However, since the 1950s the problem of teenagers has been seen not only as a problem for the parents raising them, but also a problem for society as a whole. That is, those problems that result in conflicts between parents and teenage children in individual families are perceived as indicative of problems between the adult and adolescent generations in the broader society.

A euphemism that many of us are familiar with—**the generation gap**—captures this perception. Why does a generation gap exist between adults and teenagers? According to this widespread perception, the generation gap is certainly not because of the adults. It is because of the teenagers—they are the problem that needs to be controlled. Adolescence itself has come to be defined as a time in the life cycle that is inherently deviant. We can see this perception reflected in the media; for instance, in an article titled "Your Teenager: An Owner's Manual (For the Bewildered Parent)," a popular Canadian women's magazine refers to adolescence as a time that is characterized by four "technical glitches" (*Canadian Living*, August 2006, p. 162), implying that there is something inherently wrong with teenagers. Several large-scale surveys of adults also reveal that teenagers are stereotypically perceived as embodying a range of negative characteristics; they are seen as sexually active, substance using, materialistic, emotional, awkward, anxious, confused, easily influenced by friends, rebellious, rude, and difficult to get along with (Buchanan, cited in Arnett, 1999; Buchanan & Holmbeck, 1998). Because perceptions of adolescents are based on these types of characteristics, considerable social control or regulation is seen as necessary.

We can see the formal regulation of adolescents in debates over the value of school uniforms in high schools, community curfews for those under the age of 18, special laws for teenagers (e.g., in Canada, the Youth Criminal Justice Act), special risk management programs in many junior high and high schools, and more. In all of these instances, the intent is to regulate, monitor, and control what is perceived as the inherently problematic nature of adolescence. We can see informal regulation in the changed approaches to parenting once adolescence arrives, the greater monitoring of teenagers in retail stores, the desire to sit as far away from a group of teenagers on the subway as possible, and the informal conversations we hear about "those kids today." Such forms of formal and informal social control are intended to manage the deviant nature of adolescence and the subsequent "generation gap."

The Generation Gap: The Past

The perception of youth as a problem in need of control is nothing new, extending back thousands of years. Socrates complained that youth "contradict their parents" and "tyrannize their teachers" (cited in Arnett, 1999, p. 317). Aristotle (384–322 B.C.) described youth as having an absence of self-control (especially sexual self-control), being prone to angry emotional outbursts, spending too much time with friends, and thinking they know everything (*Rhetoric, Book II*). At the turn of the twentieth century, psychologist G. Stanley Hall (1904) spoke of the **sturm und drang** (storm and stress) of adolescence, suggesting that individual development mirrors the evolution of the human species. According to Hall, the process of growing up is a transition from "beast-like" to "human-like," where the period of adolescence mirrors the evolutionary stage of primitive man. The problems of adolescence could not be avoided, but with the appropriate controls to deal with that stage of psychological development and to minimize the damage adolescents might do, adolescents would eventually "grow out of it" as they reached the civilized stage of adulthood.

The "original" teenagers of the 1950s (Doherty, 1988, p. 45) were born during and immediately after World War II. They differed from previous generations in terms of their sheer number, economic prosperity, and generational cohesion in that they had an "awareness of themselves as teenagers" (Doherty, 1988, p. 45). Society accorded them a particular social status—"teenager"—and this group became part of a recognized youth culture. There was some dismay at the arrival of the teenager and its associated youth culture, which "cultural guardians . . . likened to *barbaric hordes descending upon a city under siege* [italics added]" (Doherty, 1988, p. 51).

Research in the mid-twentieth century frequently concluded that teenagers were a distinct and oppositional subculture, and that the future of society was at risk. For example, research found that for teenage boys, being a star athlete was of ultimate importance, and for teenage girls, being popular was most important. These kinds of empirical results reinforced the perception that teenagers were as different from adults as possible, and that all adolescents were "troubling," a threat to the social order (Tanner, 1992). Other researchers (e.g., Berger, cited in Tanner, 1992), who suggested otherwise, were largely ignored in popular discourse. They claimed that the generations are far more similar than they are different, that most parents and their teenage children get along fairly well, and that there are many issues on which they agree. Berger suggested that it is parents who bring the emphasis on sports to their sons' lives, and the emphasis on popularity to their daughters' lives. Furthermore, interests in sports and peer acceptance are not limited just to the lives of teenagers, but pertain to adult lives as well (Tanner, 1992). Moving to present day, we can still see the reality of Berger's claims.

The Generation Gap: The Present

Why do children get involved in organized sports? They play sports because their parents get them involved, and this occurs at increasingly younger ages. How many 3- or 4-year-olds are actually the ones insisting to their parents that they want to play T-ball? Parents enrol these young children in sports because they are quite adorable to watch. Where do children learn that sports are important? Again, they learn this from the adults in their lives—parents, teachers, coaches, and the media. Children's sporting leagues have had to institute regulations governing parental behaviour, simply because of the preponderance of cursing at the officials, name calling of children on other teams, and even physical violence (including assault and even murder).

The extreme behaviour of parents at children's sporting events demonstrates to children from an early age how important sports are. The importance of sports is also emphasized by the fact that some of the most highly paid people in North America are professional athletes who make millions of dollars every single season. Entire channels are devoted to sports, as are entire sections in the daily newspaper. If sports are important to teenagers, it is only because their parents and other adults put so much stress on them. Berger (1963) made this basic claim 40 years ago, but in contemporary society this pattern is even more evident than it was then.

Why is popularity important to teenagers? Again, it is because adults have made it so. Parents, teachers, and other adults encourage children to "make friends," and express concern if their children have too few friends. At a very young age, how many of us have heard adults say, "You must share your toys *or the other kids won't like you*," or "You have to be nice, *or the other kids won't want to play with you anymore*"? The importance of having the other kids like you and want to play with you is made clear before a child even enters Grade 1.

Popularity is also important in the adult world, although we are unlikely to use the word "popularity" to describe it. The phrase "keeping up with the Joneses" refers to adults who want the same status of car, house, boat, or vacation as their neighbours or co-workers. An acquaintance of mine once told me of having to buy a new car upon starting a new job because hers was the only "clunker" in a parkade filled with brand new, expensive sedans. In my own neighbourhood, once two or three families had garages built, everyone else immediately began building garages as well (although oddly enough, few people seem to actually park their cars in them).

This begs the question of whether these examples are really any different than teenagers who want the same kind of clothes or shoes as their peers. Many of us have felt obligated to go along with a group of co-workers for drinks or coffee after work, even when we would rather have gone straight home. As adults, when we move to a new city or some traumatic life change occurs (e.g., divorce), the advice we are given is to join clubs or community organizations so we can make new friends—as if finding more friends is the solution to our problems. And recent research being widely reported in the media points out the link between physical health and the extent of one's social network; these popular magazine articles are telling us we have to "make friends" because our lives really do depend on it!

Adults and youth are more similar than early research claimed. Most teenagers conform to the larger society. Most get good grades in school. Most go on to post-secondary education. Most never get into trouble with the law, use drugs, or get pregnant (or get someone else pregnant). In fact, by taking a closer look at families, we see that parent–teen conflict is not as large a problem as popular images suggest. Disagreements are quite common, with 39% of teenagers saying they have disagreements with parents at least once per week (Bibby, 2009). However, conflicts are usually over smaller daily issues rather than large life-altering issues (Smetana, 1988). When conflicts do occur, they frequently relate to social life, peer group, social customs, and household responsibilities, rather than educational plans, career goals, or moral issues (Laursen, 1995).

A survey of teenagers in 2000 (Bibby, 2001) finds the single most common source of parent–teen conflict to be household tasks, but even then only slightly more than half of teens say they argue about this issue "fairly often" or "very often." Even though conflicts do increase during adolescence (Arnett, 1999), 67% of teenagers say family life is "very important" to them (the highest proportion in the more than 30 years that sociologist Reginald Bibby has been conducting regular surveys of Canadian adolescents), 80% say they get a "high level" of enjoyment from interactions with their mothers, and 89% say that their mothers have a high level of influence in their lives (82% say the same about their fathers) (Bibby, 2009). In the end, the vast majority of teenagers turn out all right. In fact, Bibby finds that in many ways, today's Canadian adolescents are doing better than ever.

Thus, some scholars say that the concept of the "generation gap" is an exaggeration, facilitated by stereotypes of teenagers, sensationalistic media portrayals that will attract an audience, and moral panics stimulated by interest groups who want to advance a political or economic agenda. Even research itself tends to focus on problems with teenagers rather than on the rather mundane everyday lives of mainstream teenagers. Although Bibby's research finds that contemporary teens are doing remarkably well compared to other cohorts over the last 30 years, concerns about adolescents are more prevalent than ever. For instance, Bibby says, "I've sometimes been appalled at the negative reaction of people involved in the drug field when I bring some good news about drug use being down—or the wincing of teachers when I suggest students are feeling more positive about school than they did in the past. I am treated like the bearer of bad news" (Bibby, 2009, pp. 67–68). Our cultural focus on problems leads us to lose sight of the fact that most families and most teenagers are doing just fine.

The Generation Gap: The Question of the Future

Although a considerable amount of research has claimed that the concept of the "generation gap" and the notion that adolescence is an inherently deviant time in the lifecycle are exaggerations, the teenage years are accompanied by increases in "storm and stress," such as conflicts with parents (Laursen, Coy, & Collins, 1998), extremes of emotion (Larson & Richards, 1994), and risk-taking behaviour (Arnett, 1992). Some social analysts are now expressing the concern that, given contemporary social patterns and family trends in particular, the possibility of a significant generation gap may arise in the near future.

Contemporary family life is frequently characterized by a culture of busy-ness, where scattered work, education, and extracurricular schedules of family members often mean that they spend little time with each other. Hersch (1998) says the following with regard to the lives of contemporary teenagers: "[They are] a vague mass of kids growing up in a world that rushes past them until one of them steps out of the shadows and demands attention by doing something extraordinarily wonderful or troublesome, outrageous or awful. The rest of the time, especially for the average, everyday kid who goes along not making any waves, the grown-up world doesn't pay much attention . . ." (p. 11).

It is in this aloneness that the potential for a new and significant generation gap emerges. In living, to some extent, separate lives, the possibility of similar values, similar interests, and an enjoyment of time spent together declines. Furthermore, considering the central roles that parenting factors (like the quality of parent–teen relationships) and community structures (that support and integrate youth) play in the emergence of youth crime, gang involvement, and substance use, adolescents' aloneness may set the stage for such "troubling" and "troubled" behaviours to emerge in the future.

"The new generation gap has nothing to do with social change, with intellectual questioning or opposition to causes. Instead it arises from a new social reality. Today's kids have an abundance of that 'space' that sixties kids coveted, enough to do their 'own thing' with great regularity. Their dramatic separation from the adult world is rarely considered a phenomenon in its own right, yet it may be the key to that life in the shadows. It creates a milieu for growing up that adults categorically cannot understand, because [it is] their absence that causes it." (Hersch, 1998, p. 23)

The exaggerated generation gap of the past may become a reality in the future, although Bibby's research suggests that this may not be the case. But even if a growing generation gap does emerge, will it be because of the inherently deviant and problematic nature of adolescence itself? It may be that just as in the past, today's teenagers are simply living the lives that adults are creating for them. Youth who end up being "troubled" or "troubling," and those who are identified as being "at risk," then require social control. But even more significant is that the perceived "deviant" nature of adolescence and youth culture may be reinforced by the resulting realities of their lives.

TIME TO REVIEW

■ What leads groups of youth to be considered "at risk," and how has the science of risk expanded in recent years?

■ What does the "generation gap" refer to, and what has traditionally been considered the cause of the generation gap?

■ How are teenagers perceived and socially controlled in society?

■ How were youth perceived in ancient Greece, at the turn of the twentieth century, and in the 1950s?

■ What led some mid-twentieth-century researchers to conclude that teenagers formed a distinct and oppositional subculture?

■ Why do some people claim that youth are *not* an oppositional subculture?

■ Why might a new and significant generation gap emerge in the future?

CHAPTER SUMMARY

■ Youth and deviance seem to go hand in hand in Canadian culture. Of particular concern are "troubling" youth, "troubled" youth, and "at-risk" youth; however, to some extent, all youth are perceived as deviant.

■ The "troubling" youth who receive the greatest attention are those involved in crime and those who are members of gangs. However, a gap exists between popular images of youth crime and gangs and their actual prevalence and nature. The media particularly contributes to a moral panic, from which various groups potentially benefit.

■ Concerns over those youth who *are* involved in crime and gangs have stimulated a wealth of research on the causes of youth crime. Research has highlighted the role of family factors in explaining youth crime and a complex set of individual, family, educational, and community factors in explaining the emergence of and involvement with gangs. The social control of gangs is intertwined with the control of youth crime more generally, which has shown considerable variation over the past century.

■ "Troubled" youth who are of particular concern in contemporary society are those who use various substances. Although almost all youth have used alcohol by the time they graduate from high school, fewer youth regularly use tobacco, marijuana, or other drugs. Over the past decade, binge drinking on university campuses has drawn widespread attention, resulting in a wide range of social control efforts. Questions about their effectiveness remain.

■ The concept of "at-risk youth" is a recent formulation that integrates various types of "troubling" and "troubled" youth. The science of risk attempts to identify those youth who are at greater risk of negative outcomes in their lives, and then target risk management efforts at those youth.

■ To some degree, *all* youth are perceived as being deviant and in need of social control. Adolescence is seen as an inherently deviant time in the life cycle, creating a "generation gap" between teenage and adult generations. Although the generation gap may be more of an exaggeration than a reality, some researchers suggest that current social patterns open the door for a real generation gap to emerge.

DEVIANCE IN PRINT

Bibby, R. W. (2009). *The Emerging Millenials: How Canada's Newest Generation is Responding to Change and Choice.* Lethbridge, AB: Project Canada Books.

Hersch, P. (1998). *A Tribe Apart: A Journey into the Heart of American Adolescence.* New York: Ballantine Books.

DEVIANCE AT THE MOVIES

Hughes, J. (Director). (1985). *The Breakfast Club.* United States: Universal City Studios. (97 minutes).

Included on many movie lists as the best teen movie of all time, it portrays five very different teenagers (e.g., the "jock," the "nerd") being held in school detention together. Their conversations address social differences, teen angst, and the complexity of their adolescent thoughts.

Ray, N. (Director). (1955). *Rebel Without a Cause.* United States: Warner Bros. (111 minutes).

James Dean portrays a "troubling" youth, newly arrived in the community. The movie's tagline says it all: "Teenage terror from today's headlines."

ENDNOTE

1 The notion of "troubling" and "troubled" youth is drawn from Tanner (2001).

KEY TERMS

troubling youth, **p. 139**
troubled youth, **p. 139**
youth, **p. 139**
moral panics, **p. 141**
parenting style, **p. 143**
ethnographic research, **p. 146**
material incentives, **p. 146**
recreation, **p. 146**
a place of refuge and
    camouflage, **p. 146**
physical protection, **p. 146**
a time to resist, **p. 147**
commitment to the community, **p. 147**

gang, **p. 145**
the "gang problem," **p. 149**
racialize, **p. 149**
parens patriae, **p. 152**
young offenders, **p. 152**
binge drinking, **p. 160**
prevention paradox, **p. 164**
at-risk youth, **p. 165**
risk society, **p. 165**
science of risk, **p. 166**
generation gap, **p. 167**
sturm und drang, **p. 168**

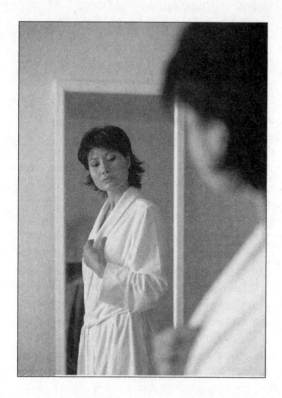

Looking Deviant: Physical Appearance

Learning Objectives

After reading this chapter, you should be able to

■ Explain the role of "body projects" in people's lives, and what the appearance of people's bodies tells us.

■ Describe the different kinds of information that are obtained about body modification when studied from various locations along the objective–subjective continuum.

■ Define the "ideal" body weight according to scientific standards and social standards, and describe how many people are "too fat" and "too thin" according to these standards.

■ Explain how people who are overweight are perceived and treated, and describe the range of social control measures targeted at "too fat."

- Explain how people who are underweight are perceived and treated, and describe the range of social control measures targeted at "too thin."
- Describe the various ways that the social typing of "too fat" and "too thin" as deviant characteristics is resisted.

"Talent counts thirty percent; appearance counts seventy." (Chinese proverb)[1]

If you had not been told where the above quotation was from, you might have thought it was a contemporary quotation. Indeed, we do live in a culture where physical appearance is important. Some people would say that looks are of the utmost importance. Think of your own physical appearance and how you maintain it. You have chosen a particular hairstyle and perhaps even hair colour. Every morning, you might blow dry, straighten, curl, gel, or spray your hair in order to achieve a specific look. Perhaps you put on makeup. Then you choose certain clothes, depending on what your plans are for the day. Are you going to work, school, a job interview, a date, dinner with your grandparents, a rave, or to write a final exam? For all but the last item on that list, you probably choose your clothes carefully. Maybe you have a tattoo, piercings, or some other type of body art. Perhaps you are dieting to lose weight, working out to become more sculpted, or taking supplements to increase muscle mass. As one of a select few, you may be gulping milkshakes in order to gain weight. You may even be contemplating plastic surgery to fix your nose, lift your eyes, suck the fat out of your love handles, or increase the size of your breasts. The time, effort, and money we spend on our physical appearance illustrate how important it is to us.

Our appearance is important to us in part because we wish to express ourselves and paint a picture of who we are. But our appearance is also important because we know people judge us by how we look. The way we look can affect whether we get hired for a job, what our grandparents think of us, who will and will not want to start a conversation with us, whether we are asked on a date by the person we are interested in, and whether people stare at us as we walk down the street.

Physical appearance is the stimulus for the social typing we do every day, and to which we are subject every day. But social typing based on physical appearance goes beyond our own individual likes and dislikes. Regardless of our own personal preferences for appearance, there are larger patterns of social typing that occur in our society. For instance, we all know that our chances of being hired are small if we appear at a job interview wearing sweatpants. Similarly, we know that someone wearing Dockers and a button-down shirt is far less likely to be stared at or teased than is a person dressed in a goth style—and yet, that person chooses to dress in a goth style anyway, despite (or perhaps because of) that social reaction.

Voluntary and Involuntary Physical Appearance

Some forms of physical appearance that are socially typed as deviant and subsequently made subject to measures of social control are voluntarily adopted— hairstyles, clothing, makeup, and body art. Precisely which forms of voluntary physical appearance are considered deviant depends on the sociohistorical context. Slicked-back hair, "dungarees" (jeans), and leather jackets were perceived so negatively in the 1950s that they were prohibited in many high schools. Men with long hair who wore beads were considered deviant in the 1960s and 1970s. Some store windows contained signs saying "No Hippies Allowed."

During most of the twentieth century, people with tattoos were viewed negatively, and were presumed to have other negative characteristics as well (Sanders, 1989). However, by the end of the twentieth century, tattoos and other forms of body art (e.g., body piercing) were less stigmatized, and in many other cultures, body art has been commonplace for centuries. Voluntary aspects of physical appearance that may be deviantized also include those associated with certain lifestyle groups, such as goths (Tait, 1999), ravers (Wilson, 2002; Weber, 1999), and punk rockers (Baron, 1989; Davies, 1996; Mattson, 2001). In these cases, appearance is only one aspect of an overall lifestyle based on political, philosophical, and/or social foundations.

Other forms of physical appearance are involuntary in nature, such as height, the size of one's nose or shape of one's eyes, or visible disabilities. Although individuals have little or no choice regarding these aspects of their physical appearance, they may be still stigmatized in our society—stared at, laughed at, teased, or excluded from opportunities, activities, and relationships (Westbrook, Legge, & Pennay, 1993; Gardner, 1991). In Nazi Germany, people with visible disabilities were even targets for genocidal efforts (Mostert, 2002).

However, the boundary between voluntary and involuntary forms of physical appearance is somewhat blurred. Some forms of physical appearance combine voluntary and involuntary aspects. A good example of this is body weight. People choose how much to eat and how much physical activity to participate in (voluntary); however, psychological factors, social factors, and biological factors may influence those outcomes (involuntary). Furthermore, what is considered to be "voluntary" or not varies across cultures and over time, and may even vary across subgroups within a single culture. For instance, in Canada today, members of particular ethnocultural or religious groups may adhere to dictates of clothing or hairstyle. In contemporary Canadian society, forms of body modification such as tattooing, piercing, and branding are voluntary; however, historically, slaves since at least the time of ancient Greece have been forcibly branded as a sign of ownership. Similarly, criminals were tattooed in many cultures around the world, as were concentration camp prisoners during the Nazi era.

Handwritten margin notes: "BODY PROJECTS", "camouflaging", "extending", "adapting", "redesigning", "(C.A.R.E.)"

Ask Yourself

We all engage in various types of body projects. What types of body projects do you engage in, and why? What makes your body projects similar to or different from those of people you see around you? What does your body say about you? What does it say about your social relationships? What does it say about Canadian society?

Shilling (1993) uses the term **body projects** to refer to the ways that each of us adapts, changes, or controls characteristics of our bodies, and whether those characteristics are voluntary or involuntary. If you have poor eyesight, you may get glasses; if you do not like the look of glasses, you might get contact lenses. If you think you are too short, you may wear shoes with higher heels; if you think you are too tall, you may slouch as you walk. If you consider yourself too fat, you may start working out or go on a diet; if you consider yourself too thin, you may begin taking supplements to build muscle mass.

There are four different categories of body projects. First are **camouflaging** projects—"normative . . . techniques of body manipulation, learned in socialization processes" (Atkinson, 2003a, p. 25). Examples include makeup, clothing, and hairstyle. Second are **extending** projects that attempt to overcome one's physical limitations, such as in the case of using contact lenses or a cane. Next are **adapting** projects, where "parts of the body are removed or repaired for a host of aesthetic . . . or medical . . . reasons" (p. 26). These include weight loss, muscle building, and laser hair removal. Finally, there are **redesigning** projects that "reconstruct the body in lasting ways" (p. 26), such as plastic surgery, tattoos, and body piercing. Various body projects may change the functioning of our bodies (e.g., contact lenses) or modify the appearance of our bodies (e.g., weight loss). This chapter emphasizes the latter, not only because physical appearance is important in our culture, but also because the appearance of people's bodies tells us something.

What is it that people's bodies tell us? The answer depends on one's location along the objective–subjective continuum. When looking at the issue from the more objective end of the continuum, bodies tell us about the characteristics of individuals involved in particular body projects, such as their age, sex, socioeconomic status, family structure and functioning, academic performance, personality, and psychopathology. Moving toward the more subjective end of the continuum, bodies tell us about the self, identity formation, and how people come to understand themselves and attribute meaning to their physical appearance. In other words, body projects "are integral in constructing and representing identity over the life course" (Lévi-Strauss, cited in Atkinson, 2002, p. 219).

From this more subjective vantage point, bodies also tell us about the characteristics of the broader society and culture. They are "text[s] upon which social reality is described" (Foucault, cited in Schildkrout, 2004, p. 319). For example, Lévi-Strauss explained the purpose of tattooing in the Maori culture of New Zealand as "not only to imprint a drawing onto the flesh but also to stamp onto the mind all the traditions and philosophy of the group" (1963, p. 257) (cited in Schildkrout, 2004, p. 321).

Among the endless variety of body projects that can affect physical appearance, two types are noteworthy. First, there are redesigning projects commonly known as body modification or body art—activities such as tattooing, piercing, branding, and scarification. These activities have become increasingly common over the past few decades, as well as increasingly accepted. They are an interesting illustration of how perceptions of what is deviant and normal change over time. Second, there are adapting projects related to body size or body weight. The social typing of body weight saturates all of us living in Canadian society today, permeating the fields of medicine, media, commercial industry, education, and even our daily interactions. Because the social typing of body size is so pervasive and affects so many lives, it is an interesting illustration of how the social construction of deviance and normality is an ongoing part of all of our lives.

With all forms of physical appearance that may be socially typed as deviant, it is not necessarily appearance itself that generates a negative reaction, but rather the meanings, stereotypes, and interpretations that are attached to that appearance. Physical appearance constitutes what Howard Becker (discussed in Chapter 3) called a **master status**, a category we immediately place people in upon first seeing them, which subsequently defines who the person is. The auxiliary traits we attach to master statuses are what make them significant. Thus, people with disabilities were systematically killed by the Nazis not simply because of their appearance, but because they were perceived as a drain on society. Similarly, people who are obese are not stigmatized because of their appearance per se, but because that appearance is presumed to be indicative of laziness, a lack of self-control, and psychological problems. Some forms of body modification are socially typed as deviant in part because they are perceived as being associated with other risk-taking behaviours and with a broader opposition to the social order.

Body Modification

The history of tattooing, piercing, branding, and scarification is a long one, perhaps as long as the history of humanity itself. Whether forms of body modification have been stigmatized or considered acceptable has varied across cultures and over time. Body modification has been "variously used to mark outlaw status and nobility, insiders and outsiders, soldiers and slaves" (Schildkrout, 2004, p. 325).The remains of a 5 000-year-old "Iceman" discovered in the Alps had several visible tattoos (Spindler, cited in Schildkrout, 2004), and throughout the world archaeologists have found evidence of tattooing and piercing on bodies and represented on artifacts (Schildkrout, 2004).

In the early Christian and medieval eras, some Europeans had tattoos representing their religious affiliations and dedication (Atkinson, 2003a; Schildkrout, 2004). The processes of European colonization brought such practices to broader public awareness. As European explorers found new lands and new peoples, and European governments colonized those lands, innumerable body modification practices were discovered (Atkinson, 2003a; Schildkrout, 2004). In diverse cultures, tattooing, branding, piercing, scarification, and implanting served as rites of passage, ritual initiations, or symbols of sexuality (Stirn, 2003).

However, European discourses that supported colonization emphasized the "civilized" and "evolved" nature of European societies in contrast to the "primitive" and "backward" nature of other cultures. From this perspective, body modification was equated with savagery, primitiveness, and heathenness (Atkinson, 2003a). Colonization also meant Christianization, and the Old Testament dictates that "Ye shall not make any cuttings in your flesh for the dead nor print any marks upon you" (Leviticus 19:28, cited in Cronin, 2001, p. 380). Although body modification was socially typed as deviant in Euro-dominant societies, the public's fascination with "primitive" cultures meant a growing interest in it, however. During the late eighteenth and early nineteenth centuries, people with extensive body modifications were featured in carnival side shows, partially nude and frequently dressed as savages (Atkinson, 2003a; Schildkrout, 2004).

Over time, body modification left the carnival community and entered society at large (Atkinson, 2003a). This transition is especially evident with changes in attitudes toward tattooing. By the 1950s, tattoos had become an established means of symbolizing masculinity and brotherhood in working-class communities and the military (Sanders, 1989). In the 1960s, criminal communities also increasingly adopted tattooing, with male convicts, motorcycle gangs, and street gangs using tattoos to indicate their memberships and allegiances. The countercultural era of the 1960s and 1970s brought the emergence of a number of youth subcultures, who used tattooing and other types of body modification as "collective representation" (Atkinson, 2003a, p. 41) of their subcultures and political/social ideologies.

Since that time, both tattooing and piercing have increasingly entered female and middle-class communities (DeMello, 2000). By 1997, body modification was in the top six fastest growing industries in the United States (Stirn, 2003). In the twenty-first century, body modification is pervasive within popular culture, from tattooed celebrities to television series (e.g., Inked). The commodification of body modification, particularly tattoos, becomes especially evident when one sees the range of tattoo-related products targeted at children, "such as Tattoo Barbie, The Sesame Street Talent Show: Tattoo Tales, Around the World in Tweety Time: Tattoo Storybook, and the Power Puff girls' Ruff n' Stuff Tattoo Book, that include tattooed figures, color-in tattoo kits, and temporary tattoos . . . " (Kosut, 2006).

In this marketplace, body modification has become more prevalent (Atkinson, 2003a; Burger & Finkel, 2002). Most research has focused on tattooing and piercing, and has found both to be particularly common among adolescents and young adults. Mayers and Chiffriller (2008) found that 22% of university undergraduates have tattoos, and 51% have piercings (other than earlobes). Among youth, females are more likely to have tattoos and piercings. In one sample of 12- to 18-year-olds in Quebec, 10% of females had tattoos (compared to 6% of males) and 44% had piercings (compared to 11% of males) (Deschesnes, Demers, & Finès, 2006). The increasing prevalence of body modification, especially among youth,

The practice of tattooing spans a wide range, from individuals who obtain one small tattoo to elite tattoo collectors who display "artwork" across their bodies.

has caused an upsurge in research on its participants. There is consensus that body modification conveys important information, but there are different points of view on precisely what that message is.

AN INTERNET MOMENT

You can find more information about different types of body modification at www.bodymod.org. The site contains articles and information about body modification, an online community for people with body modifications, and photos of the newest and most popular designs from mainstream tattoos and piercings to "hardcore" (e.g., surgical modification, implants, and suspension). There are explicit photographs of certain forms of body modification, so view this site at your own discretion.

What Do Modified Bodies Tell Us?

Characteristics of Body Modifiers: Risk and Motivation

As we move from one end of the objective–subjective continuum to the other, we learn that bodies with tattoos, piercings, and other forms of body modification can potentially provide us with a great deal of information. Beginning at the far objective end, we hold the individual under the microscope—tattooed and pierced bodies tell us about the characteristics of that individual. Research that emerges from this viewpoint focuses on two central issues: risk and motivation. Within this framework, the presence of tattoos and piercings (above all, among youth) is associated with a broader range of risk, such that youth who have forms of body modification are perceived as being "at risk" more generally. For instance, Roberts and Ryan (2002) suggest that youth with tattoos and piercings are more likely to come from single-parent homes, belong to the lowest income quartile, have parents with high-school diplomas or less, and have peers who use various substances. However, the prevalence of body modification in university and university populations (e.g., Armstrong, Roberts, Owen, & Koch, 2004) calls these conclusions into question.

Much of the risk-oriented research highlights psychological and behavioural risk, analyzing the association between body modification and other problematic characteristics such as risky sexual behaviour, substance use, violence, eating disorders, educational difficulties, and suicide (Hicinbothem, Gonsalves, & Lester, 2006; Carroll, Riffenburgh, Roberts, & Myhre, 2002; Burger & Finkel, 2002). Roberts and Ryan (2002) found that in comparisons of youth with and without tattoos, those who had modified their bodies were much more likely to smoke, be sexually active, have joined a gang, use marijuana, binge drink, have had a recent physical fight, and be failing in school.

However, research that explores the relationship between body modification and other types of risk is inconsistent. Frederick and Bradley (2000) compared people ages 16 to 30 with and without tattoos or piercings on several psychological measures such as depression, anxiety, vitality, psychopathy, and self-esteem. When comparing individuals with and without piercings, no significant differences emerged, although age of first piercing was associated with greater psychopathy (those who had obtained a piercing in early adolescence scored higher). When comparing individuals with and without tattoos, the only significant difference to emerge was that those with tattoos actually had higher self-esteem.

From this more objectivist vantage point, tattooed and pierced bodies tell us about the psychology and the behaviours of individuals who have them, although there is debate about precisely what characteristics such individuals have. The proposed association between body modification and other risks is directly linked to social control efforts. Many publications about youth and body modification are found in journals directed at pediatric professionals, and contain explicit directives for clinical practitioners to consider the presence of tattoos or piercings as an indicator of potential psychological and behavioural problems and to conduct assessments for other high-risk behaviours (e.g., Carroll, Riffenburgh, Roberts, & Myhre, 2002; Burger & Finkel, 2002).

Researchers with a more objectivist orientation also draw attention to the potential harms of body modification, although Mayers and Chiffriller (2008) found that only 19% of individuals in their sample who had piercings (and no individuals who had tattoos) experienced any medical complications. Numerous health risks are associated with tattooing and piercing, such as bacterial infections, hepatitis B and C, cracked teeth (related to facial piercings), and problems with X-rays (Burger & Finkel, 2002; Schnirring, 2003; Selekman, 2003). Given the potential risks of harm inherent in body modification, the question then becomes one of motivation or causation. Why would an individual engage in a behaviour that carries these risks?

For some people, aesthetic motivations predominate; they acquire tattoos or piercings in order to improve their appearance or because they think body modification is attractive to the opposite sex, referring to their modifications as beauty, fashion, or art (Deschesnes, Demers, & Finès, 2006; Wohlrab, Stahl, & Kappeler, 2006; Claes, Vandereycken, & Vertommen, 2005; Stirn, 2003).

Issues related to identity inspire others. One type of identity is social identity, the portion of the person's identity that is based on the groups to which the person belongs. Body modification may symbolize our affiliations with particular groups and thus contribute to the development of our social identities (Carroll & Anderson, 2002; Claes, Vandereycken, & Vertommen, 2005). Specific forms of body modification have been found to serve as indicators of group affiliation in prison, motorcycle, and street gangs (Atkinson, 2003a), among elite collectors of tattoos (Irwin, 2003), the straightedge youth subculture (Atkinson, 2003b), modern primitives (Atkinson, 2001), and cyberpunks (Millanvoye, 2001).

A second type of identity is individual in nature, and many studies of adolescents and young adults have found individual identity formation and development to be the primary motivation for body modification; that is, they wish to express themselves or feel unique (Wohlrab, Stahl, & Kappeler, 2006; Caliendo, Armstrong, & Roberts, 2005; Claes, Vandereycken, & Vertommen, 2005). Because identity formation is particularly important among youth, some researchers recommend that youth practitioners develop an understanding of the role body art plays in identity development (e.g., Armstrong, Roberts, Owen, & Koch, 2004), even though others advise pediatric practitioners to associate body modification with risk.

Individual and social identity are also explored as we begin to move toward the subjective end of the objective–subjective continuum. However, subjective researchers treat identity differently. In a more subjectively oriented analysis of body modification, bodies are not perceived as telling us about the characteristics of individuals who have tattoos and piercings, but rather telling us about the development of understanding and meaning, processes of social interaction, and structures of power. Subsequently, in contrast to the more objectively oriented analysis of identity as a "cause" of body modification, a more subjectively oriented analysis examines identity in terms of understanding the self. In this context, researchers investigate the role of body modification in understanding and developing meanings of the self in relation to others and within a broader societal and cultural framework.

The Self and Society: Understanding, Meaning, and Resistance

Body projects are "integral in constructing and representing identity over the life course" (Atkinson, 2002, p. 219). That is, the physical body reflects the individual's understandings of self and society. However, according to interpretive approaches, the self is not purely individual in nature, but emerges via processes of social interaction. As we interact with those with whom we are close (significant others) and with society in general (the generalized other), we try to see society from their points of view. Their points of view, and their views of us in particular, influence how we understand ourselves and our places in the world.

Thus, through our interactions with others we come to understand what role body modification will play in our lives. From a dramaturgical perspective, the decisions about whether to engage in body modification and the precise nature of any body art are all part of constructing our "front stage" selves and "back stage" selves (see Chapter 3). We decide on the image that we intentionally project to others and whether we want body art to be a part of that image. People with body art engage in impression management surrounding that art, deciding how large it will be, where it will be located, and to whom it will be displayed (Armstrong, Roberts, Owen, & Koch, 2004). Will the tattoos, piercings, or brandings be visible to the general public, co-workers, and parents on the front stage? Or will the modifications be visible only to intimate partners on the back stage? Will it be part of the costume on all front stages or only on certain ones (e.g., at a rock concert, but not at work)?

Interactions with family members and peers are particularly significant. In general, the disapproval of one's family and friends makes body modification less likely (Koch, Roberts, Cannon, Armstrong, & Owen, 2005), although interactions with different people play varied roles. Within families, interactions with parents have an influence on the individual's decisions about whether to obtain body art, its design, and its location (Atkinson, 2003a). If people perceive their parents as disapproving of body art, they may select a design their parents are less likely to disapprove of (e.g., a small tattoo of a flower) or a location that can be easily hidden from their parents (e.g., nipple or genital piercing). But at the same time, among adolescents body modification is often an expression of protest against parents and/or the parents' generation (Wohlrab, Stahl, & Kappeler, 2006).

However, having body art that they know their parents disapprove of or having to continually hide it from their parents can have an impact on people's perceptions of self (Atkinson, 2003a). Peers play somewhat different roles. Individuals are more likely to actively seek the opinions of their peers when deciding whether to engage in body modification. But once the decision to obtain some form of body art has been made, individuals intentionally seek out more interactions with peers that already have body art as well. Interviews reveal that these interactions make individuals feel better about their decisions and provide a validation of self (Atkinson, 2003a). The attitudes of co-workers or employers have much less of an effect on feelings about oneself; however, they play a considerable role in decisions regarding body art display and the distinction between front-stage and back-stage selves. For many people with body modifications, the workplace is a context within which body art is hidden from view, either because it is formally sanctioned or because people are concerned about threats to their professional image (Atkinson, 2003a).

Indeed, when an individual is on the front stage playing a professional role, the audience may react negatively to the presence of tattoos or piercings. For example, one study examined patients' perceptions of facial piercings in physicians (Newman, Wright, Wrenn, & Bernard, 2005). Approximately half of patients surveyed indicated that facial piercings are "inappropriate" for physicians, and more than half said it would personally bother them to have a physician with a facial piercing.

Patients who had engaged in body modification themselves had more positive attitudes, but even then, 33% considered a facial piercing to be inappropriate. Patients' attitudes are not solely based on physical appearance; they are also affected by meanings or auxiliary traits attached to that appearance. For example, survey participants perceived doctors with facial piercings as less competent and less trustworthy. Thus, although body art is central to self and "symbolically represent[s] and physically chronicle[s] changes in one's identity, relationships, thoughts, or emotions over time . . ." (Atkinson, 2001, p. 118), the expectations associated with one's professional role may place constraints on the nature and extent of self-expression. In the case of physicians, their desire for self-expression must be balanced with their obligation to make patients feel comfortable, to put them at ease, and to reduce their anxiety (Newman, Wright, Wrenn, & Bernard, 2005).

In addition to our professional or occupational roles, each of us holds numerous other roles as well. The nature of each different role we play influences people's perceptions of and reactions to any body art we may have. That is, people's attitudes toward body modification may vary depending on whether the modified body is that of a physician or rock star, university student or professor, financial advisor or landscaper, neighbourhood teenager or their children's babysitter. But at an even more fundamental level, whether one is male or female influences perceptions of body art.

Women and Tattoos. Tattooing has a long-standing association with male communities and masculinity. Even though there has been a significant increase in the prevalence of tattooing among females, females with tattoos remain stigmatized, being perceived as more promiscuous, less attractive, and heavier drinkers (Swami & Furnham, 2007). Hawkes, Senn, and Thorn (2004) presented Canadian undergraduate students with various written scenarios about a female university student. The scenarios varied in terms of the presence of a tattoo, its size, and its visibility. Researchers found that, overall, tattooed females were perceived more negatively than non-tattooed females. Females with large or highly visible tattoos were perceived more negatively than those with small or non-visible tattoos. It appears that tattoos continue to be perceived as violating some of the standards of feminine appearance.

Gender plays another part in the social interactions surrounding body modification as well, in terms of the gender of the observer. In the above study, men had more negative perceptions of tattooed females than women did. Furthermore, the gender of the observer interacts with whether he or she has a tattoo as well, as illustrated in Table 6.1.

Men with tattoos reacted negatively to females with large tattoos but not small ones, while women with tattoos were unlikely to react negatively to females with tattoos of any size. Men without tattoos reacted negatively to females with

Table 6.1   NEGATIVE REACTIONS TO WOMEN WITH TATTOOS, BY GENDER AND TATTOOING OF OBSERVER

		Types of Tattoos Observed on Women		
		Large Tattoos	Small Tattoos	Highly Visible Tattoos
Observers' reactions (if negative, indicated with x)	Men with Tattoos	X		X
	Women with Tattoos			X
	Men without Tattoos	X	X	X
	Women without Tattoos	X		X

Adapted from information in Hawkes, Senn, and Thorn (2004).

tattoos of any size, while women without tattoos reacted negatively to large tattoos. However, highly visible tattoos were perceived negatively by both men and women with and without tattoos (Hawkes, Senn, & Thorn, 2004). The reaction to women with tattoos is further complicated by gender role attitudes. That is, men and women who expressed lower levels of support for the women's movement had more negative attitudes toward females with tattoos of any type. Thus, reactions were determined by a multitude of interacting factors—gender of the observer, presence/absence of a tattoo in the observer, size of the target female's tattoo, visibility of the target female's tattoo, and gender role attitudes of the observer (Hawkes, Senn, & Thorn, 2004).

The fact that gender role attitudes influence people's perceptions of women with tattoos points to the importance of discourses of gender in the larger society, which affect people's attitudes toward others' body projects. But in addition to influencing attitudes toward the body projects of others, discourses of gender also play a significant part in people's own body projects and the relationship between those projects and the development of a gendered self. For instance, Atkinson (2002) has found that tattooing is utilized by women in the development of their gendered identities, which emerge from and have an impact on structures of power in society.

Some women use tattooing in the development of an established femininity, while others use it in the development of a resistant femininity. **Established femininity** embodies the dominant cultural constructions of what a female body should look like. Thus, some women interviewed by Atkinson used tattooing to enhance their femininity. Their thoughts about how men would perceive their bodies played a role in their initial decision to get a tattoo. One women said, "I think it looks sexy, and so do all my male friends" (p. 224). They spoke of their tattoos as making them more attractive to their boyfriends or to men in clubs, and perceived too many tattoos or too-large tattoos as unattractive and unfeminine.

Their choice of images reflected the desire to enhance their femininity—e.g., small flowers, celestial motifs, and insects such as ladybugs—as did their chosen tattoo locations, i.e., sexualized parts of the female body such as the back of the shoulder. Thus, just as with breast implants and extreme dieting, some women's use of tattooing reinforces traditional gender ideals where the female body is an object for men's desires (Bordo, cited in Atkinson, 2002).

Resistant femininity opposes dominant gender ideals, and thereby serves as a form of resistance to existing structures of power in society. For some women, tattooing is part of this resistance. They get tattoos precisely because of the association with male communities. These women select larger designs, more "masculine" images (e.g., daggers), and more visible locations to actively express the self and resistance to patriarchal power relations. One woman stated, "My temple [body] is worked with symbols that read—a strong and independent woman lives here . . . forever" (p. 228). For other women, their statement of resistance is private rather than public, a negotiation between established and resistant femininity. Their tattoos are a form of personal liberation from traditional discourses of gender, yet their concern about possible stigmatization leads them to get their tattoos in concealable locations.

But whether women's tattoos are an expression of negotiation, resistance, or conformity, they are telling us about discourses of gender and structures of power in society. We can learn more about the larger society by examining other groups of body modifiers as well, such as the straightedge subculture.

Straightedge Tattoos.   You were first introduced to the straightedge subculture in Chapter 3. Although it consists of various divergent subgroups, its core ideology is one of resistance to the perceived hedonism and self-indulgence of the modern world (Irwin, 1999; Wood, 1999, 2001). In response, straightedgers build lives around physical purity and control of one's body—no drinking or drugs, no casual sex, and for some, no caffeine, no prescription drugs, and no over-the-counter drugs.

However, their ideology is about more than just lifestyle and individual identity; it is about actively trying to change the society within which hedonism and self-indulgence have emerged. In addition to their punk-style clothing and hairstyles, tattoos are a reflection of their ideology (Atkinson, 2003b). The most common type of design is comprised of "symbols of lifestyle declaration" (p. 210), a clear signal of their group membership (e.g., "Straightedge," "sXe," and "XXX"). The next most common are "symbols of pacification" (p. 212), signifying having control of one's body (e.g., "poison-free," "100% pure"). Finally, there are "symbols of indictment" (p. 213), declarations of what is wrong with society (e.g., "nation of zombies"). Their tattoo designs spread specific messages; thus, though the design may vary, the process of tattooing is itself intertwined with straightedge ideology.

Because tattooing has been associated with various groups of rebels and protestors, tattooing is intentionally used by straightedgers to draw attention to their message. In addition, enduring the physical pain of tattooing demonstrates that they have control over their bodies rather than their bodies having control over them (Atkinson, 2003b). So not only are messages about the larger society (its hedonistic nature) and straightedge subculture (its ideology of purity and control) visible on straightedge bodies in a passive manner, straightedgers actively and intentionally use their bodies as a medium for conveying those messages and for living out their ideals.

Conclusion

Tattoos, piercings, and other forms of body modification convey many different messages to us, depending on the point along the objective–subjective continuum from which one is examining modified bodies. Body modification may tell us something about the individuals who have body art, such as their likelihood of substance use or violence, their desire to look attractive, or their need for self-expression. They may tell us about the role of body art in developing an understanding of the self and how interactions with various others have an influence. They may tell us something about the broader society, such as the expectations associated with different social roles, discourses of gender, the structure of power, and how body modification can be used as a form of resistance. Furthermore, they tell us something about the "dance" that surrounds what are considered "deviant" and "normal" bodies.

Whether or not we have body art, and the nature of any body art we do have, influences others' perceptions of and reactions to us. However, most of us still do not have tattoos, piercings, or other types of body modification. Although the proportion of the population with body modification is growing, these are simply not body projects that the majority of Canadians have undertaken. But in our society today there is one aspect of the social construction of deviant and normal physical appearance that is part of every one of our lives on a daily basis—body size or weight.

TIME TO REVIEW

- What are the differences between voluntary and involuntary physical appearance?
- What are the different types of body projects?
- In what way does one's location along the objective-subjective continuum determine one's perception of what people's bodies can tell us?
- How have body modification practices changed over time?
- Based on the more objective end of the continuum, what risks are associated with body modification, and what motivations are involved in modification practices?

- How can the dramaturgical perspective be applied to an understanding of body modification, and what role do social interactions play in the development of "front-stage" and "back-stage" selves?
- How are physicians with facial piercings and women with tattoos perceived?
- Considering both women and the straightedge subculture, what do tattoos tell us about the larger society, and how can tattoos be used as a form of resistance?

Weight: "Too Fat," "Too Thin," and "Ideal"

"You can never be too rich or too thin." (Wallis Simpson)[2]

The above phrase was uttered long ago. But in the twenty-first century, does that phrase still hold true? Is thinner better? Is it possible to be too thin? In any culture at any specific time in history, only a certain range of body sizes are perceived as normal, conforming, or ideal. A body outside of that ideal is considered unacceptable, deviant, and requiring modification—overweight or underweight or, using more popular terminology, "too fat" or "too thin."

Take a moment to look at the *Ask Yourself* exercise. Once you have done so, consider the image that first emerged in your mind. If the ideal body you initially pictured was a female body, you should not be surprised. Weight is more likely to be used as an evaluative criterion for women than men. For the latter, a wider range of body types are perceived as acceptable (Rabak-Wagener, Eickhoff-Shemek, & Kelly-Vance, 1998). But even though men tend to have more freedom in what is considered an acceptable body, at some point they are subject to the judgments of others based on their weight or the size of their bodies, just as women are. What is the ideal body according to our current cultural standards? To some extent, the answer to that question depends on whose criteria we are using—the criteria used by physicians in their evaluations of health, or the criteria used by average people in their judgments of people's physical appearance.

Ask Yourself

Take a moment to picture the ideal body. Notice the details. What does the ideal body look like? Is it a female body? If so, who does that body type most closely approximate—a runway model like Kate Moss, an actress like Halle Berry, a "plus-size" model like Emme, a competitive athlete like a member of the Canadian women's hockey team, or the average woman you see on the street? If it is a male body, who does that body most closely approximate—action hero Vin Diesel, a competitive bodybuilder, heartthrob Brad Pitt, a male figure skater, or the average man you see on the street?

The Ideal Body According to Science

In the field of medicine, acceptable and deviant body weights are determined on the basis of "risks" for negative health consequences. Relative risk can be measured in a number of ways, such as waist–hip ratio and simple height/weight tables. However, the most common measurement tool used by physicians and scientists today is the **Body-Mass Index (BMI)**. An individual's BMI is determined through a comparison of height and weight according to the following formula:

[weight in pounds/(height in inches × height in inches)]

× 703

The standards of the World Health Organization (2002a) categorize a BMI between 18.5 and 24.9 as "acceptable," because it is associated with the lowest health risks. A BMI between 25.0 and 29.9 is considered **overweight** due to increased risks of high cholesterol, type 2 diabetes, heart disease, high blood pressure, arthritis, and more. A BMI of 30.0 and higher is categorized as **obese**, with considerable risks for these illnesses. A BMI of 18.4 and lower is considered **underweight** due to greater risks of heart problems, lowered immunity, anemia, depression, and death.

According to these standards, being overweight is a significant problem throughout much of the world, and obesity is defined as an "epidemic" (World Health Organization, 2002a; International Obesity Task Force, 2003). Approximately 1.7 billion people in the world are overweight, and 300 million of those are obese. Two million people in the world die each year from complications arising from being overweight and/or sedentary (Obesity Association, 2003). In Canada, 35% of adults are overweight and another 24% are obese (Statistics Canada, 2006c). Even among children, obesity has been defined as a serious problem. In Canada, 18% of children are overweight, and another 8% are obese (Shields, 2005b). Throughout much of the world, children are developing diseases related to being overweight (e.g., type 2 diabetes, high cholesterol, cardiovascular disease), diseases that used to be limited to adults (World Health Organization, 2002a; Health Canada, 2002a; DeMont, 2002; International Obesity Task Force, 2003).

The number of people worldwide who are underweight is not as widely known. In Canada, only 1.7% of adults are considered underweight based on BMI standards (Statistics Canada, 2006c). However, the problem of being underweight is greater among adolescents, and may signal the presence of anorexia, which is considered a mental disorder by the American Psychiatric Association (1994). The diagnostic criteria for **anorexia nervosa** can be seen in Box 6.1.

International definitions go a step further than the DSM by pointing out that the weight loss must be self-induced through extreme calorie restrictions and/or intense exercise. International definitions also refer to **atypical anorexia**, in

---

Box 6.1 Diagnostic Criteria for Anorexia Nervosa

The *DSM-IV* (*Diagnostic & Statistical Manual*) defines anorexia nervosa in the following way:

- At least 15% below normal body weight
- Extreme fear of becoming fat
- For females, must have missed at least three consecutive periods

- Abnormal self-perception of body, consisting of at least one of the following:
  - Undue emphasis on weight or shape in self-evaluation
  - Denial of seriousness of weight loss
  - Distorted perception of body shape or weight

which many but not all of the above symptoms are present. For example, some females may have not yet missed any periods or their weight may not yet have fallen to 15% below normal body weight (Shuriquie, 1999).

Based on the DSM criteria, 5% of young women in Canada have anorexia (Canadian Paediatric Society, 1998), and another 10–20% have many of the symptoms (Marble, 1995). The majority of people with anorexia are female, although the incidence among males is increasing. It is estimated that approximately 10% of individuals with anorexia will die as a result of the physical complications that arise. Among males, **muscle dysmorphia** is more common than anorexia, and is sometimes called "bigorexia" (Leone, Sedory, & Gray, 2005, p. 352). This refers to a preoccupation with being too thin or small, and results in an obsession with weightlifting accompanied by anxiety/mood disorders, extreme body dissatisfaction, distorted eating attitudes, and anabolic steroid use.

The negative health and social consequences of anorexia, muscle dysmorphia, being overweight, or being obese have stimulated an abundance of research on how people come to have these experiences. Genetic, psychological, family, and larger sociocultural factors have all been areas of focus for those researchers who take a more objective approach to these conditions by searching for causes (e.g., Sandbek, 1993; Gordon, 2000; Caldwell, 2001; Levy, 2000). Research on being overweight consistently identifies consuming more calories than are being expended as the direct cause, but the factors underlying that cause are multifaceted—e.g., the inability to deal with negative emotions effectively, the way that unhealthy food saturates our culture, and the simple formation of bad habits.

Research on being underweight, and in particular anorexic, identifies four general categories of causal theories (McLorg & Taub, 1987). First are the **ego-psychological theories**, which emphasize impaired psychological functioning emerging from the child–mother relationship. Second are **family systems theories**. These theories suggest that anorexia is facilitated by emotionally enmeshed, rigid, overly controlling families. The third type of explanation is **endocrinological** in nature, exploring various hormonal defects. The last category of explanations is **sociocultural**, looking at social norms emphasizing thinness, media images, and social learning/modelling. The causes of muscle dysmorphia are just beginning to be explored. Some explanations emphasize psychological factors while others focus on media images (Leone, Sedory, & Gray, 2005).

The research on causation and prevalence that emerges from scientific definitions of the ideal body is positioned on the more objective end of the objective–subjective continuum. Deviance specialists working from the more subjective end shift their attention elsewhere—to social definitions of the ideal body, the social control of body weight, and the implications of those social messages. While scientific definitions are based on medical implications, social definitions have a very different foundation. Social judgments of body weight more typically emerge from tacit definitions of the ideal body rather than scientific definitions; that is, when we react to our own weight or the weight of people we see, health risks are rarely the stimulus for our responses.

Figure 6.1   THE "IDEAL" FEMALE BODY: CURRENT CULTURAL STANDARDS

Figure 6.2   THE "IDEAL" MALE BODY: CURRENT CULTURAL STANDARDS

The Ideal Body According to Social Standards

As we judge the physical appearance of others or as our own physical appearance is judged, medical standards such as BMI or DSM criteria rarely come into the picture. Instead, social standards determine the nature of the social typing process. These standards vary across cultures and over time, but at any given cultural moment we can identify what standards constitute the ideal body (see Figures 6.1 and 6.2).

Looking at our current cultural standards, you can see that only a small range of bodies is considered "ideal." Note that the ideal body leans toward the "thin" side of the continuum; our current cultural standards define a greater degree of "thinness" than "fatness" as being acceptable. You will also note that the ideal range is thinner for females than for males. While the ideal female is tall, very thin, and toned, the ideal male is medium-sized and muscular (Rabak-Wagener, Eickhoff-Shemek, & Kelly-Vance, 1998; Salusso-Deonier, Markee, & Pedersen, 1993).

A body outside of this ideal range is judged as in need of fixing—popular discourse labels it as either "too thin" or "too fat." At the extreme ends of the continuum are "anorexic" and "obese"; however, the popular usage of these terms does not necessarily correspond to the medical criteria for those conditions. This thin ideal for women and the muscular ideal for men are the ideals reflected in magazines, on television, and in movies. One study of male and female university students found strong support for the statements "adult models in advertisements have an ideal body size and shape," and women or men "would look more attractive if their body size or shape looked like most of the models in advertising." They consider that media images represent the ideal, even though they acknowledge that looking like those images would not necessarily be good for one's health (Rabak-Wagener, Eickhoff-Shemek, & Kelly-Vance, 1998). Even children consider the adult body images portrayed in the media as the desirable ideal. The Kaiser Family Foundation (1997) found that 70% of girls want to look like a female on television, even though 61% realize that women on television are much thinner than women in the "real world."

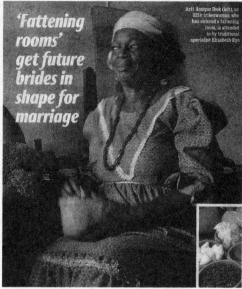

The "ideal" body weight according to current North American standards is very different than in many other parts of the world.

In other cultures, ideal body weight can be substantially different than our own. The slender ideal for women is characteristic of industrialized countries where food is plentiful. In contrast, in developing countries where food availability is less consistent, larger bodies are idealized. Once those cultures that have traditionally valued plumpness become more permeated with American media influences, the standards for the ideal body weight (especially for women) become considerably thinner (The Futurist, 2004; Shuriquie, 1999).

"Too Fat": Commercialization, Societal Reaction, and Social Control

Perceptions of People Who Are Overweight

Although approximately 60% of Canadian and American adults are either overweight or obese, people who are overweight face considerable stigmatization. They are stereotyped as emotionally and socially handicapped, lazy, sad, and lacking in self-control (Schwartz, Vartanian, Nosek, & Brownell, 2006; Roehling, 1999; Price et al., 1987). Approximately one quarter of schoolteachers say that "the worst thing that can happen to a person" is obesity, and a similar proportion of nurses say they are "repulsed" by obese people (Puhl & Brownell, 2001). Even health professionals who specialize in treating obesity stereotype obese individuals as lazy, unattractive, ugly, and bad (Puhl & Heuer, 2009).

Among the general population, 46% of adults say they would rather die one year earlier than be obese, and 30% would prefer divorce over obesity (Schwartz, Vartanian, Nosek, & Brownell, 2006). The stigma we attach to people who are overweight is overwhelmingly clear when looking at the perceptions of children. Children in Grades 3 and 4 say they would rather lose a parent, get cancer, or live through a nuclear war than be fat (National Eating Disorder Information Centre, 2003). Latner & Stunkard (2003) presented children in Grades 5 and 6 with photographs of various types of disabled children (on crutches, in a wheelchair, with an amputated hand, and with a facial disfigurement) and overweight children. The overweight children were rated as the least desirable as friends.

The negative way that "too fat" is perceived in our society is also widely evident with media portrayals of body weight. The average female fashion model is 20% thinner than is healthy, and is significantly thinner than 50 years ago (International Size Acceptance Association, 2003). Portrayals of women in all forms of media have become much thinner over the past several decades (Wiseman et al., 1992; Spitzer, Henderson, & Zivian, 1999; Owen & Laurel-Seller, 2000). Since the 1950s, *Playboy* centrefolds have become thinner (Owen & Laurel-Seller, 2000; Wiseman et al., 1992), such that they are at their lowest weight ever. Almost all centrefolds are underweight according to health standards, and approximately 30% meet the weight criteria for anorexia (Spitzer, Henderson, & Zivian, 1999). Miss America pageant winners have also become much thinner since the 1950s, with 17% currently meeting the weight criteria for anorexia (Spitzer, Henderson, & Zivian, 1999).

During this period of time, the gap between the body size of women in the media versus the average woman in society has grown and is continuing to grow (Spitzer, Henderson, & Zivian, 1999). An analysis of the 10 most popular television series during the 1999–2000 season found that 10% of female characters were overweight and 3% were obese (Greenberg, Eastin, Hofschire, Lachlan, & Brownell, 2003), compared to more than 25% of real-life American women who are overweight and 33% who are obese (Tjepkema, 2005). Approximately one third were underweight (Greenberg et al., 2003), compared to less than 5% of real women (Tjepkema, 2005). Among male characters, 17% were overweight and 7% obese (Greenberg et al., 2003), compared to 41% and 27% of real American men (Tjepkema, 2005) (see Figure 6.3). In fact, a recent analysis of children's television shows and characters on Discovery Kids, Nickelodeon, and The Disney Channel found that overweight characters are more likely to be portrayed in negative ways, such as lonely, lacking in friends, and unattractive (Robinson, Callister, & Jankoski, 2008).

The analysis of media portrayals of male bodies is complicated by the fact that the media focus on a combination of weight and muscularity. In various forms of media, images of men have become larger and more muscular since the 1950s (Wroblewska, 1997). Over the past two decades, male centrefolds in *Playgirl* magazine have actually increased in body size. Because of greater muscularity, no male centrefolds are underweight (Spitzer, Henderson, & Zivian,

Figure 6.3   BODY WEIGHT OF TV CHARACTERS COMPARED TO "REAL" PEOPLE (1999–2000)

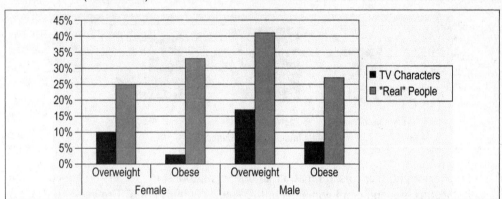

1999). An analysis of male images in *GQ*, *Rolling Stone*, and *Sports Illustrated* between 1967 and 1997 illustrates the emergence of the muscular ideal (Law & Labre, 2002). The proportion of "very muscular" images increased over that period of time from 9 to 35%, while the proportion of "not muscular" images declined from 42 to 16%. The proportion of "somewhat muscular" images remained relatively stable at 49% (see Figure 6.4).

The popular perceptions of people who are overweight and the media's portrayal of ideal body size constitute the evaluation component of the social typing process. Of course, this leads to our discussion of the third component of the process: prescription. Various social control measures, both informal and formal, are directed at people who are deemed to be "too fat."

Social Control

Negative perceptions of people who are overweight are accompanied by particular behaviours or forms of social control. Children and adolescents who are "too fat" most frequently experience direct and intentional teasing or name-calling by classmates. Less intentional negative comments by family members are also common (Neumark-Sztainer, Story, & Faibisch, 1998). In fact, Puhl and Brownell (2001) found that overweight youth receive less financial support for university from their parents than normal-weight youth do (controlling for grades and family income). Critical comments and name-calling have a significant impact on adolescents' own perceptions of weight and their feelings about their own bodies. Youth say that media messages, comments from peers, and comments from family members (respectively) have the greatest impact (Wertheim et al., 1997). In adulthood, teasing and name-calling may become less frequent, replaced by subtler messages from peers and strangers such as staring and whispering.

Behaviours extend beyond the casual comments of peers, family members, and even strangers. Research has consistently found that people who are

Figure 6.4   MALE IMAGES IN MAGAZINES, 1967 AND 1997

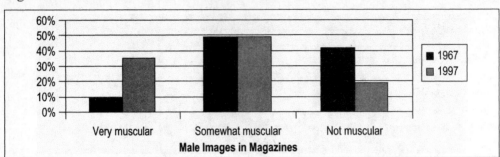

overweight face discrimination in the institutions of society—i.e., education, health care, and employment (Puhl & Heuer, 2009; Puhl & Brownell, 2001). For example, potential employees who are overweight are perceived more negatively than those who are former psychiatric patients or even ex-cons (Kennedy & Homant, 1984). In lab settings, several studies have asked participants to pretend to be employers making hiring decisions. They were provided with hypothetical resumés and photographs of job applicants. The results of these studies conclude that people who are overweight are significantly less likely to be hired for jobs, even given equivalent qualifications as normal-weight applicants. As a result of discrimination in hiring and promotion, wages are affected (Puhl & Heuer, 2009). Mildly obese women have an average wage that is 6% lower, and significantly obese women have an average wage 24% lower than that of normal-weight women (Roehling, 1999). The implications for men's wages are not as significant. Obesity lowers men's wages only at extreme levels; in fact, the average wage of mildly obese men is actually higher than that of normal-weight men.

A number of social control measures are directed specifically at trying to "fix" people who are "too fat." Some measures aim to reduce the health risks associated with the scientifically defined categories of overweight and obese, while others are based on reinforcing the overly thin social standards that define the ideal body. All of these control efforts ultimately are related to self-regulation; in the end, we are supposed to monitor and control our own body weight. However, the media, the commercial industry, medicine, government, and community programs all make efforts to "fix fatness."

Media.   Mass media permeates our lives. Not only does it contain images of the ideal body, it also tells us how to control our bodies. Magazines are one of the principal media sources of social control efforts. In any given month at a magazine stand, you can find at least one magazine cover that shares the secret of how to get a body just like that of a particular celebrity—see, for example, "Bikini Boot Camp: The Stars Share Their Secrets to Building the Perfect Beach Bod" (*Us Weekly*, June 21, 2006). There are entire magazines for both men and women devoted to creating the perfect body (e.g., *Shape*, *Men's Fitness*, *Fitness*). In women's magazines, morality is frequently linked to body weight, fitness, and food choices (Pongonis & Snyder, 1998). The "right" body, fitness level, and eating habits are represented as indicators of strong morality, while the "wrong" physical characteristics are indicative of a lack of morality in the individual. For example, ads for a certain type of low-fat breakfast bar have a photograph of a woman with a giant pastry around her waist or cinnamon buns protruding from her hips. The tag line reads, "Respect yourself in the morning," suggesting that only by eating this low-fat breakfast bar can a women respect herself—eating a pastry means a woman is undeserving of respect.

Exercise Your Mind

Take a trip to the nearest magazine stand and look at the covers of the women's and men's magazines. First, take note of the women and men featured on the covers and what they look like. Then look at the headlines for the main stories in each magazine. How many headlines regarding body size and shape do you see? What messages do these magazines give?

An important aspect of the media's control of body size lies in its integration of advertisements and commercials for weight-loss and fitness products. The commercialization of weight loss exists not only in the media, but outside of the media as well.

Commercialization. Commercial industry provides a massive range of products for controlling body size—books, videos and DVDs, packaged foods, weight-loss programs, gym memberships, fitness equipment, pills, powders, patches, and more. In the United States alone, it is estimated that between $40 billion and $100 billion are spent on the diet industry each year—"more than the combined value of the government's budget for health, education, and welfare" (Cummings, 2003, para. 4). Just as weight loss is highly commercialized, especially for females, so is muscle growth—especially for males. Gym memberships, protein shakes, anabolic steroids, and pills that purport to increase muscle mass are all aspects of controlling the muscular aspect of body size. It is in the best interests of commercial industry to attract as many consumers as possible; thus, the more of us who can be convinced that our bodies are lacking in some way, the more money the diet and fitness industry makes.

Medicalization. Despite the profit-driven motives of the diet and fitness industries, which may distort facts through their efforts to convince people they are overweight, there is no doubt that being overweight is a health risk. The World Health Organization and many national governments emphasize these health risks. Heart disease is the number one cause of death in adults in North erica, and being overweight is one of the central risk factors for heart disease. sequently, the medical community is heavily involved in the social control of ple who are "too fat." The most common forms of social control directed at weight patients by doctors are instructions to decrease calories (92%), suggestions to join a commercial weight-loss program (84%), referrals to a dietician or nutritionist (76%), and suggestions to engage in regular aerobic exercise (75%) (Price et al., 1987). Most of these forms of medicalization are based on the goal of reducing the health risks associated with being overweight.

However, the medical control of people who are "too fat" sometimes steps outside the realm of health and into the realm of physical appearance—in the past, for example, doctors told women who wanted to lose weight to take up smoking! From the 1950s through the 1970s, amphetamines were prescribed for weight loss. Beginning in the 1980s, other medications that decrease appetite were developed. In the 1990s, some of these medications were taken off the market due to health complications (and deaths), but were replaced by new drugs. A recent commercial for one of these weight-loss drugs lists its possible side effects as nausea, vomiting, headaches, and uncontrollable bowel movements. The complications from weight-loss surgery are even more frightening. Even the normal consequences of gastric bypass surgery sound unappealing, to say the least: only a few tablespoons of food can be eaten at one time: "one bite of the wrong thing or even a morsel too much of the right thing, can cause vomiting, explosive diarrhea, or a frightening attack of cramping and faintness known as dumping" (Dunleavey, 2001, p. 174). Liposuction, which is surgery that uses a vacuum-like instrument to suck fat cells out of specific parts of the body, has nothing to do with health and is based solely on physical appearance. In fact, medical criteria for the procedure say that liposuction should not be done on someone who is medically overweight.

Governments. The health risks associated with obesity and being overweight have a significant impact on the health of the world's population. By negatively impacting the health of large numbers of people, nations experience economic drains due to consequences like health care costs, absenteeism from work due to illness, and lost tax revenue. Katzmarzyk & Janssen (2004) calculated the annual costs of overweight and obese populations in Canada to be $4.3 billion, and the annual costs of physical inactivity (which is associated with being overweight, but which can occur in normal-weight individuals as well) to be $5.3 billion. As a result, several governments have recently initiated considerable efforts to reduce the proportion of overweight people in their countries.

In Canada, the federal government's Integrated Pan-Canadian Living Strategy has set 2015 as a target date for increasing by 20% the proportion of Canadians with a "normal" Body Mass Index, who engage in daily physical activity, and who make healthy food choices (Health Canada, 2005c). Some provinces have a mandatory amount of daily physical activity in schools, and parents can have tax deductions for their children's sports activities. But federal, provincial, and territorial governments are not the only bodies developing effective programs and policies for weight loss: so are individual communities.

Communities. Individual communities have developed a wide range of measures to reduce the proportion of people who are overweight. In the Aboriginal communities of the Interlake region of Manitoba, an integrated program run by the Anishinabe Mino-Ayaawin has been implemented. The Aboriginal people of these communities are at a much higher-than-average risk of weight-related health complications such as heart disease and diabetes. As a result, a comprehensive program was initiated to (a) educate children and adults in a variety of settings about nutrition and physical fitness, (b) provide healthy breakfast and lunch programs in schools, and (c) build new recreational facilities for people of all ages (DeMont, 2002).

Efforts to reduce the proportion of overweight children have also been integrated into a number of school programs elsewhere in Canada. For example, at Evangeline Middle School in New Minas, Nova Scotia, all children are required to play intramural sports; however, this school program goes one step further by having intramural games played during regular classroom hours rather than at lunchtime or after school. The gymnasium remains open every evening, every weekend, and throughout the summer for those students and parents who want to use the facilities (DeMont, 2002).

Informal interactions, community programs, government programs and policies, members of the medical community, commercial industry, and the media all interact to create a complex web of social control for body size and shape. Some of these control measures emerge from concerns over the health consequences of being overweight. However, the regulation of body size extends beyond health to concerns over physical appearance for those who are perceived as "too fat" (by others or by themselves), regardless of whether they are overweight.

AN INTERNET MOMENT

The website for Health Canada can be found at www.healthcanada.gc.ca. Along the left-hand side, select "Healthy Living." On this page you can choose to look at "Healthy Eating" and "Physical Activity." This will provide you with an overview of and links to several federal government programs designed to improve the health of Canadians who are overweight and/or physically inactive. Once you have looked at a number of these health-based social control measures, go to the internet search engine of your choice and search for "weight loss." This will bring up a number of weight-loss sites, some of which represent health-based social control measures and some of which represent appearance-based measures. Contrast the health-based and appearance-based control measures. What types of information do they provide? What types of images are contained on the sites? How hard is it to distinguish between those measures that focus on health and those that focus on appearance?

Consequences of Social Control

We are surrounded by a multitude of measures to control body size, with consequences for people's perceptions of their own bodies, psychological and physical health, and dieting patterns. Once again, we find that the media is particularly influential. Girls and women feel much worse about their own bodies, experience declines in their self-esteem, and show increases in depression and sadness after seeing images of models (Stice & Shaw, 1994; Crouch & Degelman, 1998), or even the female characters on the television show *Friends* (Want, Vilkers, & Amos, 2009). Recent research also finds that men experience greater body dissatisfaction and higher levels of depression after seeing magazine advertisements or television commercials featuring the images of the muscular-yet-lean male ideal (Baird & Grieve, 2006; Agliata & Tantleff-Dunn, 2004).

The official position of the Canadian Paediatric Society is that the media has an unhealthy influence on adolescents, providing them with "information [that is] dubious and unreliable, motivated less by scientific evidence than by fad trends and financial incentives. The net result is that many teenagers feel the cultural pressure to be thinner than is required for good health, and may try to achieve this goal through poor and sometimes dangerous nutritional choices" (2004, p. 287).

A significant proportion of people are currently dieting, in either healthy or unhealthy ways. The National Eating Disorder Information Centre in Toronto (2008) reports that at any given time, 70% of women and 35% of men are dieting. Furthermore, between 41% and 66% of adolescent girls and between 20% and 31% of adolescent boys have dieted at some point in their lives (Daee & Robinson *et al.*, cited in Canadian Paediatric Society, 2004, p. 487). Many of these children are not in need of losing weight for health reasons. One study found that more than one third of teenage girls with healthy body weights had dieted (Boutelle, Neumark-Sztainer, Story, & Resnick, 2002). Among adolescent boys, the use of steroids is increasing in their efforts to attain the ideal body— between 3% and 8% of high-school boys are using anabolic steroids (Bahrke, Yesalis, Kopstein, & Stephens, 2000). The long-term health consequences as these boys grow into adulthood remain to be seen.

The pressure placed on youth by the media is particularly intense, and influences body image and dieting practices (Wertheim et al., 1997). However, comments by or pressure from peers and family members have consequences as well. Overweight youth report that comments made by family members are hurtful (Neumark-Sztainer, Story, & Faibisch, 1998). Girls whose parents encourage them to lose weight are more dissatisfied with their bodies, more likely to want to lose weight, and more likely to be dieting (in healthy and unhealthy ways) (Thelen & Cormier, 1995).

Comments made by others trigger the adoption of a "fat" identity in individuals. Even people who may have been overweight since early childhood do not come to see themselves as "fat" until external cues give them that indication (Degher & Hughes, 2003). External cues may be of an active type (e.g., comments from others) or a passive type (e.g., seeing one's own reflection in a store window), but it is the active type of cues that have the greatest influence. Comments from others lead to the personal recognition that one does not have a "normal" body but a "fat" body. A deviant definition of the self is subsequently internalized, and a "fat" identity emerges. Being subjected to the social typing process by others thus leads people to socially type themselves, changing an individual's understanding of self.

The social controls placed on body size, especially the controls exerted by media, peers, and family members, have considerable influence on the way people feel about themselves, their self-esteem, and their self-regulation practices (like dieting or using anabolic steroids). However, over the past two decades, as public control measures for body size have burst onto the scene in a magnitude never before seen, the proportion of both adults and children who are overweight or obese has actually grown rather than declined.

"Too Fat": Resistance to Social Typing

The fact that being overweight has become so stigmatized in society and that the social definition of what constitutes "too fat" has reached absurd standards has done more than simply raise a few eyebrows. Many individuals and various organizations are taking active steps to curb this social typing process. A number of "fat acceptance" groups have formed in Canada, the United States, and Western Europe (e.g., the National Association to Advance Fat Acceptance). They provide information on current obesity research, facts about and dangers of weight-loss drugs and surgeries, and litigation updates. They also facilitate advocacy, by, for example, providing instructions on writing effective complaint letters and leading activism efforts. Other organizations have created beauty magazines, websites, and clothing lines for people who are overweight.

Although the media is one of the primary social control agents for "too fat" and the central reproducer of overly thin body images, at times it also integrates aspects of resistance to the social typing process. Some women's magazines have profiled women who have suffered weight-loss surgery disasters (Dunleavey, 2001), provided information on "wacky weight loss products" and their ineffectiveness (Seligson, 2001), and pointed out that women who lose weight are not necessarily happier (First for Women, 2001). However, these types of articles constitute the minority in women's magazines, and are contradicted by other elements in the magazines. For instance, on the very next page following an article pointing out that women who lose weight are not necessarily happier (First for Women, 2001), one magazine contains an advertisement for a weight-loss pill.

Fat acceptance organizations, websites, television personalities, and magazine articles are all participants in the resistance to social typing. The areas of emphasis for these resistance activities are twofold: first, to promote sound nutrition and physical fitness in pursuit of good health; and second, to remove the social stigma from people who are overweight, thus broadening the standards of physical attractiveness in our culture. Views of health and physical appearance are the two foundations (albeit sometimes contradictory ones) in the stigmatization and social control of "too fat," just as they are key elements in the resistance to these processes. Health and physical appearance are also foundations to discussions of the other deviant body size in our society—"too thin."

"Too Thin": Commercialization, Societal Reaction, and Social Control

Perceptions of People Who Are Underweight

The ideal body size in a particular society is one that is perceived as normal or conforming. In many Western industrialized societies today, widespread cultural perceptions support an extremely thin ideal. Consequently, considerable thinness is necessary before a "too thin" label is attached and the social typing process is triggered. This is especially the case when considering social definitions rather than scientific ones.

Based on scientific definitions, a relatively small proportion of the population is underweight—less than 2% of adults and a slightly higher percentage of adolescents (Statistics Canada, 2006c; National Eating Disorder Information Centre, 2008). Social definitions likely put those numbers even lower, considering the value placed on underweight females as images of beauty and the frequency of dieting among females who are at a healthy weight or even underweight. However, at some point a "too thin" label does emerge. McLorg and Taub (1987) found that among people belonging to an eating disorders support group, family members and friends did not perceive them as "too thin" or "anorexic" until they had reached the point of being emaciated. Prior to that point, family members and friends actually encouraged them in their pursuit of weight loss, and congratulated them on their successes. Once that label was finally attached, social control measures kicked in.

Social Control

Medicalization, Education, and Formal Intervention. "Too thin" is socially controlled at various formal levels. The medical community, frequently in conjunction with social agencies and programs, makes people who are at the most extreme end of thinness (anorexic) subject to social control efforts. When an individual is in immediate danger of sudden death, the medical community pursues intervention. The difficulty in preventing and treating anorexia and other eating disorders has resulted in a range of approaches that are employed at different points in the progression of this condition (British Columbia Eating Disorders Association, 2003; Lock, 2001; Matthews, 2001; Levenkron, 2000; Levine & Maine, 2005). A summary of the range of treatments can be found in Box 6.2.

Physicians, psychiatrists, psychologists, and nurses carry out some of the formal social control measures described in Box 6.2, while social agencies and programs carry out others. For example, at Eastwood Collegiate Institute in

Box 6.2 Preventing and Treating Anorexia

1. Prevention

You know the old saying: "An ounce of prevention is worth a pound of cure." Preventing eating disorders is emphasized by many different social organizations (British Columbia Eating Disorders Association, 2003; Costin, 1999; Levine & Maine, 2005). **Primary prevention** involves efforts to prevent eating disorders from occurring in the first place. It entails school and community programs that raise awareness of eating disorders and their associated dangers as well as the unrealistic body ideals portrayed in popular culture (British Columbia Eating Disorders Association, 2003; Matthews, 2001). However, primary prevention also must go much farther than this. At a societal level, the culture's obsession with thinness must be chipped away at, the gendered norms that constrain both men and women must be changed, and institutions (e.g., schools) must adopt processes that facilitate the development of self-esteem and efficacy in a wide range of areas (Levine & Maine, 2003; Lock, 2001; Levenkron, 2000). **Secondary prevention** involves identifying those young men and women who may be in the very early stages of an eating disorder. This kind of prevention entails educating parents, teachers, and coaches about the warning signs of eating disorders and effective means of intervention (e.g., National Eating Disorder Association, 2003).

2. Treatment

An extensive range of treatments is available, though which treatments are most effective depends entirely on the individual. People with eating disorders may choose from diverse forms of therapy and counselling—psychotherapy, group therapy, family counselling, and cognitive behavioural therapy (Lock, 2001; Levenkron, 2000; Costin, 1999; Levine & Maine, 2005 British Columbia Eating Disorders Association, 2003). For therapy to be effective, it must deal not only with the eating disorder itself, but also with the psychological, familial, and cultural factors that contributed to the eating disorder in the first place (Levine & Maine, 2005). There are medications that can help some individuals with eating disorders, such as anti-anxiety drugs or anti-depressants. Support groups are useful tools. The nature of support groups is quite varied, with some following a program pattern similar to Alcoholics Anonymous (e.g., Anorexia and Bulimics Anonymous). When severe health dangers are imminent, hospitalization or residential programs may be necessary so that medical monitoring and health supports are available around the clock (British Columbia Eating Disorders Association, 2003; Levine & Maine, 2005; Levenkron, 2000).

Kitchener, Ontario, guest speakers are brought into the school to talk to girls about eating disorders and body image. Eating disorder associations frequently sponsor group meetings and peer support for people who have eating disorders like anorexia. People who work with adolescents in a variety of arenas—schoolteachers, coaches, school counsellors, and youth care workers—are educated about the signs of anorexia and other eating disorders. Even governments are becoming involved in the control of extreme thinness; for example, politicians in Israel have proposed a ban on underweight models, acknowledging the influence fashion models have on female body images and dieting behaviours (MacKinnon, 2004).

Media.   The social control of "too thin" is evident in the media as well, although to nowhere near the extent of the social control of "too fat." For example, magazine cover stories often ask questions about the health of shrinking celebrities such as Nicole Ritchie, Keira Knightley, and Lindsay Lohan. Kim Kardashian's ample bottom, initially the subject of media jokes, is now described as a "sexy" alternative to the waif-like look of many other female celebrities. Extremely thin celebrities are now having negative labels attached to them—"Rwandan chic" (in reference to the appearance of people living through thefamine in the African country of Rwanda), and "lollipop heads" or "lollipop girls" (referring to stick-like bodies topped by comparatively large-looking heads).

Changing Ideals, Interactions with Family and Friends, and Informal Controls.
Although common media representations of thin ideal bodies influence the stigma and stereotyping of the overweight in society, there are indications that some people's perceptions of the ideal body may be changing. In a popular survey of adult men and women, participants were shown four different female body types: curvy and fit (e.g., an actress from Baywatch), a toned athlete (e.g., professional volleyball players), "skinny" (e.g., a runway model), and muscular (e.g., Ms. Fitness America). Participants were asked which of those body types they found the most and least attractive. The most attractive body type, according to more than half of the men and women, is curvy and fit, and the toned athlete was ranked second. The least attractive body type is the muscular woman, according to approximately half of female and male participants. The attractiveness of the "skinny" runway model was ranked between the toned athlete and the muscular woman, although more men than women considered that body type to be attractive (Fleming, 1999).

Although the "skinny" body type was not considered the most attractive in this survey, the fact that this body type was considered more attractive than the muscular body type illustrates that, to some degree, the value placed on a thin female body continues to be high. More recently, interviews with female aerobic exercisers and instructors similarly found the perceived ideal body type to be lean, toned, curvy—"like the supermodels in the Victoria's Secret catalogue—but not too muscular" (Greenleaf, McGreer, & Parham, 2006, p. 192). In fact, women who are hyper-muscular (i.e., competitive female bodybuilders) are perceived as having a variety of negative attributes when compared to the "average woman": having fewer feminine interests and a more masculine gender identity, less intelligent, less educated, less popular, less sexually attractive, less romantically attractive, and less likely to be a good mother (Forbes, Adams-Curtis, Holmgren, & White, 2004).

Because female bodybuilders oppose the socially ideal female body, and in what is perceived as a masculinized way, some researchers interpret these body projects as expressions of resistance against traditional norms of femininity (e.g., Shea, 2001)—just as with women who have larger and/or more masculine images in their tattoos. Regardless of whether muscular women are resisting traditional gender norms that oppress women, research on people's perceptions of female body types shows us that it is better for a woman to be extremely thin than to be extremely muscular.

When individuals are finally socially typed as "too thin," everyday interactions with family members and friends exert measures of control (McLorg & Taub, 1987). Individuals' eating habits are closely watched and then openly identified as the cause of everything bad that happens in their lives, such as falling grades and the loss of friendships. People with more moderate degrees of "too thin" may have food pushed on them, as family members and friends try to get them to eat more. Once others identify them as "anorexic," on the other hand, people may not offer them anything to eat or drink, even at social gatherings. Friends and family members withdraw from interactions with them, making them feel increasingly isolated and stigmatized. Even so, many people who have anorexia nevertheless feel that the stigma attached to their emaciated appearances and strange eating patterns is preferable to the stigma of being overweight. It is through these everyday social interactions, however, that people with anorexia eventually develop an "anorexic" identity. McLorg and Taub (1987) apply Lemert's labelling theory (discussed in Chapter 3) to this process. Identifying friends or family members as "anorexic" leads to the distinct types of treatment described above. People labelled in this way are isolated from "normal" relationships in their lives, and even say that others come to expect them to act anorexic. An "anorexic" identity forms and a lifestyle becomes entrenched—processes that are the hallmarks of the transition from primary to secondary deviance.

"Too Thin": Resistance to Social Typing

Although "too thin" is considered deviant and made subject to measures of social control largely because of severe and immediate health dangers, there is still resistance to this process of social typing. While resistance to the social typing of overweight people includes efforts to increase "fat acceptance" (change societal norms governing body ideals), measures that are intended to increase extreme thinness (and even anorexia) constitute the bulk of resistance to the social typing of "too thin."

The idea that you can never be too rich or too thin, for example, illustrates resistance to the idea that thinness is deviant and in need of social control. The extent to which weight-loss products and messages permeate our media and commercial industry reinforces this notion. The fact that magazine articles about the dangers of diet pills are frequently followed by advertisements for those very same diet pills maintains this idea as well. And although most of us would agree that the extreme thinness of anorexia is in need of both preventative and retroactive measures of control, resistance to the social typing and social control of anorexia is evident in some arenas, including the internet.

In the last few years, popular discourse has come to include "Ana." Dozens of websites are devoted to "Ana,"

Ask Yourself

How is the appearance of your body affected or socially controlled by other people in your life, groups you belong to, and cultural norms? What influence does the appearance of your body have on other people, groups you belong to, and the larger society?

which refers to anorexia. These websites do not provide help with and support for ending anorexia; rather, they help maintain anorexia. They include photographs of models and actresses as motivation for continuing the pursuit of weight loss. There are tips for losing weight faster, charts listing the calorie count of different foods and the calories burned by different activities, and advice for maintaining motivation. Additional advice tells people how to dress so that others will not detect their extreme weight loss and how to fool others into thinking they are eating normally. Avoiding a deviant label is important because detection results in social control measures, which interfere with weight loss. There even are tips on how to resist active control efforts, such as how to avoid weight gain while hospitalized for treatment. Chat rooms and discussion groups provide an arena for support in resisting the deviantization of anorexia. "Ana" websites themselves have now been identified as dangerous, and efforts are underway to control them. Several internet providers remove pro-anorexia sites once they are discovered.

Look in the mirror. Is your body "too fat," "too thin," or "just right"? The process of answering that question has our cultural standards of the ideal body as a foundation. The bodies we see in the media and elsewhere around us, as well as people's responses to those bodies, tell us what "too fat," "too thin," and "just right" entail. The medical community, commercial industry, social agencies and organizations, and the individual people we encounter in our lives let us know the status of our own bodies, and exert means of control if our bodies need to be "fixed" in some way. In the end, we are expected to self-regulate our bodies—i.e., realize when we are "too fat" and take steps to lose weight, or notice when we are "too thin" and take steps to gain weight.

Body weight is only one of many aspects of physical appearance that can potentially be socially typed as deviant and made subject to measures of social control. Additional aspects include tattoos, piercings, and other forms of body modification. The appearance of our bodies is an expression of other characteristics we may have (e.g., personality traits), our selves and identities, our culture's (or subculture's) norms and ideologies, and structures of power in society. Our bodies say a great deal—what does your body say?

TIME TO REVIEW

- How is the ideal body defined according to scientific standards and social standards? How prevalent are "deviant" bodies according to each of these standards?
- What are the causes of overweight/obesity, anorexia, and muscle dysmorphia?
- In what way are ideal male and female bodies reflected in the media, and how has that changed over time?
- How are overweight people perceived and how are they socially controlled by the media, commercial industry, medicine, government, and communities?
- How is "too thin" socially controlled at a formal level, by the media, and by family/friends?
- How are the social typing of "too fat" and "too thin" each resisted?

CHAPTER SUMMARY

■ Physical appearance is extremely important. All of us engage in body projects that change our bodies' functioning or appearance. Social scientists propose that the appearance of people's bodies can convey many important messages.

■ A growing proportion of people alter their appearance through body modification. Body modification may tell us about the characteristics of individuals, the processes involved in coming to understand the self, and the discourses and structures of power in the larger society.

■ Other body projects are based on body weight/size. Body size/weight is a nexus for social typing that occurs everywhere around us on a daily basis. The "ideal" body weight can be defined scientifically on the basis of health risks, or socially on the basis of social standards.

■ People who are considered "too fat" are perceived negatively in our society and subjected to a wide range of informal and formal social controls. Informal social interactions, discriminatory practices, the media, commercial products, medical services, government programs, and community services all target "too fat."

■ A label of "too thin" is usually not attached to people until they reach an extreme level of thinness. Once that label is attached, social control efforts are initiated through formal prevention and intervention measures, the media, and personal interactions.

■ Both the social typing of "too fat" and the social typing of "too thin" are resisted in numerous ways. The former is resisted through fat acceptance organizations and some elements of the media. The latter is resisted through the "Rwandan chic" that permeates Hollywood, which suggests that there is no such thing as "too thin." Pro-anorexia sites have even emerged on the internet, providing support for people to maintain anorexia and avoid detection by others.

DEVIANCE IN PRINT

Atkinson, M. (2003). Tattooed: The Sociogenesis of a Body Art. Toronto, ON: The University of Toronto Press.

Frost, L. (2001). Young Women and the Body: A Feminist Sociology. New York: Palgrave.

Pope, H., Phillips, K. A., & Olivardia, R. (2000). The Adonis Complex: The Secret Crisis of Male Body Obsession. New York: Free Press.

DEVIANCE AT THE MOVIES

Taplan, D. C. (Director), & Torrance, J. (Producer). (2002). Shredded. National Film Board of Canada. (22 minutes).

This documentary looks at teenage boys' quests to become extremely muscular, or "shredded."

Stiller, B. (Director & Writer), & Sather, D. (Writer). (2001). Zoolander. United States: Munich Film Partners. (89 minutes).

This is a humorous film about the male modelling industry and our culture's obsession with cultivating the right image.

ENDNOTES

1 Chinese proverb. (1996). The Columbia World of Quotations. Columbia University Press. Retrieved September 11, 2006, from **www.bartleby.com/cgi-bin/texis/webinator/sitesearch?query+counts**

2 Wallis Simpson. (n.d.) In J. Klauer. (2005). *How the Rich Get Thin*. New York: St. Martin's Press. Retrieved September 11, 2006, from **http://abcnews.go.com/GMA/Diet/story?id=1467247&page=1**

KEY TERMS

body projects, **p. 178**
camouflaging, **p. 178**
extending, **p. 178**
adapting, **p. 178**
redesigning, **p. 178**
master status, **p. 179**
established femininity, **p. 186**
resistant femininity, **p. 187**
Body Mass Index (BMI), **p. 189**
overweight, **p. 190**
obese, **p. 190**

underweight, **p. 190**
anorexia nervosa, **p. 190**
atypical anorexia, **p. 190**
muscle dysmorphia, **p. 191**
ego-psychological theories, **p. 191**
family systems theories, **p. 191**
endocrinological theories, **p. 191**
sociocultural theories, **p. 191**
primary prevention, **p. 203**
secondary prevention, **p. 203**

CHAPTER 7

Mental Disorders

Learning Objectives

After reading this chapter, you should be able to

- Describe the prevalence of mental disorders in Canada and worldwide, as well as patterns of mental disorders across various social groups.
- Describe the costs of mental illness for individuals, their families, and the larger society.
- Explain how mental disorders are subject to social control through (a) the stigmatization of mental illness, and (b) the medicalization of mental disorder.
- Describe the efforts to reduce the stigmatization of mental illness, and to improve the resources that are available to people with mental disorders.
- Explain why the diagnostic handbook used by mental health professionals is criticized.
- Describe Rosenhan's classic study on mental illness, and explain the consequences of his research.

"When terms like abnormal or mentally ill are spoken, what kinds of images come to mind? Usually, images of difference and alienation, suggesting that 'they' are not as competent, human, or safe to be around as the rest of 'us.' And often, 'abnormal' and 'mentally ill' are equated with 'crazy,' a label that calls forth images of someone who is out of control, out of touch with 'reality,' incapable of forming a good relationship, untrustworthy, quite possibly dangerous, and probably not worth one's attention, time, or energy." (Caplan, 1995, p. 11)

The concept of mental disorder consists of two different dimensions. First, it entails the experience of the disorder itself—the ways that the illness affects people's thoughts, feelings, or behaviours. But, as the above quotation illustrates, mental disorder also has a social dimension, i.e., the ways that others perceive and treat those with mental illnesses. Via both dimensions, mental disorder enters the realm of deviance. Research on mental disorder reflects both of these dimensions as well, and emerges from various points along the objective–subjective continuum. It includes research on the prevalence and patterns of mental disorder, the costs of inadequately treated mental illness, stigmatization, and medicalization. Contemporary sociological research on mental disorder tends to lean toward the more subjective end of the continuum, focusing on stigmatization, experiences of self, and the social construction of mental illness, with a strong interactionist theoretical foundation.

Mental disorder, by definition, is a psychological, biological, or behavioural dysfunction that interferes with daily life—"alterations in thinking, mood or behaviour . . . associated with significant distress and impaired functioning" (Health Canada, 2002b, p. 7), such as "impaired judgment, behaviour, capacity to recognize reality, or ability to meet the ordinary demands of life" (*Alberta Mental Health Act*, p. 7). The "bad day" (or "bad week") that all of us have at times is not sufficient to

Exercise Your Mind

You can find a copy of the revised edition of the *DSM-IV* (the *DSM-IV-TR*) in the DSM Library at www.psychiatryonline.com. Browse through the diagnostic categories to see what types of thoughts, moods, or behaviours are defined as constituting mental illness. Select three different diagnostic categories—a psychotic disorder, a mood disorder, and an anxiety disorder—and look at their descriptions and lists of symptoms. How do these three different disorders encapsulate the "distress" and "impaired functioning" that definitions of mental illness focus on? How do you think the daily lives of people with these symptoms would compare to your own daily life in terms of differences and similarities?

be considered mental illness; the distorted thoughts, moods, and behaviours must be of a magnitude and duration substantial enough to interfere with our daily functioning. The *Diagnostic and Statistical Manual of Mental Disorders (DSM)*, the diagnostic handbook created by the American Psychiatric Association, clearly outlines precisely what types of thoughts, moods, and behaviours constitute mental illness, and under what circumstances. Mental health professionals use the *DSM*'s checklist of symptoms to determine which (if any) mental disorder a given individual may have (e.g., schizophrenia; generalized anxiety disorder; gender identity dysphoria; major depressive disorder).

Who Has Mental Disorders?

"If you have a brain, you can have a mental illness." (Canadian Mental Health Association)[1]

Mental disorders can strike anyone, and affect the majority of Canadians either directly (through experiencing a mental disorder themselves) or indirectly (by having a friend, family member, or co-worker with a mental disorder). Health Canada (2002b) has found that approximately 20% of adult Canadians have a mental illness, and 80% of Canadians know someone with a mental illness.

Although most national data on mental illness is drawn from medical treatment records (e.g., hospitalization records), some smaller scale general population surveys have also addressed the topic of mental disorders, enabling researchers to identify the proportion of the population that has not sought professional assistance for their psychological problems. For example, one survey found that more than one third of Canadians say they have experienced depression or anxiety (Health Canada, 2002b).

Worldwide, the extent of the problem of mental illness is staggering. The World Health Organization (2001) has found that mental disorders affect 25% of the world's population at some point in their lives: at any given point in time, more than 450 million people are experiencing a mental disorder. The most common mental disorders—depressive disorders, anxiety disorders, and somatic complaints—strike 1 in 3 individuals. In 2001, more than 120 million people in the world suffered from depression, and 24 million were living with schizophrenia. In total, mental disorders constitute more than one third of all disabilities in the world (World Health Organization, 2001).

Although mental illness can strike anyone, some social groups are more susceptible than others. Early research done in the United States and Britain claimed that more women than men experienced mental disorders. However, later research found that the surveys underlying these conclusions were methodologically flawed. By focusing their questions on the types of psychological distress that are more common in women and excluding questions on the types of distress that are more common in men, these surveys overestimated women's mental health problems and underestimated men's (Simon, 2002). Today, researchers agree that the overall rates of mental disorder are virtually identical in men and women, but recognize that there are distinct differences in the patterns and types of mental illness (Simon, 2002; World Health Organization, 2001).

Antisocial personality disorder, substance abuse dependency disorders, and conduct disorders are much more common in men. For example, antisocial personality disorder is three times more common in men than in women (Simon, 2002; Health Canada, 2002b; World Health Organization, 2001). Those disorders that are classified as the "common mental disorders" (or CMDs)—depression and anxiety—are much more common in women (Piccinelli & Homen, 1997; Health Canada, 2002b). The reasons why women in countries throughout the world are more likely to experience depression and anxiety are largely sociocultural in nature. Although there are strong arguments for biological predeterminants of many, if not most, mental illnesses, including depression and anxiety, CMDs have been consistently linked to particular life stressors and negative life events—ones that on average, are more prevalent in women's lives than men's—low income or income inequality, low or subordinate social status, extensive responsibility for the daily care of others (spouses, children, elderly parents), and victimization by violence (World Health Organization, 2001; Roberts *et al.*, 1998; Patel *et al.*, 1999).

Although socioeconomic status interacts with gender, both women and men of low socioeconomic status have higher rates of most types of mental illness, and especially depression and anxiety (World Health Organization, 2001; Dohrenwend *et al.*, 1992; Miech *et al.*, 1999; Patel *et al.*, 1999; Williams & Takeuchi, 1992). A longstanding question about the relationship between socioeconomic status and mental illness has been about the direction of causation. The **social causation hypothesis** suggests that more life stresses and fewer resources characterize the lives of the lower class, contributing to the emergence of mental disorders.

This was, in fact, mentioned in Robert Merton's strain theory (discussed in Chapter 2). Although his theory and its later applications largely focus on crime, he did suggest that mental illness can emerge in response to the gap between institutionalized goals and the legitimate means for attaining those goals. The mode of adaptation that he labelled **retreatism**, wherein people give up on pursuing the goals as well as the legitimate means of attaining those goals, can include alcoholism, drug use, or mental illness. In contrast, the **social selection hypothesis** proposes the reverse—that people with mental disorders fall into lower economic strata because of their difficulties in daily functioning (Eaton, 2001).

Although some debate continues among mental health experts, recent research finds that the direction of causation depends on the specific mental disorder in question. Individuals with schizophrenia, conduct disorders, and attention deficit disorder are more likely to fall into the lower socioeconomic strata and are less likely to be able to rise out of the lower strata, supporting the social selection hypothesis. Conversely, social causation appears to underlie depression, anxiety, substance use disorders, and antisocial personality disorder. The life stresses associated with economic difficulties contribute to the emergence of these disorders (Kessler *et al.*, 1994; Dohrenwend *et al.*, 1992; Turner, Wheaton, & Lloyd, 1995).

Independent of socioeconomic status and gender, age is also correlated with mental illness. Mental illness is more prevalent among adolescents and young adults, and most mental disorders first emerge during this time in life (Health Canada, 2002b). Biological factors play a role in this pattern, as do psychological and social factors such as the struggles involved in identity formation during this time, the dramatic nature of the transitions that occur after graduating from high school, and the stresses associated with developing an "adult" role (e.g., deciding what type of education and career to pursue, becoming financially independent, and participating in the mate-selection process). The demands of university are particularly stressful, resulting in a higher prevalence of psychological distress among university students; for example, a survey of almost 8 000 Canadian university students recently found that more than 30% reported significant levels of psychological distress (Adlaf *et al.*, 2001).

Age, socioeconomic status, and gender are significant factors related to the prevalence and/or patterns of mental illness. But although certain types of mental illness are more prevalent in particular social groups, mental disorders can affect anyone. American research claims that half of the people in the United States will experience a psychological disorder at some point in their lives (Kessler *et al.*, 1994). The resulting costs of mental illness are substantial.

The Costs of Mental Illness

Mental disorders have a considerable impact on both people's lives and the larger society. Research that emerges from the more objective end of the objective–subjective continuum shows us that having a mental disorder can contribute to a wide range of negative life outcomes. For example, having a mental disorder is associated with higher rates of teen pregnancy and early marriage, and a greater risk of marital instability, all of which contribute to difficulties for the children being raised in those environments (Kessler, cited in Ettner, Frank, & Kessler, 1997). Children being raised by parents with mental illnesses are more likely to have problems in cognitive development as well (World Health Organization, 2001). Mental illness is also associated with lower levels of educational attainment, lower employment rates, and lower incomes. For example, each year, individuals with mental disorders earn thousands of dollars less than those without mental disorders (Ettner, Frank, & Kessler, 1997). Individuals with mental illnesses, along with their families, must bear direct and indirect financial costs (e.g., the costs of health care or the costs associated with unemployment) (World Health Organization, 2001).

Some mental illnesses are correlated with other physical ailments; for example, depression is related to a higher risk of heart disease. Furthermore, people with mental disorders are less likely to comply with medical instructions for other physical ailments, such as high blood pressure, diabetes, and cancer, resulting in poorer health overall and a greater likelihood of complications (World Health Organization, 2001). Finally, the emotional burden of living with a mental disorder creates a considerable challenge to all aspects of daily living and influences the quality of life overall.

Beyond the level of individuals and their families, insufficiently treated mental disorders also have a considerable impact on society. Five of the ten leading causes of disabilities in Canada are mental illnesses (Alberta Alliance on Mental Illness & Mental Health, 2003). Depression alone is the fourth leading global disease burden, and by 2020 it is projected to be the second leading global disease burden, behind only heart disease (Murray & Lopez, 1996; World Health Organization, 2001). Health care expenses, absences from work, and lost tax revenues due to mental illness cost the Canadian economy more than $14 billion each year (Stephans & Jorbert, 2001).

This substantial impact is not limited to Canada alone. The cost in the United States is $148 billion per year, 2.5% of their gross national product (World Health Organization, 2001). In Great Britain, it is estimated that 15 to 30% of illness-related absences from work are due to mental disorders (Lewis & Bebbington, 1998). Economies experience lost productivity due to the following: (a) premature deaths from suicide; (b) absenteeism from work due to illness; (c) inability to be employed; (d) decreased productivity while on the job during manifestations of the illness; and (e) family members' absence from work or withdrawal from the labour force in order to provide full-time care (World Health Organization, 2001; Lewis & Bebbington, 1998). Untreated mental disorders may also result in the costs associated with criminal and/or violent behaviour.

The magnitude of these various impacts means that effective treatment of mental illness would benefit the individuals who have mental illnesses, their families, and society as a whole. However, in North America, estimates are that only half, or even fewer, of those with mental disorders ever see health professionals (Sareen et al., 2005; Mosher, 2002; Health Canada, 2002b). Worldwide, two thirds of people who have mental disorders are never treated (World Health Organization, 2001), for a variety of reasons including the lack of services (e.g., long waiting times), perceptions of treatment being inadequate, discomfort with the level of self-disclosure that accompanies diagnosis and treatment, perceptions of stigmatization, or neglect within their own families and communities (Sareen et al., 2005; Mosher, 2002; World Health Organization, 2001).

Coming from a more subjectivist perspective, Wolff (2007) suggests that cost-of-illness estimates should be viewed with some level of caution. First, she points out that these estimates "are not just a product of biochemistry; biochemistry interacts with economics and social norms" (p. 73). For example, if drug costs were lower, then the costs of mental disorder would be lower as well. Second, she points out that these estimates fail to take into account the many ways that individuals with mental disorders contribute to society as parents, neighbours, and volunteers. That is, cost-of-illness estimates themselves are, in part, reflective of the negative attitudes that surround mental illness. Overall, she argues that cost-of-illness estimates only take on social meaning when we look at "the ways in which we collectively view and treat people with mental illness" (p. 75).

Controlling Mental Disorder: Perceptions, Stigmatization, and Treatment

The reactions of other people are an integral part of the experience of having a mental disorder. As we have already seen, one of the main reasons that people with mental disorders do not seek assistance from health professionals is because of the presumed reactions of other people, as well as the general stigma that is associated with mental illness in our society. The *stigmatization of mental illness* constitutes one of the major dimensions of social control; this will be the first aspect of social control that we will explore. The second major dimension of control, which we will explore later in the chapter, is embodied by the *medicalization of mental disorder*.

Stigmatization and Perceptions of Mental Illness

". . . [I]t's sort of like having 'crazy bitch' stamped across my forehead and everybody treats you differently . . . " (cited in Bassett, Lampe, & Lloyd, 1999)

More than 50 years ago, researchers were already identifying the prejudice and discrimination that people with mental disorders face (Scheff, 1966). Since that time, attitudes have not significantly improved, and some researchers suggest they have even worsened (Bourget & Chenier, 2007; Sayce, 2000). We have only to look at the media to see the way mental illness continues to be stigmatized. When mental illness is addressed in the media, it is portrayed in an exceedingly negative light and is typically associated with violent behaviour (Hannigan, 1999; Wahl, 1992; March, 1999). For example, one study found that 72% of those dramatic characters on prime time television who were portrayed as having a mental illness were associated with violence or evil (Signorielli, cited in March, 1999).

This type of media imagery has a notable impact on people's own perceptions of mental illness. Granello, Pauley, and Carmichael (cited in March, 1999) found that one-third of the undergraduate students they surveyed said the media is their primary source of information about mental illness and the number-one influence on their own attitudes toward people with mental disorders. Given the biased portrayals of mental illness in the media and their impact, it is not surprising that public attitudes toward mental illness are negative as well.

Studies conducted in countries around the world have consistently found extreme prejudice against people with mental disorders. This prejudice manifests itself in the forms of social rejection and discrimination (Sayce, 2000; Wahl, 1999; Read & Harre, 2001). A recent Health Canada (2002b) survey found that more than one-third of adult Canadians believe that others would think less of them if they had a mental disorder, such as depression or anxiety—and, unfortunately, they are right! People with mental disorders are perceived as being unpredictable, violent, dangerous, and uncontrollable (Dobson, 1996; Stip, Caron, & Lane, 2001). As a consequence of these stereotypes, more than two-thirds of people surveyed express reservations about dating someone with a mental disorder or even living next door to one (Read & Harre, 2001). In Great Britain, 34% of people with mental illnesses say they have been fired or forced to resign. Almost half have been abused or harassed by strangers in public, and 14% have been physically attacked (Dobson, 1996).

These attitudes are not limited to uneducated or uninformed laypersons, but are also found within the medical community itself (Lawrie *et al.*, 1998; Monahan, 1992). Approximately half of people with mental disorders say health professionals have treated them unfairly, particularly in dealing with the individual's physical complaints. When their own doctors fail to lend credence to their physical complaints—instead, blaming those symptoms on the mental disorder—actual physical illnesses remain untreated, only to worsen and potentially threaten patients' lives.

Mental illness can even be stigmatized by some mental health professionals who frequently admit that they try to avoid having to treat patients with more severe mental illnesses (Overton & Medina, 2008; Mental Health Commission of Canada, 2009; Read & Harre, 2001). Corrigan (cited in Overton & Medina, 2008) goes as far as to say that "most well-trained professionals subscribe to the same stereotypes about mental illness as the general public" (p. 146), and fall into an "us" versus "them" mindset that is conductive towards stigmatization (Martin and Johnston, 2007).

At a personal level, stigmatization has a negative impact on the quality of life of people with mental disorders. The sense of loneliness and isolation that accompanies social rejection can amplify psychological symptoms, actually making mental illnesses worse. Kroska and Harkness (2006) find that stigmatizing personal experiences are not even necessary for these types of negative consequences. Simply being aware of negative social perceptions of mental illness lowers self-esteem and increases feelings of demoralization among those with mental disorders. This can contribute to **self-stigma** and consequences similar to those described by labelling theory; individuals internalize the label of 'mentally ill' as well as its evaluative components (e.g., uncontrollable), becoming less likely to conform to treatment regimens or even to seek treatment. Whether through stigmatization by others or self-stigmatization, the effectiveness of treatments is hindered and recovery impeded (Overton & Medina, 2008; World Psychiatric Association, 2003; World Health Organization, 2002b).

These exceedingly negative perceptions of mental disorder contribute to discrimination in employment, health care, and housing (World Health

Organization, 2001; Overton & Medina, 2008; Sayce, 2000). For those individuals residing in psychiatric institutions, their experience in many countries includes poor living conditions, inadequate care, and harmful treatment. The stigmatization of mental illness in this way affects program and policy development as well; societies that are characterized by extremely negative attitudes of mental disorder also tend not to rate mental illness as a policy or programming priority (World Health Organization, 2001, 2002b; March, 1999). Unfortunately, this is characteristic of most countries in the world (World Health Organization, 2002b) (see Box 7.1).

Box 7.1   The Status of Mental Health Programming

Despite the fact that mental illness is a leading cause of disability in the world, and hundreds of billions of dollars are lost each year as a result, mental health policies and programs are not perceived as priorities.

- 40% of countries have no mental health policy.
- 30% of countries have no mental health program.

- More than 33% of countries allocate less than 1% of their budgets to mental health.
- Another 33% of countries allocate 1% of their budgets to mental health.
- More than half of the countries in the world have only 1 psychiatrist for every 100 000 people.
- 40% of countries have less than 1 hospital bed reserved for mental health issues for every 10 000 people.

The mental health policies and programs that do exist are embedded with the two different paradigms of mental disorder—the *disease paradigm* and the *discrimination paradigm*. The **discrimination paradigm** proposes that the experience of mental illness is primarily one of prejudice, discrimination, and stigmatization. Policies and programs in this paradigm constitute forms of resistance to the stigmatization of mental illness, and will be presented within that context later in the chapter. The **disease paradigm** proposes that the experience of mental illness is primarily one of experiencing *illness*—the signs and

TIME TO REVIEW

- What is "mental illness" and how many people have mental disorders?
- How do the prevalence and patterns of mental illness vary on the basis of gender, socioeconomic status, and age? What are the explanations?
- What costs are associated with mental illness for individuals, their families, and society?
- How many people with mental disorders seek professional help, and what prevents some people from doing so?

- How is mental illness portrayed in the media, and what perceptions of mental illness are found in the general population and among medical professionals?
- How does the stigmatization of mental disorders influence quality of life, discrimination, and mental health policies/ programming?

symptoms of the disorder, which subsequently hinder the individual's effective functioning and quality of life. Policies and programs in this paradigm revolve around the medicalization of mental disorder.

The Medicalization of Mental Disorder

The medicalization of deviance has been addressed in previous chapters. For example, in the chapter on body size, we saw how medical science defines what deviant body size is, explains why those body sizes are deviant, and then provides social control measures to ameliorate those problems (e.g., prescriptions for diet pills, references to a nutritionist, and information about physical fitness). Similarly, mental disorders are also medicalized. Psychiatrists determine which thoughts or behaviours constitute mental illness and then incorporate that into the *DSM*. They explain that these particular thoughts and behaviours are deviant because they cause significant distress and impairments in daily functioning. Finally, they provide measures of social control—that is, treatments for mental disorders to improve quality of life and level of functioning. However, a historical analysis reveals that medical treatment to improve functioning has not always been the focus of social control measures.

The History of the Social Control of Mental Illness

Through much of Western history, the thoughts and behaviours that we now define as mental illness were instead seen as demonic possession, and the "treatment" was physical torture in order to drive out the demons. During the Middle Ages and early Renaissance, a refusal to conform to society's norms (even by those people who would now be considered to have mental disorders) was considered a sign of allegiance with the devil. As a result, people were labelled "witch" or "heretic," put on trial, virtually always convicted, and put to death (e.g., by burning at the stake).

As religious explanations were replaced by scientific explanations, authorities no longer saw these non-normative behaviours as signs of possession or allegiance with the devil. Families and communities took care of those individuals who exhibited "strange" thoughts and behaviours. As the size of communities grew, prisons were built to house not only criminals but also the poor and the mentally ill (Grob, 1994). In the eighteenth century, "madhouses" were created specifically for those with mental illnesses. The purpose of these madhouses was not treatment or rehabilitation, but simply warehousing the disordered so that society's "normal" citizens could feel safe and secure (Rothman, 1971; McGovern, 1985). In the late nineteenth century, madhouses were replaced by "asylums" as some doctors proposed that, with appropriate treatment, people with mental illnesses could be trained to conform to society's norms. This is the era when the medicalization of mental illness came to predominate in Western cultures (Grob, 1994). These "asylums," later to be known as "mental hospitals" or "psychiatric institutions," continued to grow well into the 1950s.

During the Middle Ages, people with mental illnesses were some of those convicted of witchcraft and burned at the stake.

The treatments for mental illnesses provided in psychiatric institutions included practices that many people now see as almost barbaric—lobotomies and fever therapies, for example (McGovern, 1985). The failure of these types of therapies to "cure" mental illness combined with social concerns about their harshness eventually led many of them to be abandoned. Broader concerns about the effectiveness of hospitalization itself began to take hold in the late 1950s as well. People began to wonder how removing individuals from their homes, from the support of their families, and from the semblance of normality that existed within their communities and instead placing them in institutions where they were dehumanized and isolated could possibly help in recovery from mental illness. These questions, along with new drug therapies that effectively controlled many forms of mental disorder, eventually led to **deinstitutionalization**—the social control of mental illness in community-based programs rather than in institutions.

Treating Mental Illness Today

The medicalization of mental disorders in contemporary society involves an extensive range of treatment options—psychotherapy, cognitive-behavioural therapy, medication, occupational therapy, and social supports. Treatment options today have become quite effective in improving functioning and the quality of life for individuals with mental disorders. Effective treatment helps 60% of people with depression fully recover, and prevents relapses in 80% of people with schizophrenia (World Health Organization, 2001).

The combination of medical support (e.g., medications) and psychosocial support (e.g., therapy, community resources) is particularly effective for even the most severe mental illnesses (World Health Organization, 2002b). For example, without any treatment, 55% of people whose schizophrenia goes into remission will have a relapse within one year. Among those who receive psychopharmaceutical treatment alone, 20 to 25% will relapse within one year. Among those who receive both psychopharmaceutical treatment and psychosocial supports for the family, only 2 to 23% will relapse within one year (World Health Organization, 2002b).

As a result of the deinstitutionalization movement, hospitalization is reserved for only the most severe cases of mental illness, and even then is perceived as a short-term intervention that will form only one small part of the overall program of treatment. Hospitalization today is primarily voluntary in nature, with individuals themselves formally consenting to be hospitalized. Involuntary admissions to hospitals for psychiatric reasons are governed by the "**least restrictive alternative**"—legislation stating that involuntary admission can occur only if there are no reasonable non-institutional alternatives (Krieg, 2001).

The Legacy of Deinstitutionalization. When the deinstitutionalization movement began in the early 1960s, it was perceived as an evolution in treatment that would bring nothing but benefits—to the individuals who would receive treatment in their own homes and communities, to society in terms of the higher rate of recovery, and to the government and taxpayers in terms of cost-savings. Indeed, many of these benefits have been realized to some extent. Treatment in the community is generally more effective in the long term than treatment in institutions, and is considerably less expensive (World Health Organization, 2002b). There is also no doubt that many people consider it to be more respectful, more humane, and less emotionally disturbing. In fact, most people with mental illnesses want to live in the community while receiving treatment, keeping their daily lives as "normal" as possible (Tanzman, 1993). However, deinstitutionalization has had its drawbacks as well. The *Ask Yourself* exercise begins to explore some of these drawbacks.

In the *Ask Yourself* exercise, perhaps you mentioned close families or friendship networks that can help provide necessary support or care. Deinstitutionalization did, in fact, emerge during an era when the image of the "ideal" family was everywhere. Popular television series such as *Leave It to Beaver, Father Knows Best,* and *Ozzie and Harriet* portrayed family life in a way that few people in reality ever experienced (Coontz, 1992). This type of popular imagery helped create the assumption that families were always caring, supportive, united, and happily willing to work together to overcome any difficulties. This was one of the key underlying assumptions of deinstitutionalization; that is, shifting the care of people with mental illnesses into the community was perceived as non-problematic

Ask Yourself

In order for people with mental illnesses to be successfully treated in the community rather than in institutions, what kinds of resources are necessary? That is, what might people with mental illnesses need if they are to successfully recover in their own homes and neighbourhoods?

because it was assumed that they would have loving families to help them (Accordino, Porter, & Morse, 2001).

Of course, many of us do not have that type of network of family relationships. Some of us are closer to our families than others are. Some of us are able to depend on our families more than others are. Some of us may have close marital relationships that are a source of support, but others do not; furthermore, the experience of any type of serious illness contributes to the dissolution of many marriages. With all of these variations in family form and quality of family relationships, the assumption that there exists a social support network for people with mental illnesses is a precarious one. Those people who have close support networks may do very well with community-based treatment, but those who are lacking such networks may not.

In your response to the last *Ask Yourself* question, you may have said that an accepting community that is free from stigmatization is necessary for successful community-based treatment. The prejudice and negative attitudes that pervade public perceptions of people with mental disorders have been addressed earlier in the chapter; stigmatization is a central obstacle to successful recovery and integration into the community (Accordino, Porter, & Morse, 2001). Although institutionalization was perceived as degrading to people with mental disorders, living in communities permeated with negative perceptions of mental illness and the resulting discrimination may be just as degrading to some individuals (Krieg, 2001).

Perhaps you listed adequately funded community resources as necessary for successful non-institutional treatment for people with mental disorders. In fact, this is one of the biggest problems worldwide that has plagued the deinstitutionalization movement (World Health Organization, 2002b). Although the intent was quite different, the reduction in hospital-based service was accompanied by insufficient increases in community-based resources. This was because of the negative social perceptions of mental illness (that make related programs and policies difficult for politicians to "sell" to voters), a lack of adequate health care funding overall, and the prioritizing of other areas of government spending (World Health Organization, 2002b; Krieg, 2001). The nature of available resources is also dependent on community size. Individuals living in large urban centers have more community mental health resources available to them than do those living in rural areas. People with mental disorders who live in rural areas have a particularly difficult time with recovery and are more likely to experience negative outcomes, including participation in and victimization by criminal behaviour (Sullivan, Jackson, & Spritzer, 1996).

"The streets and prisons are the asylums of the 21st century." (Bailey & Bronskill, 2007)

The deinstitutionalization movement has benefited many people, but others have fallen through the cracks of the mental health care system.

You may have mentioned that in order for people to have a successful recovery in their own homes, they actually need their own homes— i.e., somewhere to live. Simply having a place to live can be a considerable challenge for some people with mental disorders, especially when we consider insufficient community resources and the stigmatization that inhibits integration within communities. As a result of discrimination or the symptoms of their disorders, some are unable to find employment or housing and may become dependent on family or friendship support networks. If those networks are lacking, and the resulting stresses exacerbate the illness, possible outcomes include alcohol or drug abuse (Davidson *et al.*, 1996) and a failure to take medication prescribed for the illness. The end result can be homelessness. It is estimated that in North America, between 25% and 50% of the homeless are mentally ill (Mental Health Commission of Canada, 2008; Krieg, 2001). Research done by various organizations in Toronto finds that between 11 and 30% of the homeless there have serious psychotic disorders such as schizophrenia (Valpy, 1998).

Homelessness adds one more dimension to the social typing process that individuals must experience: not only do they face the consequences of being socially typed as mentally ill, they also must face the consequences of being socially typed as homeless. Homeless people with mental disorders who also have substance abuse problems face the additional predicament that some community resources are designed to deal with either substance abuse or mental illness, but not both. That is, some organizations help only the homeless mentally ill (and do not address substance abuse problems), while other organizations are able to help homeless people with substance abuse problems (but are not equipped to deal with those with mental illnesses).

AN INTERNET MOMENT

You can find the Government of Canada's Homelessness Partnering Strategy at www.hrsdc.gc.ca/homelessness/index.shtml, a strategy that aligns federal, provincial, and territorial governments using a "housing first" approach. That is, the first goal is to ensure that the homeless have somewhere to live, and then supports and resources are provided that are specific to the individual's needs (e.g., mental illness, substance abuse).

The costs of community-based treatment are usually described as being lower than the costs of hospital-based treatment. However, when a significant number of people fall through the cracks of the community mental health system, other costs accompany deinstitutionalization. The costs associated with reducing homelessness are compounded by the social and economic losses emerging from higher suicide rates among individuals with untreated mental illnesses, more accidents, and a greater number of untreated physical illnesses (Krieg, 2001). The symptoms of some mental disorders, difficulties in finding employment or housing, and the emotional consequences of stigmatization lead some individuals into crime (Krieg, 2001; Sullivan, Jackson, & Spritzer, 1996; Accordino, Porter, & Morse, 2001), adding another layer of costs to society.

The rate of criminal activity among people with major mental disorders is considerably higher than among those without mental disorders (Hodgins, 1993). A study at Toronto's Don Jail found that during an 18-month period, 469 of the admissions (1 in 12) involved individuals with major mental disorders, and approximately 70% of criminals with major mental illnesses had multiple jail admissions (Valpy, 1998). American estimates suggest that 16% of the prison population has a mental disorder (Wolff, 2007).

In the five mental health treatment facilities operated within the criminal justice system in Canada, 700 beds are available; this stands in stark contrast to the 1500 inmates across Canada who require daily care for serious mental disorders (Bailey & Bronskill, 2007). As with homelessness, criminality adds a second dimension to the social typing process for some individuals with mental disorders. They face the consequences of not only being socially typed as mentally ill, but also of being socially typed as criminals. Problems with mental health programming emerge in some communities, in that community resources that help people with mental illnesses may not help those with criminal records, and resources that help former criminals may not be equipped to deal with the mentally ill.

More than a half century ago, Penrose (1939) proposed that a *hydraulic* relationship exists between the mental health care system and the criminal justice system—when one contracts the other expands. Wolff (2007) argues that this is precisely what occurred when deinstitutionalization was not accompanied by sufficient community resources; the mental health care system contracted, and the prison population expanded. Conversely, expanding the extent and nature of resources within the mental health care system should reduce the prison population.

The emphasis placed on deinstitutionalization by governments in North America and Western Europe over the past few decades has resulted in another problem—the reduction in hospital services for those people who may benefit from such services. For example, in the 1950s, Ontario had 40 beds for the mentally ill for every 10 000 people; by 1995, that had been reduced to 5 beds. In comparison, in 1995, Britain had 7.4 beds for the mentally ill for every 10 000 people, Spain had 1.7, and the Middle East had 1.4 (Valpy, 1998). The World Health Organization (2002b) reports that 40% of countries in the world have less than 1 hospital bed for the mentally ill for every 10 000 people. Despite the best of intentions on the part of its exponents and the positive outcomes for millions of people with mental disorders, deinstitutionalization has also had unintended negative consequences for millions of people worldwide.

More recently, research looking at changes in the number of service spots (e.g., treatment beds) in several European countries suggests that a "new era of reinstitutionalization" (Priebe et al., 2005, p. 124) has begun. Just as the emergence of a *risk society* has had consequences for the social control of youth (the risk management strategies addressed in Chapter 5), reinstitutionalization stems from a concern with *risk containment*—reducing the risks for individuals who may have fallen through the cracks with deinstitutionalization, but also reducing the *perceived* risks for a society characterized by negative perceptions of the mentally ill.

The Deviance Dance: Resisting Stigmatization, Inadequate Care, and Psychiatry Itself

Mental disorders are socially typed as deviant at many different levels. Seen as "crazy" and "dangerous" by the general public, people with mental illnesses face stigmatization in everyday interactions and discrimination in employment, housing, and medical care. To add to this burden, sometimes the treatments offered for these conditions fail to give the mentally ill control over their own lives. It is true that once diagnosed with particular mental disorders according to the *DSM*, individuals have a wide range of treatments available to them. The nature of these treatments has changed and expanded over time, making possible the deinstitutionalization movement that began in the 1960s. The move toward community-based treatment has benefited many and is the preferred form of treatment among people with mental disorders. However, it has also had a number of unintended negative consequences for people who happen to fall through the cracks of the community mental health system. Such consequences include homelessness, criminality, suicide, substance abuse, and a lower quality of life. Individuals and groups in society are, therefore, engaging in resistance against both stigmatization and inadequate treatment, trying to change the nature of the social typing process.

The policies and programs addressing treatment and support available to people with mental disorders arise from the *disease paradigm* of mental illness, which emphasizes ameliorating symptoms that distress and impair individuals' functioning. Other policies and programs emerge out of the *discrimination paradigm* of mental illness, which emphasizes the role that stigmatization plays in the daily experiences of people with mental illnesses. These programs and policies constitute part of the "deviance dance"—i.e., people resisting and fighting back against the stigmatization of mental illness and the social rejection or discrimination faced by individuals with mental disorders.

Resisting Stigmatization

At the government level, many nations in the world have instituted legislation and policies prohibiting discrimination against people with mental disorders in housing, employment, health care, and more. Some policies target persons with mental illnesses specifically. In other cases, people with mental illnesses are included under broader human rights legislation. For example, the Canadian Charter of Rights and Freedoms guarantees equality and prohibits discrimination on (among other things) the basis of "mental and physical disability." At an international level, the Universal Declaration of Human Rights has a similar declaration. Provincial human rights codes also integrate similar policies.

The medical community is also involved in trying to reduce negative attitudes toward mental illness. For example, Alberta's "My Mental Health" campaign was created to eliminate misconceptions about mental illness, in order to reduce stigmatization and increase people's attention to their own mental health (including their willingness to seek out services). The World Psychiatric Association coordinates an international program ("Open the Doors") to reduce the stigma of schizophrenia in many countries, including China, Egypt, Greece, and India. The World Health Organization devoted 2001's World Health Day to mental health, emphasizing issues of prejudice and discrimination. Reducing the stigma associated with mental illness is one of the dimensions of their Mental Health Global Action Programme (mhGAP), whereby they will coordinate advocacy efforts in member states to educate the public about mental illness and protect or promote patient rights (World Health Organization, 2002b).

Self-help groups for people with mental illnesses can be found in many countries in the world. One of their mandates is acting to reduce the stigmatization of mental disorders through education, communication, and media information. For example, the Canadian Mental Health Association sponsors an annual Mental Health Week that is intended to dispel myths and reduce stereotypes. These types of groups also provide information about legislation, updates of mental health-related court cases, and materials to assist persons with mental illnesses in employment, housing, parenting, and more.

AN INTERNET MOMENT

On the website for the Canadian Mental Health Association (www.cmha.ca), you can usually view their current Public Awareness Campaign, which includes magazine/newspaper ads and television commercials. You can also link to a site describing that year's Mental Health Week emphasis, obtain information that dispels the myths of mental illness, and download educational literature (e.g., educating employers about mental illness).

Not only do governments, the medical community, and self-help or advocacy groups act to reduce the stigma associated with mental illness, they are also involved in the resistance to inadequate care for individuals with mental illnesses.

Resisting Inadequate and Insufficient Care

In addition to providing public awareness to reduce stigmatization, self-help groups are also involved in lobbying governments for better funding and improved services for people with mental disorders, as well as providing information to mental health consumers about the nature and appropriateness of the resources that are available to them. Support groups for specific mental disorders (e.g., depression and schizophrenia) provide detailed information about new medications that are available, the effectiveness of specific types of treatments, and research about potential negative side effects of different medications and treatments.

The medical community, of course, is continually engaged in research on new and improved treatments for different disorders. They also monitor the professional behaviours of their members, and negatively sanction those who do not provide appropriate care to patients. For example, professional associations of psychiatrists or psychologists provide ethical guidelines to their members, governing appropriate and inappropriate behaviours when counselling patients. On an international level, groups like the World Health Organization integrate their anti-stigmatization efforts with efforts to increase government funding for mental health and improve the training of mental health professionals. Their Mental Health Global Action Programme's mission is to "support Member States to enhance their capacity to reduce risk, stigma, and burden of mental disorders and to promote the mental health of the population" (2002b, p. 11). To this end, their approach includes four core strategies (see Figure 7.1).

As one of the WHO's member states, within Canada the Standing Senate Committee on Social Affairs, Science, and Technology subsequently analyzed the

Figure 7.1   STRATEGIES OF THE MENTAL HEALTH GLOBAL ACTION PROGRAMME

Information	• Coordinate an observatory of mental health • Provide information to health care workers • Create an information database • Assist with member state information systems
Policy and Service Development	• Provide guidance on policy development • Coordinate international training networks • Provide technical assistance to member states
Advocacy	• Coordinate efforts to educate the public • Coordinate efforts to protect and promote patient rights
Research	• Provide training to mental health researchers • Assist in finding sponsorship for research • Provide a forum for networking

status of mental health services, releasing its final report (*Out of the Shadows at Last*) in 2006. One of its recommendations was that a Mental Health Commission (MHCC) be created (and funded) by the federal government, to move forward on the fact that Canada was the only G8 nation to lack a national mental health policy. The foci of the MHCC are (a) an anti-stigma campaign, (b) a program to reduce homelessness, (c) a knowledge exchange centre, and (d) a mental health strategy. Extensive consultation with researchers, service providers, individuals affected by mental illness, and the general public serves as the foundation for the MHCC's work. For instance, at the time of this writing, a series of open consultations is underway across Canada to inform the creation of a national mental health strategy; in addition, the MHCC website serves as a venue for e-consultation, providing a framework document that outlines the eight goals of the strategy (see Box 7.2), as well as separate consultation "workbooks" for mental health professionals and others.

Box 7.2   Goals of the Mental Health Strategy

The goals of Canada's mental health strategy are as follows:

- People of all ages living with mental health problems and illnesses are actively engaged and supported in their journey of recovery and well-being.
- Mental health is promoted, and mental health problems and illnesses are prevented wherever possible.
- The mental health system responds to the diverse needs of all people living in Canada.
- The role of families in promoting well-being and providing care is recognized, and their needs are supported.
- People have equitable and timely access to appropriate and effective programs, treatments, services, and supports that are seamlessly integrated around their needs.
- Actions are informed by the best evidence based on multiple sources of knowledge, outcomes are measured, and research is advanced.
- People living with mental health problems and illnesses are fully included as valued members of society.

Source: Mental Health Commission of Canada (2009). *Toward Recovery and Well-Being: A Framework for a Mental Health Strategy* (pp. 18–19). Calgary, AB: Author.

Individuals and groups who are involved in reducing the stigmatization of mental illness and ameliorating the problems of insufficient and inadequate care are trying to change aspects of the social typing process. Groups involved in the former efforts are working toward removing the label of "crazy," the evaluation of persons with mental illnesses as "dangerous" and "unlikable," and reducing the social rejection and discrimination that result. Groups involved in the latter efforts are trying to improve the ways that persons with mental disorders are treated in the mental health system—ensuring that enough of a priority is placed on mental health, that there are sufficient resources available, that harmful or ineffective treatments are stopped, and that more effective treatments are instituted. However, resistance to stigmatization and to inadequate treatment is not the only way the "deviance dance" is evident in the realm of mental illness. Some people resist the medicalization of mental disorder overall, and even question the very notion of mental illness.

Resisting Medicalization

Resistance to the medicalization of mental disorder can occur at a number of levels, from criticisms of the *DSM* to criticisms of the daily practices of mental health professionals to questions about whether "mental illness" even exists.

Criticizing the *DSM*

Since its first edition, the *DSM* has been subject to some criticism. Much of the criticism has been based on the inclusion of particular disorders in the *DSM*. For example, homosexuality was included in the *DSM* from 1952 until its removal in 1973—it was first classified as a "sociopathic personality disorder" and then as a form of "non-psychotic sexual deviance." Factors contributing to its removal from the *DSM* included research demonstrating that homosexuality was not pathological and was not related to pathological outcomes, as well as the activism of gay and lesbian rights groups.

More recently, controversy has emerged over the diagnostic category "attention deficit hyperactivity disorder" (ADHD). Most experts agree that this is a disorder that affects people's lives by interfering with their abilities to concentrate on tasks, follow instructions, and sit still in situations that require it. However, critics argue that in North America, far too many children are being diagnosed. In Britain, where different diagnostic criteria are used and different attitudes prevail, a significantly smaller proportion of children are diagnosed with this disorder (McConnell, 1997). One concern is that normal childhood restlessness and inattention is being diagnosed as a mental disorder.

Another concern is that behavioural or attention problems that are actually being caused by social forces (e.g., family conflicts) are being diagnosed as mental disorders, while the true cause of the problems remain untreated (McConnell, 1997; Shute, 2000). Furthermore, some social analysts suggest that the inability to focus or pay attention is a logical outcome for children growing up in a society in which the adults pride themselves on "busy-ness" and multitasking, and where being "stressed out" is seen by many as a sign of how important you are. All of these concerns reached a climax in 2000, when a class action lawsuit was launched against the American Psychiatric Association and the pharmaceutical company that manufactured the first drug for ADHD (Ritalin) for constructing a non-existent mental illness. The lawsuit has since been dismissed (Shute, 2000; Peck, 2001).

While some critics of the medicalization of mental disorder focus their disapproval on the inclusion of specific categories of disorder within the *DSM*, other critics express concerns over the *DSM* itself and the power it holds. Caplan (1995) points out that when some research claims half of Americans experience a mental disorder at least once in their lives, it suggests that what is considered to be a "mental disorder" has escalated to ridiculous proportions. Critics of the *DSM* not only point to methodological shortcomings in its creation, but also to the role played by power (and economics) in determining what is and is not included in the list of mental disorders. This has led some critics to suggest that the *DSM* is just as much a political document as a medical document (e.g., Armstrong, 1993).

"The point is not that decisions about who is normal are riddled with personal biases and political considerations but rather that, by dint of a handful of influential professionals' efforts, those subjective determinants of diagnoses masquerade as solid science and truth." (Caplan, 1995, p. xvi)

Despite its shortcomings, there is considerable agreement that the *DSM* does capture many diagnostically useful sets of symptoms that *are* distressful to the people that experience them and that *do* impair effective daily functioning. Furthermore, there is a sizable overlap in the psychiatric diagnostic categories contained in the *DSM* and in the *International Classification of Diseases* (*ICD*) used by the World Health Organization. However, even those social analysts and health professionals who acknowledge the validity of the *DSM* recognize that problematic patterns in its usage and in other practices of mental health professionals can occur. Research finds that variables other than medical ones may influence the diagnoses and treatments for mental disorders.

Being Sane in Insane Places: Criticizing Mental Health Professions

Rosenhan (1973) was one of the early mental health professionals who documented the influence of social factors and other biases on psychiatric diagnoses. His influential study stirred tremendous controversy in the mental health community, but also motivated considerable changes in the mental health system. Rosenhan began with the question, "If sanity and insanity exist, how shall we know them?" That is, his fundamental question was whether the sane can be distinguished from the insane—whether the salient characteristics leading to diagnosis lie within the individual or in the environment. The medical view is that people present themselves with symptoms, which are then recognized by professionals as constituting a diagnosis, leading to treatment. As a parallel, people who present themselves with certain other symptoms may also be told by professionals that those are not symptoms of any mental disorder.

Rosenhan had eight research associates (including students, homemakers, and a psychiatrist) attempt to have themselves admitted to psychiatric hospitals. These "pseudo-patients" presented themselves to mental health admissions people at 12 different hospitals, claiming that they had been hearing voices for the past few weeks that were saying "empty," "hollow," and "thud." Rosenhan's underlying assumption was that if their sanity was not detected, it would indicate that the salient characteristics involved in psychiatric diagnosis reside more in the environment than within the individual. All of these research associates were admitted to hospitals with diagnoses of "schizophrenia."

Once they were admitted, they were to begin acting normally, report that the voices had stopped, and try to get discharged. In interactions with the mental health professionals, they were to be truthful about the characteristics of their lives (with the exception that those in mental health professions would allege another occupation in order to avoid special treatment)—their relationships with family members, their life histories, their frustrations and joys in life. As patients, they were completely cooperative with staff, doing everything they were told to do (although they did surreptitiously flush their medication down the toilets). In the end, the pseudo-patients spent between 7 and 52 days hospitalized prior to being discharged, with the average stay being 19 days. The psychiatrists at the hospitals never detected the pseudo-patients' sanity; they were discharged with diagnoses of "schizophrenia in remission," suggesting that their mental illness was still there, but simply dormant for the present moment.

The lack of detection was not because they were not acting "sane" enough. They received daily visitors, who were to look for any potential abnormal behavioural consequences resulting from hospitalization, but the visitors detected no abnormal behaviours. Furthermore, in many cases *other patients* detected the sanity of the pseudo-patients, saying things like, "You're not crazy" or "You must be a journalist or professor checking up on the hospital." Inside the hospitals, the mentally ill label that they had received affected the nature of all of their interactions with staff.

Normal behaviours were overlooked or misinterpreted through the lens of the diagnosis of mental illness. For example, although the pseudo-patients initially tried to hide their note-taking (for fear of being detected), it quickly became apparent that note-taking was seen as a *sign* of their mental disorder. As boredom set in and mealtime became a highlight of the day, waiting in the hallway for the cafeteria doors to be opened was described as indicative of the "oral-acquisitive nature" of schizophrenia. In a session with a psychiatrist, one male pseudo-patient spoke of how, as a little boy, he was closer to his mother, but as he progressed through adolescence he became closer to his father and more distant from his mother; psychiatric notes described this as "considerable ambivalence in relationships." When he described his marriage as generally positive, with just occasional arguments, the case notes identified those occasional conflicts as "angry outbursts."

Of course, one factor that might contribute to misdiagnosis is the desire of mental health professionals to err on the side of caution. It may be safer to mistakenly label a healthy person as ill than to mistakenly label an ill person as healthy and not provide them with the treatment they need. Rosenhan suggested that this desire to err on the side of caution can explain misdiagnosis at the initial time of admission, but is less able to account for continued misdiagnosis after a lengthy period of observation and analysis.

So, why *did* the misdiagnosis continue all the way until the time of discharge? One reason could be the lack of interaction between the mental health professionals and the patients. Nursing attendants, nurses, and even the psychiatrists actively avoided contact with the pseudo-patients. When the pseudo-patients intercepted staff members to ask them simple questions, the psychiatrists averted their eyes and walked away 71% of the time, as did 88% of the nurses and nursing attendants. Another reason, one emphasized by Rosenhan, is the power that a diagnosis of mental illness carries. He concluded that the initial "schizophrenic" label given upon admission to the hospitals provided staff with a **schema**, or mental framework, which affected their interpretations of the pseudo-patients' behaviours—*all* behaviours then came to be interpreted as indicative of pathology. In contrast, those very same behaviours exhibited by someone who had not been diagnosed as mentally ill would not be perceived as indicative of pathology. What was Rosenhan's conclusion? The salient characteristics in the diagnosis of mental illness lie more within the social context, or the environment, than within the individual.

As you can imagine, the results of this research project caused quite a stir in the psychiatric community. An outcry from psychiatric hospitals throughout the United States claimed that something like that could certainly never happen at their hospitals, suggesting that the hospitals used in Rosenhan's study must have been poorly run. Rosenhan therefore created a follow-up study to look into this possibility.

Rosenhan selected a well-known and very well-respected teaching hospital. He told administrators that within the next three months, at least one pseudo-patient would attempt to be admitted as a psychiatric patient. Hospital staff, including the psychiatrists, were asked to rate each person admitted during that time as to the likelihood that this was one of the pseudo-patients. During that period of time, a total of 191 psychiatric patients were admitted to this hospital. Of these patients, the hospital staff identified 41 as having a high likelihood of being pseudo-patients. At least one psychiatrist identified as many as 23 patients, and both a psychiatrist and at least one additional staff member identified 19 patients as being likely pseudo-patients. How many pseudo-patients had Rosenhan actually sent in? None. Rosenhan concluded that even mental health professionals have difficulties distinguishing the sane from the insane.

Rosenhan's research seemed to present a resounding critique of the efficacy of mental health professions. First, by illustrating that people without mental disorders could be kept in hospitals and not have their "sanity" detected, it raised significant concerns about those patients who had been committed to psychiatric hospitals involuntarily. It was possible that some of these patients, being kept against their wills, did not have any mental disorder. As a result of these concerns, governments throughout the Western world created or intensified legislation governing involuntary psychiatric admissions. In Canada, all provinces now have mental health legislation that outlines the conditions under which individuals can and cannot be admitted for psychiatric care against their wills, and sets procedural safeguards in place for reviewing such cases at regular periods following admission. Within the government, the role of Mental Patient Advocate is to advise involuntarily committed patients and their families of their rights in such situations.

Second, Rosenhan's research described the dehumanizing treatment that patients in psychiatric hospitals frequently faced, such as being ignored by staff when asking a question, being prescribed large numbers of pills (altogether, the eight pseudo-patients in the first study were given a total of 2100 pills during their hospital stays), and being mistreated in many other ways. For example, in one instance a nurse unbuttoned her shirt to adjust her bra right in front of a group of male patients. It was not a teasing or sexual demonstration, but rather reflected her view that it was no big deal because these were "mental patients" rather than "real" men. These observations reinforced Goffman's (1961) argument that psychiatric hospitals were *total institutions*, similar to prisons and concentration camps, wherein "inmates" had no choice but to accept restriction and dehumanization; their identities were dismantled, and new "inmate" identities created, identities that would be carried into the community following release from the institution. Although Goffman's sociological work of more than a decade earlier had pointed to the some of the negative implications of treatment within an institutional setting, Rosenhan's empirical documentation of dehumanization raised greater awareness, contributing to changes in the practices in psychiatric hospitals and the growth of mental health advocacy groups.

Third, Rosenhan's research had, and continues to have, broader theoretical implications. Rosenhan's first study illustrates important aspects of labelling theory, which emphasizes the influence that labels have on the way people are subsequently treated. In particular, it reflects the assumption that labels have negative consequences, by closing the doors of acceptance within the "normal" world. However, even though Rosenhan's research is reflective of the negative consequences of labels, stigmatization can have potentially positive consequences as well (see Chapter 3). Several decades later, debates over whether stigmatization on the basis of mental health has positive or negative effects continue. One perspective points to the harmful effects that stigmatization has on the self-concept, which has implications for treatment outcomes and the magnitude of symptoms. Opponents in this deviance dance bring attention to the fact that stigmatization can improve self-concept, in that being labelled is the key factor in opportunities for effective treatment, which improves well-being. Empirical tests of this theoretical debate find support for both points of view (Rosenfield, 1997); thus, the debate continues.

Finally, Rosenhan's research pointed to the unintentional influence of social factors on diagnostic processes. Considering the awareness stimulated by Rosenhan's research, one might think that, since that time, the influence of social factors in diagnosis has declined. Is this the case?

The Role of Social Factors in Diagnosis and Treatment

Given the way that social factors permeate every aspect of our daily lives and the subsequent influence they have over our thoughts, feelings, and behaviours, it should not be too surprising that social factors continue to have the potential to influence diagnosis and treatment. Loring and Powell (1988) presented psychiatrists with case summaries after manipulating the sex (male or female) and race (Black or white) in the cases. They found that sex and race both influenced the diagnoses and other aspects of the psychiatrists' perceptions of the individuals contained in the case summaries. For example, Black persons in the case summaries were more likely to be described as "dangerous" and "suspicious" than were white persons, even when everything in the case summary (other than the race of the individual) was identical.

Other research has found that women are more likely to be diagnosed with depression than men are, even when they present the same symptoms (Stoppe, Sandholzer, & Huppertz, 1999). However, there is some debate over the influence of sex on diagnosis, as some other studies have not detected this pattern (Gater *et al.*, 1998). Despite the continued debate about whether there are sex differences in diagnosis, the evidence is quite clear that there are sex differences in treatment—women are far more likely to be prescribed psychotropic drugs (Simoni-Wastila, 2000).

In the *Ask Yourself* exercise, you may have referred to something like stereotypes—assumptions about what people of different races and genders are like, or should be like. Because of prejudicial attitudes that continue to pervade society, Blacks and whites are perceived in different ways. So are men and women. Indeed, researchers working in the various critical theories that were explored in Chapter 3 (e.g., feminist theories) explain these research results in precisely those terms (Loring & Powell, 1988; Simoni-Wastila, 2000).

Thus far, we have looked at resistance to the medicalization of mental disorder in three different ways. One form of resistance emphasizes the ways that some normal social behaviours have been deviantized within the *DSM*. A second form of resistance launches broader critiques against the *DSM*, showing us the political dimension of the document. The third form of resistance focuses on some of the inaccuracies and biases that occur in the daily practices of mental health professionals, revealing the power of the labelling process and the influence of social factors on diagnosis and treatment.

> ### *Ask Yourself*
> Why do you think race and sex might influence the diagnosis and treatment of mental disorders?

There is one last form of resistance to the medicalization of mental illness that moves to a much broader, more abstract level, criticizing the concept of "mental illness" itself as being a false label that denies free will (Szasz, 1994). Thomas Szasz (a psychiatrist himself) acknowledges that there are physical diseases of the brain, but argues that virtually none of the disorders listed in the

DSM have been proven to be physical diseases of the brain. Instead, people use the diagnostic categories of the *DSM* to involuntarily treat people who do not want treatment and to enable others to avoid responsibility for criminal acts. Szasz's arguments have stimulated controversy since the 1950s and continue to stimulate controversy today.

However, most people agree that mental disorders *do* exist, and that some people with mental disorders do not have everything they need to successfully recover and/or achieve a high quality of functioning in daily life. The continued stigmatization of mental illness is one of the central obstacles to recovery and high functioning, and even influences the extent and quality of policies and programs available. Governments, the medical community, and self-help/advocacy groups continue to work toward improving the lives of people with mental disorders—reducing the stigma and increasing the available resources. At another level, people are bringing to the forefront the political nature of the process by which diagnostic categories are created and the social factors that can influence or bias diagnosis and treatment.

TIME TO REVIEW

- How has the social control of mental illness changed throughout Western history?
- What are the necessary prerequisites for deinstitutionalization to be successful, and why has reinsitutionalization emerged?
- What role does mental illness play in homelessness and in crime?
- What types of policies and programs emerge from the *discrimination* and *disease paradigms*?
- What criticisms have been directed at the *DSM*?

- What happened in Rosenhan's two studies and what were his conclusions?
- What were the impacts of Rosenhan's research?
- What influence do sex and race have on the diagnosis and treatment of mental disorders, and why?
- What are Thomas Szasz's criticisms of the medicalization of mental disorder?

CHAPTER SUMMARY

- *Mental illness* refers to thoughts, moods, and behaviours that cause significant distress and/or significantly impair functioning for individuals. The nature of these impairments is further delineated in the diagnostic categories listed in the American Psychiatric Association's *Diagnostic and Statistical Manual of Mental Disorders* (*DSM*).

- The estimates of the proportion of people who experience mental disorder at some point in their lifetime range from 20 to 50%. Some social groups face higher risks for mental illness than others. Women and men show equivalent overall rates—but different patterns—of mental disorder. People in low socioeconomic status groups show higher rates of mental illness, as do adolescents and young adults.

- Considerable costs are associated with mental illness for the individuals experiencing the illness, their families, and society as a whole.

- Negative perceptions of people with mental disorders are found in media representations, attitudes of the general public, and even attitudes of health professionals. These negative attitudes hinder recovery of people with mental disorders, contribute to discrimination in many areas, and result in mental health programs and policies not being seen as priorities.

- Although mental illness has been treated in various ways throughout history, in the late nineteenth century it became *medicalized*. Over the last several decades, the *deinstitutionalization* movement has helped millions of individuals with mental disorders; however, there have also been unintended negative consequences. More recently, *reinstitutionalization* has emerged.

- Mental health policies and programs are embedded within two different paradigms: the *disease paradigm* and the *discrimination paradigm*. The first paradigm emphasizes the role of symptoms of the disorders themselves in people's experience of mental illness. The second paradigm emphasizes the role of stigmatization and prejudice in people's experience of mental illness.

- The medicalization of mental disorder is also being resisted and changed in a number of different ways. Critics express concerns about the diagnostic handbook, the *DSM,* for (a) the inclusion of some normal behaviours as "disorders," such as homosexuality and ADHD, and (b) the political nature of the process by which disorders are included in the *DSM* and the subsequent power the handbook has.

- Other people have raised questions about mental health professions themselves. Rosenhan's classic study concluded that the salient characteristics in diagnosis lie more within the social context than in the individual. Decades later, researchers continue to find that social factors have an impact on psychiatric diagnosis and treatment. Thomas Szasz takes his criticisms of psychiatry the furthest, suggesting that mental illness is a "myth."

DEVIANCE IN PRINT

Caplan, P. J. (1995). *They Say You're Crazy: How the World's Most Powerful Psychiatrists Decide Who's Normal*. Reading, MA: Perseus Books.

Goffman, E. (1961). *Asylums: Essays on the Social Situation of Mental Patients and Other Inmates*. Garden City, NY: Anchor Books.

Special Senate Committee on Social Affairs, Science, and Technology (2006, May). Report on Mental Health: *"Out of the Shadows At Last": Transforming Mental Health,*

Mental Illness and Addiction Services in Canada—Full Version. Available at www.parl.gc.ca.

DEVIANCE AT THE MOVIES

Forman, M. (Director), Kesey, K. & Goldman, B. (Writers). (1975). One *Flew Over the Cuckoo's Nest*. United States: Fantasy Films. (133 minutes).

This movie, starring a very young Jack Nicholson, is a Hollywood portrayal of the dehumanizing treatment that psychiatric patients were perceived as facing. It captures the underlying mood that contributed to the deinstitutionalization movement.

Cohen, D. (Director), & James, R. (Producer). (1995). *Mistreating the Mentally Ill*. Available from Films for the Humanities & Sciences. (53 minutes).

This documentary explores the varied perceptions and treatments of people with mental disorders in the United States, Japan, India, and Egypt. It makes visible the way that the stigmatization of mental illness affects policies and treatments.

ENDNOTE

1 Canadian Mental Health Association. Retrieved June 2, 2003, from **www.cmha.ca**

KEY TERMS

mental disorder, **p. 210**
social causation hypothesis, **p. 212**
retreatism, **p. 212**
social selection hypothesis, **p. 212**
self-stigma, **p. 216**

discrimination paradigm, **p. 217**
disease paradigm, **p. 217**
deinstitutionalization, **p. 219**
least restrictive alternative, **p. 220**
schema, **p. 231**

CHAPTER 8

What Do You Believe?
Religion and Deviance

Learning Objectives

After reading this chapter, you should be able to

■ Explain how religion is related to the concept of "truth."

■ Describe what is meant by religion as deviance.

■ Describe the traditional typology that helps determine which religions are "deviant," and explain why sects and cults are considered "deviant," using examples.

■ Describe the different levels of social control that are directed at "deviant" religions, as well as the various ways that deviant labels are resisted.

■ Explain how religion serves as a social typer of deviance, using both historical and contemporary examples.

- Describe the witch persecutions, residential schooling, and the child-savers movement.

"The task of history . . . is to establish the truth of this world." (Karl Marx)[1]

In uttering this phrase, Karl Marx was condemning religion, saying that the only way to find truth is through the full abandonment of religion. He claimed that religion is the "opium of the masses," a mechanism by which society's masses are prevented from seeing the truth about the society in which they are living. Because of religion, the proletariat is incapable of rising up to resist their bourgeoisie oppressors, and religion serves as the obstacle between the people and the truth. But in another sense, we can look at religion as proclaiming truth. Although Marx would not use the above phrase in this way, one of the ways in which people throughout the world attempt to determine the truth is via the religious belief systems that are part of their lives.

Anything that you personally think is true represents one of your **beliefs**, regardless of whether it is actually true or not. Some of your beliefs might be entirely unique to you, while other people might share some of your beliefs; that is, a group of people might accept the very same truths that you do. And frequently, single beliefs are combined with other interrelated beliefs into organized sets or **belief systems** (Stebbins, 1996). Religious doctrines (e.g., Christian, Islamic), the ideologies of specific political parties (e.g., Liberals, New Democrats), and the knowledge contained in particular disciplines of science (e.g., astronomy, zoology) are all belief systems that are shared among large groups of people. Religious belief systems are those based on "truths" about "supreme beings," the "supernatural realm," "superhuman beings," or the "sacred cosmos"—a being or beings that are far more powerful and more knowing than humans are, and that are capable of influencing our lives in significant ways (McGuire, 1997, p. 10).

Various religious belief systems declare different truths—what Buddhism says is true is considerably distinct from what Islam says is true (although there are some overlapping beliefs as well). Many religions claim that their version of "truth" is the only correct one, such that individuals who fail to accept and adhere to those "truths" will face some type of negative consequence either in this world/lifetime or another. That is, refusing to follow religious "truth" results in the individual being socially typed as "deviant" and made subject to forms of social control. This social typing process can emerge when people reject the "right" belief system and instead adopt a "wrong" one, or when individuals fail to act in accordance with the moral code integrated in the belief system. But at times the social typing process can also be directed *at* a religious institution itself, or at actions taking place *within* religious institutions (Stark & Bainbridge, 1996).

The various ways that the social typing process can occur represent the two different ways that we can explore the concept of deviance in the context of religion.

Ask Yourself

Think for a moment about your own religious beliefs and what they consist of—the "truth about the world" that is encapsulated in your religious belief system. Now shift your focus to religion as a social organization or institution. Do you attend some type of organized religious functions such as those sponsored by a church, temple, or synagogue? Why or why not? What influences how often you attend? What role does your religious institution play in the community and world?

First, we can consider **religion as deviance**—i.e., acts of deviance that occur within religious groups, or religious groups themselves being considered deviant in their entirety. Second, we can look at **religion as a social typer of deviance**, wherein religious belief systems or the way those belief systems are applied dictate to us who should be considered deviant and what the consequences should/will be.

In analyzing the relationship between religion and deviance, it is important to distinguish between the belief systems themselves (theological doctrine) and the way those belief systems are operationalized within sociocultural contexts. Look at the *Ask Yourself* questions to explore this distinction within the context of your own life. It is the latter that sociologists focus their analyses on. Sociological analyses of religion *do not* make value judgments about people's religious beliefs, nor do they attempt to prove or disprove anyone's religious beliefs—religious beliefs are a matter of *faith* (McGuire, 1997). Instead, sociological analyses of religion explore the social embeddedness of religious belief systems—i.e., the processes by which religious belief systems emerge, the role that religion plays in people's lives in societies, and the relationships between religion and other social structures or processes (e.g., social stratification). Religious institutions are social organizations just like any other social organization, and, like any other social organization, religious institutions are composed of and run by people who have their own attitudes, desires, and interests. It is this aspect of religion that sociologists pay attention to. Thus, in this chapter we are not analyzing *beliefs*, we are analyzing *social organizations* that are based on religious belief systems.

In answering the *Ask Yourself* questions, you made the transition from thinking about religion as a belief system to thinking about religion as a social organization that holds a particular place in the community and in the larger society, and that carries out specific types of activities within that environment. If you are like many people, you do have religious beliefs, but you do not necessarily attend a church, temple, mosque, or synagogue on a weekly basis. Perhaps it is because of other responsibilities at work, school, or home. Perhaps it is because you do not think attending such institutions is necessary for worship. Perhaps it is because you do not approve of what religious organizations have done in the past. If you do regularly attend a place of worship, you will be aware that it holds a particular role in the community in terms of both the way it is perceived by other members of the community and the activities it may engage in within the community.

For example, your place of worship might be highly regarded in your community or, conversely, it might be looked upon with suspicion or disdain.

Maybe your place of worship is very active in the community—raising money for charity, providing the homeless with a place to sleep, running a neighbourhood daycare, hosting debates among political candidates at election time, or organizing extracurricular activities for neighbourhood youth. The larger religious organization to which your place of worship belongs may be running a school or building a well in a developing country. Historically, perhaps it participated in less admirable pursuits, such as the witch burnings of the Middle Ages or the abuses of Canada's Aboriginal peoples in residential schools. Sociologists look at all of these types of social issues—the factors that influence people to participate in organized religion, the perceptions that people have of specific religions, and the actions carried out by religious institutions. It is the sociocultural aspect of religious institutions, not religious belief systems themselves, that is the area under discussion when we explore the linkages between religion and deviance.

Religion as Deviance

When considering religion and deviance, many of you may initially think of abuses carried out by representatives of different religions, such as instances of child sexual abuse by priests and allegations that churches tried to cover up those incidents. In addition to deviant acts carried out by religious institutions or representatives of those institutions, talking about *religion as deviance* also brings to mind those religious groups that are thought of as deviant in their entirety— religions that are considered weird, strange, or bizarre. Which religions are considered deviant and which are considered normal? Traditionally, religious belief systems were categorized in various typologies based on characteristics of the particular group in question. A religious group's location in the typology determined whether it was considered deviant. More recently, these traditional typologies have been questioned and even abandoned by some researchers, resulting in quite a different view of "deviant religions."

"Deviant Religions" According to Traditional Typologies

Different scholars have proposed various typologies of religious groups (McGuire, 1997; Troeltsch, 1960; Johnson, 1963; Yinger, 1970; Stark & Bainbridge, 1996). Although the typologies can be somewhat distinct from each other, a review of the various frameworks reveals that four categories of religious groups are commonly used. Deviance is then determined by which category a religious group is said to belong to.

Ecclesias refer to state religions: a specific religious belief system is adopted at a governmental level and becomes a nation's "official" religion. Islam is an ecclesia in Iran, as is the Anglican denomination of Christianity in England and the Lutheran denomination of Christianity in Sweden. The extent to which other religions are practised in these countries depends on the particular nation in question. Some nations identify an ecclesia and yet declare freedom of religion for their citizens (e.g., England); in other cases, non-ecclesiastic religions are outlawed (e.g., in Europe during the Middle Ages).

Churches are not "official" religions of an entire society, but they are large and powerful religious groups. Those religious groups that are commonly perceived as being the world's major religions—Islam, Judaism, Hinduism, Buddhism, and Christianity—are categorized as *churches*. They are well established in society, highly bureaucratized (having complex hierarchies of leadership and administration, as well as formalized rituals and practices), and have millions of members around the world. They are further subdivided into **denominations**, such that there are different types of Christianity (e.g., Catholicism), Islam (e.g., Sunni), and Judaism (e.g., Orthodox). The same can be said of all of the other churches of the world.

Sects are smaller religious groups that have usually broken away from larger churches at some point in their history. They are less established in society than churches are, have fewer members and more rigid doctrine formed in reaction to the doctrine of the larger church, and require higher levels of commitment from their members (e.g., clothing, behaviour, and food). The Amish and the Hutterites are examples of sects that are offshoots of the larger Christian church, while the Taliban is a sect that has broken away from mainstream Islam. Scientology is usually categorized as a sect but is not an offshoot of any of the world's major religions.

Cults are usually smaller than sects, frequently having only a handful of members. Their doctrine is even more reactionary and oppositional, and intense levels of commitment are required of members. A single, charismatic leader serves as a source of inspiration, convincing followers that the secret to salvation can be found in that group. Examples of cults that you may be most familiar with include the Branch Davidians, Heaven's Gate, and the Children of God.

This framework has traditionally been used as the foundation for decisions about whether a particular religious group is deviant or not. Ecclesias, which declare an entire nation's citizens as members (at least on a theoretical level), are not considered deviant in those societies. Of course, there may be some groups in those societies that do attempt to deviantize that religion as part of the "deviance dance." Churches, with millions of members worldwide and their high level of integration in many societies, are also perceived as normal or conventional religions, although members of one church may attempt to deviantize members of another church.

For example, the "deviance dance" between the Christian church and the Islamic church was responsible, in part, for the Crusades—a series of battles lasting from the eleventh century to the sixteenth century. The "dance" continues in a sense in contemporary society, with some Islamic groups describing the Christian church as heathen, and some Christian and secular groups describing Islam as terrorist. Sects and cults—which have fewer members, are more isolated from mainstream society, and have doctrine that is more reactionary or oppositional—are the religious groups that are traditionally seen as deviant and in need of social control. In other words, those religious groups that are characterized by high levels of tension with the broader

The Amish are a Christian-based sect who reject modern technology and live in communal settings.

society are perceived as deviant, while those that are characterized by low levels of tension are seen as normal (Stark & Bainbridge, 1996).

The "Deviant" World of Sects and Cults

Although both sects and cults are perceived as deviant, thereby existing in a state of tension with wider society, the deviance of cults is of a greater magnitude than that of sects. Cults are based on novel beliefs, while sects tend to have more traditional belief systems as their foundation, creating some differences in the level of tension that exists with society and the level of social control exerted upon the religious groups (Stark & Bainbridge, 1996).

AN INTERNET MOMENT

As you progress through the remainder of the chapter, you may want to go to "The Religious Movement Homepage at the University of Virginia" (http://religiousmovements.lib. Virginia.edu/). This is a reputable and highly respected academic website that contains an abundance of information about religious groups, cults, religious freedom issues, research bibliographies, and more. You may find the site particularly useful for obtaining more information about specific religious groups that are mentioned in the remainder of this chapter. The "Profiles of Religious Groups" on the website contains an alphabetical listing of more than 200 religious groups (churches, sects, and cults). The profiles include information on each group's belief system, origins, practices, history, and any controversies involving the group.

Sects

High levels of commitment are required of members of sects, and their beliefs and life habits are strictly controlled. Members who fail to think or act in accordance with the belief system are punished, and in many sects the most extreme punishment is excommunication from the group (Wilson, 1993; McGuire, 1997; Stark & Bainbridge, 1996). Along with the nature of their belief systems, these characteristics are what make some outsiders think of sects as somewhat peculiar. For those of us who are not a part of these types of groups, it can be difficult to understand why people adhere to such beliefs and why they would be willing to tolerate such high levels of control exerted over their lives.

Although the levels of commitment required of members and the levels of control exerted over members' lives are higher in sects than in churches, there is considerable diversity among sects in these characteristics—that is, some sects have more rigid requirements than others. Similarly, the degree of tension between sects and the wider society also varies. Such tension is fundamental to the deviantization and social control of sects within society. The level of tension experienced by a particular sect is determined by three factors: (a) the magnitude of the differences between the sect and society; (b) the level of antagonism that the sect feels for society; and (c) the extent to which the sect separates itself from the larger world (Stark & Bainbridge, 1996). Lawson (1995) illustrates this variation by comparing two sects—Seventh Day Adventists and Jehovah's Witnesses. Both sects formed in the seventeenth century, inspired by apocalyptic visions, and both can now be found in countries around the world. However, since their inception, they have followed different trajectories, such that Jehovah's Witnesses experience significantly higher levels of tension with their surrounding societies than do Seventh Day Adventists.

Greater degrees of difference, antagonism, and separation have characterized Jehovah's Witnesses since their inception. They have persistently held to their original apocalyptic vision, although they have had to repeatedly revise their projected dates for the coming apocalypse (past failed dates have caused a drop in membership due to disappointment and loss of faith). Members face rigid requirements for continued membership, such as attendance at various meetings each week, reaching targets for hours spent witnessing (i.e., going door to door in an attempt to draw converts), and following behavioural guidelines (e.g., prohibitions against substance use and blood transfusions). Such requirements make the daily lives of members considerably distinct from those of the general population. Their belief system, as illustrated in their publications, is antagonistic to other religious groups, the government, and patriotic symbols. Antagonisms toward governments and patriotic symbols in particular have placed them on the receiving end of social hostilities during conflicts like the American Civil War, World War I, and World War II.

The antagonistic dimension of the Jehovah's Witness belief system contributes to the perception that their members are attacking everyone and everything outside of the sect. Because of their beliefs about the wider society, members of the Jehovah's Witnesses live in considerable isolation from it, other than their witnessing and their participation in the labour force. Labour force participation is frequently of a limited nature, because members are discouraged from pursuing higher education, and jobs are considered secondary to witnessing.

When members fail to adhere to behavioural requirements of membership, they may be excommunicated from the group, and remaining members are directed to actively shun them in any public settings. For example, if an excommunicated member is seen in the supermarket, current members may even leave their full carts behind and exit the store.

The magnitude of the tension created because of these differences, antagonisms, and separations has resulted in significant persecution in countries around the world. In various countries, members of the Jehovah's Witnesses have been physically attacked by mobs, arrested, and even put to death (for refusing to fight during wartime, for example).

In contrast, Seventh Day Adventists have undergone substantial changes over time, and these changes have contributed to lesser degrees of tension with the larger society. The notion of a coming apocalypse maintains its presence in their sect's belief system, but it no longer holds the central position that it used to, and specific date projections have been abandoned. High levels of commitment are required of members, including not eating certain foods and not consuming certain substances. However, the requirements for membership have relaxed over time, as antagonisms and the separation from wider society have declined.

Early in their history, this sect's leaders determined that compromise was necessary in order to avoid conflicts and gain acceptance in the wider society. The sect became deeply involved in creating schools, universities, businesses, hospitals, and institutions for the elderly in the early twentieth century in their desire to "claim an increasing stake in society" (Lawson, 1995, p. 375) and attract new members. Although members are encouraged to use these Seventh Day Adventist resources instead of those outside of the sect, the boundaries with the outside world are quite permeable. The pursuit of higher education is quite common, and members typically have high-status occupations in the labour force. The value placed on higher education has also indirectly contributed to the relaxing of requirements and the growing diversity of thought among members, further enhancing integration with the wider society. Members of this sect have faced persecution in several countries in the world (e.g., for working on the traditional Christian Sabbath day of Sunday or refusing to fight during wartime); however, the extent of their persecution is less than that faced by Jehovah's Witnesses. As a result of the different trajectories the two groups have followed, they are categorized differently. Seventh Day Adventists are frequently labelled a *denominational sect*, suggesting they are verging on being considered a conventional Christian denomination. Jehovah's Witnesses are considered an *established sect* because of the magnitude of the tension that continues to exist between them and the societies in which they reside.

Seventh Day Adventists and Jehovah's Witnesses are just two of the thousands of sects that exist throughout the world. Because of the similarities in their origins, contrasting these two sects is particularly useful in demonstrating the diversity that exists among the sects of the world, as well as the varying degrees of tension between different sects and the larger society. The belief systems and practices of the sects themselves contribute to that level of tension; however, the tension is not solely the result of characteristics of the sects. It is also a product of characteristics of the wider society, such as public attitudes toward the sects and how authorities have interacted with them. Tension between a sect and society is bidirectional in that a sect may have certain levels of antagonism toward society, but society may have certain levels of antagonism toward a particular sect. Furthermore, existing hostilities in society toward specific religious groups may contribute to greater polarization of a sect's belief system and even more separation from the outside world. When a deviant group becomes even more deviant as a response to hostilities or social control efforts from outsiders, it is referred to as **deviancy amplification** (Becker, 1963).

Although the tensions between different sects and the sociocultural environment vary considerably, some degree of tension must exist for a religious group to be considered a sect rather than a church. Tension is also characteristic of the types of religious groups known as *cults*. When looking at cults, the tensions with the wider society are typically of an even greater magnitude, especially in the realm of public attitudes. Simply mentioning the word "cult" fuels a flood of images in most people's minds, more so than when the word "sect" is mentioned.

Cults

Your thoughts about cults likely draw heavily on the media, particularly news stories or documentaries about specific cults. When cults are covered in the media, it is usually because some sensationalistic incident has occurred, such as the mass suicides of the People's Temple in Guyana in 1978, the Solar Temple in Canada and Switzerland in 1994, and the Heaven's Gate in the United States in 1997. You might also recall the storming of the Branch Davidians' compound in Waco, Texas, by the American government in 1993, or the allegations of the sexual abuse of children in various cults throughout the late 1980s and early 1990s. These are the kinds of cults typically represented in the media—doomsday suicide cults and cults that engage in various criminal activities, such as the sexual abuse of children.

Wright (1997) explains the selective and distorted coverage of cults as the result of (a) a lack of accurate or in-depth knowledge about cults and the groups in question; (b) the use of biased sources of information (e.g., ex-members of cults rather than social scientists who conduct research on cults); and (c) limited time or financial resources, resulting in the tendency to over report sensationalistic stories in the beginning but then ignore later developments. Sensationalist language, used to attract an audience, frequently disparages cult members. For example, after the Heaven's Gate mass suicide in 1997, news stories referred to the leader as "loony" and "crazy," while headlines screamed, "UFO Wackos Blasted Off with Vodka and

Ask Yourself

When you think of cults, what images or ideas come to mind? Who do you see as belonging to cults? What do you imagine their leaders to be like? What actions are carried out within the cults you are thinking about?

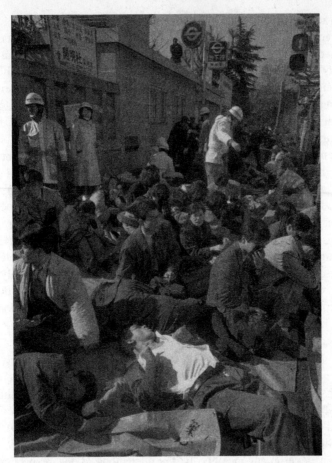

In 1995, 12 people were killed and thousands injured when members
of Aum Shinrikyô, a Japanese cult with Christian and Buddhist
foundations, released sarin nerve gas in the Tokyo subway.
Incidents like this one strongly influence public perceptions about cults.

Pills" (Hoffman & Burke, 1997, p. 63). More than 2 000 different cults exist in
the United States alone, and of these, only a handful have been involved with
violence—but each of those received extensive media coverage (Bromley &
Melton, 2002). The thousands of other cults in the world—those whose members
lead quiet, non-criminal lives—never reach public attention to influence our
images of what cults are like (Jenkins, 2000; Wright, 1997).

Consequently, public perceptions are that cults are dangerous to members, to
other individuals, and to society (Melton & Bromley, 2002; Chryssides, 1996;
Hoffman & Burke, 1997; Anthony & Robbins, 1994; Wright, 1997). In the public
mind, cults are associated with mind control, violence, mental illness, sexual
deviance, and the sexual abuse of children. Many people believe that cults carry
out mind control using secretive techniques unique to cults, and that as a result,

cult members may behave uncharacteristically during altered mental states when they are incapable of rational thought (Anthony & Robbins, 1994). Violence is commonly perceived as pervasive in cults (Melton & Bromley, 2002), either internally, such as with mass suicides (e.g., Heaven's Gate), or externally (e.g., Aum Shinrikyô).

Cults are also perceived as provoking opponents into acts of violence, such as in the 1993 Waco siege between the Branch Davidians (a group that allegedly was physically and sexually abusing children and stockpiling weapons for a final standoff with authorities) and American federal authorities. Sexual deviance has been considered characteristic of cults for more than a century, stimulated by groups advocating polygamous marriage and "free love" between all members of the group (Jenkins, 2000). Children have frequently been viewed as victims of cults. "Satanic" cults have been accused of sacrificing unbaptized babies, and cults of all forms have been associated with the ritual abuse of children, including sexual abuse (Nathan & Snedeker, 1995; deYoung, 1998; Richardson, Best, & Bromley, 1991).

Concerns over the ritual abuse of children emerged with the McMartin preschool case in California in 1984, when authorities charged that hundreds of children attending the preschool were sexually abused as part of the rituals of a Satanic cult. A moral panic followed, bringing forward more than 100 other cases of ritualistic abuse in schools and daycares in the ensuing months and years—all the way from California to Martensville, Saskatchewan. Almost all of these cases, including the McMartin preschool case, turned out to be unfounded. Investigators were accused of having posed extremely leading questions to very young children, and the various groups involved in the perpetuation of this moral panic were criticized for ignoring systematic, empirical studies, instead preferring to believe folklore (Jenkins, 2000; deYoung, 1998). By the end of the 1980s, the concept of pervasive Satanic abuse of children was debunked and the moral panic ceased. However, concerns about sexual abuse and sexual deviance in cults today continue, as the description of the Family of Love in Box 8.1 illustrates (Lewis & Melton, 1994; Kent, 1994; Bainbridge, 2002).

The public concerns that emerge as a consequence of popular images of cults are not entirely unfounded. Sexual behaviours that violate cultural norms do occur in some cults, as illustrated with the Family's concepts of *sexual sharing* and *flirty fishing*. These practices violate the norms of many cultures, especially those having more conservative sexual cultures (e.g., India). Some former child some cults that have apocalyptic or doomsday visions, especially when latent tensions between those groups and societal authorities intensify, their respective members of certain cults were sexually or physically abused as children, although this is not as common as popular images may suggest. Violence can emerge with beliefs become more polarized, and third parties are unable or unwilling to mediate the conflict (Bromley, 2002; Hall, 2002). In some groups, the leaders are able to effectively influence members' thoughts (Stark & Bainbridge, 1996) such that they are willing to engage in mass suicide. For example, an analysis of the mass suicides of the Solar Temple (1994), People's Temple (1978), and Heaven's Gate (1997) reveals parallels in the

Box 8.1 The Family of Love

The Family of Love, formerly known as the Children of God (and now calling itself "the Family" more generally), is a group that has been a target of attention for cult watchers and investigators for more than 30 years. Its founder, David "Moses" Berg, brought together a group of young hippies in the late 1960s based on his revelation from God that he would be the prophet who would play the key role in the second coming of Jesus Christ. Members fully devoted themselves to the group by abandoning all ties with their families, giving up all personal possessions, and evangelizing. Although they first lived in several communes throughout the United States, a revelation that the nation would be destroyed for its impurity led Berg to disperse all of the group's members to countries around the world. There, they continued their attempts to recruit new converts.

Controversy surrounded many of Berg's teachings, such as his concept of *flirty fishing*. Because Jesus was referred to as a "fisher of men," Berg claimed that the women in the group should also be "fishers of men," seducing and offering sexual favours to men in attempts to recruit new members. *Sexual sharing* was another component of Berg's doctrine—sex was to be freely shared among members of the group (except between

two men). Whether sex was to be freely shared between adults and children within the group is a matter of debate. Analyses of the group's own newsletters as well as the testimony of current and former members point to pedophilia and incest between Berg, his daughters, and his granddaughters. However, criminal investigations in a number of different countries have been unable to prove these allegations in court. Some civil suits have been successful.

In 1987, Berg officially banned adult-child sex and decreed that offenders would be excommunicated from the group. Flirty fishing has also been officially abandoned due to the danger of sexually transmitted diseases. However, some researchers suggest that these practices have been removed from the group's official documentation only to prevent further investigation by authorities, and that the practices actually continue (e.g., Kent, 1994). Although Berg died in 1994, the Family is alive and well, claiming more than 12 000 members worldwide. They present musical performances at youth shelters and women's shelters free of charge and participate in humanitarian efforts following natural disasters and in developing countries.

beliefs that came to permeate all of these groups, beliefs that the majority of members came to accept as truth (Introvigne & Mayer, 2002) (see Figure 8.1). First, they believed that they did not belong in this world any longer, but that they were destined to be somewhere else, somewhere better. Second, they felt increasingly isolated and estranged from the larger society, as though they did not fit in anywhere. Third, they thought society was persecuting them, denigrating their beliefs, and trying to destroy their groups. Society consisted of hostile outsiders who were a threat to them and everything they believed in. Finally, the combination of these beliefs generated one final conviction—the rules of the hostile society and the increasingly distant world did not apply to them. These beliefs open the door for the kinds of mass suicides we hear about in the media.

Although there is some foundation to the popular images of cults, such as mass suicide, violence, mind control, child abuse, and sexual deviance, these qualities are characteristic of only a small proportion of the thousands of groups in the world that

Figure 8.1   BELIEFS OF CULTS THAT COMMIT MASS SUICIDE

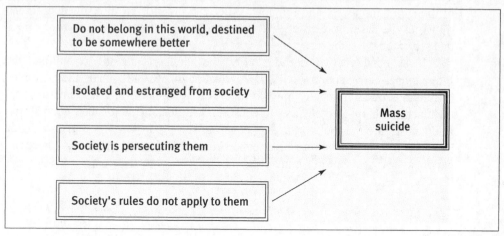

are considered "cults." Cults, like sects, are characterized by diversity in beliefs and practices, as well as the level of overt tension that exists with society. However, popular images of cults and the resulting public attitudes contribute to more overriding tensions for cults. For both cults and sects, these tensions are played out in the "deviance dance"—the various means of social control of these deviant religions and the corresponding resistance to those means of control.

TIME TO REVIEW

- What are beliefs and belief systems, and what is the difference between religions as belief systems and religions as social organizations?
- What are the two ways that deviance can be explored within the context of religion?
- What typology has traditionally been used to categorize religious groups, and which groups are socially typed as deviant?
- What factors influence the level of tension that exists between sects and the larger

society, and how do these factors vary for Seventh Day Adventists and Jehovah's Witnesses?
- How are cults represented in the media, and what factors contribute to these representations?
- What are cults typically associated with in the public mind? Are these images accurate?
- When is violence more likely to emerge in cults, and why?

Cults, Sects, and the "Deviance Dance"

Controlling "Deviant" Religions

The international community has repeatedly declared the importance of religious freedom. Many people see it as the foundation for all human rights. The United

Nations's Universal Declaration of Human Rights, created in 1948 and signed by more than 100 countries around the world (including Canada), states that freedom of thought, conscience, and religious belief and practice are fundamental human rights. In the ensuing decades, that document was followed by numerous others that reiterated the same idea.

Most notably, two decades after the United Nations declaration, the International Covenant on Civil and Political Rights (CCPR) made the guarantee of religious freedom legally binding on all of its signatories. These international documents underpinned changes to constitutional documents (or their equivalents) in countries around the world. The slogan of the group Forum 18, a worldwide network of non-governmental organizations focusing on religious freedom, captures the essence of this human right:

"The right to believe, to worship and witness. The right to change one's belief or religion. The right to join together and express one's belief." (Forum 18, 2001, p.1)

Despite the recognition of religious freedom as a fundamental human right, this right is not unbridled. Threats to public health, public order, and infringement on the rights of others constitute valid reasons for governments to violate religious freedom, according to international declarations and the documents that mirror them in most individual nations. These caveats to freedom of religion serve as the basis for the various measures of social control that target sects and cults.

During the twentieth century, a number of social organizations emerged in response to the perceived problems caused by "deviant" religions. Acting as *moral entrepreneurs* who have identified a significant social problem, they apply various measures in their efforts to control "deviant" religions. In particular, during the late 1960s and early 1970s, the **anti-cult movement** materialized (Jenkins, 2000; Bromley & Shupe, 1993; Shupe & Bromley, 1995). Initially, it consisted of parents whose hippie children had joined small, new religious groups that were part of the broader countercultural movement. Concerned about the way their children had severed ties with their families and fearful that their children would be brainwashed and led into deviant behaviours, parents coalesced into support groups.

Media stories about violent activities carried out by some of these new cults, such as the infamous Tate-LaBianca murders committed by members of the Manson "family" in 1969, seemed to validate their concerns. These support groups later became information networks working toward making other parents aware of the dangers of these new religious groups. Over time, numerous mental health, legal, and political professionals, along with academic researchers, became involved in many of the anti-cult groups, and representatives became the "experts" featured in media stories about cults. Some of these anti-cult groups offered services to parents, such as psychologists who would "de-program" their

Box 8.2   Characteristics of Destructive Cults

Although there is some disagreement over precisely what the characteristics of "dangerous" cults are, there are some common "warning signs" that are pointed out by various organizations:

- The leader of the cult places the group above the law, telling members that they are not bound by the same laws that outsiders are.
- The leader does not have to follow the same rules as the rest of the cult members.
- The leader exerts control beyond the realm of religious doctrine, extending control to members' personal lives, such as prescribing whom to marry and whether to go to university.
- "Mind control" techniques are used on members to facilitate indoctrination.
- The group follows a formal or informal policy of deceiving outsiders when recruiting, fundraising, or answering to societal authorities.
- The group is based on an apocalyptic vision in which the cult will play a key role. For example, the group may stockpile weapons to prepare for a battle with outsiders when Armageddon arrives.

children, and a few groups even provided services for kidnapping the children from cult environments in order to forcibly de-program them.

Anti-cult groups today, or what Barker (2001) calls **cult awareness groups**, engage in measures to warn everyone about the dangers of cults and to control their activities through lobbying governments and other organizations. The anti-cult movement targets only certain religious groups—those considered to be "destructive cults." In fact, the word "cult" is used in this movement to refer specifically to those religious groups that have dangerous or destructive characteristics, summarized in Box 8.2 (Lalich & Langone, 2006; Fight Against Coercive Tactics Network, 2003; Ontario Consultants on Religious Tolerance, 2003).

Although the anti-cult movement is a relatively recent construction, the **counter-cult movement** is noticeably older, going back more than a century (Bromley & Shupe, 1993; Ontario Consultants on Religious Tolerance, 2008; Cowan, 2001; Melton, 2000; Barker, 2001). Unlike the anti-cult movement, this movement does not base its philosophy on the internationally recognized legitimate limits to religious freedom discussed earlier. In fact, members of the counter-cult movement are overwhelmingly opposed to religious freedom itself. These groups primarily consist of conservative Christians drawn from evangelical and fundamentalist denominations. They are not concerned about the possibility of brainwashing or abuse in cults, but instead express a theological concern about groups utilizing the "wrong" interpretation of the Bible. Any religious group that does not follow fundamentalist, evangelical Christian doctrine is labelled a cult. Thus, not only are the groups that are commonly categorized as sects or cults targets of the counter-cult movement's control efforts, so are mainstream Christian religions (e.g. Catholicism) and all Eastern religions (e.g. Hindu, Islam, Buddhism). For example, Franklin Graham (son of the well-known evangelist

Billy Graham) referred to Islam as a "wicked and evil" religion, Jerry Vines (former president of the Southern Baptist Convention) called Islam's prophet Muhammad "a demon-possessed pedophile" (Goodstein, 2003), and Pat Robertson blamed poverty in nations like India and Bangladesh on the "demonic cults" of Islam, Buddhism, and Hinduism (Vuijst, 1995).

Counter-cult groups engage in measures to eliminate "deviant" religions, including lobbying governments and law enforcement officials to enforce the law harshly against target religions, in a larger attempt to recruit converts to their own religious groups. However, due to some of the negative perceptions that fundamentalist and evangelical Christian religious groups themselves face in society, their lobbying efforts are not as successful as those of the secular anti-cult movement. Consequently, the counter-cult movement tends to operate on a less formal level, inside communities. It also makes extensive use of the internet to spread its version of the "truth" about deviant religions, something the counter-cult movement shares in common with anti-cult groups (Dawson & Henneby, 1999).

In addition to the internet, the media is fundamental to many of the efforts of anti-cult and counter-cult groups. The relationship between these groups and the media is bidirectional. At times, groups may use the media as tools for enhancing their control efforts, but the media may also draw upon the "expertise" of members of these groups when covering news stories that may involve cults (Jenkins, 2000; Crouch & Damphousse, 1992; Bartowski, 1998).

However, the "experts" that the media use are usually not the members of academia that study these religious groups, but are often former cult members, parents of cult members, and "cult cops" (Crouch & Damphousse, 1992, p. 15). Former cult members and parents of cult members lend additional drama to a story, while police experts ("cult cops") lend legitimacy. Unfortunately, at times the perspectives of these media "experts" may be uninformed or even biased. Former cult members and parents of cult members may have only narrow views formed out of their own experiences, and these views may be contradicted by research.

The training of "cult cops" is tremendously diverse; although some might have undergone in-depth training that includes research, others might not have any specialized training at all. Furthermore, research has found that some of these law enforcement officials who specialize in cults share the religious views of the counter-cult movement, scoring higher on measures of religiosity (and fundamentalist religiosity) than police officers as a whole (Crouch & Damphousse, 1991, 1992; Victor, 1993; Hicks, 1990). When law enforcement officials who have these kinds of beliefs are the "experts" used by the media, the counter-cult movement is able to indirectly widen the influence of its social control efforts.

Independent of the anti-cult and counter-cult movements, the media has its own representations of "deviant" religions. The underlying profit motive of the media, with its corresponding need to attract larger audiences than competitors do, contributes to distorted and sensationalized coverage of news incidents involving cults or their slightly less "deviant" companions: sects (Wright, 1997). The role of the media in the creation of moral panic has been analyzed in the context of the

Satanic scare of the 1980s (deYoung, 1998; Jenkins, 2000; Crouch & Damphousse, 1992), the standoff between the Branch Davidians and federal authorities in Waco (Shupe & Hadden, 1996), and the deviantizing of voodoo (Bartowski, 1998).

In addition to having a relationship with the media, anti-cult and counter-cult groups influence governments to create legislation, policies, and programs that will curb the destructive nature of "deviant" religions. When governments do enact legislation or alternative forms of policy, they often do so under the rubric of the exceptions to religious freedom stated in international and constitutional types of documents—threats to public health, public order, and the rights of others (Forum 18, 2001; U.S. Department of State, 2008). Determining at what point governmental measures of control can be enacted without violating the right to religious freedom is an especially grey area in those nations that declare an official separation of church and state.

Thus, in many Western nations, efforts are directed at those religious groups commonly recognized as sects and cults. For example, the Canadian Security Intelligence Service (CSIS) monitors doomsday/apocalyptic cults, i.e., those cults whose members may commit mass suicide or inflict mass harm. In the United States, the FBI does the same thing. The actions of some nations, however, are not without controversy. In the late 1990s, the government of France formed the Interministerial Mission on the Fight against Sects/Cults (MILS) to monitor and control the 173 groups identified as sects or cults in a 1996 government report—groups like the Church of Scientology, Jehovah's Witnesses, Latter Day Saints ("Mormons"), and doomsday cults. After certain groups were forced to disband and members of other groups were arrested for violating pieces of the new legislation, the European Court overturned many convictions on appeal.

Measures undertaken by the German government have also raised questions in the international community and among religious freedom advocates. Germany is involved in an ongoing struggle to make the Church of Scientology an illegal organization. *Sect filters* are used by local governments in many areas as well as by some private firms in weeding out Scientologists when hiring or awarding contracts (U.S. Department of State, 2008).

Concerns about violations of religious freedom at the hands of government are of considerable interest to the international community. The U.S. Department of State releases an annual report on the state of religious freedom in the world, as does the international advocacy group Forum 18. Each year, organizations like these document violations of religious freedom in specific countries and the measures being taken to improve religious freedom in other countries. Five barriers to religious freedom throughout the world have been identified (U.S. Department of State, 2008). These barriers have been created by governmental measures to socially control many religious groups (see Figure 8.2).

First, some governments exert *authoritarian measures to control religious beliefs and practices*. This is currently occurring in countries like China, Cuba, and Vietnam. For example, under China's Religious Affairs Bureau, religious beliefs and groups are divided into three categories (Forum 18, 2001).

Figure 8.2   GOVERNMENTAL BARRIERS TO RELIGIOUS FREEDOM

Governmental Barriers to Religious Freedom				
Authoritarian measures to control religious beliefs	Hostility toward non-approved religions	Neglect of discrimination against non-approved religions	Stigmatization by wrongful association with dangerous cults and sects	Discriminatory legislation or policies

Communism is the only *orthodox and legal teaching* in China. Taoism, Buddhism, Islam, Protestantism, and Catholicism are *unorthodox but legal religious groups*. All other religious groups, including Christian sects, are categorized as *heterodox and illegal religious groups*; their members are subject to harassment, arrest, imprisonment, and even death. The politically active meditation-based group Falun Gong has had tens of thousands of its members arrested, and thousands of them have died while in prison.

The government monitors the "unorthodox but legal" religious groups—all of their activities are monitored, individual baptisms are documented, and their religious leaders must be approved or selected by the government. Despite the fact that they are recognized as legal groups, their presence is unwelcome in the officially atheist state, and several mosques and temples have been closed. Islam is the object of particular disdain, and the law states the government alone may print Islam's religious literature. The Chinese constitution guarantees religious freedom, as do international human rights documents; however, it legitimizes its actions on the basis of threats to public order and public health. The right to religious freedom does not extend to children under the age of 18, and anyone who teaches anything other than Communism to children is subject to arrest. Members of the Communist party are also not entitled to religious freedom, and any member who expresses a religious belief is kicked out of the party. The U.S. Secretary of State has declared China to be a "Country of Particular Concern" (CPC) in its annual report on religious freedom every year since 1999 (U.S. Department of State, 2008).

The second barrier to religious freedom is *hostility toward non-approved religious groups*. In these instances, governments try to intimidate members of these groups so that they will either convert to a state-approved religion or leave the country altogether. Examples include Iraq under the leadership of Saddam Hussein, Iran, Saudi Arabia, and Uzbekistan. For instance, although the Iranian government "accord[s] full respect" to non-Shi'a Islamic groups and declares

Christians, Jews, and Zoroastrians as "protected religious minorities," members of those groups "have reported imprisonment, harassment, [and] intimidation . . ." (U.S. Department of State, 2008. para. 36).

The third barrier emerges due to *state neglect of the problem of discrimination against non-approved religions*, such as in Guatemala, India, and Nigeria. In these countries, although laws may exist to prohibit discrimination based on religious beliefs and practices, the government does not actually enforce those laws. In India, although religious freedom is protected by law, attacks by extremists on minority religious sites have become increasingly commonplace due to "ineffective investigation and prosecution" (U.S. Department of State, 2008, para. 34).

The fourth barrier to religious freedom is *discriminatory legislation or policies disadvantaging certain religions*, such as in Israel and Russia (U.S. Department of State, 2008). In Russia, 70 years of Communist rule made Russia an officially atheist state. Following the fall of Communism, Russian leaders feared that naive citizens were at risk of being lured into "deviant" sects and cults because of a lack of religious knowledge. Consequently, the government declared Christianity, Buddhism, Judaism, and Islam as the country's official religions, but gave local authorities control over which religious groups would be legal and which would be labelled "cults." Those determined to be cults "must register with the government and meet a long list of requirements to win the right to meet, rent property or even hand out leaflets" (Webster, 2001, p. 28). Jehovah's Witnesses, the Church of Scientology, the Baptist church, the Pentecostal church, and even the Salvation Army have been labelled "cults" and made subject to strict controls (Webster, 2001).

The fifth barrier to religious freedom is the *stigmatization of certain religions by wrongfully associating them with dangerous "cults" or "sects"* (U.S. Department of State, 2008). The controversial policies recently created in Belgium, France, and Germany are examples of this barrier. Human rights groups and cult defender groups, active in countries throughout the world (Barker, 2001), are just some of the many groups engaged in ongoing efforts to have these government policies revoked.

Resisting a Deviant Label

Anti-cult groups, counter-cult groups, the media, and governments all act as social control agents in minimizing the perceived dangers of "deviant" religions. However, their efforts are counteracted to some extent by acts of resistance. The right to religious freedom is an international concept that serves as a nexus for many of these measures of resistance, but the social typing of "deviant" religions is resisted in numerous other ways as well.

Individual religious groups defend themselves against accusations of deviance both inside and outside of court. For example, individuals and groups targeted for control under France's new anti-sect laws have taken their cases all the way to the highest European Court and have frequently won (Forum 18, 2001; U.S. Department of State, 2008). During the Waco standoff between the Branch

Davidians and federal authorities, Seventh Day Adventists hired public relations people to make it clear to the public (via the media) that the Branch Davidians were a "cult" that had distorted Seventh Day Adventist teachings and were in no way representative of the larger group (Lawson, 1995). "The Family" not only defended itself in court cases and child custody hearings against allegations of sexual abuse, it also (a) changed its publications to remove any portions that might be perceived as indicating approval of pedophilia, (b) issued a statement declaring sexual relations between adults and children in the group to be forbidden, and (c) tried to improve the group's image by using its website to highlight humanitarian efforts within the community (Lewis & Melton, 1994; Kent, 1994; Bainbridge, 2002). Individual groups also resist the social typing process by continuing to recruit new members (Chryssides, 1996; Dawson & Henneby, 1999).

One of the most significant forms of resistance to the social typing of "deviant" religious groups comes not from the groups themselves, but from academia. The traditional distinction among ecclesias, churches, sects, and cults was used for most of the twentieth century. The distinctions among these different types of religious groups were not questioned, although debates would sometimes emerge about how a specific religion should be categorized. However, as time passed, questions about these distinctions were raised and criticisms grew. Ecclesias were easily recognized in that official state religions are identified in legislation. By contrast, with continued discussion it became evident that the boundaries between churches, sects, and cults may not be as definitive as they seem.

What Are "Deviant" Religions? The Traditional Distinction Reconsidered

As you have read through the chapter thus far, you might have already begun to feel somewhat confused about what religions are actually deviant. We began with academic definitions of cults and sects, but as the chapter progressed, we saw that different kinds of religious groups were labelled in this way at various times. The anti-cult movement prefaces the term "cult" with the descriptor "destructive," identifying as cults only those groups that have certain characteristics, such as mind control. Critics now question, however, whether brainwashing is even a scientific reality (e.g., Richardson, 1995; Richardson & Introvigne, 2001).

The counter-cult movement uses the term "cult" to refer to the theology of certain religious groups—i.e., that theology which does not adhere to fundamentalist Christian doctrine. We also saw that when the media use the word "cult," they usually do so in the context of a distorted image of cults—those religious groups involved in destructive events captured in the news. Finally, we saw that in an international context, any religious groups that a particular government does not approve of are categorized as cults.

The boundaries between churches, sects, and cults become blurred even further when we incorporate a historical perspective. All of the world's major religions, now categorized as churches, began as cults—small groups of highly committed members who followed a single charismatic leader and whose doctrine was oppositional to a society's conventional belief system at the time (Jenkins, 2000; Hadden & Bromley, 1995). As these religious groups became more established, attracted larger numbers of members, and became integrated in a society's power structure, they progressed to being churches. In fact, many sects become recognized as denominations of major churches over time. For instance, the Church of Jesus Christ of Latter Day Saints ("Mormons") is usually categorized as a sect. However, many would argue that with almost 12 million members worldwide, the Latter Day Saints should more logically be considered a denomination of the Christian church (Church of Jesus Christ of Latter Day Saints, 2003).

Even when we temporarily set aside the debates over which groups are cults or sects, the notion of *religion as deviance* crosses all boundaries. Every religious belief system in the world has been considered deviant at some time, in some place. There is no group of religious believers that has not at some moment in history been persecuted or perceived as evil, dangerous, and a threat to the social order. This is evident in looking at the former Soviet Union, where *all* religion was at one time prohibited, but is also apparent when looking at historical events such as the Crusades, the Israel/Palestine conflicts, the bloodshed between Protestants and Catholics in Europe over hundreds of years, the religious dimension of European colonization of indigenous peoples throughout the world, and more.

For all of these reasons, many contemporary academics have abandoned the traditional terminology of ecclesias, churches, denominations, cults, and sects, and instead use more encompassing terms, such as "ideological groups." Some scholars who wish to distinguish the world's major religions from more recent religious groups that may exist in some tension with society use the term **new religious movements** (Chryssides, 1994; Jenkins, 2000). Although some scholars find the traditional typology valid and, for various reasons, continue to use it, a historical and global perspective shows us that *any* religion can be socially typed as "deviant" and made subject to measures of social control.

TIME TO REVIEW

- In what ways do the anti-cult movement and the counter-cult movement differ in terms of who their members are, which religious groups they target in their efforts, and their ideologies?
- What is religious freedom and what are its exceptions? What are the governmental barriers to religious freedom that are found in some countries?

- In what ways have "deviant" religious groups themselves acted in resistance to social typing?
- What limitations are there in the traditional typology that distinguishes between churches, sects, and cults?
- Why can we say that any religion can be socially typed as deviant and made subject to social control efforts?

Religion as a Social Typer of Deviance

While various religions have been socially typed as deviant at different times and in different places, religious belief systems also play a role in the social typing *of* deviance. That is, their proclamations of truth incorporate moral truths as well— i.e., dictums of what is considered right and wrong. At the individual level, the religious belief systems we adhere to present us with guidelines for our own behaviour. Some religious groups prohibit the use of caffeine, alcohol, tobacco, or drugs (e.g., Latter Day Saints). Others dictate rules about appropriate and inappropriate foods (e.g., Seventh Day Adventists, Judaism, Hinduism). Religious doctrine may dictate aspects of dress (e.g., Sikhism, Islam) or restrict the use of certain medical treatments (e.g., Jehovah's Witnesses). Behavioural guidelines may govern marriage, sexual relations, and parenting. Religiosity has been found

Its belief system established as "law," the Christian church was central to the persecution of witches from the fourteenth to the seventeenth centuries.

to influence behaviours as diverse as smoking (Bush *et al.*, 2003) and the use of contraception (Orji & Onwudiegwu, 2002). Among American high school students, positive attitudes toward religions and regular religious attendance are related to less drug use, fewer school attendance problems, positive attitudes toward parental involvement, better grades, and positive attitudes toward school (Trust & Watts, 1999).

Not only do the moral "truths" contained in religious belief systems influence the behaviour of followers, they also dictate to followers how they should evaluate and deal with the behaviours of others. The same moral guidelines that influence our own behaviours have an impact on our judgments of others. And even more broadly, our religious belief systems influence the way we approach the events of the day and the way we interact with people. For example, if you adhere to a religious belief system that has the characteristics of forgiveness and kindness as its foundation, that will govern your interactions with others.

Beyond the individual level, religious belief systems also serve as social typers of deviance at the societal level. This is of particular interest when the boundaries between religious and political belief systems become blurred; that is, when a particular religious belief system becomes institutionalized by the government and serves as the foundation for the construction of governmental policy and law. Those people and behaviours considered deviant according to religious beliefs thereby become the people and behaviours considered deviant at the political level. Historically, the witch persecutions that occurred throughout many parts of Europe from the fourteenth through the seventeenth centuries are a classic example of the lack of boundaries between religious and political belief systems.

Religion and Politics in History

The Witch Persecutions

From the fourteenth through the seventeenth centuries, the Christian church was essentially the core of government in Europe. It either served as the main governing body itself or acted in a key advisory capacity for governing bodies in most of Europe. Thus, its belief system was the foundation for law and governance. It was in this capacity that the "witchcraze" occurred (Anderson & Gordon, 1978; Barstow, 1994; Quaife, 1987).

It is estimated that during this time, between 40 000 and 100 000 "witches" were persecuted, sometimes by being burned at the stake. One of the best-known victims was Joan of Arc, who was convicted of witchcraft and burned at the stake in 1431. Witches were declared to be in league with Satan and responsible for plagues, floods, stillborn babies, infertility, crop failures, and any other unfortunate events in families or communities.

Those accused of witchcraft included a wide range of people, the list growing longer as the witchcraze snowballed. Followers of the pre-Christian religions were suspect in their refusal to convert to Christianity (although many people combined Christian and Pagan beliefs). Women who violated new cultural norms were suspect—i.e., those who were financially independent, those who met with other women after dark, or those who outlived their husbands. Midwives were suspect, because in their use of herbs and other natural techniques they eased the pain of childbirth; according to church doctrine at the time, this use violated God's plan because the pain of childbirth was women's punishment for Eve's sin in the Garden of Eden. Village "wise women," who used herbs in healing illness and injury, were also suspect. Peasants were often accused of witchcraft. Overall, the majority of people prosecuted as witches were women; however, there were considerable regional variations (e.g., in Iceland, 90% of the accused were male) (Briggs, 1996). At the peak of the witchcraze (1550–1650), *anyone* could potentially be accused of witchcraft (except for church leaders)—all it would take was a report from a disgruntled neighbour.

Once arrested, torture was used to elicit confessions. The torture was so horrendous (e.g., having one's toenails pulled out or being stretched on the rack) that many people did confess. The content of their confessions was virtually guaranteed, given that a handbook (the *Malleus Maleficarum*) had been written with approval by the Pope in 1486 about how to question and torture witches. The nature of the questions asked typically led to specific types of responses, and torture would progress until that point. Upon being found guilty, the witch was put to death via hanging, decapitation, burning at the stake, or other means. With the invention of the printing press, church documents about the "witch problem" flooded the educated classes. Various witch-hunting manuals, church sermons, and pamphlets made people aware of the extent of the problem, frequently exaggerating the magnitude of persecution in order to gain more support and strike more fear into the populace.

AN INTERNET MOMENT

The *Malleus Maleficarum* (translated into English) can be found in its entirety at www.malleusmaleficarum.org. This book outlines the religious and pragmatic rationales for hunting witches and the step-by-step process for arresting, trying, questioning, torturing, and killing accused witches. The site contains a search engine for the document as well.

The witchcraze was not a uniform phenomenon throughout Europe. Witch trials occurred far more often in some countries than in others, ranging from 26 000 deaths in Germany to 4 deaths in Ireland (Briggs, 1996). Ben-Yehuda (1980) explains that following the Protestant Reformation, witch persecutions flourished in the regions of Europe where the Catholic church had weakened (e.g., Germany), while they were rare in those countries where Catholicism continued to hold its traditional power (e.g., Italy, Spain); however, both the Catholic and Protestant churches participated in the persecutions, each using the trials to demonstrate their religious dominance.

In some regions, the Christian church was directly responsible for the arrest and trial of witches, while in other regions it was local authorities that searched for and tried them. In these latter instances, even though the church was not directly involved, church doctrine provided the theological foundation for persecution. In some regions, local authorities steered the witch trials, while in other regions it was national authorities; capital punishment was virtually guaranteed in the former, while in the latter it was possible to hold onto one's life by turning in fellow witches to the authorities. Witch persecutions frequently followed peasant rebellions against the political elite, or preceded them in an attempt to distract peasants from rebellion. As Quaife (1987, p. 208) concludes, the witch hunts were the result "of either the godly zeal of the political and religious elite and their peasant allies or the furious rage of her discomforted and ill-fortuned neighbours." As political change progressed, as Christian doctrine was transformed, and as philosophical and scientific ideas grew, the witch hunts faded away. But for those few hundred years, religious belief systems were the foundation of political belief systems, with the end result in this particular instance being the loss of up to 100 000 lives.

Residential Schooling

Following the colonization of North America, European colonizing governments began to establish a long list of laws and policies designed to assimilate the Aboriginal people. An apple analogy was used to convey the idea that after going to a residential school, an Aboriginal person would still be "red" on the outside but "white" on the inside. An integral part of the assimilation process was "Christianizing" natives (Miller, 1996; Milloy, 1999; Fournier & Crey, 1998). Every aspect of Aboriginal cultures was perceived as deviant and in need of elimination.

Efforts on this front began when, upon settlement, Christian missionaries were among the first Europeans sent to North America. At a later point, laws prohibiting various Aboriginal spiritual practices were enacted, and spiritual leaders faced up to 30 years in prison for violating some of these laws. In 1879, the Canadian government adopted a **residential schooling** policy that it hoped would guarantee assimilation. Aboriginal children would be removed from their homes and families and taken to residential boarding schools where they would be given an education—not only in reading, writing, and arithmetic, but also in Christianity and learning to act "white." Taking children from their homes would remove the "heathen" influence and facilitate greater assimilation. Residential schools were a part of government policy and were funded by the government but were operated by Christian churches. Residential schooling occurred for more than a century, beginning in 1879; the last residential school closed in 1996. Approximately 150 000 children went through these schools.

One of the mandates of residential schools was to provide Aboriginal children with an education so that they would be equipped with the knowledge and skills necessary for success in the industrial economy. In fact, this was the main rationale provided to Aboriginal parents when they were approached for consent to having their children taken. However, parental consent was not actually considered necessary by the government. In many instances, Aboriginal communities that refused to have their children removed were threatened with the loss of government resources and even arrest. In some instances, government and law enforcement authorities forcibly removed the children. Although formal education was one of the mandates, in many of the schools the children received formal teaching for only half of the day; for the rest, the children had to engage in physical labour on school grounds or nearby farms. But even more important than learning to read, write, and do math was learning to adopt Euro-Canadian beliefs and practices.

Any behaviours related to traditional Aboriginal spirituality or culture were prohibited and children were punished if caught engaging in these behaviours. What was perceived as being normal punishment in that environment, however, is now seen by many as actually having been physical abuse; and many students were victims of what, even during that era, would have been perceived as abuse. Furthermore, thousands of children were sexually abused in some of these schools. Of the 150 000 children who went to residential schools, 91 000 have reported being physically and/or sexually abused. The psychological abuse the children experienced is also too great to even be estimated. Many children went years without being able to see their parents; some never saw their parents alive again. On a daily basis, many children were told that their parents, having not found God, would burn in hell for eternity—as would they if they did not do as they were told.

One of my students told me about her grandfather, who had only recently begun to talk about his years at a residential school. Upon his arrival there at the age of 8, he was slapped in the face by the minister who ran the school for having dared to look him in the eye. At the school there were only two sizes of shoes, so that most of the children had to wear shoes that were far too big or far too small. It was more than two years before his mother was able to arrange to visit him because the school was hundreds of miles away from his community. Before she arrived, he was given instructions for the visit. If he spoke anything other than English, the visit would be ended and he would be punished. His mother did not speak English, so she was unable to understand anything he said. If there was any physical contact between them, the visit would be ended and he would be punished. The school authorities supervised the entire visit to watch for violations.

In the 1990s, government and religious authorities acknowledged the damage caused by the residential schooling initiative, recognizing the high rates of substance abuse, suicide, and family violence as well as the loss of traditional cultures. The United Church of Canada, Anglican Church of Canada, and Presbyterian Church of Canada have all issued formal apologies to the Aboriginal people of Canada. The Roman Catholic Church (via the Pope) has also apologized for the ethnic and racial injustices inflicted on some groups in the world by members of the Catholic church, though they have not mentioned residential schools specifically, and their apology is directed to God rather than the victims

(Ontario Consultants on Religious Tolerance, 2003). Meanwhile, on June 11, 2008, Prime Minister Stephen Harper offered a formal apology, on behalf of the government:

". . . it was wrong to forcibly remove children from their homes and we apologize for having done this . . . .it was wrong to separate children from rich and vibrant cultures and traditions . . . in separating children from their families, we undermined the ability of many to adequately parent their own children and sowed the seeds for generations to follow, and we apologize for having done this . . . far too often, these institutions gave rise to abuse and neglect and were inadequately controlled, and we apologize for failing to protect you . . . the burden of this experience has been on your shoulders for far too long. The burden is properly ours as a government and as a country. There is no place in Canada for the attitudes that inspired the Indian residential schools system to ever again prevail." (www.cbc.ca/canada/story/2008/06/11/ pm-statement.html)

The government and churches have not only issued formal apologies for residential schooling, but are also offering restitution. The federal government will give each former residential school student $10 000 plus $3 000 for each year spent in a residential school; in addition, it has invested $10 million in an existing commemoration initiative, will give $125 million to the Aboriginal Healing Foundation, and has established the Truth and Reconciliation Commission to further analyze the legacy of residential schools. A number of churches (e.g., the Anglican Church of Canada), in conjunction with Aboriginal communities, are also embarking upon various church and community programs designed to undo some of the damage that was done by residential schooling.

 AN INTERNET MOMENT

The website for the Canadian Broadcasting Corporation (CBC) includes an in-depth report on residential schooling and its consequences, including historical and contemporary audio and video clips, Stephen Harpers's full apology, and information on the federal government's resolution package (www.cbc.ca/news/background/truth-reconciliation/).

The Victorian Child-Savers

At the same time as residential schooling was being implemented in Canada, the Victorian **child-savers movement** was at its apex, another example of religious belief systems influencing political belief systems. During the late nineteenth and early twentieth centuries, this movement played an essential role in child welfare reforms, compulsory education legislation, prohibition, and many other government policies in Canada, the United States, and Britain (Platt, 1977; Jordon, 1998; Valverde, 1991). An aspect of Protestant theology known as the Social Gospel largely informed the child-savers movement, whereby Christian principles were applied in real-world settings to solve social problems (providing humanitarian aid to the less fortunate in society was seen as one way of achieving salvation). The child-savers consisted primarily of ministers of local churches, and upstanding (primarily female) members of those congregations.

The child-savers were especially interested in social problems that involved children. The Protestant belief system had changed, so that children were now perceived as pure and innocent instead of born in sin. Children were corrupted by growing up in immoral homes, leading to drunkenness, poverty, and vice. The child-savers thought that it was the state's responsibility to provide a moral environment for children whose parents were unwilling or unable to do so. Child abuse and neglect were deviantized, and over time, the efforts of the child-savers led to legislation dictating that children whose parents were abusive or neglectful should be removed from their homes. They were placed in foster homes with morally upstanding families who could teach the children the path to good citizenship and to salvation.

The path to citizenship and salvation was, however, based on the beliefs and norms of the Protestant middle class. Interpretations of Protestant doctrine at the time suggested that God rewarded strong morality with material success. Thus, the fact that people of the middle class had material success meant that whatever beliefs and norms they adhered to were the "moral" ones, i.e., those ordained by God. People who were members of the lower classes or who lived in poverty were automatically considered immoral—after all, if they were moral, they would be rewarded by God and would not be lower class! Consequently, simply being of a lower socioeconomic class was automatically considered deviant, so virtually all of the efforts of the child-savers were directed at lower-class families.

Since lower-class parents were seen as inherently immoral, it was primarily their children who were removed to receive the care of the state. Single mothers, who violated middle-class norms by virtue of being unmarried, were also considered inherently deviant and were targeted for social control efforts by the child-savers. Lower-class parents and single mothers were threatened with the removal of their children to motivate them to adopt middle-class beliefs and practices. For many child-saver groups, alcoholism was perceived as the foundation for lower-class immorality. Consequently, there was considerable overlap in membership between the child-savers and the social reformers who led the temperance movement. Their efforts eventually resulted in prohibition (discussed in Chapter 1).

Conclusion

A historical perspective provides excellent examples of blurred boundaries between religious and political belief systems. With the witchcraze, residential schooling, and the Victorian child-savers, those behaviours, beliefs, and people that were considered deviant within specific religious belief systems came to be socially typed as deviant in political belief systems as well. As components of religious beliefs were incorporated into the political realm, social control shifted to legislation and other forms of government policy.

Looking back, most of us consider what happened during the witch hunts and with residential schooling to be overwhelmingly negative examples of what can happen when religious beliefs serve as the foundation for governance of a society. Perhaps you believe that these two historical events are not only instances of religion serving as a social typer of deviance, but are also examples of *religion as deviance*, wherein religious institutions or their representatives have done something "deviant" themselves. The case of the Victorian child-savers, for example, had both positive and negative aspects. On one hand, part of the movement's foundation did lie in prejudice and was based on social characteristics like class, race, and family structure. Movement activists did, in fact, attempt to impose their own middle-class norms and values on everyone in society. On the other hand, they also provided assistance to children who were abused or neglected and the historical efforts of the child-savers underlie our modern-day child abuse and neglect laws, the child welfare and social assistance systems, and compulsory education for children.

Religion and Politics Today

Perhaps you think that the blurring of religious and political belief systems is something relegated to the distant past, something that occurred when people were less educated, less aware, and less informed. In fact, the influence of religion and politics continues throughout the world today. It is most obvious in those societies we looked at earlier, where the government exerts authoritarian control over religious beliefs and practices or attempts to intimidate members of non-approved religions (e.g., in Vietnam, Iran, Saudi Arabia). Another example where the eradication of religious and political boundaries is obvious is Afghanistan under Taliban rule. During that time, the laws were based on the Taliban's fundamentalist interpretation of Islam. Behaviour considered criminal included dancing, listening to music, and proselytizing (i.e., expressing any other religious beliefs to another person), as well as the failure of women to be fully covered (including their faces) when outside their homes and allowing themselves to be seen through windows when inside their homes.

The blurring of religious and political boundaries is also evident in the United States today in the influence of the Christian Coalition (Watson, 1997; Vuijst, 1995; Ontario Consultants on Religious Tolerance, 2003; Boston, 1996). The precursor to the Christian coalition was the Moral Majority, a politically active religious group comprised of ultra-right-wing conservative fundamentalist Christians. Televangelist Pat Robertson founded this group, whose symbolic leader was fellow televangelist Jerry Falwell. The Moral Majority's political efforts culminated in Pat Robertson's run for president of the United States in 1988.

After his attempt at the presidency failed, it appeared that the Moral Majority had lost steam, leading Stebbins (1996) to conclude that the ultra-right-wing

Christian conservative political movement had essentially disappeared by the end of the 1980s. In fact, it had not disappeared—it was simply reborn in 1990 as the Christian Coalition, with Pat Robertson as its founder. It was registered as a "social welfare organization" that would provide assistance to the needy. On this basis, it received tax-exempt status. As a requirement for tax-exempt status, it could not be active in the political agenda of any single political party. Its members could express political beliefs, but the organization could not give money to any particular party; nor could it be active in lobbying for any specific party. In time, it became clear that the Christian Coalition was engaging in precisely these prohibited activities, and in 1999 its tax-exempt status was removed (MacDonald, 1999).

After Pat Robertson's failed attempts at the presidency, the Christian Coalition determined that it would be more successful at a local level. Subsequently, it refocused its efforts on state and local politics (school boards, town councillors, etc.). Using what have been called **stealth tactics**, during election time political candidates avoid religious agendas and focus on non-religious issues. The Christian Coalition makes ultra-right-wing fundamentalist Christian voters aware of its candidates by distributing voter guides, primarily through fundamentalist Christian churches, on the Sunday before election day. Prior to the 2000 presidential election, they distributed more than 70 million voter guides throughout 50 states (Christian Coalition of America, 2003). The voter guide lists all of the candidates in a district and evaluates them on the basis of the Coalition's "pro-family agenda"; in practice, the only candidates likely to be approved in the voter guide are the most conservative of Republicans.

Rival political candidates and other critics have accused the Coalition of lying about rivals' positions on various issues in order to increase the likelihood of the candidate they support being elected. The Coalition runs political training workshops for members who want to run for political office, as well as workshops teaching other members the most effective ways to convince voters whom to vote for. For example, a segment of the documentary *Onward Christian Soldiers* captures a meeting held for church ministers (Vuijst, 1995). At this meeting, the Coalition representative tells his fellow ministers that although he cannot tell his own parishioners whom to vote for, he can tell them whom he is voting for. He then tells them they can do the same in front of their parishioners, and if they are good leaders, the parishioners will follow and vote for the same person.

These stealth tactics resulted in a period of extreme success for the Coalition. Scholars and political analysts suggest the Christian Coalition essentially controls the Republican Party, and that a Republican candidate cannot get elected without the support of the Coalition. Various groups have formed in opposition to the Christian Coalition (e.g., "Fight the Right"), and civil rights organizations (e.g., the American Civil Liberties Union) are involved in opposition as well. Their core concern is that because of the Coalition's power and influence, their religious belief system will come to be reflected in law and government policy. Many think that the institutionalization of the Coalition's belief system within government would violate human rights legislation, although this is disputed by the Coalition.

Leaders of the Christian Coalition have stated, however, that they are opposed to the separation of church and state and want to incorporate a particular form of religion into the public school system (e.g., avoiding teaching evolution in science classes). Concerned critics fear these beliefs will be turned into law if the Coalition fully succeeds. However, with the election of Barack Obama as president of the United States, the political power of the Coalition, and of the ultra-conservative Christian right in general, seems to have waned. Some representatives of this religious-political view (although not necessarily representatives of the Coalition itself) "have admitted that their association with George W. Bush has not only hurt the cause of social conservatives, but contributed to the failure of the key objectives of its 30-year struggle" (*Edmonton Journal*, April 11, 2008).

TIME TO REVIEW

- What role does religion play as a social typer of deviance in terms of individuals' own behaviours and their evaluations of others?
- How did religion act as a social typer of deviance in terms of (a) residential schooling, and (b) the Victorian child-savers movement?
- What happened during the witchcraze? How did religion serve as a social typer of deviance during this time?

- What are some contemporary examples that show how the boundaries between religious and political belief systems become blurred?
- In what way is the Christian Coalition an example of religion influencing politics? Why have some critics and scholars been concerned?

Exercise Your Mind

Is the blurring of religious and political boundaries evident in Canadian politics in any way, or is it limited to the American context? A good place to start your investigation is the website of the Canadian Family Action Coalition at www.familyaction.org. This organization, located in Calgary, encourages Christians to be politically active, and their website focuses on current political and legal issues. What political themes emerge on their site? Can you find other groups, perhaps associated with non-Christian religions, that also bring religious beliefs to bear on political attitudes and actions? Compare this organization and any other organizations you find with the Christian Coalition (www.cc.org). What similarities and differences can you detect between the groups? Finally, what are the possible positive and negative outcomes that could occur if any of the religious belief systems you looked at were to influence legislation and government policy?

CHAPTER SUMMARY

■ Two types of relationship exist between religion and deviance. Religion as deviance refers to religious institutions (or their representatives) that commit deviant acts, and to religious groups that are considered deviant in their entirety. Religion as a social typer of deviance describes religion when it serves to tell us who or what should be considered deviant.

■ Traditionally, the typology distinguishing between *ecclesias, churches, sects, and cults* has been used to determine which religions are deviant. Sects are perceived as deviant because of a combination of rigid belief systems and high levels of commitment required of members.

■ The media presents distorted images of cults, which influence public attitudes toward those religious groups. Cults are considered deviant because of the presumed brainwashing, sexual deviance, and dangers they present to members and to outsiders.

■ Deviant religions are subject to a wide range of social control measures. The *anti-cult movement* and *counter-cult movement* are active in reducing the threat they consider cults present. The media exerts control over cults in conjunction with these movements and in their representations of cults. Governments control deviant religions, but precisely which religions are considered deviant and the manner in which they are controlled vary across countries.

■ Numerous forms of resistance to the social typing of deviant religions occur as well, with the internationally recognized right to *freedom of religion* as the nexus of this resistance. Individual religious groups try to demonstrate that they are not deviant. Human rights groups and religious freedom groups also resist the social typing of deviant religions. Today, academics even call into question the traditional distinctions between churches, sects, and cults.

■ Religion serves as a social typer of deviance on many levels. Individually, our religious beliefs provide guidelines for our own behaviour and how to evaluate the behaviour of others. At a societal level, religion can socially type deviance when the boundaries between religious and political belief systems become blurred. Historically, this occurred during the witch persecutions, with residential schooling, and with the Victorian child-savers movement. In contemporary society, one example is the power held by the Christian Coalition in American politics.

DEVIANCE IN PRINT

Jenkins, P. (2000). *Mystics and Messiahs: Cults and New Religions in American History.* New York: Oxford University Press.

Shupe, A. (2008). *Rogue Clerics: The Social Problem of Clergy Deviance.* New Brunswick, NJ: Transaction Publishers.

DEVIANCE AT THE MOVIES

Gray, J. (Director), Bugliosi, V., & Gentry, C. (Writers). (2004). *Helter Skelter*. United States: Lakeside Productions and Warner Bros. Television. (137 minutes).

This made-for-TV movie portrays infamous "cult" leader Charles Manson, who led his teenage followers on a killing spree in the late 1960s. The spree resulted in the murder of director Roman Polanski's wife, Sharon Tate, who was 7 months pregnant at the time.

Ewing, H., & Grady, H. (Directors). (2006). *Jesus Camp*. Toronto, ON: Distributed by Mongrel Media.

This film goes behind the scenes at a summer camp where children are trained as religious-political "soldiers" who will "take back America for Christ" (www.mongrelmedia.com).

ENDNOTE

1 Karl Marx. [1844]. *Contribution to the Critique of Hegel's Philosophy of Right. In Deutsch-Französische Jahrbücher*, February 1844. Retrieved September 16, 2006, from **www3.baylor.edu/~Scott_Moore/texts/Marx_Contr_Crit.html**

KEY TERMS

beliefs, **p. 238**

belief systems, **p. 238**

religion as deviance, **p. 239**

religion as a social typer of deviance, **p. 239**

ecclesia, **p. 240**

churches, **p. 241**

denominations, **p. 241**

sects, **p. 241**

cults, **p. 241**

deviancy amplification, **p. 245**

anti-cult movement, **p. 250**

cult awareness groups, **p. 251**

counter-cult movement, **p. 251**

new religious movements, **p. 257**

residential schooling, **p. 261**

child-savers movement, **p. 263**

stealth tactics, **p. 266**

CHAPTER 9

Scientific Belief Systems

Learning Objectives

After reading this chapter, you should be able to

- Describe the components of science.
- List the different forms of deviance in science, and provide examples.
- Describe the contrasting explanations for deviance in science.
- Define deviant science, and provide examples.
- Describe the power science holds as a social typer of deviance, and give historical and contemporary examples of science acting as a social typer.
- Describe the contemporary debates over the science of genetics.

"The wise man regulates his conduct by the theories both of religion and science. But he regards these theories not as statements of ultimate fact but as art forms." (J.B.S. Haldane, 1892–19641)

Religion Compared to Science

The above quotation indicates that both religious and scientific belief systems are vital parts of our daily lives. It also suggests that these belief systems can, and indeed should, serve social control functions, and that if we are wise, we will act on the basis of religion and science. In the quote, Haldane also points to the subjectivity of religious and scientific belief systems. Although these belief systems proclaim truths, they emerge through processes of social construction or creation, just as art does. In the preceding chapter, we saw that religion is subjected to measures of social control and also steers processes of social control—it is socially typed, but also socially types other people, behaviours, and characteristics.

> ## Ask Yourself
>
> In your own life, what roles are played by the truths proclaimed by the religious belief system you adhere to and scientific belief systems? Which of these belief systems plays a larger role in your life?

In this chapter, we will see that the same is true for scientific belief systems. Science serves a social control function, dictating to us what is deviant and providing a means for controlling that deviance. It is also made subject to social control itself in order to prevent and resolve deviance. That is, there are two different relationships between deviance and science—**science as deviance** (i.e., when deviance occurs within science) and **science as a social typer of deviance** (i.e., when science tells us what is or should be considered deviant).

Science can be broadly defined as "knowledge or a system of knowledge covering *general truths* of the operation of general laws especially as obtained and tested through *scientific method* [italics added]" (Merriam-Webster, 2003). Looking at this definition, we can see that science consists of both **scientific belief systems** (proclaimed truths) and **technologies** (techniques and methods used to obtain that knowledge) (Ben-Yehuda, 1990). Belief systems in the sciences are twofold. First, there are claims about the nature of reality—i.e., the way the world works. Second, there are ethical and moral claims embedded in the scientific belief system. For example, in cloning research, claims are being made about both the biological or genetic foundations of cloning and the implicit morality of cloning.

Some beliefs are characteristic of science as a whole (e.g., that the truths about nature can be discovered), but other beliefs are specific to each of the disciplines or sub-disciplines of science. For instance, biology and sociology each have their own distinct truths based on the specific objects of study. The same can be said for technologies. The technology known as the *scientific method* is broadly shared among sciences, but specific techniques and methods are also used within each sub-discipline of science, such as in physics and genetics.

Science as Deviance

"Science's major effort is to find, describe, and analyze . . . the truth." (Ben-Yehuda, 1990, p. 196)

In the pursuit of this ultimate goal, scientists can be thought of as deviant in two instances. First, scientists may be socially typed when they engage in scientific misconduct or violate ethical guidelines; this is **deviance in science**. Second, scientists may be considered deviant when they are part of a discipline that is not recognized by the scientific community as being real science; this can be called **deviant science**.

Deviance in Science

Forms of Deviance in Science

In any occupation or profession, there are some individuals who engage in deviant acts. Some elite members of the business world embezzle funds or participate in insider trading, some retail employees steal products from stores, and some police officers use excessive force. Similarly, some scientists engage in acts of scientific misconduct.

Precisely what does *deviance in science* consist of? Nineteenth-century physicist Charles Babbage (cited in Judson, 2004) identified several forms of behaviour that are commonly considered deviant in the scientific community. First is **forging**, which refers to scientists who falsify their data, reporting observations that never really occurred. Forging is involved in a second form of deviance in science, **hoaxes**, but hoaxes are distinct in that it is expected they will be discovered (Judson, 2004) or they are intended to be similar to practical jokes (Ben-Yehuda, 1986).

A scientific hoax with Canadian origins was discovered in 2000. In 1999, the curator of the Royal Tyrrell Museum, Philip Currie, brought a paleontological find to the attention of *National Geographic*. A fossil found in China was purported to be a new species that bridged birds and dinosaurs, and a photograph of the fossil was published in the magazine. It did not take long for fellow scientists to declare that the fossil had to be a hoax, and an investigation determined that it indeed was. The fossil had been created by putting together pieces of fossils from various different species.

Knowing this, the curator (via X-rays of the fossil) reported the "finding" to *National Geographic* anyway (Parker, 2000). Representatives of the museum declared this to be a mistake and the curator was able to keep his position. This incident bears a striking resemblance to the Piltdown Man hoax in 1912; the partial skull and jawbone of an unknown form of early stone-age human were actually taken from separate species, put together, and treated with a chemical to make them look older (Judson, 2004). More recently, another scientific hoax was brought to the public's attention. Scientists working for the company Clonaid contacted the media claiming that they had successfully cloned a human being; however, the rest of the scientific community declared this to be a hoax and the Clonaid scientists have refused to come forward to offer evidence of their cloning success.

A third type of deviance in science is **trimming**, which means manipulating real observations so that they will support a theory in question. A fourth type is **cooking**—that is, selectively reporting only that data that supports a theory in question and suppressing or ignoring remaining data. Since Babbage first described these infractions more than a century ago, science has grown and become considerably more complex, and, some suggest, so have the means of engaging in scientific deviance. Judson (2004) describes fabrication, which is equivalent to forging and hoaxes, and falsification, which includes trimming, cooking, combining two experiments into one set of results, "and so on through all permutations the imp of the perverse can whisper" (p. 5).

Some scholars mention **ethical violations** as another form of scientific deviance. The various disciplines of science are governed by different codes of ethics. The code of ethics you may be most familiar with is that used by some medical doctors—the Hippocratic oath—whereby doctors vow to balance the protection of their patients with the pursuit of science and the practice of the art of medicine. But all scientific disciplines are governed by codes of ethics. For example, the Canadian Sociological Association has a code of ethics governing various aspects of research and professional practice, addressing such issues as (a) how research is done, (b) protecting research participants from harm, (c) relationships with academic peers, students, and the discipline of sociology, and (d) harassment and exploitation. Although each scientific discipline may have its own specific codes of ethics, all scientists working in academic institutions are subject to the Research Ethics Boards of their institutions. Before any faculty member at a university begins a research project on human participants (e.g., observations, interviews, surveys, clinical treatments), a research proposal must be submitted to the Research Ethics Board. The proposal must describe the project, its rationale, the research methods that will be used, and the efforts being undertaken to protect any vulnerable populations that will be affected by the project. Board approval is required before the faculty member may begin research.

There is a diversity and complexity of forms of *deviance in science*. For the purposes of simplicity, **scientific misconduct** can be used as the umbrella term to refer to fabrication, falsification, breaches of ethics, plagiarism, and any other scientific practices deemed unacceptable or inappropriate. Concerns about the nature and extent of scientific misconduct intensified in the late 1970s, partially due to the 1974 Patchwork Mouse incident. This incident involved a researcher who claimed to have grafted skin from a black mouse onto a white mouse, but had actually drawn patches on the white mouse using a black marker (Bleicher, 2003; Judson, 2004). The resulting concern with how to prevent, detect, and punish scientific misconduct has steadily grown since that time.

Cases of scientific misconduct are now regularly reported in science journals, some of which publish an annual review of cases (e.g., *Nature*). For example, in just the first six months of 2003, several instances of misconduct were revealed. A British cardiologist was suspended from practice for one year because of his fraudulent research claims. He falsely claimed that following a first heart attack, men of Indian descent had a higher risk of death than men not of Indian descent (Kerr, 2003). A neurologist was reprimanded for falsifying data about the effectiveness of a particular drug in the treatment of diabetes. The drug's manufacturer had promised the neurologist 0.5% of the profits from the drug if it became marketable (Dyer, 2003).

A physicist who had published several high-profile articles on his research was found to have falsified data when two fellow researchers were unable to reproduce his findings (Ball, 2003). A well-known environmental scientist who published a book that was far more optimistic about the environmental future than other research was determined to have falsified and distorted data, plagiarized other people's work, and deliberately misrepresented research findings (White, 2003). The Office of Research Integrity (an American federal organization that handles allegations of, and provides education about, misconduct in research funded by the public health service) also reports recent cases of misconduct in its quarterly newsletter. In its March 2009 issue alone, four cases of falsification resulting in punitive measures were reported; in one case, it was determined that a researcher associated with Harvard Medical School, Brigham and Women's Hospital, California Institute of Technology, and Massachusetts Institute of Technology falsified data in not just one instance, but "in seven published papers, three submitted papers . . . one submitted book chapter, and multiple presentations . . ." (Office of Research Integrity, 2009, p. 7).

The social sciences and other disciplines outside of the hard sciences are not immune to such instances of fraud. Several of the twin studies and adoption studies from the 1970s and 1980s that claimed genetic determinants to various psychological and behavioural characteristics (e.g., criminality, personality traits) have since been called into question, and accusations of scientific misconduct made in some instances (Joseph & Baldwin, 2000). Cases of fabrication, falsification, and ethical violations have been found in the social sciences, health services (e.g., nursing), and human services (e.g., counselling) (Gibelman & Gelman, 2005). However, misconduct continues to be associated primarily with the hard sciences, especially biomedical research (Gibelman & Gelman, 2005)— not because misconduct is necessarily more common in these fields, but because it is more likely to be looked for and detected.

Ben-Yehuda (1986, p. 18) suggests that deviance is far more likely to be detected in research on hot issues and in breakthrough research because of the interest that is generated—in the twenty-first century, these terms often characterize biomedical research. Furthermore, it is this type of research that receives the most funding from external agencies (Gibelman & Gelman, 2005), and accountability of funds is another factor that stimulates greater interest in potential research misconduct. The U.S. Office for Research Integrity (cited in Langlais, 2006) reports that "the financial cost of gross misconduct in the biomedical fields has been estimated to be as high as $1 million per case" (para. 3). A recent example of scientific misconduct in a heavily funded breakthrough area of research is the case of scientist Dr. Hwang Woo Suk (see Box 9.1).

Any of the described types of scientific misconduct can be combined with yet another type—that of **junk science**. Junk science refers to the ungrounded claims of people with little or no scientific background or people using their scientific credentials alone to try to convince people of the validity of their claims.

Box 9.1   The Rise and Fall of Dr. Hwang Woo Suk

In May 2005, Dr. Hwang Woo Suk, a professor at Seoul National University in South Korea, was a national celebrity and famed international scientist. By the end of that same year, he was under investigation by the university and criminal prosecutors for scientific misconduct and fraud.

Hwang was propelled to fame when he published an article claiming he had successfully cloned human embryos and extracted stem cells from them. His research appeared to be the first step in developing customized cures for various diseases and repairs for spinal cord injuries (Associated Press, 2006; *The Lancet*, 2005; Onishi, 2006). Soon, his research was featured on a Korean postage stamp, Korean Air provided him with free airline travel anywhere in the world, the government provided him with bodyguards and gave him tens of millions of dollars for further research, and the Korean public treated him as a national hero (Onishi, 2006).

However, it wasn't long before anonymous web postings and a call to a television news program claimed Hwang had fabricated at least some of his research data (Onishi, 2006). An investigation began at Seoul National University, and its final report revealed that Hwang's data on human cloning and stem cells had been falsified. He quickly lost his status and credibility, a loss that was compounded by his emotional public apology on Korean national television. Seoul National University fired him.

Then in May 2006, he and five other members of his research team were indicted for embezzlement and bioethics law violations (Associated Press, 2006). Hwang initially denied responsibility for the misconduct, claiming that junior researchers at one of the labs he was working with had provided him with fraudulent data without his knowledge. Since then he has admitted to falsifying data, though he still claims his fellow researchers are just as guilty as he is.

Not only has this case received worldwide media attention, it has also stimulated tremendous discussion and debate within the scientific community (*The Lancet*, 2006). Many questions are being asked. For example, how did this fraud fall through the cracks of the peer-review process at the journal that published his articles? Who should hold ultimate responsibility for preventing and detecting scientific misconduct? And how widespread is this problem? Is Hwang simply one "bad apple"? Or is he the "tip of the iceberg"?

It is frequently used in courtrooms and in front of other legislative bodies as lawyers and junk scientists form a coalition in the joint pursuit of profit (Huber, 1991). The tobacco industry has been a target of *junk science* accusations and, in fact, has been accused of many other forms of scientific misconduct as well.

The Tobacco Industry.   One has only to think of the scientists who have worked for tobacco companies for many years, claiming that their research showed that smoking was neither addictive nor harmful, to see many possible forms of *deviance in science* (Ramsey, 2002; Rampton & Stauber, 2000b, 2001). Were they using research data fraudulently? Were they seeing what they wanted to see in the data, either intentionally or unintentionally? Were they simply using their scientific credentials to convince people of the truth of their claims? Were public relations firms simply using scientific credentials to convince people of the tobacco companies' claims?

It is possible to say that various forms of fabrication, falsification, and junk science have all characterized the scientific claims of the tobacco industry, "which has arguably done more to corrupt science than any other industry in history" (Rampton & Stauber, 2000a). The tobacco industry did not finally admit that smoking is harmful until 1999. Critics say they then turned their sights on the research that was showing a link between secondhand smoke and health problems. In their efforts to discredit that research, they had their own scientific experts label it *junk science*, and even established The Advancement of Sound Science Coalition (TASSC) to explain to people the difference between invalid *junk science* and valid sound science (Rampton & Stauber, 2000a, 2000b, 2001; Ong & Glantz, 2001).

Initially, the fact that this coalition was created and funded by Philip Morris (a leading tobacco firm) was hidden. Of course, the scientists from TASSC consistently showed that the research linking secondhand smoke with physical harm was invalid science. The scientific claims made by TASSC typically conclude that research showing evidence of harm due to any environmental toxins (e.g., arsenic in water supplies, airborne pollutants) is all *junk science*. Critics of TASSC comment on how its research always comes down in favour of the tobacco industry, and opposed to any environmental legislation that would regulate that industry. So although claims of *junk science* are frequently directed at the tobacco industry, similar claims are directed by the tobacco industry at its critics.

The Extent of the Problem.   The prevalence of scientific misconduct is difficult to determine (Judson, 2004) and is a matter of some debate. Some scholars claim these actions are quite rare in the scientific community due to the search for truth that most scientists pursue in their work. However, other researchers suggest these behaviours are far more frequent than empirical studies can capture (Ben-Yehuda, 1986; Park, 2000; Dyer, 2005; *The Lancet*, 2006). Barrett and Jay (2005) found that widespread scientific fraud forced one pharmaceutical company to shut down seven of its research centres in one European country, suggesting that the problem may be of considerable proportions.

A survey of 3 200 medical researchers in the United States found that one-third admitted to engaging in at least 1 of 10 "serious" forms of research misconduct, including overlooking "colleagues' use of flawed data," plagiarizing other people's ideas, changing "the design or results of a study under pressure from a funding source," and ignoring or erasing data "that would have contradicted the results of the research process" (Martinson, cited in Dyer, 2005, p. 1465). Another survey of more than 2 000 researchers found that over the previous three years, they had observed 201 cases of suspected misconduct within their own departments; more than one third of those incidents were never reported to anyone (Titus, Wells, & Rhoades, 2008). Whether scientific misconduct is perceived as a relatively rare or relatively common occurrence determines the explanation that is offered for it. Thus, the debates over the extent of the problem are directly related to debates over explanations of the problem.

Explanations for Deviance in Science

The essence of the debate over why scientific misconduct occurs lies in the contrast between **bad apple/bad person theory** and **iceberg theory** (Ben-Yehuda, 1986; Bechtel & Pearson, 1985; James, 1995). For many years, deviant acts committed by scientists were explained on the basis of individual factors—the *bad apple/bad person theory* of scientific deviance (Ben-Yehuda, 1986; Bechtel & Pearson, 1985). Just as a few "bad" people commit crimes because of psychological disturbances, personality factors, or free choice, a few "bad" scientists commit deviant acts in their work for similar reasons. This theory suggests that we need to find those few bad apples and throw them out so they do not spoil the whole barrel. For example, an editorial in *The Lancet* (2006) about the Hwang Woo Suk incident points out that the structure of science itself is sound: "The fact that Hwang's work has so quickly been shown to be fake is proof that the system of oversight currently in place has the power to self-correct when a transgression occurs" (p. 1).

In contrast, the *iceberg theory* of scientific deviance claims that the structure within which scientists work actually encourages deviance, making it likely to occur (Titus, Wells, & Rhoades, 2008; Nylenna & Simonson, 2006; Ben-Yehuda, 1986). Sleight (2004) proposes that many cases of scientific misconduct "are prompted by ambition/publication pressures" (p. 33). That is, scientists today face an incredible amount of "pressure to publish." The number of publications that a scientist has can determine hiring, increases in salary, promotion, likelihood of receiving research grants, and the degree of status within the scientific community. All of these pressures increase the chance that scientists will use deviant means of getting these publications. Furthermore, the institution of science exists within a particular societal context. For instance, an analysis of Hwang Woo Suk's misconduct points out that broader cultural characteristics are reflected within the scientific culture of South Korea: "Knowledge acquisition in South Korea has close connections to hierarchies of status and prestige; and . . . South Korean work ethos imposes a severe workload on junior researchers" (Kim, 2008, p. 397), creating a foundation upon which this misconduct occurred.

Another factor contributing to scientific misconduct is that it is unlikely to be detected. Most known cases of misconduct are discovered by accident rather than as a function of institutional processes or safeguards (Judson, cited in McCarthy, 2004). In the instances of scientific deviance that Barrett and Jay (2005) have been called upon to investigate, most of the scientists had been engaging in misconduct for 5 to 10 years prior to being caught. Unless research is controversial or about a particularly hot issue, it is unlikely to stimulate questions and efforts at replication, because replicating someone else's research does not add much to the prestige of scientists.

Because the chances of being caught are remote, there is little motivation to refrain from deviant acts. Finally, although organizational structures and committees have been put in place to investigate reports of *deviance in science*, their investigations are often fraught with controversy themselves (e.g., White, 2003), and even if scientists' misconduct is detected, sanctions are not likely to be of sufficient severity to deter other potential offenders. For example, the curator at the Royal Tyrrell Museum may have had his reputation tarnished for his participation in the hoax described earlier, but he was able to keep his position as curator of this prestigious museum. Combined, these characteristics of the scientific community create a structure that actually encourages rather than deters *deviance in science*. After finding that one third of scientists who were surveyed admitted to engaging in various forms of misconduct, Martinson (cited in Dyer, 2005) concludes the following: ". . . we've shown that it's about more than just fraud, and we shouldn't be looking for a few bad apples. It may be that competition in science in this country has reached dysfunctional levels" (p. 1465).

The scholars who consider the detected cases of *deviance in science* to be just the tip of the iceberg have applied various specific theories that we addressed in Chapter 2 to explain this form of deviance. For example, Ben-Yehuda (1986) proposes that *techniques of neutralization* (Sykes & Matza, 1957) play an important role in scientific deviance. Techniques like *denial of injury* or *denial of responsibility* help scientists to justify their actions, convincing themselves or others that what they are doing is not *really* wrong or that they are not responsible for the misconduct.

We saw this in the case of Korean scientist Dr. Hwang Woo Suk, who initially claimed that junior scientists at another lab had provided him with the fraudulent data and that he had no idea it had been fabricated. Bechtel & Pearson (1985) discuss the usefulness of Robert Merton's *strain theory*. They point out that scientific deviance can be considered an example of the mode of adaptation called *innovation*; i.e., the gap between legitimized goals and access to the legitimate means of attaining those goals leads some people to pursue those goals in "innovative" ways. Just as some people who want fancy cars will steal rather than purchase them, some scientists who want career success will falsify data (or other forms of deviance) rather than obtain it legitimately.

Gottfredson and Hirschi's (1990) *general theory of crime* has not been used to study scientific deviance specifically but has been applied to occupational deviance more generally. Research has found that *self-control* plays a role in occupational deviance, particularly when low self-control is combined with an environment in which co-workers are engaging in deviance (Gibson & Wright, 2001). If co-workers appear to be rewarded for their deviance, such as by receiving promotions or large research grants for their productivity in publishing, the pull toward deviance may be even greater.

Exercise Your Mind

Go back to the various theories discussed in Chapters 2 and 3. Select the ONE theory from each of these chapters that you think best explains scientific misconduct. What makes each of those theories preferable to the others in those chapters?

Misconduct and the Corporatization of Science

The prevalence and reasons for scientific misconduct are influenced by ties with corporate industry. A growing proportion of scientific research is funded by commercial industry, especially in biomedical fields. These scientist-industry partnerships can result in scientific misconduct that is steered by the funding source, or done by the funded scientists without the funder's knowledge. Corporate funding and the nature of the research results frequently go hand in hand (Born, 2004; Caulfield, 2004).

Martinson (cited in Dyer, 2005) found that 15% of 3 200 medical researchers surveyed had "changed the design or results of a study under pressure from a funding source" (p. 1465). And resulting publications from industry-sponsored research are far more likely to report positive findings than those sponsored by public (i.e., government) funds (Krimsky, cited in Thompson, Baird, & Downie, 2005). This pattern is most evident in therapeutic/drug research sponsored by pharmaceutical companies. For example, "an analysis of 70 studies of specific cardiac drugs showed that 96% of authors with ties to the pharmaceutical company produced favorable results, while only 37% of independently funded studies *of the same drugs* showed favorable results" (Stelfox, Chua, O'Rourke, & Detsky, cited in Born, 2004, para. 12).

In many cases, the contracts between pharmaceutical companies and researchers stipulate that the company retains the right to determine which research results do and do not get published (Born, 2004). Even in those instances where the company does not retain that right to publish, the company may delay the publication of negative results (Thompson, Baird, & Downie, 2005), which enables the company to "quickly fund a new study that produces a favorable response and then publish only the positive results" (Born, 1994, para. 14).

In addition, most clinical drug research is now done by commercial centres hired by the pharmaceutical companies, compared to 15 years ago when it was done in university research departments, a phenomenon that has been labelled *post-academic science* (Ziman, cited in Montgomery and Oliver (2009). This creates a structure within which researchers face considerable pressure to obtain the results that will make their funding sources happy, a structure that is conducive to scientific misconduct.

While the pharmaceutical company itself may not be aware of misconduct, when it is detected they can face economic sanctions. For instance, in 2004, the manufacturers of the anti-depressant Paxil® settled a lawsuit claiming they had hidden data showing that the drug increased suicidal thoughts in children. They paid a US$2.5 million fine and agreed to make all of their clinical trial data available online; in this way, they were able to avoid criminal charges (Levine, 2005). To most of us, US$2.5 million seems like a large sum of money. However, three years earlier, the very same company had been ordered to pay US$6.4 million to the family of a man who had committed suicide after taking Paxil® for only 48 hours. That larger fine obviously did not deter the company from future misconduct.

The profitability of the pharmaceutical industry is such that fines of even millions of dollars seem little more than a proverbial "slap on the wrist" (Levine, 2005, para. 3). By the turn of the twenty-first century, the pharmaceutical industry had become "the most profitable industry in the United States . . . with an 18.6% return on revenues" (Conrad & Leiter, 2004, p. 161). An industry that spends more than $4 billion each year just on public advertising in the United States alone (Mintzes, 2006) is difficult to control with light economic sanctions.

One distinct form of *deviance in science* that is suggested to be quite prevalent in research sponsored by pharmaceutical companies is that of **ghostwriting** (Barnett, 2003; Kelton, 2005; Thomas, 2004). The pharmaceutical company itself (or a subcontractor) conducts research into a particular drug or other therapy, has an employee of the company write an article about the results of the research, and then pays external scientists to put their names on the article as authors. Healy (cited in Thompson, Baird, & Downie, 2005) claims that "at least 50% of academic publications in therapeutics [are] now ghost written, in particular . . . in the most prestigious medical journals" (para. 17). Journal editors will not publish articles that they know have been ghostwritten, but as with other forms of scientific misconduct, detection may occur by accident. For instance, the *New England Journal of Medicine* retracted a ghostwritten article, but discovered it had been ghostwritten only "when German cardiologist Dr. Hubert Seggewiss, one of the eight listed authors, called the editor of the journal to say he had never seen any version of the paper" (Barnett, 2003, para. 5).

Controlling Scientific Misconduct

Scientific misconduct can be controlled in a number of ways. Scientists found to have engaged in misconduct can face temporary or permanent disbarment from public research funding and from serving on public research bodies, and may face a loss of credibility among their peers. However, preventative social control is even more important. Just as effective efforts to curb binge drinking on university campuses must target the whole environment rather than just those students who are problem drinkers (see Chapter 5), reducing scientific misconduct also requires a population prevention approach (Nylenna & Simonsen, 2006). This approach includes the following: regular informational and educational seminars at research institutions; focusing on misconduct at its broadest level, rather than only on fabrication, falsification, and plagiarism; mentoring of young researchers in order to transmit guidelines; investigation mechanisms at the national level; and a restructuring of the academic reward system to remove the climate of publish-or-perish (Nylenna & Simonsen, 2006).

Population prevention is a relatively recent approach to controlling scientific misconduct. Montgomery and Oliver's (2009) analysis of the discourses (or what they call "institutional logics," p. 139) of the regulation of scientific misconduct reveals three distinct time periods. Prior to 1975, the institutional logic emphasized science as self-governing, based upon the assumption that science was inherently about objectivity and the search for truth. Sociologist Robert Merton (1973) described this as the *normative structure of science*, and listed four norms of science: **communism** (not referring to Marxist politics but to the idea that scientists freely give up rights to the knowledge that they create so that this knowledge can be shared by all); **skepticism** (all ideas must be subjected to rigorous scrutiny); **disinterestedness** (scientific work is done in the name of truth rather than for any personal gain or vested interests); and **universalism** (knowledge is free from any biases based on characteristics such as race, gender, or religion). Although Merton himself recognized that not all scientists would necessarily adhere to these norms, the institutional logic of the time suggested that normative pressures within the scientific community would be sufficient to prevent misconduct.

However, with the growing awareness of specific cases of misconduct (such as the 1974 Patchwork Mouse incident described earlier in this chapter), and of questionable ethical practices (e.g., Stanley Milgram's studies on obedience), it became increasingly clear that the normative structure of science was not sufficient to prevent acts of misconduct. Consequently, from 1975 to 1990, the institutional logic became one of coercive measures to both punish and prevent misconduct. This heralded an era when institutional research boards emerged, and research institutions that received public research funding were required to implement procedures for investigating allegations of misconduct.

Since 1990, the growth of private research funding (through scientist–industry partnerships) over public funding has removed some of the power behind the coercive social control mechanisms of the previous time period; it has also subjected scientists to new and different pressures that can increase the likelihood of misconduct (as discussed on pp. 278–279).

As a result, the institutional logic has once again shifted from a focus on preventing/punishing misconduct to an emphasis on "promoting research integrity" (Montgomery & Oliver, 2009, p. 146). This entails a cooperative, multifaceted effort, among governmental organizations, universities, professional academic societies, credentialing associations, and academic journal editors. It is within this discourse, and its resulting network of stakeholders, that the population prevention approach has emerged.

The history of scientific misconduct is almost as long as the history of science itself (Judson, 2004). But with the proliferation of science over the last century, we have also seen the escalation of scientific misconduct. From the Piltdown Man of 1912 to some of the industry-sponsored research of today, the list of instances of scientific misconduct continues to grow, as does the debate over how to best control *deviance in science.*

TIME TO REVIEW

- What are the components of science, and what are the possible relationships between science and deviance?
- What are some of the forms of deviance in science, and what are some examples?
- What types of scientific misconduct has the tobacco industry been accused of, and how have they responded?

- How is deviance in science explained by bad apple/bad person theory and iceberg theory?
- In what way may the relationship between commercial industry and science promote scientific misconduct?
- How have the institutional logics of social control changed over time?

Deviant Science

As we have seen thus far, deviance can occur in science when scientists engage in particular behaviours that are deemed deviant by fellow members of the scientific community (i.e., *deviance in science*). Another form that *science as deviance* can take is when a whole discipline of science is perceived as deviant in its entirety— the notion of *deviant science* (Ben-Yehuda, 1990).

Figure 9.1   THE DEVIANT SCIENCE / REAL SCIENCE CONTINUUM

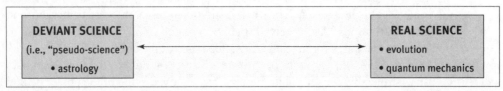

Source: Adapted from Shermer's (2001) model of the science/pseudo-science continuum.

An entire science may be socially typed as deviant when its belief system and/or technologies are significantly called into question. If subject to enough doubt, the belief system and/or technologies may be determined not to be a science at all; instead, they may be labelled a "non-science." Particular combinations of belief systems and technologies can be thought of as falling along a continuum.

At one end of the continuum lie those belief systems, such as astrology, magnetic therapy, and Bible codes (i.e., *pseudo-sciences*), that have not been supported by empirical research using scientific methods. At the other end of the continuum are those belief systems that have been consistently supported by the most research evidence, such as evolution and quantum mechanics. Falling at various points between these two extreme ends of the continuum is the bulk of other belief systems/technologies, such as those involved with human cloning (Shermer, 2001).

Astrology is an interesting example of a deviant science. Its belief system proposes that people's personalities, interests, strengths, and weaknesses are determined by the position of the various planets at the time of birth. The solar system is divided into different sections, or "houses" (and correspondingly labelled Leo, Aquarius, etc.). Astrology's techniques include complex mathematical calculations and some techniques borrowed from astronomy. Based on the date and time of a person's birth, natal astrologers determine where each planet was (in which "house") at the moment of birth. The positions of planets are claimed to determine personality, abilities, and life events.

Some ancient scientists and philosophers, such as Aristotle and Ptolemy, were proponents of astrology, but today astrology is perceived as a pseudo-science or anti-science (Saliba, 2001/2002; Emery, 2001; *Skeptical Inquirer*, 1999; Clarke & Gabriels, 1996; Maddox, 1994). However, some scientists have begun using scientific methods to study whether some of the claims of astrology might actually be valid. For example, Clarke and Gabriels (1996) investigated whether personality traits like extroversion and emotionality were associated with astrological signs, and found no relationship between these variables. However, other research has found some support for astrological claims.

One research study compared scientists who had won Nobel prizes in medicine and physiology with scientists who had not won such prizes but who worked in reputable academic institutions. This study found a statistically significant relationship between astrological sign and Nobel laureate status: the Nobel-winning scientists were likely to have had the sun sign of Gemini, while scientists with the sun sign of Leo were the least likely to have won Nobel prizes in medicine and science (Pollex, Hegels, & Ban, 2001). More recently, a study of more than 15 000 people found no association between birth date and individual differences in personality or intelligence (Hartmann, Reuter, & Nyborg, 2006).

Despite the fact that astrology has tried to establish itself as a science for hundreds (or even thousands) of years (Pruzhinin & Scanlan, 1995), it continues to be viewed as a pseudo-science. The question of its scientific nature aside, many non-scientists continue to subscribe to some of the claims of astrology. Feher's

Astrology has been considered a "deviant" science for many years. However, some scientists are now finding support for some of astrology's claims.

(1992) study of believers in astrology finds them to be very mainstream people with above-average levels of education. Meanwhile, though astrology continues to be widely viewed as a deviant science by the scientific community, its beliefs are studied in other ways—for example, as a religious belief system and as philosophy. For example, the Sophia Project, whose aim is to promote the development of skilled and prestigious contemporary philosophers in the British post-secondary system, emphasizes, in part, the study of astrological beliefs (see www.sophia-project.org.uk).

The media plays an important role in reproducing pseudo-scientific beliefs (Yam, 1997). The stranger the scientific claim, the more likely it is to be reported in the media—unusual scientific claims are sensationalistic and can reliably attract an audience. The media ties into commercialization as well. Belief systems that are frequently labelled as deviant science are often linked to companies selling a marketable product or service related to those claims (Yam, 1997). Astrological charts, magnetic insoles for your shoes, and homeopathic remedies are just some of the services and products available.

Determining what is a deviant science or a pseudo-science may initially appear to be quite straightforward. However, as with religious belief systems, determining which ones really are deviant is challenging. A science that may be perceived as deviant at one time may become an accepted science at a later date. This is what happened with radio astronomy in the early twentieth century (Ben-Yehuda, 1986, 1990). Radio astronomy essentially claims that scientists can identify events that are occurring in the solar system by measuring the radio waves the events emit. Those of you who are familiar with this field may ask how radio astronomy can be a deviant science when its claims are entirely accepted in the scientific community. Well, though this may be true today, it was not always the case. The scientists who argued for the validity of radio astronomy initially faced considerable censure. They had tremendous difficulty in finding a research journal willing to publish their article, and for a number of years they were stigmatized in the scientific community. Eventually, other astronomers conducted research and concluded that their claims were, in fact, valid; thus radio astronomy entered the realm of mainstream science.

Because of instances in which the claims made by a deviant science eventually came to be adopted by the scientific community, proponents of deviant sciences today claim that the same might eventually become true of their belief systems. They argue that the methods for investigation in mainstream science have not evolved sufficiently to properly evaluate the claims being made (Shermer, 2001). Ben-Yehuda (1986, 1990) points out that one of the reasons that a science may first be considered deviant and later become accepted is the conservative character of the scientific community.

Although scientists pursue innovation via their research efforts, the tendency to resist change can sometimes prevail. Senior scientists who have become well established are usually the members of the scientific community who determine whether new ideas are viewed as valid or not—i.e., whether the new claims are characteristic of science or pseudo-science. The cynical view they have developed as part of the scientific world view (presuming that a claim is *not* true until it is proven beyond a doubt) contributes to this conservative dimension. The conservative aspect of science then increases the likelihood that any claim outside of the mainstream will, at least initially, be looked upon with suspicion.

Some disciplines are considered deviant because the claims they make about the nature of reality are questioned or empirical support cannot be found for them. But at other times disciplines may be considered deviant even when their claims about the nature of reality are considered to be true. In these cases, it can be the ethical and moral claims with which the discipline is intertwined that lead to a deviant label. For example, the scientific community accepts the claim that cloning is possible by certain means. But the claims made by scientists about *human* cloning in particular are currently subject to more questioning (Mayor, 2003). What is considered particularly deviant about cloning, however, are the ethical and moral claims that serve as the foundation for cloning research, i.e., claims that suggest cloning humans is morally appropriate. The dubiousness of the underlying ethics is such that a number of governments have begun to explore legislation to exert tight control over human cloning research or even to prohibit it.

Pseudo-science surrounds us in our daily lives, whether in the form of the horoscope in the newspaper each morning, the magazine advertisement for magnetic insoles that will heal our illnesses, or the new remedies on drugstore shelves. The prevalence of scientific claims we see being made, especially in the media, makes it important that we be able to distinguish between scientific and pseudo-scientific claims. Organizations that educate the public about destructive/doomsday cults echo this concern, because of the scientific claims that are sometimes integrated in cults' belief systems. These organizations suggest that the best tool for detecting a pseudo-science is knowledge about science itself, particularly knowledge of the methods, checks, and balances used in the various disciplines of science. By knowing how science actually works, people can more easily detect claims that fall short of scientific requirements. A fact sheet on how to distinguish a pseudo-science from a science can be found on the website of the International Cultic Studies Association (http://icsahome.com/infoserv_articles/astop_science_vs_pseudoscience.htm).

AN INTERNET MOMENT

A number of websites address the issue of pseudo-science. An informative but fun resource is *The Skeptical Inquirer*, at www.csicop.org/si/. It has online articles about Dracula, alien abductions, crop circles, and much more!

Conclusion

In the last chapter we saw how religions can be socially typed as deviant and made subject to social control. In this chapter, we have explored how science can also be socially typed as deviant and made subject to social control. Sometimes this occurs when scientists engage in specific actions that are considered deviant within the scientific community, such as using data fraudulently, hoaxing, and violating codes of ethics. At other times, the claims about reality or the ethical and moral assumptions of a discipline are called into question themselves. When this happens, the entire science is labelled deviant and made subject to control.

TIME TO REVIEW

- What is a deviant science?
- Who determines whether a science is considered deviant?
- What is the nature of the continuum that describes science and pseudo-science?
- What is astrology? Why is astrology called a deviant science?
- What have scientists investigating the claims of astrology found?

Science as a Social Typer of Deviance

The Power of Scientific Social Typing

For most of history, religious belief systems have been the foundation for the dominant moral codes of societies. The truths proclaimed in religion dictated to followers who or what should be considered deviant and the nature of social controls to be exerted. Following the Renaissance and the scientific revolution, religion began to slowly lose some of its grip as a legitimate claims-maker for the truth. In contemporary Western societies, science has now surpassed religion as a creator of the dominant moral codes of society by which deviance and normality are judged (Conrad, 1992). Any statement or person that can claim to be scientific is automatically granted additional legitimacy.

Ask Yourself

Where do you see "experts" being used in order to legitimize claims to truth?

In his book *Power/Knowledge*, Michel Foucault (1980) proposed that a relationship exists among knowledge claims, the power of people making those knowledge claims, and the resulting influence those knowledge claims have. Thus, when claims to truth come from individuals or groups in society that have high levels of institutionalized power, those claims also become institutionalized—people believe the claims being made, simply because those claims are coming from "experts." This is the position that science holds in our culture today, such that the social typing done by scientists tends to be effective: "Laypeople generally hesitate to question those who seem to be experts in a mystifying or highly technical field; to do such questioning can feel like asking the clergy if there really is a God" (Caplan, 1995, p. xxii).

Although the first half of this chapter explored scientific misconduct and deviant sciences such as astrology, the social typing of deviance is associated with *all* science, not just questionable science. The examples of science serving as a social typer of deviance are so numerous that it is not possible to address them all; however, we can look at a few examples, both historical and contemporary.

Scientific Social Typing in History: Social Darwinism, Eugenics, and the Nazis

In the previous chapter, we briefly explored the European colonization of North America and the role that religious belief systems played in the government initiative for residential schooling, a policy that caused long-term damage to Aboriginal individuals, their families, and their cultures. European colonization did not occur just in North America, it took place all over the world—e.g., in Africa, Asia, Australia, Central America, and South America—missing only Japan, Korea, Turkey, Iran, Thailand, Saudi Arabia, and (to some extent) China.

What all of these instances of colonization have in common is that indigenous populations were encouraged, and usually coerced, into abandoning traditional beliefs and cultural norms and adopting the European beliefs and norms of their colonizers (e.g., Abernethy, 2001; Jaimes, 1992). Religious beliefs were central to the push toward colonization, serving as the primary rationalization for several centuries. However, by the end of the nineteenth century, scientific theory also provided a rationale for the last several centuries of European colonization and a justification for government policies regarding indigenous peoples for years to come.

Social Darwinism, exemplified by the work of sociologist Herbert Spencer, applied the Darwinian concept of *evolution* to an understanding of history and society (Asma, 1993; Jones, 1998). The theory proposed that just as biological species evolve over time, so do human societies, from "primitive" to "civilized." Although ancient Athenian society was seen by many social Darwinists as the most evolved in history, European societies were seen as the most evolved in the nineteenth century. Thus, the colonization of more "primitive" societies was justified as benefiting indigenous peoples; in other words, European colonizers were seen as helping these cultures to evolve at a more rapid rate than they were doing on their own. Government policies based on the principle of assimilation also justified moving the evolution of indigenous cultures forward.

Social Darwinism was soon popularized as the science of **eugenics** (Asma, 1993; Jones, 1998; Jones, 1986; Kevles, 1995). Similar principles were applied, but to various individuals and groups within particular societies. Recent biological developments were used to support the argument that some social groups were more evolved than, and therefore biologically superior to, other groups. Although eugenics is most often associated with Nazi Germany (Kuhl, 1994), governments in Britain (Jones, 1986), the United States (Seldon & Montagu, 1999), Australia (Jones, 1998) and Canada (McLaren, 1990) also pursued eugenic ideals. The science of eugenics had multiple related purposes, as the following excerpt from a 1922 sociology textbook on eugenics illustrates:

"The problem of eugenics is to make such legal, social and economic adjustments that (1) a larger proportion of superior persons will have children than at present, (2) that the average number of offspring of each superior person will be greater than at present, (3) that the most inferior persons will have no children, and finally that (4) other inferior persons will have fewer children than now." (Popenoe & Johnson, 1922)

Over time, "inferior" persons came to include non-whites, Eastern and Southern Europeans, "mental defectives," criminals, the poor, and the morally suspect (Dennis, 1995; Beaud & Prevost, 1996; McLaren, 1990; Kevles, 1985; Buchanan, 1997). Social activists drawn primarily from the scientific and social reform communities engaged in a number of measures to increase reproduction in "superior" people and decrease reproduction in "inferior" people. Local fairs held "family fitness competitions" (Whiting, 1996; Seldon & Montagu, 1999), referring not to physical fitness but to genetic and evolutionary fitness. In many universities, biology and sociology students studied from eugenics textbooks just like the one quoted above. In churches, ministers presented sermons on eugenic ideals and competed for awards from local eugenics societies (Seldon & Montagu, 1999). Eugenics societies influenced restrictions on immigration policies, legislation enforcing racial segregation and prohibiting interracial marriages, and involuntary sterilization (Seldon & Montagu, 1999; Dennis, 1995; McLaren, 1990).

AN INTERNET MOMENT

If you are interested in the history of the eugenics movement, this is a website you cannot miss! The Eugenics Archive at www.eugenicsarchive.org/eugenics/list3.pl is an award-winning website that documents the history of eugenics, emphasizing the United States. It includes material on the social origins of eugenics, its scientific foundations, its popularization, and the various forms of its implementation. The text is complemented by images of eugenics documents from the time, such as photographs of the winners of family fitness contests, posters advertising the local eugenics boards, and scientific figures and charts explaining the necessity for eugenics.

The history of involuntary sterilization and the eugenics movement reached widespread public attention in Canada in the 1990s, when Leilani Muir launched a lawsuit against the Alberta government for wrongful sterilization. In 1928, the Alberta government set up a eugenics board and instituted the *Sexual Sterilization Act*. The board would evaluate "mental defectives" when they reached puberty, and after an interview of only a few minutes, would determine if they should be sterilized. When Muir was a pre-teen, her alcoholic and abusive mother dropped Muir off at the Provincial Training School in Red Deer. Shortly thereafter, she was classified as a "mental defective" and, without her knowledge or permission, sterilized. After leaving the training school and embarking upon a normal life, she sought medical advice to determine why she had been unable to become pregnant. In the words of Buchanan (1997), "The doctor described her insides as 'being as if she'd been through a slaughterhouse.' Then, when she tried to adopt, she was refused because of the stigma of being a former inmate of Red Deer" (p. 46). Muir won her lawsuit and was awarded an undisclosed amount of money for the pain and suffering she had endured (Whiting, 1996; Buchanan, 1997; Grekul, 2002). Shortly thereafter, the Alberta government introduced legislation to prohibit individuals from being able to sue the government.

The eugenics board attached the label "mental defective" to an extremely wide range of people—e.g., those with low IQs, those who had lifestyles deemed to be "immoral" (the board presumed that only a "mental defective" would live an immoral lifestyle), immigrants unable to speak English, those who were considered burdens because of their poverty, and poverty-stricken women who dared to have children. In a significant proportion of cases, the "mental defectives" who were sterilized were people who had simply violated social norms (Grekul, 2002). For example, one young woman had been gang raped by local boys, and as a result was

The eugenics movement reached its historical apex in Nazi Germany, with millions of people killed in concentration camps. However, eugenic ideals were also being pursued to lesser degrees in Canada, Britain, Australia, and the United States.

labelled "sexually immoral" and entered into the juvenile justice system herself. Her father, unable to live with what had happened, placed her in the Provincial Training School, where she was sterilized (Buchanan, 1997).

The act was not repealed until 1978, thus lasting far longer than in other countries that used sterilization in pursuit of eugenic ideals. Even following World War II, at a time when "Nazis were being hung for their eugenic programs, 'lessons from this dark period of human history appeared to have little or no impact on the operation of the Alberta Eugenics Board'" (Wahlstein, cited in Buchanan, 1997, p. 46). Thus, even though governments throughout the world (including Canada's) considered the Nazis' pursuit of eugenic ideals to be deviant (Proctor, 1988; Weiss, 1988), the ongoing pursuit of those ideals through sterilization continued to be practised in Canada.

Of course, the Nazis in Germany went much further in their application of eugenics (Proctor, 1988; Weiss, 1988). They sterilized between 350 000 and 400 000 people in the period from Hitler's election in 1933 to the beginning of World War II in the late 1930s. Initially, the world community viewed the size of the Nazi sterilization program in a positive light, setting it as a standard they could attempt to approximate themselves (Proctor, 1988). However, as the drive for "racial purity" progressed under the Nazis, genocidal measures were implemented, including the killing of millions in concentration camps—i.e., people who were Jewish, Romany, trade unionists, homosexual, or mentally or physically disabled. A large-scale science program was established as well, and significant strides were made in the area of genetics; thus, torturous medical experimentation (e.g., on twins) served as the basis for these scientific advancements (Proctor, 1988).

Today, some scientists continue to make claims about evolutionary differences among the races, such as in terms of intelligence (e.g., Phillippe Rushton, founder of the Charles Darwin Research Institute). Their scientific claims are heavily criticized (e.g., Brace, 1996; MacEachern, 2006) as racist and based on faulty science, but are widely used by white supremacist groups to support these groups' ideals. Thus, although history provides us with rather dramatic illustrations of the power of science, the role that science plays in the social typing of deviance is not limited to the past.

TIME TO REVIEW

- What is social Darwinism, and how is it related to the social typing of deviance?
- What is eugenics, and what were the goals of the eugenics movement?

- In what countries were eugenic ideals pursued, and how? Provide specific examples.

Scientific Social Typing Today: Medicine, Psychiatry, and Genetics

Medicalization

Science continues to play a role in the determination and control of deviance. Medical science, in particular, plays a central role; in fact, some scholars claim that medicine is the form of science that most underlies our culture's dominant moral codes (Conrad, 1992; Turner, 1987). As you have progressed through this textbook, the medicalization of deviance has been one of the central themes. In the chapter on physical appearance, we addressed the role that medical science plays in defining "too fat" and "too thin," and then the various ways that doctors exert social control over those "deviant" populations.

In the chapter on mental disorders, the role of the psychiatric community in the medicalization of deviance was evident. Members of the psychiatric community determined the symptoms that constitute deviance through their creation of the *Diagnostic and Statistical Manual of Mental Disorders* (American Psychiatric Association, 1994). They then use the manual to diagnose people with those disorders and provide treatment in the amelioration of symptoms. Precisely what mental deviance consists of varies over time, as some characteristics are removed from the diagnostic manual (e.g., homosexuality) and new ones are added (e.g., ADHD, gender identity disorder). Therefore, there are ongoing debates over the diagnostic categories of mental deviance, its political nature, and the absolute guardianship that psychiatrists have over it (Caplan, 1995).

Earlier in this chapter, we briefly looked at the tobacco industry and the "science wars" that surround it. As a consequence of research done by the anti-smoking medical activists, smoking has become successfully medicalized. Direct smoking was the first behaviour to be medicalized, and with medical research as a foundation for their views, anti-smoking activists have had a tremendous impact on society. Their efforts have resulted in warning labels on cigarette packages, bans on cigarette commercials on television, restricted sponsorship of events by tobacco companies, and anti-smoking programs in schools. More recently, secondhand smoking has essentially been medicalized and has resulted in many community bylaws prohibiting smoking in various places.

There is no doubt that medicine is of tremendous importance to people's health throughout the world. Being overweight or underweight *does* increase health risks. Advances in psychopharmaceuticals *have* cured many people of mental disorders such as depression and have enabled many people with ongoing mental disorders to lead high-quality, high-functioning lives. Smoking *is* dangerous to smokers and people around them. However, the primacy given to medical science in determining deviance has led to numerous questions and concerns (Conrad, 1992), not the least of which is whether *social* characteristics are being medicalized.

This concern in particular is illustrated by the practice of giving liposuction to patients solely for the purpose of physical appearance, by the categorization of social groups (e.g., immigrants, people who did not follow social norms) as "mental defectives" under the science of eugenics, and by the individualization of social problems in the widespread diagnosis of ADHD in North America. Today, concerns about the possible implications of the social nature of medicalization are especially widespread, particularly with regard to genetic testing and genetic manipulation.

Genetic Testing and Genetic Manipulation

The Human Genome Project, an international effort involving governments, universities, and private industry, has now created a map of the human genome. The success of this project has generated almost limitless hopes among scientists. They are making promises reminiscent of science fiction (Carlson & Stimeling, 2002)—for example, that the science of genetics will be able to prevent and cure illness, increase longevity and intelligence, and allow us to ensure that our children begin life with the best possible chance in the world (Carlson & Stimeling, 2002; Stock, 2002). Some proponents have even suggested that social problems such as homelessness will be solved (Koshland, cited in Beckwith, 1993). At the same time, ethicists are raising questions about whether this science is simply eugenics in twenty-first-century clothing (Ward, 1993).

There are several different positions in the debates over genetic testing and genetic manipulation (Sinsheimer, 1990): (a) those who advocate the complete abandonment

Ask Yourself

If you could create a "designer baby" through the science of genetics, what characteristics would you select? What might some of the implications be, not just at an individual level, but at a societal level?

of the Human Genome Project; (b) those who claim that beneficial gains can be made through this science, but because of the great danger also involved, scientists should select only a handful of areas in which to make use of it; (c) those who do want to give science freedom to advance, but advocate caution on the part of scientists and a slow pace of implementation; and (d) those who would set no limits on the science of genetics or its implementation.

Arguments for the complete abandonment of this science are frequently based on religious or other stringent moral belief systems. The human genetic structure and the genes possessed by specific individuals are perceived as a matter of "divine will" (Sinsheimer, 1990, para. 4). Humanity, and particularly science, has no place in altering the will of God (or the will of nature, depending on the fundamental belief system).

Awareness of the potential social dangers of the misuse of genetic science serves as the foundation for advocacy of strict controls or extreme cautions. Memories of the Nazi genetic program serve as a reminder of the possible outcomes of ranking some biological characteristics as "superior" to others (Beckwith, 1993; Proctor, 1988). Although what happened in Nazi Germany may not happen again, the fact that "Nazi racial policy . . . was played out, at least in part, in the spheres of science and medicine [has] forever taint[ed] genetic research, at least in the public mind, with a sinister aspect" (*Wilson Quarterly*, 1992, para. 7). The complex intertwining of science with both politics and commerce today creates a structure wherein the misuse of genetic science is possible and of concern (Sinsheimer, 1990; Stock, 2002; Carlson & Stimeling, 2002).

More abstract and more specific questions about the possible implications of this science abound. Who will decide which genes are desirable and which are undesirable (Stock, 2002; Carlson & Stimeling, 2002)? For example, will being short, brown-eyed, and dark-skinned be considered problematic? Will having artistic abilities be seen as inferior to having scientific abilities? Will people with Down syndrome or other genetic disorders simply no longer be born? The issue of power is central to answering these questions. The decisions are likely to be made by medical scientists themselves, given the degree of power that medical science holds in society today, as we have seen. But what safeguards will control the decisions made by these scientists?

Of course, the hope is that genetic research will eventually be able to cure disease rather than eliminate individuals. However, the lag between the ability to diagnose genetic problems and the ability to treat those genetic problems is significant, and likely to grow even larger (Ward, 1993). The Human Genome Project was extraordinarily expensive for numerous corporate entities; the quickest and most profitable means of recouping these costs is through the mass marketing of tests for specific genetic conditions rather than through continued research into finding "cures." Furthermore, critics point out that very few diseases and conditions are purely genetic in origin. In most cases, disease emerges from the interaction between biology, environment, and lifestyle. Thus, they claim that genetic science will *not* be able to significantly alter the presence of disease and disability in society (Beckwith, 1993; Dunne & Warren, 1998).

The suggestion that social problems such as homelessness can be solved by genetic science (because of the prevalence of mental illness among the homeless) is criticized as ignorant and uninformed (Beckwith, 1993). As we saw in the chapter on mental disorders, homelessness is not caused by mental illness, but by the structure of the health care system, wherein people with mental illnesses fall through the cracks. This has happened due to the unintended consequences of deinstitutionalization and a lack of sufficient funding for community-based treatment programs. By suggesting that genetic manipulation is the solution, attention is drawn away from the non-biological factors that are involved in social problems, and changes that would make society a better place are not given a priority (Beckwith, 1993). Some critics have even indicated that the trillions of dollars that have been spent on the Human Genome Project would have been better spent on social improvements throughout the world.

The largest issues that are raised in relation to genetic testing and genetic manipulation emphasize human rights. Some nations (e.g., Iceland) are trying to implement national banks of genetic information, wherein citizens will have no choice but to undergo genetic testing (Jones, 2001). Voluntary genetic testing is considered an important human rights issue, yet the results of Dunne and Warren's (1998) research question whether such testing is actually voluntary.

Genetic counsellors advise certain groups of pregnant women about potential genetic defects in their fetuses. The counsellors are expected to provide women with enough information from all sides of the issue to decide whether or not they want genetic testing done. All too often, the genetic counsellors provide only the negative information about the specific disease or condition involved, rather than all of the information (Dunne & Warren, 1998). That is, instead of telling women about the resources that are available to them if they do decide to have a child that has a genetic condition (e.g., support groups, educational programs, medical treatments), they may provide information only on the negative aspects of the condition. Thus, the deviant label that is attached to genetic conditions by members of the medical community means that the information provided to patients may be biased, unduly influencing the nature of decisions they make about whether to get tested, and, if tested, whether or not to continue with a pregnancy.

There is also the realistic concern that the results of genetic testing could be used for the purposes of discrimination in insurance and employment (Ward, 1993; Beckwith, 1993; Carlson & Stimeling, 2002). In fact, the Council for Responsible Genetics (2001) found instances of genetic discrimination to be on the rise. For example, consider the following case: "Seven-year-old Danny is in perfect health, but a genetic test reveals that he has a gene predisposing him to a heart disorder. Even though he takes medication that lowers his risk of a heart attack, he is denied health insurance. His insurance company argues that since his gene has been present since birth, it qualifies as a pre-existing medical condition" (para. 5).

The various concerns involving the possible implications of genetic testing have resulted in social control measures being directed at the scientific community itself. Groups of scientists have come together to raise issues, ask questions, and issue guidelines for scientific work—e.g., "Science for the People," the "Council for Responsible Genetics," and the "Union of Concerned Scientists" (Beckwith, 1993). For example, the Council for Responsible Genetics has adopted a Genetic Bill of Rights, which outlines fundamental principles that they believe genetic research and implementation should be based on. It includes "the right to a world in which living organisms cannot be patented," "the right to protection against eugenic measures such as forced sterilization or mandatory screening aimed at aborting or manipulating selected embryos or fetuses," and "the right to be free from genetic discrimination" (Council for Responsible Genetics, 2000).

International coalitions of governments are also addressing the issues and discussing appropriate control measures. In 1997, the United Nations Educational, Scientific, and Cultural Organization (UNESCO) adopted the Universal Declaration on the Human Genome and Human Rights, which makes declarations similar to those made by the Council for Responsible Genetics. Significant aspects of the declaration include prohibitions against human cloning, guidelines for scientists declaring that "they should seek to ensure that research results are not used for non-peaceful purposes," and the statement that the "uniqueness and diversity" of individuals must be respected (UNESCO, 1997). Individual governments have also developed guidelines for genetic research and its application. What most of these organizational, international, and national guidelines share are the fundamental principles that underlie their policies (Jones, 2001):

- respect for human dignity
- the right to genetic privacy
- health protection and promotion
- genetic equality
- public participation in decision-making processes

Given the rapid pace at which this science is developing and the growing discussion of ethical and legal science issues, policy and law are constantly changing. New genetic advances continue to be made, new ethical issues emerge, and lawsuits involving some aspect of genetic testing, research, or manipulation are ongoing in countries throughout the world. It can be difficult to keep up with these developments. However, the World Health Organization, UNESCO, and organizations like the Council for Responsible Genetics are all reliable sources of information about the current state of affairs with respect to ethical, scientific, and legal issues involving the science of genetics.

AN INTERNET MOMENT

The website of the Council for Responsible Genetics is located at www.gene-watch.org. It contains a wealth of information on genetic determinism, genetic testing and discrimination, human genetic manipulation and cloning, biotechnology and agriculture, and biowarfare.

Like religious belief systems, scientific belief systems also have extensive relationships with the concept of deviance. Certain practices that occur in science can be considered deviant, and entire bodies of science can be considered deviant. However, science also serves as a powerful social typer of deviance—perhaps the most powerful social typer in society today. That power does not go unquestioned, and controls are being exerted on the social typing that occurs in science. Both religious and scientific belief systems are governing forces in the lives of billions of people in the world. The truths that they proclaim are a foundation for our own behaviours, as well as our judgments of others. But as the quote at the beginning of this chapter suggests, both types of belief systems are socially constructed. The subjective dimension of religion and science means that neither belief system should operate unbridled or without question.

TIME TO REVIEW

- What are some contemporary examples of how science serves as a social typer of deviance?
- What are the different positions involved in the debate over genetic testing and genetic manipulation?
- What are the potential benefits and the potential dangers of the science of genetics?
- How have scientific organizations, governments, and the international community responded to the potential dangers of the science of genetics?

CHAPTER SUMMARY

- Science consists of belief systems and technologies. Like religious belief systems, science also exists in different types of relationships with deviance: science as deviance and science as a social typer of deviance.

- Science as deviance occurs in two different ways: deviance in science and deviant sciences. Various forms of scientific misconduct characterize deviance in science. Bad apple/bad person theories propose that individual characteristics are the cause of deviance in science, such that some people are simply more prone to deviance than others. The iceberg theory claims that the structure of the scientific community itself sets the stage for deviance to occur. The increasing corporatization of science creates a context that promotes scientific misconduct. The nature of control of misconduct changes over time, as the institutional logics governing science change.

■ Deviant sciences are those in which the claims being made about the nature of reality (e.g., astrology) or the implicit ethical/moral claims (e.g., cloning) are questioned in their entirety. As a result, the entire science is labelled deviant, or pseudo-science. What is considered to be a deviant science can change over time.

■ Science also serves as a social typer of deviance. Historical examples include social Darwinism, the eugenics movement, and certain scientific pursuits in Nazi Germany. Instances of contemporary social typing are evident in a number of topics addressed in earlier chapters (e.g., mental disorder, body size, sexuality). An especially controversial issue today is the actual and potential social typing that occurs in the science of genetics.

DEVIANCE IN PRINT

Krimsky, S., & Shorett, P. (Eds.) (2005). *Rights and Liberties in the Biotech Age: Why We Need a Genetic Bill of Rights*. New York: Rowman & Littlefield.

McLaren, A. (1990). *Our Own Master Race: Eugenics in Canada 1885–1945*. Toronto: McClelland and Stewart.

DEVIANCE AT THE MOVIES

Maltby, D. (Director & Writer), & Abraham, C. (Writer). (2002). *DNA and Dollars*. Available from the National Film Board of Canada. (47 minutes).

This documentary looks at Canada's genetics research groups and industry, contrasting the search for cures with the growing commercialization of genetic science.

Niccol, A. (Director & Writer). (1997). *Gattaca*. United States: Columbia Pictures. (101 minutes).

This film starring Uma Thurman is about a futuristic dystopia where genetic manipulation has created two classes of human beings.

Reitman, J. (Director & Writer) & Buckley, C. (Writer). (2005). *Thank You for Smoking*. United States: Room 9 Productions. (92 minutes).

This comedy follows the struggles of a lobbyist for the tobacco industry, whose job it is to minimize people's perceptions of the dangers of smoking.

ENDNOTE

1 J. B. S. Haldane. [1927]. "Science and Theology as Art-Forms," in *Possible Worlds and Other Essays*. London: Chatto & Windus. From the Columbia World of

Quotations. (1996). New York, NY: Columbia University Press. Retrieved September 19, 2006, from **www.bartleby.com/66/11/26511.html**

KEY TERMS

science as deviance, **p. 271**
science as a social typer of
deviance, **p. 271**
science, **p. 271**
scientific belief systems, **p. 271**
technologies, **p. 271**
deviance in science, **p. 272**
deviant science, **p. 272**
forging, **p. 272**
hoaxes, **p. 272**
trimming, **p. 273**
cooking, **p. 273**
ethical violations, **p. 273**

scientific misconduct, **p. 273**
junk science, **p. 275**
bad apple/bad person theory, **p. 277**
iceberg theory, **p. 277**
ghostwriting, **p. 280**
communism, **p. 281**
skepticism, **p. 281**
disinterestedness, **p. 281**
universalism, **p. 281**
social Darwinism, **p. 288**
eugenics, **p. 288**

CHAPTER 10

The "Deviance Dance" Continues

Learning Objectives

After reading this chapter, you should be able to

- Describe how more objective and more subjective approaches to studying deviance have been reflected in the chapters in this textbook.
- Describe how the notion of the social typing process has been reflected in the topics explored in this textbook.
- Explain how the importance of *power* has been addressed in the chapters in this textbook.
- Explain how the concept of the "deviance dance" has been integrated into the topics explored in this textbook.
- Cite examples of human rights legislation, and explain how these documents can determine when it is and is not appropriate to attach a deviant label to people, behaviours, or characteristics.

"Conformity makes everything easier, if you can still breathe." (Mason Cooley)[1]

"You have to be deviant if you're going to do anything new." (David Lee)[2]

These are the two quotations that this textbook began with. The first quotation suggests that conforming will make our lives run more smoothly; at the same time, it points out that **conformity** is restricting. The second quotation suggests that we can achieve innovation and change only if we're willing to risk being thought of as **deviant**. Now that you have reached the last chapter, this is a good time to reflect upon these concepts. In this chapter, we will look back at some of the main ideas that were introduced in the first chapter, and explore how those ideas have been reflected in the various substantive topics that have been addressed—i.e., sexuality, youth, physical appearance, mental disorder, religion, and science. As you read through this chapter, you will be asked to do a lot of thinking on your own. This is the time when you can reflect on the topics you have learned about and the ideas you had during this course.

> **Ask Yourself**
>
> Let's return to some of the questions raised in Chapter 1: Who are the conformists in our society and in our world? Is life easier for them? Are their thoughts, behaviours, and identities limited by their conformity? Who are the deviants? Are they really the deviants of our world, or do they represent some type of problem that we need to control? What is it that differentiates a "deviant" from a "conformist"? How can we distinguish between them? Given what you have learned during the course, and the ideas that the course material has stimulated, spend some time thinking about how you would answer these questions now.

The Objective–Subjective Continuum

Various researchers approach the study of deviance differently. Although the differences among researchers have traditionally been characterized as a dichotomy or dualism (Adler & Adler, 2003; Ben-Yehuda, 1990), most deviance specialists today combine some aspects of both objective and subjective approaches (e.g., Evans, 2001). Even looking back at earlier research reveals that the distinctions between these approaches were not as clear-cut as has been suggested (e.g., Becker, 1963). Thus, we can think of deviance research as falling along a continuum, wherein virtually all scholars fit somewhere between the two extreme ends. Some deviance specialists lean to the more objective side of the continuum, while others lean to the more subjective side.

Scholars who lean to the more **objective** side of the continuum focus their analytical spotlight on the deviant act itself. For these scholars, the deviant act exists *a priori* to the analysis, and can be recognized by specific characteristics such as a negative societal reaction, harm, statistical rarity, or a violation of norms. With an overarching **positivist** interest in explaining the variation in human behaviour, they focus on causation—what makes people act in deviant ways. Due to their focus on explaining the deviant act, they find that particular types of theories are more useful to them than to the scholars who lean toward the more subjective side of the research continuum. These were the theories addressed in Chapter 2: functionalist theories, social learning theories, and social control theories (Ashley & Orenstein, 2001).

Deviance specialists who lean to the more **subjective** side of the continuum focus their analytical spotlight on the social processes by which certain people, actions, or characteristics come to be perceived as deviant and treated accordingly. They suggest that we cannot recognize deviance in any objective sense, but instead must be taught that certain people, actions, and characteristics are deviant (Becker, 1963). Power is perceived as central to determining what is deviant. Due to their emphasis on explaining the social processes that underlie deviant labels, particular types of theories are more useful to them than to scholars who lean toward the more objective side of the research continuum. These were the theories addressed in Chapter 3—interpretive theories and critical theories (Ashley & Orenstein, 2001).

Combining the results of both the more objective and more subjective research provides us with the most comprehensive understanding of deviance, wherein we learn something about the deviant act (why, when, and how it occurs) and the processes by which that act has come to be perceived and treated as deviant. Throughout this textbook you have seen many instances of each of these areas of emphasis.

In the chapter on sexuality (Chapter 4), a historical context surrounded our exploration. In looking at the sexual cultures of fifth-century B.C. Athens (Arkins, 1994), the Sambia of New Guinea (Herdt, 1984), traditional Aboriginal cultures (Newhouse, 1998), and North America before, during, and after industrialization (D'Emilio & Freedman, 1997; Razack, 2002; Valverde, 1991), we saw the various norms (i.e., a more objectivist interest) that shaped people's sexual behaviours. For example, we saw that ritualized homosexual acts with young boys occur in Sambian society because of cultural norms emerging out of their spiritual belief system (Herdt, 1984).

In contemporary society, we explored cultural norms that if violated are considered deviant (e.g., age of the sexual partner). We also saw that the Supreme Court of Canada has shifted the definition of obscenity to one based on social harm. From a more subjectivist point of view, an historical context also enabled us to look at the culturally specific processes by which certain people, acts, or characteristics come to be labelled deviant. In Chapter 4, our discussion of the tremendous diversity in sexual cultures around the world and throughout history illustrated that what is considered sexually deviant stems not from the acts themselves, but from the evaluations of particular acts based on the dominant moral codes in society at the time.

In the chapter on youth (Chapter 5), the objective and subjective dimensions were reflected in the various topics of youth-related deviance that were addressed—i.e., crime, gangs, substance use, and the nature of adolescence itself. An abundance of more objectivist research has been conducted on the causes of youth crime (e.g., Davies, 1994), gang emergence and involvement (e.g., Jankowski, 1991; Grekul & LaBoucane-Benson, 2007), smoking, alcohol use, and drug use (e.g., Roberts *et al.*, 2001). We explored some of the theoretical and empirical research that explains these "deviant" behaviours. Differential association theory, social control theories, and social learning theories have been applied to understandings of many of these acts, and empirical research reveals the complex web of factors that contributes to them as well. For instance, characteristics of family life (especially the balance of parental expectations and parent–child affection) are consistently found to play an important role in youth crime (Milan, 2000; Brook *et al.*, 1999). Because these behaviours emerge from the interaction of personal, family, school, and community factors, the programs and policies designed to reduce the frequency of these behaviours must address such multilevel factors. Shifting our focus to the more subjectivist interest in the social processes that underlie the deviantization of youth, we also explored how the gap between the perceptions and actual prevalence of youth crime or the "gang problem" contributes to particular ways of trying to control these problems (Tanner, 2001; Fasiolo & Leckie, 1993). In looking at the way in which youth itself, as a stage in the life cycle, is considered deviant, we saw that adolescents live the lives that we, as adults, create for them. The exaggerated generation gap of the past may become a reality in the future; however, it is not because of the deviant nature of adolescence, but because of the structure of society as created by adults. Even so, the misperceptions that all youth are both troubling and troubled influences the ways that youth are treated in society (Bibby, 2009).

Body size was the one of the areas of emphasis for the chapter on physical appearance (Chapter 6), which addressed body images such as "too fat," "too thin," and "ideal." Certain body sizes are indeed associated with significantly higher risks of health problems (World Health Organization, 2002a; Health Canada, 2002a), and scholars with more objectivist interests have therefore analyzed various biological, psychological, and social factors in their attempts to determine why people become obese or anorexic and what treatments will help them (Caldwell, 2001; McLorg & Taub, 1987). However, scholars with more subjectivist interests reveal that popular social perceptions of "too fat," "too thin," and "ideal" have little to do with health risks and much to do with current cultural standards of beauty—standards that critics say have reached alarmingly thin proportions (Owen & Laurel-Seller, 2000; Spitzer, Henderson, & Zivian, 1999). These standards of beauty vary considerably across cultures and over time, so that what is seen as being a "deviant" body size in twenty-first-century Canada is very different than in twenty-first-century Ghana, or nineteenth-century Canada (Shuriquie, 1999). Body modification was another area of emphasis in the chapter. More objectivist-based research has explored the motivations for obtaining tattoos or piercings, and other risk factors with which body modification is associated. From a more subjectivist point of view, scholars have explored what body modification tells us about social interaction (e.g., impression management) and the larger society (e.g., discourses of gender).

Like obesity and anorexia, discussed in Chapter 6, mental disorders are medicalized forms of deviance. In the chapter on mental disorders (Chapter 7), the more objective approach to deviance was reflected in the material on prevalence, causes, and treatments of mental illness. We saw that mental illness affects most Canadians either directly (through their own experiences of mental illness) or indirectly (by having a friend, family member, or co-worker with a mental illness) (Health Canada, 2002b). The social and economic costs of mental disorders are tremendous not only in Canada but throughout the world (Ettner, Frank, & Kessler, 1997; Murray & Lopez, 1996; Stephans & Jorbert, 2001). Therefore, a wide range of therapeutic techniques—counselling, medication, and family supports—are used to treat the combined biological and social aspects of mental disorders (World Health Organization, 2002b).

The more subjective approach to deviance is reflected in the research that emphasizes the political and social aspects of diagnosis and treatment. Although there is considerable overlap between North American and international diagnostic tools, scholars point out that there is a political aspect to determining what constitutes psychological deviance (Caplan, 1995). For example, homosexuality is no longer categorized as a mental disorder, but other behaviours (e.g., gender identity dysphoria) now are. Some critics suggest that *social* problems are being medicalized and treated as illnesses. For example, the high rate of ADHD diagnoses in North America may have more to do with the multi-tasking that characterizes modern life than with a psychological disorder in particular children (McConnell, 1997; Shute, 2000).

The objective and subjective dimensions of deviance research are reflected in the chapter on religious belief systems as well (Chapter 8). More objective research is reflected in the search to understand sects and cults. Researchers have explored why "deviant" religious groups form, what conditions foster acts like mass suicides, and what factors contribute to sect or cult violence (Lewis & Melton, 1994; Bromley, 2002; Hall, 2002). Specialists in the study of cults have investigated specific groups (e.g., "the Family"), testified in court as expert witnesses, and created guidelines for people to use in determining whether a specific religious group may be dangerous (Barker, 2001). Scholars with more subjective interests in deviance have questioned the traditional distinction between churches, sects, and cults, and have demonstrated that political factors frequently determine which groups are treated as deviant within a particular society (Jenkins, 2000; Chryssides, 1994). They have also pointed out the power that religion has frequently had as a social typer of deviance—i.e., that it dictated to us who or what should be considered deviant—and the potential dangers of the boundaries between religion and politics becoming blurred (Boston, 1996).

Marshall Applewhite, founder of the Heaven's Gate cult. Deviance scholars with a more objective approach to research try to explain why mass suicides occur in some cults.

Like religion, science now has great influence over what society considers deviant. Chapter 9, therefore, addresses science as social typer of deviance as well as deviance in science. Researchers with more objective interests have studied "deviant" acts that occur in science, broadly referred to as **scientific misconduct** (e.g., Park, 2000). Many of them have concluded that these acts are more common than might be suspected. Some explanations of "deviant" scientific acts focus on individual factors (the **bad apple/bad person theory**), but others emphasize that the characteristics of the scientific community itself set the stage for "deviant" acts (the **iceberg theory**) (Ben-Yehuda, 1986; Bechtel & Pearson, 1985; James, 1995). In the latter approach, a number of specific theories have been applied, such as differential association theory, Merton's strain theory, and social control theories. The subjective dimension of deviance is explored in the analysis of science as a powerful social typer of deviance, telling us who or what should be considered deviant. When scientists make claims to truth, many of us automatically believe them and would likely never dare to question them. Although in many cases the efforts of scientists benefit us all (e.g., regarding the health dangers of obesity), we must also remember the central role that science played in the eugenics movement and the horrors of what occurred in Nazi Germany.

Social Typing, Social Control, and Powerful Groups

The notion of deviance emerges out of the **social typing process** (Rubington & Weinberg, 2008). The first component of social typing is **description**, wherein a label is attached to a person, behaviour, or characteristic. The second component is **evaluation**, in which a judgment is attached to the person, behaviour, or characteristic as a result of the initial label. The last component is **prescription**, where the person is treated in specific ways only because of the label and the judgment that have been attached. This last component of the social typing process refers to measures of **social control** or **regulation**. Deviance can be met with **informal controls** (through everyday social interactions) or with **formal controls** (at the hands of an institution or organization) (Rubington & Weinberg, 2002). The social control of deviance may be **preventative** (preventing a deviant act in the first place, such as through socialization) or **retroactive** (following a deviant act) (Edwards, 1988). **Self-control** is another form of regulation, wherein we all monitor our own behaviours to prevent and fix our own deviance (Edwards, 1988; Foucault, 1995).

The social typing of deviance is most effective when done by someone who has some institutionalized power in society (Rubington & Weinberg, 2002). Five different groups in society are especially powerful in that they are able to influence our decisions about who or what is "deviant," and able to exert potent measures of social control: the media, commercial enterprise, government, religion, and science. At times, these powerful groups act as **moral entrepreneurs** themselves by trying to influence or change society's dominant moral code in relation to a particular issue. At other times, these powerful groups serve as tools used by other groups of moral entrepreneurs in their efforts.

The central role that the media play in the daily lives of billions of people makes it the locus of claims-making in the struggles over moral codes and deviance. Commercial enterprise is another powerful group involved in the social typing process. Its efforts are intertwined with the media in two different ways. First, although there is a small non-profit element in Canadian broadcasting, the media are predominantly a form of commercial enterprise, i.e., an industry that is driven by the profit motive. Second, commercial enterprise uses the media as a tool for selling its products, via advertising, commercials, and product placement in television shows or movies.

Another group using the media is, of course, politicians and government, who have ultimate power vested in them. In their hands lies the power to create or revoke legislation, to construct social policies that will be implemented through various means, and to influence the enforcement of society's dominant moral codes. Politicians may act as moral entrepreneurs or may be lobbied by interest groups acting as moral entrepreneurs. The work of politicians also exists in a bidirectional relationship with the media, where the media follow the work of politicians, and

Ask Yourself

Social typers frequently rationalize the labelling of certain people, actions, or characteristics as deviant on the basis of notions of statistical rarity, social harm, negative societal reaction, or normative violation. As you read through the review of how social typing was addressed in the substantive topics in this textbook, consider the rationales that were used for the social typing of deviance in each of the various instances.

politicians use media to influence the public mind. There are two other groups of moral entrepreneurs, however: religion and science. Religious institutions have played a vital role in the creation of dominant moral codes throughout history, maybe more so in the past than today. Finally, the power of scientists in the social typing process is perhaps granted more legitimacy than any other group is. Science is seen by many people as a purely objective discipline, such that its claims to truth are frequently considered unaffected by political, religious, or commercial interests.

Chapter 4, on sexuality, revealed that in any given culture at any particular time in history, certain sexual behaviours are socially typed as deviant and made subject to social control measures. In fifth-century B.C. Athens, sexual relationships between males were accepted, but only if the males were of different social statuses; if two males of equal status had a sexual relationship, they would be subject to informal sanctions. Males who received money for engaging in anal intercourse had their citizenship revoked and lost their right to participate in political life (Arkins, 1994). Following European colonization, Aboriginal sexuality was socially controlled through religion (e.g., the teachings of local missionaries) and government (e.g., through legislation banning polygamy) (Newhouse, 1998; Razack, 2002).

Over the past several hundred years, what has been socially typed as deviant sexuality has varied based on the cultural norms of the time (D'Emilio & Freedman, 1997). When sexuality was perceived as solely for the purpose of procreation, any non-procreative sexual acts (e.g., heterosexual coitus involving contraceptive use, homosexuality, masturbation) were socially typed as deviant. This is considerably different from society today, wherein personal fulfillment is perceived as the purpose of sexuality.

Although there is more freedom in sexual norms today than in the past, certain sexual acts are still socially typed as deviant (e.g., sex with a minor, having sex "too frequently," or being "kinky") (Goode, 1997). The way that sexuality is socially controlled has changed as well. During the sixteenth and seventeenth centuries, sexual deviance was primarily a religious and familial concern; for example, sexual deviance could result in excommunication from the church, and fathers would enforce "shotgun" weddings following premarital pregnancy. Today, religion has lost its hold over sexuality and has been succeeded by a diversity of social control measures. We have legislation that governs certain aspects of sexuality (e.g., degree of consent and age), medicalization (e.g., encouraging "safer" sex and the designation of "sexual disorders" as mental disorders), social organizations that try to encourage abstinence and contraceptive use in adolescents, and the pervasiveness of sexuality in all forms of the media.

In Chapter 5, on youth, we saw that certain behaviours and characteristics of youth are socially typed as deviant and made subject to social control. Youth crime is defined and controlled by government and the criminal justice system. Youth gangs are considered a widespread social concern, which is reflected in media reports of youth street gangs, specialized law enforcement units to monitor gang members, as well as various educational programs that discourage gang membership (Fasiolo & Leckie, 1993; Tanner, 2001). The science of "risk management" attempts to intervene with youth who are seen as "at risk" of gang membership, criminal involvement, homelessness, substance abuse, teen pregnancy, and more. Law enforcement, social workers, psychologists, educators, health professionals, government, and social organizations all participate in such "risk management" (Bessant, 2001). Youth substance use is socially typed as deviant, seen as both a medical and a social problem. Public service campaigns via the media; education and intervention programs within various social organizations; and medical treatment are all means by which substance use is controlled (Roberts *et al.*, 2001). Binge drinking in university is controlled through diverse programs that include peer education and support, university policies, and, in some cases, even "dry" campuses (Keeling, 2000, 2002).

Chapter 6 addresses how certain types of voluntary and involuntary physical appearances are socially typed as deviant. Those who choose particular hairstyles, makeup, and clothing (e.g., "goths") may find it difficult to find employment, because of employers' attitudes and biases. Body modification that may be considered acceptable in some groups may be considered unacceptable in others (e.g., in physicians). People who stray beyond the "ideal" body size are socially typed as "too fat" or "too thin," although there is much more leeway for thinness before a deviant label is attached.

Body size is regulated in the realms of medicine for health reasons, but is controlled in other arenas as well. The media is a powerful social typing and social control agent for "too fat," with media imagery having a significant influence on people's perceptions of body size, feelings about themselves, and efforts at weight loss (Stice & Shaw, 1994; Garner, 1997). Commercial industry permeates social control over "too fat." Books, magazines, videos, pills, potions, and patches all promise to help us lose weight and look great. In the realm of everyday interaction, people who are considered "too fat" are controlled through stigmatization (e.g., name-calling), prejudicial attitudes, and overt discrimination (e.g., in employment) (Puhl & Heuer, 2009; Puhl & Brownell, 2001). Government programs target people who are overweight and/or out of shape, trying to encourage people to adopt healthier lifestyles (e.g., Health Canada, 2003). Even some schools are attempting to reduce the proportion of children who are overweight by instituting daily fitness activities (DeMont, 2002).

Chapter 7 discusses the social typing of psychological deviance as mental disorder, which occurs at both formal and informal levels. Mental disorder today is highly medicalized. The fields of psychiatry and psychology are intimately involved in social typing, determining what the "descriptions" are (e.g., "depression"), what the evaluation is (i.e., "ill"), and what the treatments should be (e.g., therapy, medication, hospitalization).

In the past, mental illness was perceived quite differently. For example, for several centuries, people who are now seen as "mentally ill" were instead perceived as being possessed by the devil or guilty of witchcraft. Control measures included religious rituals to exorcise the devil (in the case of possession) or, in the case of witchcraft, executions carried out by religious or governmental authorities. Over the last several decades, the **deinstitutionalization** movement has characterized most Western nations, with a shift from hospital-based treatments to community-based ones. Deinstitutionalization has worked very well for those people who have strong support networks and who live in communities with sufficient resources. However, for people lacking support networks and community resources, deinstitutionalization has meant a lack of medical treatment (Krieg, 2001; Sullivan, Jackson, & Spritzer, 1996). People with mental illnesses who do not receive medical treatment frequently end up being socially controlled as homeless persons or criminals (Belcher, 1989; Hodgins, 1993).

In Chapter 8, on religion, we saw that many different religious groups are socially typed as deviant by governments, scientific "experts," or other religious groups. For example, the government of Germany labels Scientology as deviant, and does not hire its adherents (Forum 18, 2001). The Chinese government closely monitors and controls the few legalized religions in that country: adults are legally prohibited from teaching any religion to children, members of the Communist Party are not permitted to hold any religious beliefs, and religious leaders are frequently appointed by the government (Forum 18, 2001).

The **anti-cult movement** socially types certain religious groups as deviant, emphasizing those groups thought to use mind control techniques and authoritarian leadership. Organizations that are part of this movement provide information on cult awareness, support groups for parents of cult members and, in some cases, deprogramming services for former cult members (Barker, 2001). The **counter-cult movement** consists of certain fundamentalist Christian groups that identify all non-fundamentalist Christians and all non-Christian religions as deviant. They spread their messages via the internet, at church meetings, and through publications that teach members how to convince adherents of specific cults to leave those groups (Bromley & Shupe, 1993).

Chapter 9, on science, notes that one of the ways that social typing, social control, and power made themselves evident was in the concept of deviant sciences or pseudo-sciences (Shermer, 2001). The scientific community itself determines which belief systems are not "real" sciences,

---

Ask Yourself

An important aspect of social typing is who benefits from the social typing process—the social typers themselves, particular groups in society, society as a whole, or sometimes even the people who have been socially typed. Select one specific issue from each of the substantive topics covered in the textbook—sexuality, youth, physical appearance, mental disorder, religion, and science—and ask yourself who has benefited from the social typing in that instance.

such as astrology. Although the scientific community is the most qualified entity to evaluate scientific claims being made by others, some scholars suggest that its inherent conservatism often leads it to automatically reject anything that is new or too different from the status quo (Ben-Yehuda, 1990). This is particularly apparent in those instances where claims that were initially rejected as deviant later come to be accepted. The astronomy community socially typed the first radio astronomers as deviant; consequently, they had difficulty getting their work published and became outcasts in the astronomy community. At a later point, however, that same scientific community determined that radio astronomy was a "real" science after all (Ben-Yehuda, 1990).

The "Deviance Dance"

Another theme throughout this textbook is the notion of the "**deviance dance**." This refers to the idea that with any particular person, action, or characteristic that has been socially typed as deviant, there will be differing points of view, debate, and resistance. The dance surrounding deviance is sometimes uniform (like a country line dance), with virtually everyone agreeing on the issue and what should be done with it; everyone moves in the same direction in pursuit of the same goal. At other times, the dance is more waltz-like, where various groups work toward the same goal, but everyone is not taking the same steps to reach that goal. At yet other times, the dance is more like a mosh pit, with groups pushing, shoving, and slamming into each other in order to reach their own particular goals.

Every substantive topic we have looked at involves the "deviance dance." Our historical review of sexuality in Chapter 4 revealed that although a dominant sexual culture exists in any given society, there are always differences, resistance, and disagreement within such sexual cultures. For example, although sexual relationships between aristocratic men and adolescent boys were normative in the dominant sexual culture of fifth-century B.C. Athens, there were groups of people within Athenian society who considered such relationships inappropriate and dangerous for the boys involved. They implemented efforts to regulate these relationships, such as legislation barring contact between the hours of dusk and dawn (Arkins, 1994).

In contemporary society, we see debate over various aspects of sexuality, such as how often is "too often" or "not often enough," whether pornography is harmful, and how old is "too creepy" for sexual activity (Goode, 1997). There are even different points of view as to whether or not certain acts (e.g., exotic dancing) are "sexual acts." We can also see resistance to legislation that prohibits sexual contact between adults and children; despite the fact that such behaviours are widely abhorred in Canadian society, the North America Man/Boy Love Association (NAMBLA) tries to convince people that consensual sexual relationships between adults and children are not harmful (NAMBLA, 2002).

At times, the struggle over deviance is characterized by intense debate and conflict.

In Chapter 5, on youth, different opinions, debates, and resistance are evident also. For example, critics say that virtually every adolescent ends up being perceived as "at risk" within the knowledge and practices of "risk management" (Bessant, 2001; Ericson & Haggerty, 2001). That is, adolescence itself has become defined as a time of inherent risk. The "deviance dance" is also apparent in the debates that occur between politicians or interest groups that proclaim youth crime to be out of control and in need of tougher legislation, and those groups that point out the public image of youth crime is tremendously overblown. Differing points of view are present with regard to problems that *are* generally recognized, as well. For example, although most university administrators see binge drinking among students as problematic, they can have very different approaches to controlling it (Wechsler *et al.*, 2000). The most controversial approach has been the "dry campus," where all alcohol is prohibited. This has met with resistance from students who oppose university alcohol programs or policies that are directed *at* them rather than created *with* them. It has also been criticized by a number of substance abuse experts, who claim that prohibitionist approaches are ineffective and simply move binge drinking off campus (Keeling, 2002).

The topic of body size embodies differing views and resistance as well. Although the cultural ideal of thinness continues to be perpetuated in the media and public opinion, various organizations are trying to change cultural ideals to accommodate a wider range of body sizes, and are lobbying the media to integrate more realistic representations of the female body. Anorexia is an extremely dangerous disorder that frequently requires immediate medical intervention. However, recent media images (e.g., of *Playboy* centrefolds) actually promote anorexic ideals, and "Ana" websites even provide tips to people with anorexia to enable them to continue their pursuit of weight loss. Like the behaviours of these lobbyists and even the "Ana" websites, body modification may also be seen as a form of resistance to social typing. For example, women may get tattoos in order to reject traditional discourses of gender in society (Atkinson, 2002), and straightedgers use their bodies as statements against the hedonism and self-indulgence of the modern world (Atkinson, 2003b).

In the chapter on mental disorders, Chapter 7, the "deviance dance" is most apparent in debates surrounding specific diagnostic categories contained in the American Psychiatric Association's *Diagnostic and Statistical Manual of Mental Disorders* (e.g., Caplan, 1995). For example, in contemporary society, debates over the extent to which ADHD is being diagnosed in North America are common. However, some groups have even gone a step further, suing the American Psychiatric Association for "manufacturing" a mental illness (Shute, 2000; Peck, 2001). Debates over whether gender identity disorder is a mental illness are also common today. Some scholars resist the medicalization of mental disorders even more profoundly, by arguing that the concept of mental illness itself is a "myth" (Szasz, 1994).

The deviance dance is perhaps at its most obvious in situations involving religion (see Chapter 8)—those in which particular groups have been socially typed as being sects or cults, and then actively resist those labels. In France, more than one hundred groups have been socially typed in this way by the French government. Some members of these groups have taken their cases all the way to the European Court, where the judges' decisions have frequently opposed the claims made by the French government (U. S. Department of State, 2008). Throughout the world, as Jehovah's Witnesses resist the "deviant" label that has been attached to them (and the discriminatory actions they have faced as a result, including arrest), they also claim that all religious groups other than their own are deviant (Lawson, 1995). In the United States, the Christian Coalition attempts to influence government policy on the basis of their own beliefs about the people, actions, and characteristics that are "deviant." Conversely, various individuals and groups who are concerned about the Coalition's influence on the Republican Party and the blurring of religious and political boundaries oppose the Coalition's actions (e.g., Boston, 1996).

Difference, debate, and resistance are even evident in the world of science. Ongoing debates have characterized scientific claims in relation to the tobacco industry. For example, the industry's scientists label the work of their opposition as **junk science**, while scientists whose research shows the dangers of smoking launch similar claims at the industry (Rampton & Stauber, 2000a; Ong & Glantz, 2001). Historically, although the eugenics movement had considerable influence in Canada, the United States, Britain, and Germany, there were also scientists and social organizations in each of those nations who were critical of eugenic ideals. In contemporary society, while some groups of scientists proclaim the benefits that genetic testing and manipulation will bring to the world, others disagree, and some claim that modern genetics is nothing more than eugenics in twenty-first-century clothing (Ward, 1993; Carlson & Stimeling, 2002).

Exercise Your Mind

The examples included in this chapter barely scratch the surface of how certain themes that were introduced in the first chapter have been embodied in the rest of this textbook. You may want to look back at a particular chapter or small segments of several chapters to look for the numerous other instances of these themes: the objective–subjective continuum, social typing, social control, power, and the "deviance dance."

TIME TO REVIEW

- How have more objective research interests been reflected in the chapters of this textbook?
- How have more subjective research interests been reflected in the chapters of this book?
- What are some examples of how social typing and social control are evident with each of the substantive topics explored in the textbook?
- How are notions of power embedded in the chapters of the textbook?
- In what way is the "deviance dance" apparent in the topics we have looked at?

The Search for Standards

Throughout this textbook, we have seen that, to some extent, "deviance" is in the eye of the beholder. That is, there is far more to the concept of deviance than the inherent nature of the person, act, or characteristic. The cross-cultural and historical examples that we have looked at show us that power is fundamental to determining what or who will be considered deviant in society. Actions considered criminal in certain cultures at specific historical moments are seen as acceptable actions in other cultures and at other historical times. For example, homosexual acts were seen as criminal throughout North America a century ago, but today they are not considered criminal in Canada, although they are criminalized in several American states.

Conversely, during most of the nineteenth century, child abuse and spousal abuse were seen as legally, socially, and morally acceptable, but today are considered crimes in much of the world. The sexual relationships between boys and adult men in Sambian society would constitute pedophilia according to Canadian standards. Adultery, while merely frowned upon in North America, is considered criminal in other nations (Mackay, 2000). A half-century ago, youth (but not adults) could run afoul of the criminal justice system for misbehaviours like truancy, sexual promiscuity, and incorrigibility; today, the list of offences is identical for youth and adults.

Historically, acts that were carried out by societal authorities with wide support from the rest of the community would now be considered deviant by contemporary standards. The witch persecutions that swept much of Europe for centuries are now looked upon with disdain as an instance of religious and political authorities preying on the superstitious populace in order to further their own goals of power. Residential schooling is perceived as a regrettable event in Canadian history, even by those societal institutions that participated in it— i.e., the federal government and several church bodies. Formal apologies have been given, reparations are underway, and programs have been instituted to assist Aboriginal communities in beginning the healing process (Ontario Consultants on Religious Tolerance, 2003).

Social Darwinism and the subsequent eugenics movement, popular in Canada, the United States, Britain, and other nations during the late nineteenth and early twentieth centuries, targeted numerous social groups for forced sterilization. The

The United Nations is one international body that develops universal human rights standards.

eugenics movement itself is now looked upon as a deviant use of science and politics. The apex that the eugenics movement reached in the Holocaust is widely perceived as one of the most horrific events in human history; however, it is important to remember that for several years during the 1930s, the rest of the world (including Canada) looked upon the success of Nazi eugenics with admiration.

After exploring cross-cultural and historical variations, as well as the debate and differing points of view that exist within a single society at any given time, some people may understandably begin to think that there are no transcendent standards by which people, behaviours, or characteristics can be evaluated—and that no group has the right to impose its subjective standards of behaviour on any other group. Because deviance is in the eye of the beholder, "anything goes." Of course, if that belief were fully realized, anarchy would reign in society. So how can balance be achieved? How can we determine whether it is appropriate to socially type specific groups of people as deviant, and subject them to measures of social control?

To some extent, subjectivity will always be involved in the social typing of deviance. Regardless of what norms, policies, programs, or legislation exist, there will always be some people (no matter how few) who will be in opposition. However, one place to begin a search for possible universal standards is with documents that emphasize the notion of human rights.

The Universal Declaration of Human Rights, adopted by the member states of the United Nations on December 10, 1948, is the foundational document for other modern human rights policies, programs, and legislation throughout the world (including the Canadian Charter of Rights and Freedoms). A larger sample of human rights documents can be found in Box 10.1.

Box 10.1   A Sample of Human Rights Documents

- The Magna Carta (see the British Library website for scanned pages of the original Magna Carta, and an English translation, at www.bl.uk/collections/treasures/magna.html)
- Declaration of the Rights of Man and Citizens (from the French Revolution)
- Universal Declaration of Human Rights
- Canadian Charter of Rights and Freedoms
- Convention on the Rights of the Child
- International Covenant on Civil and Political Rights
- International Covenant on Economic, Social, and Cultural Rights
- European Convention on Human Rights
- Universal Declaration of Sexual Rights

- Universal Declaration on the Human Genome and Human Rights
- Declaration on the Elimination of All Forms of Intolerance and of Discrimination Based on Religion and Belief
- Declaration on the Rights of Disabled Persons
- Principles for the Protection of Persons with Mental Illness and the Improvement of Mental Health Care
- Convention Concerning Indigenous and Tribal Peoples in Independent Countries

All of these documents can be found, in their entirety, on the internet. A good source of information for human rights documents is the National Center for Human Rights Education at www.nchre.org.

AN INTERNET MOMENT

Go to the British Library's website, listed in Box 10.1, and look at the *Magna Carta*, which was written back in the thirteenth century. Then select a handful of the other human rights documents listed in Box 10.1 and find them on the internet. Look for some of the ideas that these human rights documents share, as well as some of the distinct components of specific documents.

A number of themes run through the range of human rights documents that can be found in countries around the world. One of these is the right to **human dignity**, which is the right to be treated with respect. Numerous issues that have been addressed in this textbook can be considered in relation to this human right. The way that certain social groups were targeted by the eugenics movement can certainly be considered a violation of human dignity, as can the Nazis' racial hygiene program. European colonization and residential schooling also involved infringements on the dignity of Aboriginal people. The notion of human dignity underlies other international documents as well, such as the Universal Declaration of Sexual Rights (World Association for Sexology, 1999), and UNESCO's Universal Declaration on the Human Genome and Human Rights (UNESCO, 1997). The former document emphasizes that consensual adult sexual activities should not be deviantized, and that the freedom to sexual expression must prevail. The latter document suggests that certain genetic traits should not be considered superior or inferior to other traits; that is, individuals with specific genetic traits should not be deviantized.

Another theme in human rights documents is the prohibition of differential treatment on the basis of group membership (i.e., **discrimination**). The characteristics that are commonly listed in relation to this right are race, sex, ethnicity, colour, nation of origin, religion, political membership, and language; however, other categories (e.g., sexual orientation) are included in some human rights documents as well. The Canadian Charter of Rights and Freedoms and various pieces of provincial human rights legislation address the notion of discrimination in Canadian society. The World Health Organization's constitution declares that the right to physical, mental, and social health applies to all social groups, such as those just listed (World Health Organization, 2003). The Universal Declaration on the Human Genome and Human Rights prohibits discrimination on the basis of genetic characteristics (UNESCO, 1997).

Historically, the right to freedom from discrimination was infringed upon in the eugenics movement and during European colonization. In contemporary society, people who are considered "too fat" face discrimination in employment, housing, health care, and education (Puhl & Brownell, 2001). Members of certain religious groups are discriminated against in several countries, such as the groups identified by the government of France as cults (e.g., Jehovah's Witnesses, Scientology) (U. S. Department of State, 2002). Members of the Christian Coalition have voiced narrow views of a number of different social groups, including non-whites, members of other religious groups, and immigrants; their influence in the political realm has the potential to turn those prejudicial beliefs into overt discrimination (Boston, 1996; Vuijst, 1995).

Security of person and property are also prevalent in human rights documents. Violent crimes (e.g., assault) and property crimes (e.g., theft) violate security of the person and property. The World Health Organization's constitution declares that the universal right to physical, mental, and social health is necessary for peace and security, not specifically for individuals, but in societies and throughout the world (World Health Organization, 2004); thus, the failure to provide the necessary means for achieving health for any group is seen as unacceptable. The involuntary sterilization of "mental defectives," the torture and death involved in the Holocaust, the abuse suffered by tens of thousands of Aboriginal children in residential schools, and the witch persecutions (wherein witches were not only executed but also had their property seized to pay for their arrest, torture, trial, and execution) can all be seen as infringements upon the right to security of the person and of property. When, in World War II, the Canadian government defined Japanese-Canadians as "enemy aliens," it placed thousands of Japanese-Canadian citizens in internment camps and subsequently seized their property and auctioned it to the highest bidder. Security of person and security of property were again violated by the Canadian government.

Human dignity, freedom from discrimination, and security of person and property are three of the core themes that are integrated into various types of human rights policies and legislation. Given the influence of subjectivity and power that has been involved in the social typing of deviance across cultures and throughout history, human rights policies represent some basic standards that we may be able to apply in determining whether it is appropriate to label anyone or anything as deviant. However, a level of subjectivity also exists in determining whether human rights have been violated in any particular instance. Human rights documents themselves state that there are circumstances where someone's human rights may legitimately be violated; typically, this is when there are threats to social order, morality, or other people's human rights. For example, although freedom of religion is a basic human right, many governments monitor, regulate, and even ban specific religious groups that are perceived as a threat to social order or morality (Forum 18, 2001; U. S. Department of State, 2008).

Although freedom of expression is a universal human right, Canada, the United States, and numerous other countries have hate crime or human rights legislation that prohibits spreading hatred or advocating the genocide of identifiable social groups. For instance, some leaders and members of white supremacist groups have been charged with spreading hatred, even though charging them with that offence is a violation of their right to freedom of expression. International human rights documents condone this as a legitimate violation of that freedom, based on threats to the social order and violations of other people's human rights.

"Never doubt that a small group of thoughtful committed citizens can change the world. Indeed, it's the only thing that ever has." (Margaret Mead)[3]

Box 10.2   Are You Interested in Human Rights?

If you want to learn more about human rights, or wish to become active in the pursuit of human rights, you may find the following organizations and information centres useful:

- Human Rights Watch (www.hrw.org)
- Amnesty International (www.amnesty.org)
- International Gay and Lesbian Human Rights Commission (www.iglhrc.org)
- Women's Human Rights Resources (www.law-lib.utoronto.ca/diana/)
- African Human Rights Resource Center (www.umn.edu/humanrts/africa/)

CHAPTER SUMMARY

- Certain ideas that were introduced in Chapter 1 represent themes that have been carried through the various chapters in the textbook. One of these themes is the blending of *objective* and *subjective* approaches to the study of deviance. In various chapters, the *positivist* interest in causation that characterizes more objective approaches was explored, such as in explanations of youth crime and substance use.

- The *interpretive* and *critical* interests in the social processes by which deviance is assigned, which characterize more subjective approaches, was addressed throughout the chapters as well. For example, we looked at the *moral panics* surrounding youth crime and gangs, and the social standards that define "too fat."

- A second theme throughout this book is the notion of the *social typing process*. Power plays a critical role in determining who or what will be considered deviant, and what social control measures are directed at them. Governments, the media, religious institutions, scientists, and commercial industry are all intimately involved in the social typing and social control of various aspects of deviance.

- The *deviance dance* can be seen throughout this book as well. Regardless of the specific issue in question, various individuals and groups have differing points of view on whether something or someone is deviant, how deviant they are, and what the most effective means of social control will be.

- Given the role of subjectivity in understanding deviance, does that mean "anything goes"? Does it mean that we cannot legitimately socially type anyone or anything as deviant? The concept of *human rights* is one place where we can begin looking at whether any standards can be applied. Numerous international human rights documents exist, and they give some indication of criteria that may be used to determine who should and should not be deviantized.

DEVIANCE IN PRINT

Sweet, W. (2003). *Philosophical Theory and the Universal Declaration of Human Rights*. Ottawa: University of Ottawa Press.

Schulz, W. (2003). *Tainted Legacy: 9-11 and the Ruins of Human Rights*. New York: Thunder's Mouth Press.

British Medical Association (2000). *The Medical Profession and Human Rights: Handbook for a Changing Agenda*. London: Zed Books.

DEVIANCE AT THE MOVIES

Read, D. (Director), Armstrong, M., Pettigrew, M., & Johansson, S. (Producers). (1990). *The Burning Times*. (Available from the National Film Board of Canada.) (56 minutes).

This documentary about the witch persecutions was recommended in Chapter 1. It might be interesting to revisit the film in order to see the greater complexity with which you are now able to analyze the events presented.

ENDNOTES

1 Mason Cooley [b.1927]. Columbia World of Quotations. City aphorisms, fourteenth selection. New York. Retrieved August 23, 2006, from **www.bartleby.com**

2 David Lee (producer of Frasier). Rand Lindsly's quotations, from The Quotations Page. Retrieved August 23, 2006, from **www.quotationspage.com**

3 Margaret Mead. [1901–1978]. Laura Moncur's quotations, from The Quotations Page. Retrieved July 4, 2003, from **www.quotationspage.com/quote/33522.html**

KEY TERMS

conformity, **p. 300**

deviant, **p. 300**

objective, **p. 300**

positivist, **p. 301**

subjective, **p. 301**

scientific misconduct, **p. 304**

bad apple/bad person theory, **p. 304**

iceberg theory, **p. 304**

social typing process, **p. 305**

description, **p. 305**

evaluation, **p. 305**

prescription, **p. 305**

social control, **p. 305**

regulation, **p. 305**

informal control, **p. 305**

formal control, **p. 305**

preventative control, **p. 305**

retroactive control, **p. 305**

REFERENCES

Abernethy, D. B. (2001). *The Dynamics of Global Dominance: European Overseas Empires, 1415–1980*. New Haven, CT: Yale University Press.

Accordino, M. P., Porter, D. F. & Morse, T. (2001). Deinstitutionalization of Persons with Severe Mental Illness: Context and Consequences. *Journal of Rehabilitation Medicine, 67*(2), 16–21.

Adlaf, E. M., Demers, A. & Gliksman, L. (Eds.) (2005). *Canadian Campus Survey 2004*. Toronto, ON: Centre for Addiction and Mental Health.

Adlaf, E. M., Gliksman, L., Demers, A. & Newton-Taylor, B. (2001). The Prevalence of Elevated Psychological Distress Among Canadian Undergraduates. *Journal of American College Health, 50*(2), 67–72.

Adlaf, E. M. & Paglia-Boak, A. (2007). *Drug Use Among Ontario Students, 1977–2007*. CAMH Research Document Series No. 21. Toronto, ON: Canadian Association for Mental Health.

Adler, P. A. & Adler, P. (2006a). *Constructions of Deviance: Social Power, Context, and Interaction* (5th ed.). Toronto, ON: Thomson Wadsworth.

Adler, P. A. & Adler, P. (2006b). The deviance society. *Deviant Behavior: An Interdisciplinary Journal, 27*(2), 129–148.

Adler, P. A. & Adler, P. (2003). *Constructions of Deviance: Social Power, Context, and Interaction* (4th edition). Belmont, CA: Wadsworth.

Agliata, D. & Tantleff-Dunn, S. (2004). The Impact of Media Exposure on Males' Body Image. *Journal of Social and Clinical Psychology, 23*(1), 7–22.

Agnew, R. (1992). A Foundation for a General Strain Theory of Crime and Delinquency. *Criminology, 30*, 47–87.

Agnew, R. (1998). A General Strain Theory of Crime and Delinquency. In F. T. Cullen & R. Agnew (Eds.), *Criminological Theory: Past to Present* (pp. 152–156). Los Angeles, CA: Roxbury.

Agnew, R. A. (2006). *Pressured into Crime: An Overview of General Strain Theory*. Los Angeles, CA: Roxbury.

Agnew, R. & Brezina, T. (1997). Relational Problems with Peers, Gender, and Delinquency. *Youth & Society, 29*, 84–111.

Agnew, R., Cullen, F., Burton, V., Evans, T. D., & Dunaway, R. G. (1996). A New Test of Classic Strain Theory. *Justice Quarterly, 13*, 681–704.

Akers, R. L. (1977). *Deviant Behavior: A Social Learning Approach*. Belmont, CA: Wadsworth.

Akers, R. L. (1991). Self-Control as a General Theory of Crime. *Journal of Quantitative Criminology, 7*, 201–211.

Akers, R. L. (1998). *Social Learning and Social Structure: A General Theory of Crime and Deviance*. Boston, MA: Northeastern University Press.

Akers, R. L. (2000). *Criminological Theories: Introduction, Evaluation, and Application* (3rd ed.). Los Angeles, CA: Roxbury.

Akers, R. L. (2006). *Social Learning and Social Structure: A General Theory of Crime and Deviance*. Boston, MA: Northeastern University Press.

Alberta Alliance on Mental Illness & Mental Health. (2003). Homepage. Retrieved April 19, 2003, from **www.aamimh.ca**.

Alberta Mental Health Act. (n.d.). Retrieved June 1, 2003, from **www.qp.alberta.ca/574.cfm?page=M13.cfm&leg_type=Acts&isbncln=9780779741168**.

American Psychiatric Association. (1994). *Diagnostic and Statistical Manual of Mental Disorders–IV*. Washington, DC: Author.

Anderson, A. & Gordon, R. (1978). Witchcraft and the Status of Women—The Case of England. *British Journal of Sociology, 29*, 171–184.

Anthony, D. & Robbins, T. (1994). Brainwashing and Totalitarian Influence. In S. Ramachandran (Ed.), *Encyclopedia of Human Behavior* (Vol. 1) (pp. 457–471). San Diego, CA: Academic Press.

Apatow, J., (Writer/Director), & Carell, S. (Writer), (2005). *The 40-Year-Old-Virgin*. United States: Universal Pictures.

Arkins, B. (1994). Sexuality in Fifth-Century Athens. *Classics Ireland, 1*, 1–8.

Armstrong, L. (1993). *And They Call It Help: The Psychiatric Policing of America's Children.* Reading, MA: Addison-Wesley.

Armstrong, M. L., Roberts, A. E., Owen, D. C. & Koch, J. R. (2004). Toward Building a Composite of College Student Influences with Body Art. *Issues in Comprehensive Pediatric Nursing, 27,* 277–295.

Arnett, J. (1992). Reckless Behavior in Adolescence: A Developmental Perspective. *Developmental Review, 12,* 339–373.

Arnett, J. J. (1999). Adolescent Storm and Stress Reconsidered. *American Psychologist, 54*(5), 317–326.

Aseltine, R. (1995). A Reconsideration of Parental and Peer Influences on Adolescent Deviance. *Journal of Health and Social Behavior, 3*(6), 103–121.

Asma, S. T. (1993). The New Social Darwinism. *Humanist, 53*(5), 10–12.

Ashley, D. & Orenstein, D. M. (2001). *Sociological Theory: Classical Statements* (5th ed.). Boston, MA: Allyn & Bacon.

Associated Press. (2006, May 21). Disgraced Korean Cloning Scientist Indicted. *The New York Times.* Retrieved June 7, 2006, from **www.nytimes.com**.

Atkinson, M. (2001). Flesh Journeys: Neo Primitives and the Contemporary Rediscovery of Radical Body Modification. *Deviant Behavior, 22,* 117–146.

Atkinson, M. (2002). Pretty in Ink: Conformity, Resistance, and Negotiation in Women's Tattooing. *Sex Roles, 47*(5/6), 219–235.

Atkinson, M. (2003a). *Tattooed: The Sociogenesis of a Body Art.* Toronto, ON: University of Toronto Press.

Atkinson, M. (2003b). The Civilizing of Resistance: Straightedge Tattooing. *Deviant Behavior: An Interdisciplinary Journal, 24,* 197–220.

AuCoin, K. (2005). Children and Youth as Victims of Violent Crime. *Juristat, 25*(1). Statistics Canada Catalogue No. 85002XIE.

Bahrke, M. S., Yesalis, C. E., Kopstein, A. N. & Stephens, J. A. (2000). Risk Factors Associated with Anabolic-Androgenic Steroid Use Among Adolescents. *Sports Medicine, 29*(6), 397–405.

Bailey, S. & Bronskill, J. (2007, January 30). Prisons, 'Open-Air Asylum' Home to Mentally Ill. *Edmonton Journal.* Retrieved September 3, 2008 from **www.canada.com**.

Bainbridge, W. S. (2002). *The Endtime Family: Children of God.* New York: State University of New York Press.

Baird, A. L. & Grieve, F. G. (2006). Exposure to Male Models in Advertisements Leads to a Decrease in Men's Body Satisfaction. *North American Journal of Psychology, 8*(1), 115–122.

Ball, P. (2003). Physicists Fail to Find Saving Grace for Falsified Research. *Nature, 421*(6926), 878.

Bandura, A. (1986). *Social Foundations of Thought and Action: A Social Cognitive Theory.* Englewood Cliffs, NJ: Prentice Hall.

Barker, E. (2001). Watching for Violence: A Comparative Analysis of the Roles of Five Types of Cult-Watching Groups. Paper presented at the annual meeting of the Center for Studies in New Religions.

Barnett, A. (2003, December 7). Pharma Ghostwriting Revealed: How Drug Firms 'Hoodwink' Medical Journals. *The London Observer.* Retrieved May 19, 2006, from **http://proliberty.com**.

Baron, S. W. (1989). Canadian West Coast Punk Subculture: A Field Study. *Canadian Journal of Sociology, 14*(3), 289–316.

Barrett, J. & Jay, P. (2005). Clinical Research Fraud: A Victimless Crime? *Applied Clinical Trials, 14*(2), 44–46.

Barsley, M. (1967). *The Other Hand: An Investigation into the Sinister History of Left-Handedness.* New York: Hawthorn Books.

Barstow, A. L. (1994). *Witchcraze.* San Francisco: Pandora.

Bartowski, J. P. (1998). Claimsmaking and Typifications of Voodoo as a Deviant Religion: Hex, Lies, and Videotape. *Journal for the Scientific Study of Religion, 37(4),* 559–579.

Bassett, H., Lampe, J. & Lloyd, C. (1999). Parenting: Experiences and Feelings of Parents with a Mental Illness. *Journal of Mental Health, 8(6),* 597–604.

Baumrind, D. (1991). Parenting Styles and Adolescent Development. In R. Lerner, A. Peterson, & J. Brooks-Gunn (Eds.), *Encyclopedia of Adolescence.* New York: Garland Publishing.

Beaman, L. G. (2000). *New Perspectives on Deviance: The Construction of Deviance in Everyday Life.* Scarborough, ON: Prentice Hall.

Beaud, J. P. & Prevost, J. G. (1996). Immigration, Eugenics, and Statistics: Measuring Racial Origins in Canada, 1921–1941. *Canadian Ethnic Studies, 28(2),* 1–23.

Bechtel, K. & Pearson, W. (1985). Deviant Scientists and Scientific Deviance. *Deviant Behavior: An Interdisciplinary Journal, 6,* 237–252.

Beck, M. (2001, November). Embracing Your Inner Brat. *O Magazine,* p. 69.

Beck, U. (1992). *Risk Society: Towards a New Modernity.* London: Sage.

Beck, U. (1999). *World Risk.* Cambridge: Polity Press.

Becker, H. (1963). *Outsiders: Studies in the Sociology of Deviance.* New York: Free Press.

Beckwith, J. (1993). A Historical View of Social Responsibility in Genetics. *Bioscience, 43*(5), 327–333.

Belcher, J. R. (1989). On Becoming Homeless: A Study of Chronically Mentally Ill Persons. *Journal of Community Psychology, 17,* 173–185.

Bell, S., Cossman, B., Ross, B. L., Gottell, L., & Janovicek, N. (1998). Bad Attitude/s on Trial: Feminism, Pornography, & the Butler Decision. *Journal of Canadian Studies, 33*(1), 163-172.

Bell, S. J. (2002). *Young Offenders and Juvenile Justice: A Century After the Fact* (2nd ed.). Scarborough, ON: Nelson Thomson.

Benard, B. (1991). *Fostering Resilience in Kids: Protective Factors in the Family, School, and Community.* Portland, OR: Northwest Regional Educational Laboratory.

Benda, B. B. (1994). Testing Competing Theoretical Concepts: Adolescent Alcohol Consumption. *Deviant Behavior: An Interdisciplinary Journal, 15,* 375–396.

Ben-Yehuda, N. (1980). The European Witch Craze of the 14th to 17th Centuries: A Sociologist's Perspective. *American Journal of Sociology, 86*(1), 1–31.

Ben-Yehuda, N. (1986). Deviance in Science. *British Journal of Criminology, 26(1),* 1–27.

Ben-Yehuda, N. (1990). *The Politics and Morality of Deviance: Moral Panics, Drug Abuse, Deviant Science, and Reversed Stigmatization.* Albany, NY: State University of New York Press.

Benson, M. (1985). Denying the Guilty Mind: Accounting for Involvement in White-Collar Crime. *Criminology, 23(4),* 589–599.

Beres, M. A. (2007). 'Spontaneous' Sexual Consent: An Analysis of Sexual Consent Literature. *Feminism & Psychology, 17*(1), 93–108.

Berger, B. (1963). Adolescence and Beyond. *Social Problems, 10,* 294–408.

Bernberg, J. G. & Krohn, M. D. (2003). Labeling, Life Chances, and Adult Crime: The Direct and Indirect Effects of Official Intervention in Adolescence on Crime in Early Adulthood. *Criminology, 41*(4), 1287–1318.

Bessant, J. (2001). From Sociology of Deviance to Sociology of Risk: Youth Homelessness and the Problem of Empiricism. *Journal of Criminal Justice, 29,* 31–43.

Best, J. (2003). Constructionism in Context. In. E. Rubington & M. S. Weinberg (Eds.), *The Study of Social Problems: Seven Perspectives* (6th ed.) (pp. 351–356). New York: Oxford University Press.

Bibby, R. W. (2001). *Canada's Teens: Today, Yesterday, and Tomorrow.* Toronto, ON: Stoddart.

Bibby, R. W. (2009). *The Emerging Millenials: How Canada's Newest Generation Is Responding to Change and Choice.* Lethbridge, AB: Project Canada Books.

Bleicher, P. (2003). Is Change Afoot? 21 CFR 11 in Transition. *Applied Clinical Trials, 12*(6) 34–36.

Bloch, E. (2001). Sex Between Men and Boys in Classical Greece: Was It Education for Citizenship or Child Abuse? *Journal of Men's Studies, 9*(2). Retrieved October 2, 2001, from Expanded Academic ASAP database.

Blumer, H. (1986). *Symbolic Interactionism: Perspective and Method.* Berkeley, CA: University of California Press.

Bochenek, M. & Brown, A. W. (2001). *Hatred in the Hallways: Violence and Discrimination Against Lesbian, Gay, Bisexual, and Transgender Students in U.S. Schools.* New York: Human Rights Watch.

Born, L. (2004). Fast-Tracking the Plague: Drugging America to Death. *International Socialist Review, 33*. Retrieved May 19, 2006, from **www.isreview.org**.

Bortner, M. (1988). *Delinquency and Justice: An Age of Crisis*. Toronto, ON: McGraw-Hill.

Boston, R. (1996). *The Most Dangerous Man in America? Pat Robertson and the Rise of the Christian Coalition*. Amherst, NY: Prometheus Books.

Bourget, B. & Chenier, R. (2007). *Mental Health Literacy in Canada: Phase One Report Mental Health Literacy Project*. Ottawa, ON: Canadian Alliance on Mental Illness and Mental Health.

Bourgois, P. (1995). *In Search of Respect: Selling Crack in El Barrio*. Cambridge, UK: Cambridge University Press.

Boutelle, K., Neumark-Sztainer, D., Story, M. & Resnick, M. (2002). Weight Control Behaviors Among Obese, Overweight, and Non-Overweight Adolescents. *Journal of Pediatric Psychology, 27*, 531–540.

Boyce, W., Doherty, M., Fortin, C., & MacKinnon, D. (2003). *Canada Youth, Sexual Health and HIV/AIDS Study*. Toronto, ON: Council of Ministers of Education Canada.

Brace, C. L. (1996). Racialism and Racist Agendas. *American Anthropologist, 98*(1), 176–177.

Braithwaite, J. (2000). Shame and Criminal Justice. *Canadian Journal of Criminology, 42*(3), 281–298.

Brandt, A. M. (2007). *The Cigarette Century: The Rise, Fall, and Deadly Persistance of the Product that Defined America*. New York: Basic Books.

Briggs, R. (1996). *Witches and Neighbors: The Social and Cultural Context of European Witchcraft*. New York: Viking Penguin.

British Columbia Eating Disorders Association (2003). Homepage. Retrieved May 17, 2003, from **http://webhome.idirect.com/~bceda/ index.html**.

British Medical Association. (2000). *The Medical Profession and Human Rights: Handbook for a Changing Agenda*. London: Zed Books.

Broidy, L. M. & Agnew, R. (1997). Gender and Crime: A General Strain Theory Perspective. *Journal of Research in Crime and Delinquency, 34*, 275–306.

Bromley, D. G. (2002). Dramatic Denouement. In D. G. Bromley & J. G. Melton (Eds.), *Cults, Religion, and Violence* (pp. 11–41). Cambridge, UK: Cambridge University Press.

Bromley, D. G. & Melton, J. G. (Eds.). (2002). *Cults, Religion, and Violence*. Cambridge, UK: Cambridge University Press.

Bromley, D. G. & Shupe, A. D. (1993). Organized Opposition to New Religious Movements. In D. G. Bromley & J. K. Hadden (Eds.), *The Handbook of Cults and Sects* (pp. 177–198). Greenwich, CT: JAI Press.

Brook, J. S., Brook, D. W., De La Rosa, M., Whiteman, M. & Montoya, I. D. (1999). The Role of Parents in Protecting Colombian Adolescents from Delinquency and Marijuana Use. *Archives of Pediatrics & Adolescent Medicine, 153*(5). Retrieved October 7, 2002, from Expanded Academic ASAP database.

Brounstein, P. J. & Zweig, J. M. (1999). *Understanding Substance Abuse Prevention: Toward the 21st Century: A Primer on Effective Programs*. Rockville, MD: U.S. Department of Health and Human Services.

Brower, A. M. (2002). Are College Students Alcoholics? *Journal of American College Health, 50*(5), 253–255.

Brower, R. (1999). Dangerous Minds: Eminently Creative People Who Spent Time in Jail. *Creative Research Journal, 12*(1). Retrieved August 6, 2001, from Academic Search Premier database.

Bruinsma, G. J. N. (1992). Differential Association Theory Reconsidered: An Extension and its Empirical Test. *Journal of Quantitative Criminology, 8*, 175–187.

Buchanan, C. M. & Holmbeck, G. N. (1998). Measuring Beliefs About Adolescent Personality and Behavior. *Journal of Youth & Adolescence, 27*, 609–629.

Buchanan, E. (1997). A School for Sterilization. *World Press Review, June*, 46.

Burger, T. D. & Finkel, D. (2002). Relationships Between Body Modifications and Very High-Risk Behavior in a College Population. *College Student Journal, 36*(2), 203–213.

Burgess, R. & Akers, R. (1966). A Differential Association Reinforcement Theory of Criminal Behavior. *Social Problems, 25*, 128–147.

Burton, V. S. & Cullen, F. T. (1992). The Empirical Status of Strain Theory. *Journal of Crime and Justice, 15*, 1–30.

Burton, V. & Dunaway, R. G. (1994). Strain, Relative Deprivation, and Middle-Class Delinquency. In G. Barak (Ed.), *Varieties of Criminology: Readings from a Dynamic Discipline* (pp. 79–96). Westport, CT: Praeger.

Bush, J., White, M., Kai, J., Ranking, J., & Bhopal, R. (2003). Understanding Influences on Smoking in Bangladeshi and Pakistani Adults: Community Based Qualitative Study. *British Medical Journal, 326*, 962–965.

Buzzell, T. (2005). Holiday Revelry and Legal Control of Fireworks: A Study of Neutralization in Two Normative Contexts. *Western Criminology, 6*(1), 30–42.

Caldwell, W. (2001). *Obesity Sourcebook*. Detroit, MI: Omnigraphics.

Caliendo, C., Armstrong, M. L. & Roberts, A. E. (2005). Self-Reported Characteristics of Women and Men with Intimate Body Piercings. *Journal of Advanced Nursing, 49*(5), 474–484.

Canadian Broadcasting Corporation (2001). PM Blasts MP for Blocking Mandela Honour. *CBC News*, June 8. Retrieved May 7, 2009, from **www.cbc.ca/canada/story/2001/06/07/Mandela_mp010607.html**.

Canadian Broadcasting Corporation (2007). Same-Sex Rights: Canada Timeline. *CBC News Indepth*. Retrieved January 4, 2009 from **www.cbc.ca/news/background/samesexrights/timeline_canada.html**.

Canadian Broadcasting Corporation (2008). Prime Minister Stephen Harper's Statement of Apology. Retrieved January 2, 2009 from **www.cbc.ca/anada/story/2008/06/11/pm-statement.html**.

Canadian Living. (2006, August). Your Teenager: An Owner's Manual (For the Bewildered Parent). *Canadian Living,* 159–162.

Canadian Paediatric Society. (1998). Eating Disorders in Adolescents: Principles of Diagnosis and Treatment. *Paediatric & Child Health, 3*(3), 189–192.

Canadian Paediatric Society. (2004). Dieting in Adolescence. Position Statement AH-2004-01. Retrieved August 1, 2006, from **www.cps.ca**.

Caplan, P. J. (1995). *They Say You're Crazy: How the World's More Powerful Psychiatrists Decide Who's Normal*. Reading, MA: Perseus Books.

Carlson, R. J. & Stimeling, G. (2002). *The Terrible Gift: The Brave New World of Genetic Medicine*. New York: PublicAffairs.

Carroll, L. & Anderson, R. (2002). Body Piercing, Tattooing, Self-Esteem, and Body Investment in Adolescent Girls. *Adolescence, 37*(147), 627–637.

Carroll, S. T., Riffenburgh, R. H., Roberts, T. A. & Myhre, E. B. (2002). Tattoos and Body Piercings as Indicators of Adolescent Risk-Taking Behaviors. *Pediatrics, 109*(6), 1021–1027.

Caulfield, T. (2004). The Commercialisation of Medical and Scientific Reporting. *PLoS Medicine, 1*(3), 178–179.

CCTV User Group (2008). How Many Cameras Are There? Retrieved May 12, 2009, from **www.cctvusergroup.com**.

Center on Alcohol Marketing and Youth (2004). *Clicking with Kids: Alcohol Marketing and Youth on the Internet*. Washington, DC: Author.

Chambliss, W. J. & Seidman, R. (1982). *Law, Order and Power* (2nd ed.). Reading, MA: Addison-Wesley.

Chappell, A. T. & Piquero, A. R. (2004). Applying Social Learning Theory to Police Misconduct. *Deviant Behavior, 25*, 89–108.

Chatterjee, J. (2006). *A Research Report on Youth Gangs: Problems, Perspectives, and Priorities*. Ottawa, ON: Research and Evaluation Branch, RCMP.

Childress, S. A. (1991). Reel "Rape Speech": Violent Pornography and the Politics of Harm. *Law & Society Review, 25*(1), 177–214.

Christian Coalition of America. (2003). Homepage. Retrieved July 7, 2003, from **www.cc.org**.

Chryssides, G. D. (1994). New Religious Movements—Some Problems with Definition. *Diskus: Web Edition, 2*(2). Retrieved February 19, 2003, from **http://web.uni-marburg.de/religionswissenschaft/journal/diskus/chryssides.html**.

Chryssides, G. D. (1996). New Religions and the Internet. *Diskus: Web Edition, 4*(2). Retrieved February 19, 2003, from **www.uni-marburg.de**.

Church of Jesus Christ of Latter Day Saints (2003). Main page. Retrieved June 7, 2003 from **www.lds.org**.

Claes, L., Vandereycken, W. & Vertommen, H. (2005). Self-Care Versus Self-Harm: Piercing, Tattooing, and Self-Injuring in Eating Disorders. *European Eating Disorders, 13*, 11–18.

Clarke, D. & Gabriels, T. (1996). Astrological Signs as Determinants of Extroversion and Emotionality: An Empirical Study. *Journal of Psychology, 130*(2), 131–140.

Clinard, M. B. & Meier, R. F. (2001). *Sociology of Deviant Behavior* (11th ed.). Fort Worth, TX: Harcourt College Publishers.

Cloward, R. A. & Ohlin, L. E. (1960). *Delinquency and Opportunity: A Theory of Delinquent Gangs*. New York: Free Press.

Cohen, A. J. (1955). *Delinquent Boys*. New York: Free Press.

Cohen, D. (Director) & James, R. (Producer). (1995). *Mistreating the Mentally Ill*. Available from Films for the Humanities & Sciences.

Cohen, S. (1973). *Folk Devils and Moral Panics*. London: MacGibbons and Kee.

Condon, B. (Director). (2004). *Kinsey*. United States: Fox Searchlight Pictures.

Conrad, P. (1992). Medicalization and Social Control. *Annual Review of Sociology, 18*, 209–232.

Conrad, P. & Leiter, V. (2004). Medicalization, Markets and Consumers. *Journal of Health and Social Behavior, 45*(Extra Issue), 158–176.

Conservative Party of Canada (2006). *Stand Up for Canada: Conservative Party of Canada Election Platform 2006*. Retrieved August 10, 2006, from **www.conservative.ca**.

Contemporary Sexuality. (2001). Among Drowning Dot-Coms, Cybersex Sails. *Contemporary Sexuality, 35*(5), 8.

Coontz, S. (1992). *The Way We Never Were: American Families and the Nostalgia Trap*. New York: Basis Books.

Cooper, A. (Ed.). (2002). *Sex and the Internet*. New York: Brunner-Routledge.

Copelton, D. A. (2007). "You are what you eat": Nutritional norms, maternal deviance, and neutralization of women's prenatal diets. *Deviant Behavior: An Interdisciplinary Journal, 28*(5), 467–494.

Costin, C. (1999). *The Eating Disorder Sourcebook*. Los Angeles, CA: Lowell House.

Council for Responsible Genetics. (2000). Genetic Bill of Rights. Retrieved June 17, 2006, from **www.gene-watch.org**.

Council for Responsible Genetics. (2001). Genetic Discrimination: Position Paper. Retrieved June 17, 2006, from **www.gene-watch.org**.

Council for Responsible Genetics (2003). Homepage. Retrieved July 5, 2003, from **www.gene-watch.org.**

Cowan, D. E. (2001). From Parchment to Pixels: The Christian Countercult on the Internet. Paper presented at the 2001 Conference of the Center for Studies on New Religions, April 20, London.

Cowan, P. (Director). (2000). *Give Me your Soul . . . .* Available from the National Film Board of Canada.

Cromwell, P. & Thurman, Q. (2003). The Devil Made Me Do It: The Use of Neutralization by Shoplifters. *Deviant Behavior, 24(6)*, 1–16.

Cronin, T. A. (2001). Tattoos, Piercings, and Skin Adornments. *Dermatology Nursing, 13*(5), 380–383.

Crouch, A. & Degelman, D. (1998). Influence of Female Body Images in Printed Advertising on Self-Ratings of Physical Attractiveness by Adolescent Girls. *Perceptual & Motor Skills, 87*(2), 585–586.

Crouch, B. & Damphousse, K. (1991). Law Enforcement and the Satanism-Crime Connection: A Survey of "Cult-Cops." In J. T. Richardson, J. Best, & D. Bromley (Eds.), *The Satanism Scare* (pp. 191–204). New York: Aldine de Gruyter.

Crouch, B. M. & Damphousse, K. R. (1992). Newspapers and the Anti-Satanism Movement. *Sociological Spectrum, 12*, 1–20.

Cullen, F. T. & Agnew, R. (1998). *Criminological Theory: Past to Present*. Los Angeles, CA: Roxbury.

Cummings, L. (2003). The Diet Business: Banking on Failure. *BBC News*. Retrieved August 1, 2006, from **www.bbc.co.uk**.

Das Gupta, T. (2000). Families of Native People, Immigrants, and People of Colour. In N. Mandell & A. Duffy (Eds.), *Canadian Families: Diversity, Conflict, and Change* (2nd ed.) (pp. 146–187). Scarborough, ON: Nelson Thomson.

Davidson, L., Hoge, M. A., Godleski, L., Rakfeldt, J. & Griffith, E. I. H. (1996). Hospital or Community Living? Examining Consumer Perspectives on Deinstitutionalization. *Psychiatric Rehabilitation Journal, 19*(3), 49–58.

Davies, J. (1996). The Future of "No Future": Punk Rock and Postmodern Theory. *Journal of Popular Culture, 29*(4), 3–25.

Davies, K. A. (1997). Voluntary Exposure to Pornography and Men's Attitudes Toward Feminism and Rape. *Journal of Sex Research, 34*(2), 131–137.

Davies, L. (1994). In Search of Resistance and Rebellion Among High School Drop-Outs. *Canadian Journal of Sociology, 19*(3), 331–350.

Dawson, L. L. & Henneby, J. (1999). New Religions and the Internet: Recruiting in New Public Space. *Journal of Contemporary Religion, 14*(1), 17–39.

Degher, D. & Hughes, G. (2003). The Adoption and Management of a "Fat" Identity. In P. A. Adler & P. Adler (Eds.), *Constructions of Deviance: Social Power, Context, and Interaction* (pp. 211–221). Belmont, CA: Wadsworth.

Delaney, T. (2005). *American Street Gangs*. Upper Saddle River, NJ: Prentice Hall.

DeMello, M. (2000). *Bodies of Inscription: A Cultural History of the Modern Tattoo Community*. Durham, NC: Duke University Press.

D'Emilio, J. & Freedman, E. B. (1997). *Intimate Matters: A History of Sexuality in America* (2nd ed.). Chicago: University of Chicago Press.

DeMont, J. (2002, August 5). Growing Up Large. *Maclean's, 115*(31), 20–26.

Dennis, R. M. (1995). Social Darwinism, Scientific Racism and the Metaphysics of Race. *Journal of Negro Education, 64*(3), 243–252.

Dennis, A. & Martin, P. J. (2005). Symbolic Interactionism and the Concept of Power. *The British Journal of Sociology, 56*(2), 191–213.

Deschesnes, M., Demers, S., & Finès, P. (2006). Prevalence and Characteristics of Body Piercing and Tattooing Among High School Students. *Canadian Journal of Public Health*, *97*(4), 325–329.

Des Rosiers, N. & Bittle, S. (2004). Introduction. In the Law Commission of Canada (Ed.) *What Is a Crime? Defining Criminal Conduct in Contemporary Society* (pp. vii–xxv). Vancouver, BC: UBC Press.

Deutschmann, L. B. (2002). *Deviance and Social Control* (3rd ed.). Scarborough, ON: Nelson Thomson Learning.

deYoung, M. (1998). Another Look at Moral Panics: The Case of Satanic Day Care Centers. *Deviant Behavior: An Interdisciplinary Journal, 19,* 257–278.

Dobson, R. (1996, November 30). Mentally Ill People Face Discrimination. *British Medical Journal, 313*(7069), 1352.

Doherty, T. (1988). *Teenagers & Teenpics: The Juvenilization of American Movies in the 1950s*. Boston: Unwin Hyman.

Dohrenwend B. P., Levav, I., Shrout, P. E. & Schwartz, S. (1992). Socioeconomic Status and Psychiatric Disorders: The Causation Selection Issue. *Science, 255,* 946–952.

Downes, D. & Rock, P. (2003). *Understanding Deviance* (4th ed.). New York: Oxford University Press.

Dunleavey, M. P. (2001, April). Would You Have Surgery to Lose Weight? *Self,* pp. 172–175, 199–200.

Dunne, C. & Warren, C. (1998). Lethal Autonomy: The Malfunction of Informed Consent Mechanism Within the Context of Prenatal Diagnosis of Genetic Variants. *Issues in Law & Medicine, 14*(2), 165–202.

Durex (2005). *Global Sex Survey 2005*. Author unknown.

Durkheim, E. (1933). *The Division of Labour in Society*. New York: Free Press.

Durkheim, E. (1951). *Suicide*. New York: Free Press.

Dyer, O. (2003). GMC Reprimands Doctor for Research Fraud. *British Medical Journal, 326*(7392), 730.

Dyer, O. (2005). US Survey Shows Extent of Research Misconduct. *British Medical Journal, 330,* 1465.

Eaton, W. W. (2001). *The Sociology of Mental Disorders*. Westport, CT: Praeger Publishing.

Edmonton Journal (2009, April 11). Religious Right Concedes to Obama, p. A20.

Edmonton Police Service. (2003). *Who Are Your Children Hanging With? A Resource Guide on Youth & Gangs*. Edmonton: Author.

Edmonton Police Service (2009). Traits of Gang Members. Retrieved on May 2, 2009, from **www.edmontonpolice.ca**.

Edwards, A. R. (1988). *Regulation and Repression: The Study of Social Control*. Sydney, Australia: Allen & Unwin.

Egan, R. D. (2003). I'll Be Your Fantasy Girl, If You'll Be My Money Man: Mapping Desire, Fantasy and Power in Two Exotic Dance Clubs. *JPCS: Journal for the Psychoanalysis of Culture & Society, 8(1),* 109–120.

Elliot, D., Huizinga, D. & Ageton, S. (1985). *Explaining Delinquency and Substance Use*. Beverly Hills, CA: Sage.

Emery, J. R. (2001). Cracked Crystal Balls? Psychics' Predictions for Past Year a Litany of Prognostive Failures. *Skeptical Inquirer, 25*(1), 8.

England, J. (2004). Disciplining Subjectivity and Space; Representation, Film and Its Material Effects. *Antipode, 36,* 295–321.

Erickson, K. G., Crosnoe, R. & Dornbusch, S. M. (2000). A Social Process Model of Adolescent Deviance: Combining Social Control and Differential Association Perspectives. *Journal of Youth and Adolescence, 29*(4), 395–425.

Ericson, R. V. & Haggerty, K. D. (2001). Governing the Young. In R. C. Smandych (Ed.), *Youth Justice: History, Legislation, and Reform* (pp. 104–123). Toronto, ON: Harcourt.

Erikson, K. (1966). *Wayward Puritans*. New York: Wiley.

Ettner, S. L., Frank, R. G. & Kessler, R. C. (1997). The Impact of Psychiatric Disorders on Labor Market Outcomes. *Industrial and Labor Relations Review, 51*(1), 64–83.

Evans, R. D. (2001). Examining the Informal Sanctioning of Deviance in a Chat Room Culture. *Deviant Behavior: An Interdisciplinary Journal, 22,* 195–210.

Ewing, H. & Grady, H. (Directors). (2006). *Jesus Camp*. Toronto, ON: Mongrel Media.

Fasiolo, R. & Leckie, S. (1993). *Canadian Media Coverage of Gangs: A Content Analysis*. Ottawa, ON: Solicitor-General Canada.

Featherstone, R. & Deflam, M. (2003). Anomie and Strain: Context and Consequences of Merton's Two Theories. *Sociological Inquiry, 73*(4), 471–489.

Feher, S. (1992). Who Looks to the Stars? Astrology and Its Constituency. *Journal for the Scientific Study of Religion, 31*(1), 88–93.

Fernea, E. W. (1998). *In Search of Islamic Feminism*. New York: Anchor Books.

Fight Against Coercive Tactics Network. (2003). Homepage. Retrieved July 8, 2003, from **www.factnet.org**.

First for Women. (2001, September 17). How Much Sex is Normal? *First for Women*, p. 39.

Fischer, B., Ala-Leppilampi, K., Single, E. & Robins, A. (2003). Cannabis Law Reform in Canada: Is the "Saga of Promise, Hesitation and Retreat" Coming to an End? *Canadian Journal of Criminology and Criminal Justice, 45*(3), 265–297.

Flannery, D. J., Huff, C. R. & Manos, M. (2001). Youth Gangs: A Developmental Perspective. In R. C. Smandych (Ed.), *Youth Ccrime: Varieties, Theories, and Prevention* (pp. 206–229). Toronto, ON: Harcourt.

Fleming, A. T. (1999, January). The New Ideal: What Makes a Body Beautiful? *Women's Sports and Fitness, 2*(2). Retrieved August 1, 2001, from Expanded Academic ASAP database.

Forbes, G. B., Adams-Curtis, L. E., Holmgren, K. M., & White, K. B. (2006). Perceptions of the Social and Personal Characteristics of Hypermuscular Women and the Men Who Love Them. *The Journal of Social Psychology, 144*(5), 487–506.

Ford, J. A. & Schroeder, R. D. (2009). Academic Strain and Non-Medical Use of Prescription Stimulants Among College Students. *Deviant Behavior: An Interdisciplinary Journal, 30,* 26–53.

Forman, M. (Director), B. Goldman, K. Kesey, & (Writers). (1975). *One Flew Over the Cuckoo's Nest*. United States: Fantasy Films.

Forum 18. (2001). Freedom of Religion: A Report with Special Emphasis on the Right to Choose Religion and Registration Systems. Retrieved June 2, 2003, from **www.forum18.org**.

Foucault, M. (1980). Power/Knowledge: Selected Interviews and Other Writings 1972–1977 (1st American ed.). (C. Gordon, L. Marshall, J. Mepham, & K. Super, Trans.). New York: Pantheon Books.

Foucault, M. (1978). *The History of Sexuality, Volume I: An Introduction*. New York: Vintage Books.

Foucault, M. (1995). *Discipline and Punish: The Birth of the Prison* (2nd ed.). (A. Sheridan, Trans.). New York: Vintage Books. (Original work published 1977).

Fournier, S. & Crey, E. (1998). *Stolen from Our Embrace*. Berkeley, CA: Roundhouse Publishing.

Franklin, K. (2000). Antigay Behaviors Among Young Adults: Prevalence, Patterns, and Motivators in a Noncriminal Population. *Journal of Interpersonal Violence, 15*(4), 339–362.

Frederick, C. M. & Bradley, K. A. (2000). A Different Kind of Normal? Psychological and Motivational Characteristics of Young Adult Tattooers and Body Piercers. *North American Journal of Psychology, 2*(2), 380–393.

Freud, S. (1999). The Social Construction of Normality. *Families in Society: The Journal of Contemporary Human Services, 80*(4), 333–339.

The Futurist. (2004, July/August). Western Lifestyles and South African Women.

Gabbidon, S. L. (2003). Racial Profiling by Store Clerks and Security Personnel in Retail Establishments: An Exploration of "Shopping While Black." *Journal of Contemporary Criminal Justice, 19*(3), 345–364.

Gardner, C. B. (1991). Stigma and the Public Self: Notes on Communication, Self, and Others. *Journal of Contemporary Ethnography, 20*(3), 251–252.

Garner, D. M. (1997, January/February). The 1997 Body Image Survey Rresults. *Psychology Today*, 31–44, 75–84.

Gater, R., Tnasella, M., Korten, A., Mavreas, V. G. & Olatawura, M. O. (1998). Sex Differences in the Prevalence and Detection of Depressive and Anxiety Disorders in General Health Care Settings. *Archives of General Psychiatry, 55*, 405–413.

Gibelman, M. & Gelman, S. R. (2005). Scientific Misconduct in Social Welfare Research: Preventive Lessons from Other Fields. *Social Work Education, 24*(3), 275–295.

Gibson, C. & Wright, J. (2001), Low self-control and coworker delinquency: A research note, *Journal of Criminal Justice, 29* 483–492.

Giesbrecht, N. (2000). Roles of Commercial Interests in Alcohol Policies: Recent Developments in North America. *Addiction, 95* (suppl. 4), S581–S595.

Gilmour, H. (2007). Physically active Canadians. *Health Reports, 18*(3), 45–65. Statistics Canada. Catalogue No. 82-003.

Goffman, E. (1959). *The Presentation of Self in Everyday Life.* Garden City, NY: Doubleday-Anchor.

Goffman, E. (1961). *Asylums: Essays on the Social Situation of Mental Patients and Other Inmates.* Garden City, NY: Anchor Books.

Goffman, E. (1963). *Stigma: Notes on the Management of Spoiled Identity.* Englewood Cliffs, NJ: Prentice Hall.

Gomme, I. M. (1985). Predictors of Status and Criminal Offences Among Male and Female Adolescents in an Ontario Community. *Canadian Journal of Criminology, 27,* 157–159.

Goode, E. (1997). *Deviant Behavior* (5th ed.). Upper Saddle River, NJ: Prentice Hall.

Goode, E. & Ben-Yehuda, N. (1994). *Moral Panics: The Social Construction of Deviance.* Cambridge: Blackwell.

Goodstein, L. (2003, May 27). Seeing Islam as an Evil Faith, Evangelicals Seek Converts. *New York Times.* Retrieved June 20, 2003, from **www.nytimes.com**.

Gordon, R. A. (2000). *Eating Disorders: Anatomy of a Social Epidemic.* Malden, MA: Blackwell.

Gordon, R. M. (1993). Incarcerated Gang Members in British Columbia: A Preliminary Study. Victoria: Ministry of Attorney-General.

Gordon, R. M. (1995). Street Gangs in Vancouver. In J. Creechan & R. Silverman (Eds.), *Canadian Delinquency* (pp. 311–320). Scarborough, ON: Prentice Hall.

Gordon, R. M. (2001). Street Gangs and Criminal Business Organizations: A Canadian Perspective. In R. C. Smandych (Ed.), *Youth Crime: Varieties, Theories, and Prevention* (pp. 248–265). Toronto, ON: Harcourt.

Goring, C. (1919). *The English Convict.* London: H. M. Stationery Office.

Gottfredson, M. R. & Hirschi, T. (1990). *A General Theory of Crime.* Stanford, CT: Stanford University Press.

Grasmick, H. G., Tittle, C. R., Bursik, R. J., & Arneklev, B. J. (1993). Testing the Core Empirical Implications of Gottfredson and Hirschi's General Theory of Crime. *Journal of Research in Crime and Delinquency, 30*(1), 47–54.

Greco, A. N. (1995/96). The First Amendment, Freedom of the Press, and the Issues of "Harm": A Conundrum for Publishers. *Publishing Research Quarterly, 11*(4), 39–57.

Greenberg, B. S., Eastin, M. , Hofshire, L., Lachlan, K. & Brownell, K. D. (2003). Portrayals of Overweight and Obese Individuals on Commercial Television. *American Journal of Public Health, 93*(8), 1342–1348.

Greenleaf, C., McGreer, R., & Parham, H. (2006). Physique Attitudes and Self-Presentational Concerns: Exploratory Interviews with Female Aerobic Exercisers and Instructors. *Sex Roles, 54*(3/4), 189—99.

Gregoire, L. (2003). Alberta Teens Face Smoking Fines, Price of Cartons Tops $70. *CMAJ: Canadian Medical Association Journal, 168*(7), 888.

Grekul, J. M. (2002). *The Social Construction of the Feebleminded Threat: Implementation of the Sexual Sterilization Act in Alberta, 1929–1972.* Unpublished doctoral dissertation, University of Alberta, Edmonton, AB.

Grekul, J. & LaBoucane-Benson, P. (2007). *An Investigation into the Formation and Recruitment Processes of Aboriginal Gangs in Western Canada.* Ottawa, ON: Aboriginal Corrections Policy Unit, Public Safety Canada.

Gray, J. (Director), C. Gentry, & V. Bugliosi, (Writers). (2004). *Helter Skelter.* United States: Lakeside Productions and Warner Bros. Television.

Grob, G. N. (1994). *The Mad Among Us: A History of the Care of America's Mentally Ill.* New York: Free Press.

Hackler, J. C. (2000). Strain Theories. In R. Linden (Ed.), *Criminology: A Canadian Perspective* (4th ed.) (pp. 270–300). Toronto, ON: Harcourt Canada.

Hadden, J. & Bromley, D. (Eds.) (1995). *The Handbook of Cults and Sects in America.* Greenwich, CT: JAI Press.

Hagedorn, J. M. (2007). Introduction: Globalization, Gangs, and Traditional Criminology. In J. M. Hagedorn (Ed.) *Gangs in the Global City: Alternatives to Traditional Criminology* (pp. 1–10). Chicago, IL: University of Illinois Press.

Hagmann, M. (2001). Alcohol Takes Its Toll on Europe's Youth. *Bulletin of the World Health Organization, 79*(4), 380.

Hall, G. S. (1904). *Adolescence* (Vol. I). Englewood Cliffs, NJ: Prentice Hall.

Hall, J. (2002). Mass Suicide and the Branch Davidians. In D. G. Bromley & J. G. Melton (Eds.), *Cults, Religion, and Violence* (pp. 149–169). Cambridge, UK: Cambridge University Press.

Hall, L. (2005). Steam, Stealth Selling TV Sex. *Television Week, 24*(32), 6–7.

Hannigan, B. (1999). Mental Health Care in the Community: An Analysis of Contemporary Public Attitudes Towards, and Public Representations of, Mental Illness. *Journal of Mental Health, 8*(5), 431–440.

Harkin, A. M., Anderson, P. & Goos, C. (1997). *Smoking, Drinking and Drug Taking in the European Region.* Copenhagen, DK: World Health Organization.

Harrison, M. L., Jones, S., & Sullivan, C. (2008). The Gendered Expressions of Self-Control: Manifestations of Non-Criminal Deviance Among Females. *Deviant Behavior: An Interdisciplinary Journal, 29*(1), 18–42.

Hartmann, P., Reuter, M. & Nyborg, H. (2006). The Relationship Between Date of Birth and Individual Differences in Personality and General Intelligence: A Large-Scale Study. *Personality & Individual Differences, 40*(7), 1349–1362.

Hathaway, A. D. & Atkinson, M. F. (2001). Tolerable Differences Revisited: Crossroads in Theory on the Social Construction of Deviance. *Deviant Behavior: An Interdisciplinary Journal, 22*, 353–377.

Hawdon, J. E. (1996). Deviant Lifestyles: The Social Control of Daily Routines. *Youth & Society, 28*(2), 162–188.

Hawkes, D., Senn, C. Y. & Thorn, C. (2004). Factors That Influence Attitudes Toward Women with Tattoos. *Sex Roles, 50*(9/10), 593–604.

Health Canada. (1999). *Trends in the Health of Canadian Children.* Ottawa: Author.

Health Canada. (2002a). *A Review of Weight Guidelines.* Ottawa, ON: Author.

Health Canada. (2002b). *A Report on Mental Illness in Canada.* Ottawa, ON: Author.

Health Canada. (2005a). *2002 Youth Smoking Survey: Technical Report.* Ottawa, ON: Author.

Health Canada. (2005b). Evaluation of Retailers' Behaviour Towards Certain Youth Access-to-Tobacco Restrictions. Final Report Findings 2005. Ottawa, ON: Author.

Health Canada. (2005c). *The Integrated Pan-Canadian Healthy Living Strategy.* Ottawa, ON: Author.

Health Canada (2008). *Canadian Addiction Survey (CAS): A National Survey of Canadians' Use of Alcohol and Other Drugs: Focus on Gender.* Ottawa, ON: Author.

Hefley, K. (2007). Stigma management of male and female customers to a non-urban adult novelty store. *Deviant Behavior: An Interdisciplinary Journal, 28*(1), 79–109.

Heltsley, M. & Calhoun, T. C. (2003). The Good Mother: Neutralization Techniques Used by Pageant Mothers. *Deviant Behavior: An Interdisciplinary Journal, 24*, 81–100.

Herek, G. M., Gillis, J. R., Cogan, J. C. & Glunt, E. K. (1997). Hate Crime Victimization Among Lesbian, Gay, and Bisexual Adults: Prevalence, Psychological Correlates, and Methodological Issues. *Journal of Interpersonal Violence, 12*(2), 195–215.

Herdt, G. (1993). *Ritualized Homosexuality in Melanesia* (2nd ed.). Berkeley, CA: University of California Press.

Herdt, G. (1984). Ritualized Homosexuality in the Male Cults of Melanesia, 1862–1982: An Introduction. In G. Herdt, (Ed.), *Ritualized Homosexuality in Melanesia* (pp. 1–81). Berkeley, CA: University of California Press.

Herman, N. J. (1995). Introduction. In N. J. Herman (Ed.), *Deviance: A Symbolic Interactionist Approach* (pp. 1–6). Lanham, MD: General Hall.

Herman, N. J. & Miall, C. E. (1990). The Positive Consequences of Stigma: Two Case Studies of Mental and Physical Disability. *Qualitative Sociology, 13*, 251–269.

Hersch, P. (1998). *A Tribe Apart: A Journey into the Heart of American Adolescence*. New York: Ballantine Books.

Hicinbothem, J., Gonsalves, S., & Lester, D. (2006). Body Modification and Suicidal Behavior. *Death Studies, 30*, 351–363.

Hicks, R. (1990). Police Pursuit of Satanic Crime. *Skeptical Inquirer, 14*, 276–286.

Hier, S. P. (2002). Raves, Risks and the Ecstasy Panic: A Case Study of the Subversive Nature of Moral Regulation. *Canadian Journal of Sociology, 27*(1), 33–57.

Higgins, G. E., Wolfe, S. E., & Marcum, C. D. (2008). Digital Piracy: An Examination of Three Measurements of Self-Control. *Deviant Behavior: An Interdisciplinary Journal, 29*(5), 440–460.

Hirschi, T. C. (1969). *Causes of Delinquency*. Berkeley, CA: University of California Press.

Hodgins, S. (1993). The Criminality of Mentally Disordered Persons. In S. Hodgins (Ed.), *Mental Disorder and Crime*. Newbury Park, CA: Sage.

Hoffman, B. & Burke, C. (1997). *Heaven's Gate Cult: Suicide in San Diego*. New York: HarperCollins.

Hoffman, J. P. & Su, S. S. (1997). The Conditional Effects of Stress on Delinquency and Drug Use: A Strain Theory Assessment of Sex Differences. *Journal of Research in Crime and Delinquency, 34*, 46–78.

Hollinger, R. (1991). Neutralizing in the Workplace: An Empirical Analysis of Property Theft and Production Deviance. *Deviant Behavior, 12*, 169–202.

Hone-McMahan, K., & Schleis, P. (1998, February 15). Faith No More? Religion Often Seen as Source of Misery for Gay Teens. *The Sunday Gazette Mail*, p. P10E.

Hook, H. (Director), Golding, W. (Writer) & Schiff, S. (Screenplay). (1990). *Lord of the Flies*. United States: Metro Goldwyn Mayer.

Hope, T. L., & Chapple, C. L. (2005). Maternal Characteristics, Parenting, and Adolescent Sexual Behavior: The Role of Self-Control. *Deviant Behavior, 26*, 25–45.

Hotton, T. & Haans, D. (2004). Alcohol and Drug Use in Early Adolescence. *Health Reports, 15*(3), 9–19. Statistics Canada Catalogue No. 82003XIE.

Huber, P. W. (1991). *Galileo's Revenge: Junk Science In the Courtroom*. New York: Basic Books.

Hughes, J. (Director). (1985).*The Breakfast Club*. United States: Universal City Studios.

Hunt, A. (1998). The Great Masturbation Panic and the Discourses of Moral Regulation in Nineteenth- and Early Twentieth-Century Britain. *Journal of the History of Sexuality, 8*(4), 575-615.

Ingram, J. R. & Hinduja, S. (2008). Neutralizing Music Piracy: An Empirical Examination. *Deviant Behavior: An Interdisciplinary Journal, 29*(4), 334–366.

Intercamp. (2001, October 11). *The Censorship Issue*. Edmonton, AB: Grant MacEwan Students' Association.

International Obesity Task Force. (2003). Homepage. Retrieved April 3, 2003, from **www.iotf.org**.

International Size Acceptance Association. (2003). Homepage. Retrieved April 3, 2003, from **http://size-acceptance.org**.

Introvigne, M. & Mayer, J.-F. (2002). Occult Masters and the Temple of Doom: The Fiery End of the Solar Temple. In D. G. Bromley & J. G. Melton (Eds.), *Cults, Religion, and Violence* (pp. 170–188). Cambridge, UK: Cambridge University Press.

Irwin, D. (1999). The Straight Edge Subculture: Examining the Youths' Drug-Free Way. *Journal of Drug Issues, 29*, 365–380.

Irwin, K. (2003). Saints and Sinners: Elite Tattoo Collectors and Tattooists as Positive and Negative Deviants. *Sociological Spectrum, 23*, 27–57.

Jaimes, M. A. (1992). *The State of Native America: Genocide, Colonization, and Resistance.* Cambridge, MA: South End Press.

James, W. H. (1995). Frauds and Hoaxes in Science. *Nature, 377*(6549), 474.

Jang, S. J. & Smith, C. A. (1997). A Test of Reciprocal Causal Relationships Among Parental Supervision, Affective Ties, and Delinquency. *Journal of Research in Crime and Delinquency, 34*(3), 307–336.

Jankowski, M. S. (1991). *Islands in the Street: Gangs and American Urban Society.* Berkeley, CA: University of California Press.

Jenkins, P. (2000). *Mystics and Messiahs: Cults and New Religions in American History.* New York: Oxford University Press.

Jernigan, D. H. (2001). *Global Status Report: Alcohol and Young People.* Geneva: World Health Organization.

Johnson, B. (1963). On Church and Sect. *American Sociological Review, 28*, 539–549.

Jones, D. J. (2001). *Selected Legal Issues in Genetic Testing: Guidance from Human Rights.* Ottawa: Health Canada.

Jones, G. (1986). *Social Hygiene in Twentieth-Century Britain.* London: Croom Helm.

Jones, L. (1998). Social Darwinism Revisited. *History Today, 48(8).* Retrieved October 16, 2001, from Expanded Academic ASAP database.

Jones, S. & Quisenberry, N. (2004). The General Theory of Crime: How General Is It? *Deviant Behavior, 25,* 401–426.

Jordon, T. E. (1998). Victorian Child Savers and Their Culture: A Thematic Evaluation (Mellon Studies in Sociology, Vol. 19). Lewiston, NY: Edwin Mellon Press.

Joseph, J. & Baldwin, S. (2000). Four Editorial Proposals to Improve Social Sciences Research and Publication. *International Journal of Risk & Safety in Medicine, 13,* 109–116.

Judicial Council of California (2009), Proposition 8 Cases. Retrieved April 4, 2009, from **www.courtinfo.ca.gov/courts/supreme/highprofile/prop8.htm**.

Judson, H. F. (2004). *The Great Betrayal: Fraud in Science.* Orlando, FL: Harcourt.

Kaiser Family Foundation. (1997). Reflections of Girls in the Media. Retrieved March 29, 2003, from **www.kff.org**.

Katzmarzyk, P. T. & Janssen, I. (2004). The Economic Costs Associated with Physical Inactivity and Obesity in Canada: An Update. *Canadian Journal of Applied Physiology, 29(1),* 104.

Keeling, R. P. (2000). The Political, Social, and Public Health Problems of Binge Drinking in College. *Journal of American College Health, 48(5),* 195–198.

Keeling, R. P. (2002). Binge Drinking and the College Environment. *Journal of American College Health, 50*(5), 197–201.

Kelton, E. (2005, June). Sales Tactics, Whistleblowers and *Qui Tam* Lawsuits in the Pharmaceutical Industry. Retrieved May 19, 2006, from **http://phillipsandcohen.com**.

Kendall, D., Murray, J. L. & Linden, R. (2007). *Sociology in Our Times* (4th Canadian ed.). Toronto, ON: Thomson Nelson.

Kennedy, D. B. & Homant, R. J. (1984). Personnel Managers and the Stigmatized Employee. *Journal of Employment Counseling, 21*, 89–94.

Kent, S. A. (1994). Lustful Prophet: A Psychosexual History of the Children of God's Leader, David Berg. *Cultic Studies Journal, 11*(2), 135–188.

Kent, S. L. & Jacobs, D. (2004). Social Divisions and Coercive Control in Advanced Societies: Law Enforcement Strength in Eleven Nations from 1975 to 1994. *Social Problems, 51*(3), 343–361.

Kerr, C. (2003). Phony Research Earns 1-Year Suspension. *Canadian Medical Association Journal, 168*(8), 1032.

Kessler, R. C., McGonagle, K. A., Zhao, S., Nelson, C. B., Hughes, M., Eshleman, S. *et al.* (1994). Lifetime and 12-Month Prevalence of DSM-III-R Psychiatric Disorders in the United States. *Archives of General Psychiatry, 51*, 8–19.

Kevles, D. (1995). *In the Name of Eugenics: Genetics and the Uses of Human Heredity.* Berkeley, CA: University of California Press.

Kim, L. (2008). Explaining the Hwang Scandal: National Scientific Culture and Its Global Relevance. *Science as Culture, 17*(4), 397–415.

Kitsuse, J. I. (1980). Coming Out All Over: Deviants and the Politics of Social Problems. *Social Problems, 28*(1), 1–12.

Kitsuse, J. I. & Dietrick, D. C. (1979). Delinquent Boys: A Critique. In H. L. Voss (Ed.), *Society, Delinquency, and Delinquent Behavior* (pp. 238–245). Boston: Little, Brown.

Koch, J. R., Roberts, A. E., Cannon, J. H., Armstrong, M. L. & Owen, D. C. (2005). College Students, Tattooing, and the Health Belief Model: Extending Social Psychological Perspectives on Youth Culture and Deviance. *Sociological Spectrum, 25*, 79–102.

Konty, M. (2005). Microanomie: The Cognitive Foundations of the Relationship Between Anomie and Deviance. *Criminology, 43*(1), 107–131.

Kosut, M. (2006). An Ironic Fad: The Commodification and Consumption of Tattoos. *The Journal of Popular Culture, 39*(6), 1035–1048.

Krieg, R. G. (2001). An Interdisciplinary Look at the Deinstitutionalization of the Mentally Ill. *Social Science Journal, 38*, 367–380.

Kroska, A. & Harkness, S. K. (2006). Stigma Sentiments and Self-Meanings: Exploring the Modified Labeling Theory of Mental Illness. *Social Psychology Quarterly, 69*(4), 325–348.

Kubrin, C. E., Stucky, T. D., & Krohn, M. D. (2009). *Researching Theories of Crime and Deviance*. New York: Oxford University Press.

Kuhl, S. (1994). *The Nazi Connection*. New York: Oxford University Press.

Kuhns, E. (2003). *The Habit: A History of the Clothing of Catholic Nuns*. New York: Doubleday.

Lalich, J. & Langone, M. D. (2006. Characteristics Associated with Cultic Groups—Revised. Retrieved August 11, 2009, from **www.icsahome.com/infoserv_articles/langone_michael.checklis.htm**.

The Lancet (2006, January 7). Editorial: Writing a New Ending for a Story of Scientific Fraud. Retrieved May 24, 2006, from **www.thelancet.com**.

Langlais, P. J. (2006). Ethics for the Next Generation. *Chronicle of Higher Education, 52*(19). Retrieved July 19, 2006, from Expanded Academic ASAP database.

Larsen, N. (2000). Prostitution: Deviant Activity or Legitimate Occupation? In L. G. Beaman (Ed.), *New Perspectives on Deviance: The Construction of Deviance in Everyday Life* (pp. 50–66). Scarborough, ON: Prentice Hall.

Larson, R. & Richards, M. H. (1994). *Divergent Realities: The Emotional Lives of Mothers, Fathers, and Adolescents*. New York: Basic Books.

Latner, J. & Stunkard, A. (2003). Stigmatization of Obese Children. *Nutrition Research Newsletter, 22*(4), 12.

Laurendeau, J. & Van Brunschot, E. G. (2006). Policing the edge: Risk and social control in skydiving. *Deviant Behavior: An Interdisciplinary Journal, 27*(2), 173–201.

Lauritsen, J. L. (1994). Explaining Race and Gender Differences in Adolescent Sexual Behavior. *Social Forces, 72*(3), 859–884.

Laursen, B. (1995). Conflict and Social Interaction in Adolescent Relationships. *Journal of Research on Adolescence, 5*, 55–70.

Laursen, B., Coy, K. C. & Collins, W. A. (1998). Reconsidering Changes in Parent-Child Conflict Across Adolescence: A Meta-Analysis. *Child Development, 69*, 817–832.

Law, C. & Labre, M. P. (2002). Cultural Standards of Attractiveness: A Thirty-Year Look at Changes in Male Images in Magazines. *Journalism & Mass Communication Quarterly, 79*(3), 697–711.

Lawrie, S. M., Martin, K., McNeill, G., Drife, J., Chrystie, P., Reid, A. *et al.* (1998). General Practitioners' Attitudes to Psychiatric and Medical Illness. *Psychiatric Medicine, 28*, 1463–1467.

Lawson, R. (1995). Sect-State Relations: Accounting for the Differing Trajectories of Seventh-Day Adventists and Jehovah's Witnesses. *Sociology of Religion, 56*(4), 351–378.

Lemert, E. M. (1951). *Social Pathology: A Systematic Approach to the Study of Sociopathic Behavior*. New York: McGraw-Hill.

Leon, J. S. (1977). The Development of Canadian Juvenile Justice: A Background for Reform. *Osgoode Hall Law Journal, 15*, 71–106.

Leone, J. E., Sedory, E. J. & Gray, K. A. (2005). Helping Athletes: Recognition and Treatment of Muscle Dysmorphia and Related Body Image Disorders. *Journal of Athletic Training, 40*(4), 352–359.

Levenkron, S. (2000). *Anatomy of Anorexia*. New York: W.W. Norton.

Levine, B. (2005). Behind the Paxil Scandals. *Z Magazine, 18*(4). Retrieved May 19, 2006, from **http://web.uni-marburg.de/religionswissenschaft/journal/diskus/chryssides.html**.

Levine, M. & Maine, M. (2005). Eating Disorders Can Be Prevented. *National Eating Disorders Association*. Retrieved September 12, 2006, from **www.nationaleatingdisorders.org**.

Levy, L. D. (2000). *Conquering Obesity*. Toronto, ON: Key Porter Books.

Lewis, G. & Bebbington, P. (1998). Socioeconomic Status, Standard of Living, and Neurotic Disorder. *Lancet, 352*(9128), 605–609.

Lewis, J. & Melton, J. G. (1994). *Sex, Slander, and Salvation: Investigating the Family/Children of God*. Stanford, CA: Center for Academic Publication.

Li, S. D. (2004). The Impacts of Self-Control and Social Bonds on Juvenile Delinquency in a National Sample of Midadolescents. *Deviant Behavior, 25*, 351–373.

Lianos, M., with Douglas, M. (2000). Dangerization and the End of Deviance. *British Journal of Criminology, 40*, 261–278.

Liazos, A. (1972). The Poverty of the Sociology of Deviance: Nuts, Sluts, and Perverts. *Social Problems, 20*, 102–120.

Linden, R. (Ed.) (2000). *Criminology: A Canadian Perspective* (4th ed.). Toronto, ON: Harcourt Canada.

Liska, A. & Reid, M. (1985). Ties to Conventional Institutions and Delinquency. *American Sociological Review, 50*, 547–560.

Lock, J. (2001). *Treatment Manual for Anorexia Nervosa: A Family-Based Approach*. New York: Guilford Press.

Lombroso, C. (1911). *Crime, Its Causes and Remedies*. Boston, MA: Little, Brown.

Longshore, D., Chang, E., Hsieh, S. & Messina, N. (2004). Self-Control and Social Bonds: A Combined Control Perspective on Deviance. *Crime & Delinquency, 50*(4), 542–564.

Loring, M. & Powell, B. (1988). Gender, Race and DSM-III. *Journal of Health and Social Behavior, 29*, 1–22.

Luhovy, Y. (Director & Producer). (1994). *Freedom Had a Price*. Available from the National Film Board of Canada.

Lyman, S. (2000). Accounts: Roots and Roundations. In C. D. Bryant (Ed.) *Encyclopedia of Criminology and Deviant Behavior*. Philadelphia: Brunner-Routledge.

MacDonald, G. J. (1999). Spiritual Politicking and the IRS. *Religion in the News, 2*(2). Retrieved September 29, 2006, from **http://b27.cc.trincoll.edu/mt-search=spiritual+politicking+and+the+IRS&Includeblogs=13&limit=20**.

MacEachern, S. (2006). Africanist Archaeology and Ancient IQ: Racial Science and Cultural Evolution in the Twenty-First Century. *World Archaeology, 38*(1), 72–92.

Mackay, J. (2000). Global Sex: Sexuality and Sexual Practices Around the World. Paper presented at the 5th Congress of the European Federation of Sexology, June 29–July 2, 2000, Berlin.

MacKinnon, I. (2004, December 31). Model Purge on Anorexics Makes Weight Vital Statistic. *The Times Online*. Retrieved May 17, 2006, from **www.timesonline.co.uk**.

Maddox, J. (1994). Defending Science Against Anti-Science. *Nature, 368*, 185.

Maltby, D. (Director & Writer) & Abraham, C. (Writer). (2002). *DNA and Dollars*. Available from the National Film Board of Canada.

Mandell, N. & Momirov, J. (2000). Family Histories. In N. Mandell & A. Duffy (Eds.), *Canadian Families: Diversity, Conflict, and Change* (2nd ed.) (pp. 17–47). Scarborough, ON: Nelson Thomson.

Marble, M. (1995, June 21). Many Women Athletes Suffer From Side Effects. *Women's Health Weekly*. Retrieved January 7, 2002, from **www.newsrx.com/newsletters/Womens_Health_Weekly.html**.

March, P. A. (1999). Ethical Responses to Media Depictions of Mental Illness: An Advocacy Approach. *Journal of Humanistic Counseling, Education, & Development, 38*(2), 70–79.

Marcos, A. C., Bahr, S. J. & Johnson, R. E. (1986). Test of a Bonding/Association Theory of Adolescent Drug Use. *Social Forces, 65*, 135–161.

Marshall, B. L. (2006). The New Virility: Viagra, Male Aging and Sexual Function. *Sexualities, 9*(3), 345–362.

Martin, N. & Johnston, V. (2007). *A Time for Action: Tackling Stigma and Discrimination: Report to the Mental Health Commission of Canada*. Calgary, AB: Mental Health Commission of Canada.

Marvarsti, A. (2008). Being Middle Eastern American: Identity Negotiation in the Context of the War on Terror. In E. J. Clarke (Ed.) *Deviant Behavior: A Text-Reader in the Sociology of Deviance* (pp. 648–671). New York: Worth.

Mason, A. & Palmer, A. (1996). *Queer Bashing: A National Survey of Hate Crimes Against Lesbians and Gay Men*. London: Stonewall.

Mason, G. & Tomsen, S. (Eds.). (1997). *Homophobic Violence*. Annandale, AUS: Hawkins Press.

Massey, J. L. & Krohn, M. D. (1986). A Longitudinal Examination of an Integrated Social Process Model of Deviant Behavior. *Social Forces, 65*, 106–134.

Matthews, D. D. (2001). *Eating Disorders Sourcebook*. Detroit, MI: Omnigraphics.

Matthews, J. S. (2005). The Political Foundations of Support for Same-Sex Marriage in Canada. *Canadian Journal of Political Science, 38*(4), 841–866.

Mattson, K. (2001). Did Punk Matter? Analyzing the Practices of a Youth Subculture. *American Studies, 42*(1), 69–97.

Mayers, L. B. & Chiffriller, S. H. (2008). Body Art (Body Piercing and Tattooing) Among Undergraduate University Students: "Then and Now". *Journal of Adolescent Health, 42*, 201–203.

Mayor, S. (2003). Human Cloning May Be Impossible. *BMJ: British Medical Journal, 326*(7394), 838.

Mazerolle, P. (1998). Gender, General Strain, and Delinquency: An Empirical Examination. *Justice Quarterly, 15*(1), 65–91.

Mazerolle, P., Piquero, A. R. & Capowich, G. E. (2003). Examining the Links Between Strain, Situational and Dispositional Anger, and Crime: Further Specifying and Testing General Strain Theory. *Youth & Society, 35*(2), 131–157.

McCaghy, C. H., Capron, T. A. & Jamieson, J. D. (2003). *Deviant Behavior: Crime, Conflict, and Interest Groups* (6th ed). Boston: Allyn & Bacon.

McCarthy, M. (2004). Lies, Damn Lies, and Scientific Research. *The Lancet, 364*, 1657–1658.

McConnell, H. (1997, January 21). ADHD Just Doesn't Add Up To Brit Psych Society. *Medical Post*. Retrieved August 20, 2002, from **http://mentalhealth.com**.

McGovern, C. M. (1985). *Masters of Madness: Social Origins of the American Psychiatric Profession*. Hanover, NH: University Press of New England.

McGuire, M. B. (1997). *Religion: The Social Context* (4th ed.). Belmont, CA: Wadsworth.

McKee, M. (2002). Substance Use and Social and Economic Transition: The Need for Evidence. *International Journal of Drug Policy, 13*, 453–459.

McKeen, S. (2002, March 24). An XXX-Ray of Our Psyche: Basic Instinct or Debauchery? *Edmonton Journal*, p. D6.

McLaren, A. (1990). *Our Own Master Race: Eugenics in Canada 1885–1945*. Toronto, ON: McClelland & Stewart.

McLorg, P. A. & Taub, D. E. (1987). Anorexia, Bulimia, and Developing a Deviant Identity. *Deviant Behavior: An Interdisciplinary Journal, 8*, 177–189.

Melton, D. E. (2000). Emerging Religious Movements in North America: Some Missiological Reflections. *Missiology: An International Review, 27*(1), 85–98.

Melton, J. G. & Bromley, D. (2002). Challenging Misconceptions About the New Religion-Violence Connection. In D. G. Bromley & J. G. Melton (Eds.), *Cults, Religion, and Violence* (pp. 42–56). Cambridge, UK: Cambridge University Press.

Mental Health Commission of Canada (2008). The Homeless and Mental Illness: Solving the Challenge. Presentation by Honourable Michael Kirby, Chair, Mental Health Commission of Canada at the "Collaboration for Change Forum," Vancouver, BC, April 28, 2008. *MHCC TV*. Retrieved February 19, 2009 from www.mentalhealthcommission.ca.

Mental Health Commission of Canada (2009). *Toward Recovery and Well-Being: A Framework for a Mental Health Strategy for Canada. Draft: For Public Discussion*. Calgary, AB: Author.

Merriam-Webster (2002). *Merriam-Webster's Online Dictionary*. Retrieved January 4, 2002, from **www.merriam-webster.com**.

Merriam-Webster (2003). *Merriam-Webster's Online Dictionary*. Retrieved June 17, 2003, from **www.merriam-webster.com**.

Merton, R. K. (1938). Social Structure and Anomie. *American Sociological Review, 3*, 672–682.

Merton, R. K. (1968). *Social Theory and Social Structure*. New York: Free Press.

Merton, R. K. (1973). *The Sociology of Science: Theoretical and Empirical Investigations*. Chicago, IL: University of Chicago Press.

Merton, R. K. (1995). Opportunity Structure: The Emergence, Diffusion, and Differentiation of a Sociological Concept, 1930s–1950s. In F. Adler and W. S. Laufer (Eds.) *The Legacy of Anomie Theory* (pp. 3–78). New Brunswick, NJ: Transaction Publishers.

Messner, S. F. & Rosenfeld, R. (2001). *Crime and the American Dream*. Belmont, CA: Wadsworth.

Mestemacher, R. A. & Roberti, J. W. (2004). Qualitative Analysis of Vocational Choice: A Collective Case Study of Strippers. *Deviant Behavior, 25*, 43–65.

Miech, R. A., Caspi, A., Moffitt, T. E., Wright, B. R. E. & Silva, P. A. (1999). Low Socioeconomic Status and Mental Disorders: A Longitudinal Study of Selection and Causation During Young Adulthood. *American Journal of Sociology, 104*(4). Retrieved October 23, 2001, from Expanded Academic ASAP database.

Milan, A. (2000). One hundred years of families. *Canadian Social Trends*, 56, 2-12. Statistics Canada Catalogue No. 11-008.

Millanvoye, M. (2001). Teflon Under My Skin. *The UNESCO Courier, July/August*, 57.

Miller, J. (1996). *Shingwauk's Vision*. Toronto, ON: University of Toronto Press.

Miller, J. M., Wright, R. A. & Dannels, D. (2001). Is Deviance "Dead"? The Decline of a Sociological Research Specialization. *American Sociologist, 32*(3), 43–59.

Milloy, J. S. (1999). *A National Crime: The Canadian Government and the Residential School System, 1879–1986*. Winnipeg, MB: University of Manitoba Press.

Mintzes, B. (2006). *What Are the Public Health Implications? Direct-to-Consumer Advertising of Prescription Drugs in Canada*. Toronto, ON: Health Council of Canada.

Monahan, J. (1992). Mental Disorder and Violent Behavior: Perceptions and Evidence. *American Psychologist, 47*, 511–521.

Montgomery, K. & Oliver, A. L. (2009). Shifts in Guidelines for Ethical Scientific Conduct: How Public and Private Organizations Create and Change Norms of Research Integrity. *Social Studies of Science, 39*(1), 137–155.

Moon, D. (2008). Culture and the Sociology of Sexuality: It's Only Natural? *The Annals of the American Academy of Political and Social Science, 619*(1), 183–205.

Mosher, C. E. (2002). Impact of Gender and Problem Severity upon Intervention Selection. *Sex Roles, 46*(3/4), 113–119.

Mosher, J. F. & Johnsson, D. (2005). Flavored Alcoholic Beverages: An International Marketing Campaign that Targets Youth. *Journal of Public Health Policy, 26*(3), 326–342.

Mostert, M. P. (2002). Useless Eaters: Disability as Genocidal Marker in Nazi Germany. *Journal of Special Education, 36*(3), 155–168.

Mulgrew, I. (2001). Sex in Space. *Homemakers Magazine, Feb./Mar.*, 33–39.

Murphy, E. F. (1973 [1922]). *The Black Candle*. Toronto, ON: Coles Publishing Co.

Murphy, S., Waldorf, D. & Reinarman, C. (1990). Drifting into Dealing: Becoming a Cocaine Seller. *Qualitative Sociology, 13*(4), 487–507.

Murray, J. L. & Lopez, A. D. (1996). *The Global Burden of Disease: A Comprehensive Assessment of Mortality and Disability from Diseases, Injuries, and Risk Factors in 1990 and Projected to 2020: Summary*. Boston: Harvard School of Public Health/World Health Organization.

Nakhaie, M. R., Silverman, R. A. & LaGrange, T. C. (2000). Self-Control and Resistance to School. *Canadian Review of Sociology and Anthropology, 37*(4), 443–460.

NAMBLA Homepage. Retrieved January 7, 2002, from **www.nambla1.de**.

Nanda, S. (2000). *Gender Diversity: Crosscultural Variations*. Chicago, IL: Waveland Press Inc.

Nathan, D. & Snedeker, M. (1995). *Satan's Silence: Ritual Abuse and the Making of a Modern American Witchhunt*. New York: Basic Books.

National Eating Disorders Association. (2003). Homepage. Retrieved July 8, 2003, from **http://nationaleatingdisorders.org**.

National Eating Disorder Information Centre. (2003). Homepage. Retrieved May 4, 2003, from **www.nedic.ca**.

National Eating Disorder Information Centre (2008). Statistics. Retrieved April 12, 2009 from **www.nedic.ca/ knowthefacts/statistics.html**.

Nelson, A. (2006). *Gender in Canada* (3rd ed.). Toronto, ON: Pearson Prentice Hall.

Nelson, E. D. & Robinson, B. W. (2002). *Gender in Canada*. Scarborough, ON: Prentice Hall.

Network World Canada. (2002). Sex Drive Down on Net. *Network World Canada, 12*(9). Retrieved October 7, 2002, from Canadian Business and Current Affairs database.

Neumark-Sztainer, D., Story, M. & Faibisch, L. (1998). Perceived Stigmatization Among Overweight African-American and Caucasian Adolescent Girls. *Journal of Adolescent Health, 33*(5), 264–270.

Newhouse, D. (1998). Magic and Joy: Traditional Aboriginal Views of Human Sexuality. *Canadian Journal of Human Sexuality, 7*(2), 183–187.

Newman, A. W., Wright, S. W., Wrenn, K. D. & Bernard, A. (2005). Should Physicians Have Facial Piercings? *Journal of General Internal Medicine, 20*(3), 213–218.

Newman, G. (2008). *Comparative Deviance: Perception and Law in Six Cultures*. New Brunswick, NJ: Transaction Publishers.

Niccol, A. (Director & Writer). (1997). *Gattaca*. United States: Columbia Pictures.

Nylenna, M. & Simonsen, S. (2006). Scientific Misconduct: A New Approach to Prevention. *The Lancet, 367*, 1882–1884.

Obesity Association. (2003). Homepage. Retrieved April 4, 2003, from **www.obesity.org**.

Office of Research Integrity (2009). Case Summaries. *Office of Research Integrity Newsletter, 17*(2), 1–12.

Onishi, N. (2006, January 22). In a Country That Craved Respect, Stem Cell Scientist Rode a Wave of Korean Pride. *The New York Times*. Retrieved June 7, 2006, from **www.nytimes.com**.

Ontario Consultants on Religous Tolerance. (2003). Homepage. Retrieved October 7, 2002, to July 2, 2003, from **www.religioustolerance.org**.

Ong, E. K. & Glantz, S. A. (2001). Constructing "Sound Science" and "Good Epidemiology": Tobacco, Lawyers, and Public Relations Firms. *American Journal of Public Health, 91*, 1749–1757.

Owen, P. R. & Laurel-Seller, E. (2000). Weight and Shape Ideals: Thin Is Dangerously In. *Journal of Applied Social Psychology, 30*(5), 979–990.

Orji, E. O. & Onwudiegwu, U. (2002). Prevalence and Determinants of Contraceptive Practice in a Defined Nigerian Population. *Journal of Obstetrics and Gynaecology, 22*(5), 540–543.

Ostrowsky, M. K. & Messner, S. F. (2005). Explaining Crime for a Young Adult Population: An Application of General Strain Theory. *Journal of Criminal Justice, 33*, 463–476.

Overton, S. L. & Medina, S. L. (2008). The Stigma of Mental Illness. *Journal of Counseling & Development, 86*, 143–151.

Parents Television Council (2009). Family Guide to Prime-Time Television. Retrieved January 17, 2009, from **www.parentstv.org**.

Park, K. (2002). Stigma management among the voluntarily childless. *Social Perspectives, 45*(1), 21–45.

Park, R. (2000). *Voodoo Science: The Road from Foolishness to Fraud*. New York: Oxford University Press.

Parker, S. (2000). The Tail Wagging the Bird. *Report/Newsmagazine (National Edition), 27*(12), 36–37.

Parnaby, P. F. & Sacco, V. F. (2004). Fame and Strain: The Contributions of Mertonian Deviance Theory to an Understanding of the Relationship Between Celebrity and Deviant Behavior. *Deviant Behavior, 25*(1). 1–26.

Parsons, T. & Bales, R. F. (1955). *Family, Socialization, and Interaction Process*. Glencoe, IL: Free Press.

Parsons, T. & Smelser, N. J. (1956). *Economy and Society: A Study in the Integration of Economic and Social Theory*. Glencoe, IL: Free Press.

Patel, V., Araya, R., deLima, M., Ludermir, A. & Todd, C. (1999). Women, Poverty and Common Mental Disorders in Four Restructuring Societies. *Social Science & Medicine, 49*, 1461–1471.

Peace, K. A., Beaman, L. G. & Sneddon, K. (2000). Theoretical Approaches to the Study of Deviance. In L. G. Beaman (Ed.), *New Perspectives on Deviance: The Construction of Deviance in Everyday Life* (pp. 2–17). Scarborough, ON: Prentice Hall.

Pearson, G. (1983). *Hooligan: A History of Respectable Fears*. London: MacMillan Press.

Peck, R. L., (2001). What's New with ADHD? *Behavioral Health Management, November/December*, 26–29.

Penrose, L. S. (1939). Mental Disease and Crime: Outline of a Comparative Study of European Statistics. *British Journal of Medical Psychology, 18*, 1–15.

PFLAG. (2004). From Our House to the School House. *Families and Educators Partnering for Safe Schools*. Retrieved September 8, 2006, from **www.pflag.org**.

Pfohl, S. (1994). *Images of Deviance and Social Control: A Sociological History*. New York: McGraw-Hill.

Piccinelli, M. & Homen, F. G. (1997). *Gender Differences in the Epidemiology of Affective Disorders and Schizophrenia*. Geneva, Switzerland: World Health Organization.

Piquero, N. L., Tibbets, S. G. & Blankenship, M. B. (2005). Examining the Role of Differential Association and Techniques of Neutralization in Explaining Corporate Crime. *Deviant Behavior, 26*, 159–188.

Platt, A. M. (1977). *The Child Savers: The Invention of Delinquency*. Chicago: University of Chicago Press.

Polak, H. & Celinski, A. (Directors & Producers). (2004). *The Children of Leningradsky*. Available from the National Film Board of Canada.

Pollex, R., Hegels, B. & Ban, M. R. (2001). Celestial Determinants of Success in Research. *Canadian Medical Association Journal, 165*, 12.

Pongonis, A. & Snyder, R. (1998). Links Between Body Size, Food, and Perceptions of Morality. Paper presented at the Annual Meeting of the American Psychological Association, August 14–18, San Francisco.

Popenoe, P. & Johnson, R. H. (1922). *Applied Eugenics*. New York: Macmillan.

Potts, A. & Tiefer, L. (Eds.) (2006). Introduction. *Sexualities, 9*(3), 267–272.

Presdee, M. (2001). *Cultural Criminology and the Carnival of Crime*. New York: Routledge.

Price, J. H., Desmond, S. M., Krol, R. A., Snyder, F. F. & O'Connell, J. K. (1987). Family Practice Physicians' Beliefs, Attitudes, and Practices Regarding Obesity. *American Journal of Preventative Medicine, 3*(6), 339–345.

Priebe, S. et al. (2005). Reinstitutionalization in Mental Health Care: Comparison of Six European Countries. *British Medical Journal, 330*, 123–126.

Proctor, R. N. (1988). *Racial Hygiene: Medicine Under the Nazis*. Cambridge, MA: Harvard University Press.

Pruzhinin, B. I. & Scanlan, J. P. (1995). Astrology Has Tried to Establish Itself as a Science for More Than 2000 Years. *Russian Social Science Review, 36*(5), 75–94.

Puhl, R. & Brownell, K. D. (2001). Bias, Discrimination, and Obesity. *Obesity Research, 9*, 788–805.

Puhl, R. M. & Heuer, C. A. (2009). The Stigma of Obesity: A Review and Update. *Obesity, 17*, 941–964.

Quaife, G. R. (1987). *Godly Zeal and Furious Rage: The Witch Craze in Early Modern Europe*. New York: St. Martin's Press.

Quinney, R. (1977). *The Problem of Crime: A Critical Introduction to Criminology* (2nd ed.). New York: Harper & Row.

R. v. Butler. (1992). Canadian Legal Information Institute. Retrieved May 19, 2002, from **www.canlii.org**.

R. v. Labaye. (2005). Canadian Legal Information Institute. Retrieved May 16, 2006, from **www.canlii.org**.

R. v. Sharpe. (2001). Canadian Legal Information Institute. Retrieved May 18, 2002, from **www.canlii.org**.

Raback-Wagener, J., Eickhoff-Shemek, J. & Kelly-Vance, L. (1998). The Effect of Media Analysis on Attitudes and Behaviors Regarding Body Image Among College Students. *Journal of American College Health, 47*(1). Retrieved August 14, 2002, from Expanded Academic ASAP database.

Radford, M. (Director & Writer), Orwell, G. (Writer). (1984). *Nineteen Eighty-Four*. United States: Metro-Goldwyn-Mayer.

Rampton, S. & Stauber, J. (2000a). How Big Tobacco Helped Create "the Junkman." *PR Watch, 7*(3), 5–9.

Rampton, S. & Stauber, J. (2000b). Tobacco's Secondhand Science of Smoke-Filled Rooms. *PR Watch, 7*(3), 10–11.

Rampton, S. & Stauber, J. (2001). *Trust Us, We're Experts: How Industry Manipulates Science and Gambles with Your Future*. New York: Tarcher/Putnam.

Ramsey, S. (2002). PAHO Exposes Tobacco-Industry Tactics in Latin America. *Lancet, 360*(9350), 2057.

Rapley, R. (2007). *Witch Hunts: From Salem to Guantanamo Bay*. Montreal: McGill-Queen's University Press.

Ray, N. (Director). (1955). *Rebel Without a Cause*. United States: Warner Bros.

Razack, S. H. (2002). *Race, Space, and the Law: Unmapping a White Settler Society*. Toronto, ON: Between the Lines.

Read, D. (Director), Armstrong, M., Pettigrew, M. & Johansson, S. (Producers) (1990). *The Burning Times* [videorecording]. Available from the National Film Board of Canada.

Read, J. & Harre, N. (2001). The Role of Biological and Genetic Causal Beliefs in the Stigmatisation of 'Mental Patients.' *Journal of Mental Health, 10*(2), 223–235.

Redmon, D. (2003). Examining Low Self-Control Theory at Mardi Gras: Critiquing the General Theory of Crime Within the Framework of Normative Deviance. *Deviant Behavior, 24*, 373–392.

Regioli, R. & Hewitt, J. (1994). *Delinquency in Society: A Child-Centered Approach*. New York: McGraw-Hill.

Reid, S. (2003). *Crime and Criminology* (10th ed.). Toronto, ON: McGraw-Hill.

Reitman, J. (Director & Writer) & Buckley, C. (Writer). (2005). *Thank You for Smoking*. United States: Room 9 Productions.

Reitsma-Street, M. (1989–90). More Control Than Care: A Critique of Historical and Contemporary Laws for Delinquency and Neglect of Children in Ontario. *Canadian Journal of Women and the Law, 3*(2), 510–530.

Richardson, J. T. (1995). A Social Psychological Critique of "Brainwashing" Claims Made about Recruitment to New Religions. In J. Hadden & D. Bromley (Eds.), *The Handbook of Cults and Sects in America* (Vol. 3, Part B) (pp. 75–97). Greenwich, CT: JAI Press.

Richardson, J. T., Best, J. & Bromley, D. G. (1991). *The Satanism Scare*. New York: Aldine de Gruyter.

Richardson, J. T. & Introvigne, M. (2001). "Brainwashing" Theories in European and Administrative Reports on "Cults" and "Sects." *Journal for the Scientific Study of Religion, 40*(2), 143–168.

Ritzer, G. & Goodman, D. J. (2004). *Sociological Theory* (6th ed.). New York: McGraw-Hill.

Roberts, J. (2003). Introduction: Commentaries on Policing in Toronto. *Canadian Journal of Criminology and Criminal Justice, 45*(3), 343–346.

Roberts, G., McCall, D., Stevens-Lavigne, A., Anderson, J., Paglia, A., Bollenbach, S., Weibe, J. & Gliksman, L. (2001). *Preventing Substance Abuse Problems Among Young People: A Compendium of Best Practices*. Ottawa: Health Canada.

Roberts, G. L., Lawrence, J. M., Williams, G. M. & Raphael, B. (1998). The Impact of Domestic Violence on Women's Health. *Australia and New Zealand Journal of Public Health, 22*, 796–801.

Roberts, T. A. & Ryan, S. A. (2002). Tattooing and High-Risk Behavior in Adolescents. *Pediatrics, 110*(6), 1058–1063.

Robinson, C. M. (2008). Order in Chaos: Security Culture as Anarchist Resistance to the Terrorist Label. *Deviant Behavior: An Interdisciplinary Journal, 29*, 225–252.

Robinson, T., Callister, M., & Jankoski, T. (2008). Portrayal of Body Weight on Children's Television. *Body Image, 5*, 141–151.

Rodriguez, H., Trainor, J., & Quarantelli, E. L. (2006). Rising to the Challenges of Catastrophe: The Emergent and Prosocial Behavior Following Hurricane Katrina. *Annals of the American Academy of Political and Social Science, 604*, 82–101.

Roehling, M. (1999). Weight-Based Discrimination in Employment: Psychological and Legal Aspects. *Personnel Psychology, 52*(4). Retrieved March 23, 2003, from Expanded Academic ASAP database.

Rosenau, P. M. (1992). *Postmodernism and the Social Sciences*. Princeton: Princeton University Press.

Rosenfield, S. (1997). Labeling Mental Illness: The Effects of Received Services and Perceived Stigma on Life Satisfaction. *American Sociological Review, 62*, 660–672.

Rosenhan, D. L. (1973). Being Sane in Insane Places. *Science, 179*(1973), 250–258.

Rossol, J. (2001). The Medicalization of Deviance as an Interactive Achievement: The Construction of Compulsive Gambling. *Symbolic Interaction, 24*(3), 315–341.

Rothman, D. J. (1971). *The Discovery of the Asylum: Social Order & Disorder in the New Republic*. Baltimore, MD: Johns Hopkins University Press.

Rubington, E. & Weinberg, M. S. (2008). *Deviance: The Interactionist Perspective* (10th ed.). Boston: Pearson Education.

Rubington, E. & Weinberg, M. S. (2002). *Deviance: The Interactionist Perspective* (8th ed.). Boston: Allyn & Bacon.

Sacco, V. F. (1992). *Deviance, Conformity and Control in Canadian Society*. Scarborough, ON: Prentice Hall.

Saliba, G. (2001/2002). Reading the Heavens. *Natural History, 110*(10), 80–81.

Salusso-Deonier, C. J., Markee, N. L. & Pedersen, E. L. (1993). Gender Differences in the Evaluation of Physical Attractiveness for Male and Female Body Guilds. *Perceptual & Motor Skills, 76*, 1155–1167.

Sandbek, T. J. (1993). *The Deadly Diet: Recovering from Anorexia & Bulimia* (2nd ed.). Oakland, CA: New Harbinger Publications.

Sanders, C. (1989). *Customizing the Body: The Art and Culture of Tattooing*. Philadelphia: Temple University Press.

Sareen, J., Cox, B. J., Afifi, T. O.,Yu, B. N., & Stein, M. B. (2005). Mental Health Service Use in a Nationally Representative Canadian Survey. *Canadian Journal of Psychiatry, 50*(12), 753–761.

Savoie, J. (2002). Crime Statistics in Canada, 2001. *Juristat, 22*(6). Statistics Canada Catalogue No. 85002XIE.

Sayce, L. (2000). *From Psychiatric Patient to Citizen: Overcoming Discrimination and Social Exclusion*. New York: St. Martin's Press.

Scheff, T. J. (1966). *Being Mentally Ill*. Chicago, IL: Aldine Publishing.

Schildkrout, E. (2004). Inscribing the Body. *Annual Review of Anthropology, 33*, 319–344.

Schissel, B. (1997). *Youth Crime, Moral Panics, and the Politics of Hate*. Halifax, NS: Fernwood.

Schissel, B. (2001). Youth Crime, Moral Panics, and the News: The Conspiracy Against the Marginalized in Canada. In R. C. Smandych (Ed.), *Youth Justice: History, Legislation, and Reform* (pp. 84–103). Toronto, ON: Harcourt.

Schnirring, L. (2003). Exploring Body Art Trends. *Physicians & Sportsmedicine, 31*(3), 7–8.

Schreck, C., Stewart, E., & Fisher, B. (2006). Self-Control, Victimization, and Their Influence on Risky Lifestyles: A Longitudinal Analysis Using Panel Data. *Journal of Quantitative Criminology, 22*(4), 319–340.

Schulz, W. (2003). *Tainted Legacy: 9-11 and the Ruins of Human Rights*. New York: Thunder's Mouth Press.

Schwartz, M. B., Vartanian, L. R., Nosek, B. A. & Brownell, K. D. (2006). The Influence of One's Own Body Weight on Implicit and Explicit Anti-Fat Bias. *Obesity, 14(3),* 440–447.

Seidman, S. (2002). *Beyond the Closet: The Transformation of Gay and Lesbian Life*. New York: Routledge.

Seldon, S. & Montagu, A. (1999). *Inheriting Shame: The Story of Eugenics and Racism in America*. New York: Teachers College Press.

Selekman, J. (2003). A New Era of Body Decoration: What Are Kids Doing to Their Bodies? *Pediatric Nursing, 29*(1), 77–79.

Seligson, S. V. (2001). Wacky Weight-Loss Products. *Good Housekeeping, 232*(4), 58–61.

Sellin, T. (1938). *Culture Conflict and Crime*. New York: Social Science Research Council.

Sharp, S. F., Terling-Watt, T. L., Atkins, L. A. & Gilliam, J. T. (2001). Purging Behavior in a Sample of College Females: A Research Note on General Strain Theory and Female Deviance. *Deviant Behavior: An Interdisciplinary Journal, 22*, 171–188.

Shea, B. C. (2001). The Paradox of Pumping Iron: Female Bodybuilding as Resistance and Compliance. *Women and Language, 24*(2), 42–46.

Shermer, M. (2001). *The Borderlands of Science: Where Sense Meets Nonsense*. New York: Oxford University Press.

Shields, M. (2005a). The Journey to Quitting Smoking. *Health Reports, 16*(3), 19–37. Statistics Canada Catalogue No. 82003XIE.

Shields, M. (2005b). *Measured Obesity: Overweight Canadian Children and Adolescents*. Statistics Canada Catalogue No. 82620MWE2005001.

Shilling, C. (1993). *The Body and Social Theory*. London: Sage.

Shirpak, K. R., Maticka-Tyndale, E., & Chinichian, M. (2007). Iranian Immigrants' Perceptions of Sexuality in Canada: A Symbolic Interactionist Approach. *The Canadian Journal of Human Sexuality, 16*(3/4), 113–128.

Shupe, A. (2008). *Rogue Clerics: The Social Problem of Clergy Deviance*. New Brunswick, NJ: Transaction Publishers.

Shupe, A. D. & Bromley, D. G. (1995). The Evolution of Modern American Anti-Cult Ideology. In T. Miller (Ed.), *America's Alternative Religions* (pp. 401–409). Albany, NY: State University Press.

Shupe, A. & Hadden, J. K. (1996). Copes, New Copy and Public Opinion: Legitimacy and the Social Construction of Evil in Waco. In S. Wright (Ed.), *Armageddon in Waco* (pp. 177–202). Chicago, IL: University of Chicago Press.

Shuriquie, N. (1999). Eating Disorders: A Transcultural Perspective. *Eastern Mediterranean Health Journal, 5*(2), 354–360.

Shute, N. (2000, October 2). Pushing Pills on Kids? *U S. News & World Report, 129*(13), 60.

Siegel, K., Lune, H., & Meyer, I. H. (1998). Stigma management among gay/bisexual men with HIV/AIDS. *Qualitative Sociology,* (21(1), 3–24.

Siegel, L. J. & McCormick, C. (2003). *Criminology in Canada: Theories, Patterns, and Typologies* (2nd ed.). Scarborough, ON: Nelson Thomson.

Simon, R. W. (2002). Revisiting the Relationships Among Gender, Marital Status, and Mental Health. *American Journal of Sociology, 107*(4), 1065–1098.

Simoni-Wastila, L. (2000). The Use of Abusable Prescription Drugs: The Role of Gender. *Journal of Women's Health and Gender Based Medicine, 9,* 289–297.

Simpson, N. (2004). Coming Attractions: A Comparative History of the Hollywood Studio System and the Porn Business. *Historical Journal of Film, Radio and Television, 24*(4), 635–652.

Sinsheimer, R. L. (1990). Whither the Genome Project? *Hastings Center Report, 20*(4), 5.

Skeptical Inquirer (1999). Science Needs to Combat Pseudo-Science. *Skeptical Inquirer, 23*(1), 37–38.

Sleight, P. (2004). Where Are Clinical Trials Going? Society and Clinical Trials. *Journal of Internal Medicine, 255,* 151–158.

Sloan, L. & Wahab, S. (2004). Four Categories of Women Who Work as Topless Dancers. *Sexuality & Culture, 8*(1), 18–43.

Smetana, J. G. (1988). Adolescents' and Parents' Conceptions of Parental Authority. *Child Development, 59(2),* 311–335.

Solivetti, L. M. (2003). Structural Features, Diffusion of Addiction and Addicts' Social Traits: The Case of Italy. *International Review of Sociology, 13*(1). 39–66

Special Senate Committee on Social Affairs, Science, and Technology (2006, May). Report on Mental Health: *"Out of the Shadows At Last": Transforming Mental Health, Mental Illness and Addiction Services in Canada—Full Version.* Available at **www.parl.gc.ca**.

Spector, M. (1981). Beyond Crime: Seven Methods to Control Troublesome Rascals. In L. Ross (Ed.), *Law and Deviance* (pp. 127–148). Beverly Hills, CA: Sage Publications.

Spitzer, B. L., Henderson, K. A. & Zivian, M. T. (1999). Gender Differences in Population Versus Media Body Sizes: A Comparison over Four Decades. *Sex Roles, 40,* 545–565.

Stark, C. A. (1997). Is Pornography an Action? The Causal vs. the Conceptual View of Pornography's Harm. *Social Theory & Practice, 23*(2), 277–306.

Stark, R. & Bainbridge, W. S. (1996). *A Theory of Religion.* New Brunswick, NJ: Rutgers University Press.

Statistics Canada (n. d.). Table 252-0014 Adult and Youth Charged, by Detailed Offences, Annually (Number). Using CHASS (distributor). **http://dc1.chass.utoronto.ca/chasscansim/** (accessed April 4, 2009).

Statistics Canada. (1992). Crime Trends in Canada, 1962–1990. *Juristat, 12*(7). Catalogue No: 85002XIE.

Statistics Canada. (2006b). Smoking and Diabetes Care: Results from the CCHS Cycle 3.1 (2005). Catalogue No. 82621XIE.

Statistics Canada. (2006c). Measured Adult Body Mass Index (BMI), by Age Group and Sex, Household Population Aged 18 and Over Excluding Pregnant Females, Canada, 2005. CANSIM Table 105–0407.

Statistics Canada (2007). Smokers, by Province and Territory, Age Groups 12 and Over, 2005. CANSIM Table 105-0427.

Statistics Canada (2008). Victims and Persons Accused of Homicide, by Age and Sex (Accused). CANSIM Table 253-0003.

Stebbins, R. A. (1996). *Tolerable Differences: Living with Deviance.* Toronto, ON: McGraw-Hill Ryerson.

Stephans, T. & Jorbert, N. (2001). The Economic Burden of Mental Health Problems in Canada. *Chronic Diseases in Canada, 22*(1), 18–23.

Stiller, B. (Director & Writer), & Sather, D. (Writer). (2001). *Zoolander.* United States: Munich Film Partners.

Stice, E. & Shaw, H. E. (1994). Adverse Effects of the Media-Portrayed Thin-Ideal on Women and Linkages to Bulimic Symptomatology. *Journal of Social and Clinical Psychology, 13*(3). Retrieved April 18, 2003, from Expanded Academic ASAP database.

Stip, E., Caron, J. & Lane, L. J. (2001). Schizophrenia: People's Perceptions in Quebec. *Canadian Medical Association Journal, 164*(9), 1299–1300.

Stirn, A. (2003). Body Piercing: Medical Consequences and Psychological Motivations. *The Lancet, 361,* 1205–1215.

Stock, G. (2002). *Redesigning Humans: Our Inevitable Genetic Future*. Boston, MA: Houghton Mifflin.

Stoppe, G., Sandholzer, H. & Huppertz, C. (1999). Gender Differences in the Recognition of Depression in Old Age. *Maturitas, 32*, 205–212.

Stylianou, S. (2002). Control Attitudes Toward Drug Use as a Function of Paternalistic and Moralistic Principles. *Journal of Drug Use, 32*(1), 119–152.

Sullivan, G., Jackson, C. A. & Spritzer, K. L. (1996). Characteristics and Service Use of Seriously Mentally Ill Persons Living in Rural Areas. *Psychiatric Services, 47*(1), 57–61.

Sumner, C. (1994). *The Sociology of Deviance: An Obituary*. New York: Continuum.

Sumner, W. G. (1906). *Folkways: A Study of the Sociological Importance of Usages, Manners, Mores, and Morals*. Boston: Ginn and Co.

Sutherland, E. H. (1947). *Principles of Criminology*. Philadelphia, PA: J. B. Lippincott.

Sutherland, N. (1976). *Children in English-Canadian Society: Framing the Twentieth-Century Consensus*. Toronto, ON: University of Toronto Press.

Swami, V. & Furnham, A. (2007). Unattractive, Promiscuous and Heavy Drinkers: Perceptions of Women with Tattoos. *Body Image, 4*, 343-352.

Sweet, W. (2003). *Philosophical Theory and the Universal Declaration of Human Rights*. Ottawa: University of Ottawa Press.

Sykes, G. & Matza, D. (1957). Techniques of Neutralization: A Theory of Delinquency. *American Sociological Review, 22*, 664–670.

Szasz, T. (1994). Mental Illness is Still a Myth. *Society, 31*(4), 34–39.

Tait, G. (1999). Rethinking Youth Cultures: The Case of the Gothics. *Social Alternatives, 18*(2), 15–20.

Tannenbaum, F. (1938). *Crime and the Community*. New York: Ginn.

Tanner, J. (1992). Youthful Deviance. In V. Sacco (Ed.), *Deviance, Conformity and Control in Canadian Society* (2nd ed.). Scarborough, ON: Prentice Hall.

Tanner, J. (2001). *Teenage Troubles: Youth and Deviance in Canada* (2nd ed.). Scarborough, ON: Nelson Thomson.

Tanzman, B. (1993). An Overview of Surveys of Mental Health Consumers' Preferences for Housing and Support Services. *Hospital and Community Psychiatry, 44*(5), 450–455.

Taplan, D. C. (Director), & Torrance, J. (Producer). (2002). *Shredded*. National Film Board of Canada.

Taylor-Butts, A. & Bressan, A. (2008). Youth Crime in Canada, 2006. *Juristat, 28*(3). Statistics Canada Catalogue No. 85002XIE.

Teevan, J. J. & Dryburgh, H. B. (2000). First Person Accounts and Sociological Explanations of Delinquency. *Canadian Review of Sociology and Anthropology, 37*(1), 77–94.

Thelen, M. H. & Cormier, J. F. (1995). Desire to Be Thinner and Weight Control Among Children and Their Parents. *Behavior Therapy, 26*, 85–99.

Thio, A. (1983). *Deviant Behavior* (2nd ed.). Boston: Houghton Mifflin.

Thomas, S. P. (2004). From the Editor: Drug Companies Under Investigation. *Issues in Mental Health Nursing, 25*, 751–752.

Thompson, J., Baird, P. A. & Downie, J. (2005, December 3). The Olivieri Case: Context and Significance. *Ecclectica*. Retrieved June 18, 2006, from **www.ecclectica.ca**.

Thompson, W. E., Harred, J. L. & Burks, B. E. (2003). Managing the Stigma of Topless Dancing: A Decade Later. *Deviant Behavior, 24*, 551–570.

Thornberry, T., Lizotte, A., Krohm, M., Farnworth, M. & Jang, S. (1991). Testing Interactional Theory: An Examination of Reciprocal Causal Relationships Among Family, School and Delinquency. *Journal of Criminal Law and Criminology, 82*(1), 3–33.

Tiefer, L. (2006). The Viagra Phenomenon. *Sexualities, 9*(3), 273–294.

Tittle, C. R. & Paternoster, R. (2000). *Social Deviance and Crime*. Los Angeles, CA: Roxbury.

Titus, S. L., Wells, J. A., & Rhoades, L. J. (2008). Commentary: Repairing Research Integrity. *Nature, 453*, 980–982.

Tjepkema, M. (2005). *Measured Obesity: Adult Obesity in Canada: Measured Height and Weight*. Statistics Canada Catalogue No. 82620MWE2005001.

Todd, P. (2001, October). Veiled Threats? *Homemakers, October*, 45–53.

Troeltsch, E. (1960). *The Social Teachings of the Christian Churches* (Vols. 1 and 2). (O. Wyon, Trans.). New York: Harper & Row. (Original work published 1931).

Trust, J. & Watts, R. E. (1999). Relationship of High School Seniors' Religious Participation and Behavior to Educational, Career, and Leisure Variables. *Counseling Values, 44*(1), 30–39.

Turk, A. (1969). *Criminality and Legal Order*. Chicago: Rand McNally.

Turner, B. S. (1987). *Medical Power and Social Knowledge*. London: Sage.

Turner, R. J., Wheaton, B. & Lloyd, D. A. (1995). The Epidemiology of Social Stress. *American Sociological Review, 60*(1), 104–127.

Tyyskä, V. (2001). *Long and Winding Road: Adolescents and Youth in Canada Today*. Toronto, ON: Canadian Scholars' Press.

Ullman, S. R. (1997). *Sex Seen: The Emergence of Modern Sexuality in America*. Berkeley, CA: University of California Press.

UNESCO (1997). *Universal Declaration On the Human Genome and Human Rights*. Paris: Author.

U.S. Department of Health and Human Services. (2000). *Healthy People 2010: Understanding and Improving Health*. Washington, DC: U.S. Government Printing Office.

U.S. Department of State. (2008). *International Religious Freedom Report 2008*. Washington, DC: Bureau of Democracy, Human Rights, and Labor.

Us Weekly (2006, June 21). Bikini Boot Camp: The Stars Share Their Secrets to Building the Perfect Beach Bod.

Valpy, M. (1998, March 7). Cleaning Out the Cuckoo's Nest. *Globe and Mail*, p. D1.

Valverde, M. (1991). *The Age of Light, Soap, and Water: Moral Reform in English Canada, 1885–1925*. Toronto, ON: McClelland & Stewart.

Van Rassel, J. (2009). The Evolution of Calgary's Deadly Gang War. *Calgary Herald, March 14*. Retrieved May 11, 2009, from **www.calgaryherald.com**.

Venkatesh, S. (2003). A Note on Social Theory and the American Street Gang. In L. Kontos, D. Brotherton, and L. Barrios (Eds.) *Gangs and Society: Alternative Perspectives*. New York: Columbia University Press.

Victor, J. (1992). The Search for Scapegoat Deviants. *Humanist, 52*(5), 10–13.

Victor, J. (1993). *Satanic Panic: The Creation of a Contemporary Legend*. Chicago, IL: Open Court.

Victor, J. S. (2004). Sluts and Wiggers: A Study of the Effects of Derogatory Labeling. *Deviant Behavior, 25,* 67–85.

Vold, G. (1958). *Theoretical Criminology*. New York: Oxford University Press.

Vowell, P. R. & Chen, J. (2004). Predicting Academic Misconduct: A Comparative Test of Four Sociological Explanations. *Sociological Inquiry, 74*, 226–249.

Vuijst, F. (Director & Producer). (1995). *Onward Christian Soldiers*. United States: Green Room Productions. Available from Filmakers Library, 124 East 40th Street, NY, NY 10016.

Wahl, O. F. (1992). Mass Media Images of Mental Illness: A Review of the Literature. *Journal of Community Psychology, 15*, 285–291.

Wahl, O. F. (1999). Mental Health Consumers' Experience of Stigma. *Schizophrenia Bulletin, 25*, 467–478.

Wallace, M. (2003). Crime Statistics in Canada, 2002. *Juristat, 23*(5). Statistics Canada Catalogue No. 85002XIE.

Walsh, P. & Dauvergne, M. (2009). Police-Reported Hate Crime in Canada, 2007. *Juristat, 29*(2), 1–6. Statistics Canada Catalogue No. 85002X.

Want, S., Vilkers, K., & Amos, J. (2009). The Influence of Television Programs on Appearance Satisfaction: Making and Mitigating Social Comparisons to *Friends*. *Sex Roles, 60*(9/10), 642–655.

Ward, D. E. (1993). Gene Therapy: The Splice of Life. *USA Today Magazine, 121*(2572), 63–66.

Ward, D. A., Carter, T. J. & Perrin, R. D. (1994). *Social Deviance: Being, Behaving, and Branding*. Boston: Allyn & Bacon.

Watson, J. (1997). *The Christian Coalition: Dreams of Restoration and Demands for Recognition*. New York: St. Martin's Press.

Weber, T. (1999). Raving in Toronto: Peace, Love, Unity, and Respect in Transition. *Journal of Youth Studies, 2*(3), 317–336.

Webster, P. (2001, March 26). Defending the Faith. *Maclean's*, 28–29.

Wechsler, H. & Kuo, M. (2000). College Students Define Binge Drinking and Estimate Its Prevalence: Results of a National Survey. *Journal of American College Health, 49*(2), 57–64.

Wechsler, H., Lee, J. E., Kuo, M., Seibring, M., Nelson, M. S. & Lee, H. (2002). Trends in College Binge Drinking During a Period of Increased Prevention Efforts: Findings from Four Harvard School of Public Health College Alcohol Student Surveys: 1993–2001. *Journal of American College Health, 50*(5), 203–217.

Wechsler, H. & Nelson, T. F. (2008). What We Have Learned from the Harvard School of Public Health College Alcohol Study: Focusing Attention on College Student Alcohol Consumption and the Environmental Conditions that Promote It. *Journal of Studies on Alcohol and Drugs*, *69*(4), 481–490.

Wechsler, H., Seibring, M., Liu, M. T. S. & Ahl, M. (2004). Colleges Respond to Student Binge Drinking: Reducing Student Demand or Limiting Access. *Journal of American College Health, 52*(4), 159–168.

Wegs, R. (1999). Youth Delinquency & "Crime": The Perception and the Reality. *Journal of Social History, 32*(3). Retrieved December 20, 2002, from Expanded Academic ASAP database.

Weinberg, M. S. (1967). Nudist Camp: Way of Life and Social Structure. *Human Organization*, *26*, 91–99.

Weiss, S. F. (1988). *Race Hygiene and National Efficiency: The Eugenics of Wilhelm Schallmayer*. Berkeley, CA: University of California Press.

Weitzman, E. R. & Nelson, T. F. (2004). College Student Binge Drinking and the "Prevention Paradox": Implications for Prevention and Harm Reduction. *Journal of Drug Education, 34*(3), 247–266.

Wells, E. & Rankin, J. (1991). Families and Delinquency: A Meta-Analysis of the Impact of Broken Homes. *Social Problems, 38*, 71–93.

Wertheim, E. H., Paxton, S. J., Schutz, H. K. & Muir, S. L. (1997). Why Do Adolescent Girls Watch Their Weight? An Interview Study Examining Sociocultural Pressures to Be Thin. *Journal of Psychosomatic Research, 42*(4), 345–355.

Wesely, J. K. (2003). "Where Am I Going to Stop?" Exotic Dancing, Fluid Body Boundaries, and Effects on Identity. *Deviant Behavior, 24*, 483–503.

West, G. (1991). Towards a More Socially Informed Understanding of Canadian Delinquency Legislation. In A. Leschied, P. Jaffe, & W. Willis (Eds.), *The Young Offenders Act: A Revolution in Canadian Juvenile Justice*. Toronto, ON: University of Toronto Press.

West, W. G. (1984). *Young Offenders and the State: A Canadian Perspective on Delinquency*. Toronto, ON: Butterworths.

Westbrook, M. T., Legge, V. & Pennay, M. (1993). Attitudes Towards Disabilities in a Multicultural Society. *Social Science & Medicine, 36*(5), 615–623.

Wheeler, S. (1960). Sex Offenses: A Sociological Critique. *Law and Contemporary Society, 25* (Spring), 258–278.

White, C. (2003). Environmentalist Accused of Scientific Dishonesty. *British Medical Journal, 326*(7381), 120.

Whiting, G. (1996). *The Sterilization of Leilani Muir* [videorecording]. Available from the National Film Board of Canada.

Whorton, J. (2001). The Solitary Vice. *The Western Journal of Medicine, 175*(1). Retrieved January 24, 2002, from Expanded Academic ASAP database.

Williams, D. R. & Takeuchi, D. T. (1992). Socioeconomic Status and Psychiatric Disorder Among Blacks and Whites. *Social Forces, 70*(5), 179–194.

Wilson, B. (2002). The Canadian Rave Scene and Five Theses on Youth Resistance. *Canadian Journal of Sociology, 27*(3), 373–412.

Wilson, B. R. (1993). Historical Lessons in the Study of Sects and Cults. *Religion and the Social Order, 3A*, 53–73.

Wilson Quarterly (1992). The Fateful Code. *Wilson Quarterly, 16*(2), 85–86.

Wiseman, C. V., Gray, J. J., Mosimann, J. E. & Ahrens, A. H. (1992). Cultural Expectations of Thinness in Women: An Update. *International Journal of Eating Disorders, 11*, 85–89.

Wohlrab, S., Stahl, J., & Kappeler, P. M. (2006). Modifying the Body: Motivations for Getting Tattooed and Pierced. *Body Image, 4*, 87–95.

Wolff, N. (2007). The Social Construction of the Costs of Mental Illness. *Evidence & Policy, 3*(1), 67–78.

Wood, R. (1999). Nailed to the X: A Lyrical History of the Straightedge Youth Subculture. *Journal of Youth Studies, 2,* 133–151.

Wood, R. (2001). *Straightedge Youth: Subculture, Genesis, Permutation, and Identity Formation.* Unpublished doctoral dissertation, University of Alberta, Edmonton, AB.

World Association for Sexology. (1999). *The Universal Declaration of Sexual Rights.* Retrieved August 8, 2002, from **www.worldsexology.org/about_sexualrights.asp.**

World Health Organization. (2001). Costs of Mental Illness. *Fact Sheet No. 218.* Retrieved May 7, 2002, from **www.who.int**.

World Health Organization. (2002a). Homepage. Retrieved April 15, 2003, from **www.who.int**.

World Health Organization. (2002b). *Mental Health Global Action Programme.* Geneva, Switzerland: Author.

World Health Organization (2003). *WHO Constitution.* Retrieved July 2, 2003 from **www.who.int**.

World Health Organization. (2004). *Constitution of the World Health Organization.* Retrieved September 21, 2006, from **www.who.int/governance/en.**

World Psychiatric Association. (2003). Program Against Stigmatization and Discrimination Because of Schizophrenia. Retrieved May 17, 2003, from **www.wpanet.org.**

Wortley, S. S. & Tanner, J. (2003). Data, Denials, and Confusion: The Racial Profiling Debate in Toronto. *Canadian Journal of Criminology and Criminal Justice, 45*(3), 367–389.

Wright, S. A. (1997). Media Coverage of Unconventional Religion: Any "Good News" for Minority Faiths? *Review of Religious Research, 39*(2), 101–115.

Wroblewska, A. M. (1997). Androgenic Anabolic Steroids and Body Dysmorphia in Young Men. *Journal of Psychosomatic Research, 42,* 225–234.

Yam, P. (1997). The Media's Eerie Fascination. *Scientific American, 276*(1), 100–101.

Yinger, J. M. (1970). *The Scientific Study of Religion.* New York: Macmillan.

Zeman, K. & Bressan, A. (2008). Factors Associated with Youth Delinquency and Victimization in Toronto, 2006. *Crime and Justice Research Paper Series.* Statistics Canada Catalogue No. 85561M, No. 14.

PHOTO CREDITS

Index

Social power perspective. *See* conflict view of law
Social purity movement 117
Social selection hypothesis 212
Social typing
   definition 28–29, 305
   deviance dance 31
   mental illness 307–308
   physical appearance 307
   power 305
   religion 308
   science 308–309
   sexuality 306
   youth 307
Spoiled identity 82
Sports 169–170
Stealth tactics 266
Stigmatization, responses to 82
Straightedge subculture 80, 187–188
Students' perceptions
   college alcohol policies 164
   deviance 2–3
   media images of the "ideal" body 192
   mental illness 215
Sturm und drang 168
Swingers' clubs 134

T

Tagging 79
Taliban 241, 265
Tattoos. *See* body modification
Tautology 55, 68–69
Techniques of neutralization 60–62
Teenagers, concept of 167
Teleology 54
Terrorism 7, 43–44, 49

Tertiary deviance 83
The Blind Men and the Elephant 38
Theory
   coexistance of multiple theories 37–39
   versus practice 36
Tobacco. *See* smoking

U

Universal Declaration of Sexual Rights 135

V

"Viagra culture" 128

W

Witch persecutions
   boundaries between religious and political belief systems 259–261
   functionality of deviance 42–43
   historical views of mental illness 218
   history 259–261
   religious institutions 26

Y

Young Offenders Act 152
Youth
   definition 139
   criminal victimization 141
Youth crime
   causes 142–144
   International Youth Survey 144
   parenting 143
   perceptions 141–142
   rates 140–141
Youth Criminal Justice Act 152